Everything You Need to Know About
LSAT Logic Games

Brad Leutwyler
Christine Lord, Editor
Jacqueline Maldonodo, Logic Editor

ISBN: 0-9840821-2-3
ISBN 13: 978-0-9840821-2-4

By Brad Leutwyler

CRITICAL NOTES

Read and learn every word in this book. ALL OF THEM. Cover to cover. This includes the appendices, which are highly instructive in and of themselves. If you really want to be a lawyer, or at least go to law school, your days of half-assing things are over. Be thorough. Learn it all. Know as much as you can and know it better than everyone else in the room. Nobody cares what you *think:* they care about what you *know* and what you can *prove.*

"LSAT" and "LSAC" are copyrights of the Law School Admission Council. They do not endorse this book and did not in any way participate in the production of this work, nor did they contribute to it, except in that they charge huge sums of money to use LSAT problems, which is why LSAT books and classes cost so much money. In fact, the LSAC probably hates the fact that you are about to discover that there is nothing magical about the LSAT. The test makers and law schools want you and everyone else out there to think that all of the people admitted to law schools are super-smart, inherently talented, highly capable and somewhat gifted, though all evidence is to the contrary. Actually, the LSAT is simply a *barrier to entry*, like a big fence or wall. "We gots yo' ladder right here."

NOTES ON LANGUAGE: Throughout the book the word "we" is used frequently and in at least two distinct ways. The first is a *Royal We*, like they use in hospitals, palaces and dungeons: "How are **we** today?" or, "Would we be likin' another flogging?" No reader should confuse the issue: when "we" is used royally, as in, "We should use the XXXX technique," that means that YOU should use it. This is mostly because I have already crushed the LSAT, burned up my scholarship money, been through law school and practiced as a trial lawyer. I already *know* what to do and would have to be insanely arrogant to presume that I can give me advice. Are we clear? (See how I did that? Just sort of slipped one in on you).

Second, "we" is sometimes used to refer to the author of this book. "**We** recommend that you use the XXXX technique," actually means that *I* recommend it. A long time ago (the greed and coke-addled 1980s), in a galaxy far, far away (Oregon) I had writing teachers who drilled the sentence, "Death to I," Into my head. Ever since then, no amount of therapy or alcohol can stop me from habitually using "we" when I really mean "I". There is no "we," just me. In the event the word "I" is used, it is an accident, on purpose, both or neither.

"Recommend" really means "demand." It is just a more polite way of saying that you *must* do something.... Like the way that yo' mama might say, "I recommend that you tell me the truth." She ain't *recommending* jack.

Finally, there are times when "we" deliberately choose to use words, phrases, stylistic choices, colloquialisms, idioms etc. that are not, "according to Hoyle," correct. These are all deliberate choices. Things that make you have to stop and think force your conscious awareness and attention. We frequently do this in order to make you slow down, pay attention and learn more better. See how we did that? So whatever you do, do NOT attempt to blame the editor, Jacqueline Maldonado, for such occurrences. They are on purpose and not errors or oversights by her. She is smart. Really smart. Smarter than me, or you or both of us. Honest. She's wicked awesome smart and it drives her NUTS that we deliberately allow grammatically improper elements to remain in this monograph. For being able to work past the dissonance and flow with our mojo, we owe her great tribute.

For Ava
You have given life new meaning.

IF YOU HAVE ANY SUGGESTIONS, COMMENTS, INSIGHTS, CORRECTIONS, ADDITIONS, OUTRAGED DENUNCIATIONS ETC. CONTACT BRAD AT
Brad@TestMentors.com

Preface

The Test Mentors Method is the only LSAT program designed to make sure that you have all of the skills needed to be a top-drawer law student. There are no "tricks" or "shortcuts" here. There is a proven, fool-proof method for laying waste to the logic games section by teaching you the essence of several aspects of legal reasoning and how to apply them to the "games" section of the LSAT. These are the *identical* skills that are required for reading laws (statutes, administrative regulations, judicial opinions etc.), figuring out what those laws allow, what they forbid and what they require. If you learn the Test Mentors Method you will crush the games section and go on to slay your law school curriculum. Our students do not "just get in," they get scholarships, they are at the top of their classes and they get good jobs when they graduate. This is true because of they are all very competent.

We are always amazed to find students preparing for law school who are ignorant as to what is required of them. They somehow think that if they can just "get past the LSAT," they will "kick ass" at law school. These people are severely deluded. If you cannot do well on this test, you will not do well in school, and DECADES of statistics bear this truth out well. Your LSAT score *proves* whether or not you belong in law school like nothing else does.

I. **Overview**: The Truth About LSAT Logic Games

Most inexperienced LSAT takers come to the table thinking that the logic games portions of the test is the most intractable, challenging, vexing and important part of the test to learn. They are monstrously incorrect. The truth is that logic games are easy to master. Once you know how to do them well, the answers are always one hundred percent absolutely correct, without exception. Unlike the other sections of the test where language use is integral to success (and thus problematic because word interpretation can vary from person to person, especially when there are cultural differences between the test maker and the test taker), the games boil down to the absolute, immutable and invariable laws of logic.

So how is it that the games section has taken on the mystique of the dragon that must be slain with a plastic fork? The explanation is simple: most people do not think like lawyers. That is to say that most people do not think in an analytically rigid, logically "proper" manner. Lawyers are excellent at taking factual information, organizing it, applying rules to that information and drawing inferences from those facts and rules. If you have never studied logic, math, computer science or other such logically rigorous disciplines you are at a huge disadvantage when it comes to taking the LSAT. BUT IT IS NO MAGIC TRICK to be able to do the games well. You just need to learn how to do logic, just like all of the other lawyers did.

The business of being a competent law student and then a competent lawyer is absolutely dependent upon sound analytical skills. With them, you can comply with the most important of all of the rules of life for lawyers:

FIGURE IT OUT FOR YOURSELF!

Memorize that. If you cannot figure out the answers to problems to your own intellectual satisfaction, you are always in danger of having someone else, whether it be the LSAT makers, other lawyers, judges, professors etc. lead you down a blind alley and into the jaws of humiliation, if not malpractice, which is very expensive, more so than law school. ALWAYS figure out the solution to a problem *for yourself* before you allow anybody else (including answer choices A, B, C, D and E) to pollute your mind with incorrectness.

Logic games are designed to test your ability to use logic to determine four things:
    1) What must be true at all times.
    2) What can never be true under any circumstance.
    3) What might possibly be false in a given situation.
    4) What might possibly be true in a given situation.

Two of these (what must be true and what must be false) are relatively easy to determine most of the time. It is the "might be" questions that are the more difficult to deal with, and separate those who just eek their way into law school from those who get in with a scholarship based upon their LSAT score. You *must* set your mind to one goal and one goal only: getting a score of 163 or higher. Anyone can do it, and it is relatively easy.

Can one barely scrape by the logic games, barely get a respectable LSAT score, go to a sub-mediocre law school, muddle through said law school, pass the bar exam and survive as a lawyer on minimal reasoning skills? Certainly! Look at all of the ambulance chasers in your local phone book, in television commercials during the afternoon soap operas, or do a Google search for lawyers in your area. It is easy to be a bottom-tier lawyer in the local hierarchy. We can assure you, however, that the bottom is not where **you** want to end up: graduating with minimal employment prospects and a huge pile of law school debt is not the recipe for happiness you want to be cooking from. Rather, you should be at the top of your class, or darned near it. That, dear reader, is also relatively easy.

Richard and his big blue book

Once upon a time there was a boy named Richard who wanted more than all else to be a lawyer. When counseling failed to dissuade him, his parents sent him to LSAT class. Richard thought (if you can call it that), "If I just do lots of real LSAT problems, I will be able to do well on the test." So Richard purchased a large blue book full of all of the old LSAT logic games and did them over and over until he could get every answer correct every time.

He took the LSAT. He crashed and burned. He had to re-take it.

If you buy a math book and do the same 100 problems over and over until you get the correct answers every time, does that mean that you know how to do the math? NO! If you do not learn general principles and specific rules, you will always be stuck doing the same 100 questions well and doing poorly on almost every new question that requires *actual understanding*.

The same goes for the LSAT.

DON'T BE A RICHARD.
STUDY AND PRACTICE THE RULES AND PROCESSES SO YOU CAN CRUSH ANY LOGIC GAME!

What One Fool Can Do, Another Can[1]

Every hack lawyer in the United States has taken the LSAT. So has every outstanding one. What is the difference between them? Good law students and good lawyers learned how to do logic well. There is NOTHING special about the people who achieve a high score on the LSAT. Nothing. Just in case you missed the point, we will state it again: *There is NOTHING SPECIAL about the people who achieve a high score on the LSAT.* They are no smarter than you. They are no more worthy of a better education than you. Rather, they simply have special skills that enable them to score higher. They previously learned things that low-scorers did not, much as your lawn-mower repairman has learned things you have not. You too, will learn the coveted skills of the LSAT logic games.

This brings us to the first meta-point for learning logic games:

---

[1] We quote Prof. Sylvanus P. Thompson, the original author of *Calculus Made Easy*, available from St. Martin's Press and quality bookstores world-wide.

Anyone can learn this stuff.

Say it out loud if you must. Go ahead. Take a second, look up from this book and say aloud, "Anyone, including me, can learn how to do logic games. Millions of fools have done it. I am smarter than a fool, so I can too."[2]

This brings us to big point number two:

You must actually learn the rules and processes for doing logic games.

You may not half-ass this process. This is not like an undergraduate history class, where you can memorize a few facts and then obfuscate your way through an essay answer. You have to learn the rules of logic games and you must practice them over and over again until you know them inside and out. Memorizing the rules is not enough. You must know how they work in action, and that means that you have to practice, and then practice some more and then, just for measure, practice more. You may ask yourself, "Why? Once I get into law school, I don't care about this LSAT stuff." Many a law school flunkout has had the same thought. The concepts being tested on the LSAT are the exact same skills that you need to do well in law school and as a Jedi-lawyer. So pretty please with sugar on top, get with the program, learn the rules and the processes, do them as if your future depended upon them and start planning for your future as a highly paid legal professional.

We will teach you the best, most efficient and intelligent approach to **ALL** of the different logic games that there are, and we will teach you the reasoning skills required to crush the games section. *If you do not make the most serious effort of your life* to learn and master what we are about to teach you, you will not do nearly as well on the test as any of us would like. If you do put forth a serious effort, you will be rewarded... GREATLY.[3]

There is one other meta-rule you should tattoo onto your brain right now and it goes a little something like this:

ALWAYS GO WITH WHAT YOU ALREADY KNOW.

Memorize that.

---

[2] This argument assumes that anything a fool can learn, so can you, and that being smarter than a fool will enable you to learn those things. This is an infinitely reasonable assumption set and ought to be proceeded upon with much enthusiasm. Also, get used to reading footnotes. Law school is all about the footnotes. Eventually you will come to love them like a rabid puppy or a pustule that no amount of antibiotics can make go away.

[3] Most law schools offer huge scholarships for students with LSAT scores above 160. In fact, a 164 will get you a full-ride at most law schools, and virtually anybody can, with practice, hit 165 using the Test Mentors' methods!

As it stands, we have already learned a few things and we will learn a boatload more soon. Most people look at problems and say, "I don't know how to do this." Or, "I don't know how to start solving this." They are unthinking zombies. You will know where to begin because you will have a list of steps to go through, and like any process, you begin with step number one. You will know how to walk through the steps for solving problems. You will always learn more about the game as you answer each question. Thus, you will know a lot about games generally, you will know a lot about games specifically, and in any individual game you will learn more and more about it as you go, none of which you should forget.

If and when you feel the urge to say, "I don't know...." stop yourself, smack yourself upside the head and say, ***"What do I know already?"*** By the time you reach Chapter 3, you will know enough to be able to handle 95% or more of all of the logic games ever written on the LSAT. That is, in our estimation, pretty damned cool.

The Big Lie: "Games are complex, with hundreds of possible outcomes."

Let us examine the ***fact pattern*** for a basic logic game. The fact pattern is the little paragraph at the very start of a game. It is separate and distinct from the ***formal rules*** of the game, which are listed right after the fact pattern. Memorize these two definitions, as they will be used throughout the text.

> *"Each of six people, Adam, Bobby, Cindy, David, Edward and Francine are waiting in line for a bus, and are the only people in line. They are each standing in one of six spots in a straight line, one person per spot, with the person at the front of the line being first and the person at the end being sixth. The order in which they stand is consistent with the following rules."*

Typically the uninitiated game player looks at this fact pattern and thinks, "Crud! There are a million ways you could arrange those people! If Adam is number one, then any of the remaining five can be in position number two. But if Adam is in position number two, any of the others could be in positions one, three etc...."[4] This is an incorrect understanding, BUT it is *one of the things* the test makers are checking to see whether or not you think. If you are already psyched out, you will be more apt to make mistakes, get a lower score and be deemed "un-special" by law schools!

It is *supposed* to confuse and intimidate you because you are being tested, in part, on your ability to deal with it, see through the confusion and "logic" your way through the illusion to the truth, just like lawyers do.

---

[4] The mathematically inclined reader may realize that there are 6! ways that the game can be played. More on this point in a moment.

What Logic Games Really Are

The LSAC refers to logic games as *analytical reasoning.* There is good cause for this label. The study and practice of law revolves around four basic concepts: spotting legal issues, knowing what the legal rules are, knowing how the rules apply to a given situation, and drawing conclusions about your given situation based upon the proper application of the rules. This approach, called I.R.A.C. (issues, rules, application, conclusion) is 99% of law student-ing and lawyering. Logic games are the way that law schools determine whether or not you have any skills at this.

What you do not have to know before you get into law school is anything legal. Knowledge of law, legal principles etc. is in no way necessary in order to be an top-drawer law student. Rather, the **skills** are what are important. Hence in every "game" you are given a set of "facts" (issues) and a list of conditions (rules). From them, you are tested as to your ability to apply (application) those rules to the facts where appropriate and draw inferences (conclusions). In other words, logic games are the closest analogue they can come up with to test whether you have actual lawyer skills before you set foot on a law school campus. We will say it over and over throughout this text: ANYONE CAN LEARN THESE SKILLS. You simply have to remember what the games section(s) is/are really about and be very adept at using all of the necessary skills you learn herein.

The Big Truth

Believe it or not, the LSAT has to be "fair". By "fair," we mean that the average test taker has to be able to get an average score, somewhere around 153. In other words, the curve is pre-set. In order to make this dream a reality, all of the problems in every section are tested and re-tested on thousands of guinea pigs[5] in order to determine precisely how many people will get them correct or incorrect. When you sit down to take the for-real LSAT, you are doing games that the test makers know, almost to a 100% certainty, will land the average test taker at 152/153-ish. There will be easy questions and more difficult ones, but they must all fall into patterns and follow precise, pre-ordained rules in order for ten-thousand test takers to perfectly fill the pre-set curve! They can never do something new, crafty or unknown, because that would screw up their precious little curve with 153 as its center. Just knowing this one simple fact ought to comfort you a great deal. If the curve is pre-set, *they can't put anything on the test that we haven't already seen and practiced over and over*. All we have to do is know exactly what *can* be on the test, prepare for it and crush the life out of it.

---

[5] Not actual guinea pigs: no animals are harmed in the construction of the LSAT, (or so they say). Rather, there is an un-scored, "experimental" section of the LSAT every time it is given. That section contains questions to be used on future tests and develops the statistical basis for the curve. In other words, YOU are the guinea pig. How humiliating. The good news is that this is as low as you have to go to be a lawyer. After the LSAT, it's all dignity and respect. Okay, that's not true either.

There are actually very few ways that the fact pattern for the game above can be worked out. This is true of EVERY GAME, EVERY TIME. In the previous fact pattern there are 6x5x4x3x2 = 720 ways the players can be arranged at the beginning. That sounds frightening. Read on.

As we shall soon see, after we read the fact pattern, the number of possible outcomes is usually smaller. After we read the given "formal" rules, they will further limit the possible outcomes, frequently to only two or three possible scenarios! Each question on the games section will then try to test whether or not you took the time to figure out the logical implication(s) of the rules of the game at the start, and whether or not you understand the limited number of ways to play it. Finally, they want to know whether or not you realize that if you are given just a little more hypothetical information, there are exact things that must happen, things that cannot happen and things that are possible but not necessarily required. This is exactly like lawyering.

For right now, you must memorize and repeat our personal pledge to ourselves. Yes, it is sort of new-age, crystal-hugger optimism, and many readers will not want to do "power of positive thinking," exercises. Do it anyway. Decades of research tell us that there is a huge benefit to it, and that there is no downside.[6]

"There are only SIX kinds of logic games (even though, for some idiotic "reason," there are people/organizations out there claiming that there are between 12 and 30). They are all simple. Every problem can be reduced to an exact outcome when I follow the rules precisely. I will defeat them all. "What one fool can do, so can another."

META POINT: EVERY GAME IS ABOUT ISSUES AND PATTERNS

Every game falls into one of six types, and each type of game is designed to raise certain logical issues. Because there are a limited number of these issues tested, there is a repetitive pattern amongst games of the same types. For example, in what we will come to know and love as a "Firm Ordering" game (things lined up in a definite order), often the rules will have two players, let's call them Adam and Bobby, or "A" and "B", that must be separated by a set number of spaces in line. Let us pretend that there is a rule requiring them to have exactly two spaces between them. This always raises two issues. First, do we recognize that the order of A and B can go A, space, space, B or alternatively, B, space, space, A?

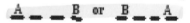

If we think that there is only one of those two possible orders available, we lose points. Second, there is frequently another rule in such games that requires two players, let us call these new players Cindy and David, or "C" and "D", to always

---

[6] http://www.nytimes.com/1987/02/03/science/research-affirms-power-of-positive-thinking.html

stand next to each other in line, and in the order C,D. So C and D are ALWAYS going to look like this:

C D

Now laugh if you must, but there are people out there who do not see one of the key "issues" raised by this: the C,D "bundle" can interlace into the two spaces between A and B or B and A. Strange to think it, but some folks out there cannot wrap their brains around that. They think that the C,D pairing must come before or after the "A, space, space, B". They too lose points.

So DO NOT FIXATE on the details of the example above... there will be plenty of stuff to fixate on soon enough. Rather, train yourself to:

ALWAYS THINK ABOUT GAMES AS HAVING REPETITIVE PATTERNS FORMED BY THE ISSUES RAISED BY THE FACT PATTERN AND FORMAL RULES.

Once you have learned the Test Mentors Method and have practiced enough games, you will recognize all of the issues and shenanigans the test makers put into any new game that you encounter.

II. The Six Types of Logic Games

MEMORIZE this list:

1) Put things in ORDER
2) Put things into BUCKETS
3) Pick WINNERS & LOSERS
4) Follow PROCEDURES
5) Make a DRAWING
6) COMBO: combination of two or more of the above

These are the ONLY kinds of logic games you are going to encounter on the LSAT. The first step in crushing any particular game is to understand precisely what kind of a game it is. Let us take a moment to understand what each kind of game is and how it works. This will enable us to quickly recognize them and launch directly into eviscerating them.

Putting things in order – "ORDERING"
The "simplest"[7] kind of game on the LSAT is the "ordering" game. In these games you will be asked to put a list of items or people or animals or "*whatevers*" into some

---

[7] "Simple" is, admittedly, rather subjective. What we mean by "simple" is that the majority of people find this type of game to be the easiest to understand and master. This does not mean that in your individual case these will be the easiest: everyone is different, thinks uniquely and sees the world in

sort of sequence. The set up for the "Bus stop" game we introduced earlier is an example of an ordering game.

There are two sub-types of ordering games. In the first type, which we shall call "FIRM," there are exact positions into which things can be assigned and those positions fall in a set, pre-defined order: think seats in a row at the theater numbered one through seven, or parking spots in a garage numbered one through six from left to right, or floors in a hotel numbered first through seventh etc. The only thing that they can do to "freak us out" is to make the pre-defined order look goofy. We will see that, much the way a cat arches it back to look big and scary to dogs, this is all just, "Trickery! Trickery! Trickery!"[8]

In the second sub-type, which we shall call "SQUISHY," we are supposed to determine relative relationships between characters: which player is more or less popular than another. There are fewer definitive *sounding* elements to these games, but notice how the word "sounding" was italicized to indicate that this is just a trick and not a reality. If "A" is more popular than "B," and "B" is more popular than "C," and "C" is more popular than "D," we know that "A" is more popular than "B," "C," and "D," and that "B" is more popular than "C" and "D". All we have to do is think a little before we use our pencils.

The essence of both firm and squishy ordering games is the same: the *order in which things can or must appear is what is being tested.*

Putting things into "BUCKETS"

This second type of game should always be thought of as sticking stuff into buckets, even when it does not sound like there are buckets to stick stuff into. For example, read over the following fact pattern.

> Two awls, two chisels, two drills, two planes and one saw, are the only tools being distributed amongst four carpenters, Willis, Xenophilius, Yancy and Zunfufu. Each carpenter receives at least one tool, and all of the tools are distributed. The following conditions determine the assignment of tools to carpenters.

Are you being asked to put things into buckets? Actually, YES! The four "buckets" are W, X, Y and Z and we are putting tools into each of them. It is very important that you get into the habit of thinking in these terms, because these kinds of games are much easier than most, but only if we think of them as "things in buckets" rather than some other abstraction or worse, the specific facts that the game uses to confuse us.

---

their own special way. Please refrain from thinking that there is something wrong with you if you find these games to be difficult. Many very bright people struggle with them.

[8] Gary Larsen, The Far Side, FarWorks, Inc.

Notice that the fact pattern was very careful to tell you precisely how many tools there are of each type. This is a key distinguishing characteristic of this type of game: we have a definitive set and number of "things" to put into a definitive set of "buckets."

Contrast the last fact pattern with the following:

> *Awls, chisels, drills, planes and saws, are the only tools being distributed amongst four carpenters, Willis, Xenophilius, Yancy and Zunfufu. The following conditions determine the assignment of tools to carpenters.*

It is the same set of people and the same kinds of tools as before, however it is slightly different. Here, we are not told *how many* of each tool there are: there could be one saw or there could be ten. Neither have we been told whether or not each person gets a tool: perhaps one of our carpenters will have no tools to work with, which, despite sounding grossly inefficient, is completely possible in LSAT land (and in reality, where a supervising carpenter might enjoy pastries whilst underlings toil). It is also possible at this point that every carpenter gets one of every tool type, another possibility that cannot be overlooked. The test maker is relying upon these sorts of ambiguities to intimidate and confuse you. We have an iron-clad way of dealing with them however, and just like all other games, we will reduce the possible outcomes to exact answers. Ultimately, we are just putting things (tools) into buckets (people).

Picking WINNERS AND LOSERS
Consider the following fact pattern:

> *An awl, chisel, drill, plane and saw are the only tools that might be in Willis the carpenter's tool chest. Which tools are in the chest is determined by the following conditions:*

The set up is short; frighteningly so. Again, the test maker is trying to either lull you into a trap ("This looks simple and easy."), intimidate you by using the wide-opened nature of the fact pattern to make you believe that the game can go a million different ways, or both. In the end, we are just determining what is in the chest, and thus what must not be in it. It is distinct from a BUCKET game in that there is only one bucket, i.e. the tool chest, and that would not make for a very challenging test of one's reasoning abilities. The conditions of the game, as dictated by the rules, are aimed at a different objective: which tools are used (winners) and which are not (losers).

The rules for these kinds of games tend to be a bit tricky to master. We will learn how to understand them precisely and we will learn how to do some logical operations that yield a much deeper understanding of those rules, an understanding that makes us so much more than average. Every single time we encounter these games we will get every question correct. Along the way we will refresh some fundamentals of logic that you may not have seen for some time. If you have never seen them, you will learn them. They aren't that tough. This logic will have application to other parts of the LSAT, to law school and to the practice of law as well... We are throwing that in as a bonus!

Follow the PROCEDURE/ Make a DRAWING

Though tested very infrequently, these problems, when they show up, will be a snap to pound out. Here is an example of a fact pattern:

> *"Awls, chisels, drills, planes and saws are the only tools which may be used by a carpenter. Over the course of several days the carpenter builds a cabinet, with at least one tool being employed each day. The procedure for selecting the tools used and the days upon which they are used is as follows:"*

Here we have a hugely ambiguous fact pattern. How many days does the carpenter work? No idea. How many tools are used? No idea. Can a carpenter work with more than one tool at a time? No idea. Can the carpenter use two tools on the same day? How about three? We know zilch. All of these kinds of questions and more float through the mind of the test taker.

Not so for you. You will be given a list of rules that describe the process of building the cabinet. Typically the rules will tell us the process that must be followed on a day-by-day basis, and then we are asked about specific days. That forces us to figure out and understand what happened during the preceding days, which we can logically and easily determine.

Combinations - COMBO

Finally, there will be games that ask you to do two of the game types at the same time. For example, we might be asked to put things into buckets and then put the buckets into a particular order. Other times we might be asked to pick winners and losers and then to put the winners into buckets. Two tasks at the same time sounds tougher. Again, this is sheer trickery. For most people this kind of game is the most frightening, but it ought not be. By the time we are done, you will see that they are actually easier overall because of this fundamental principle of the logic game: *"The more information we have and the more rules and requirements that there are, the fewer possible outcomes there can be."* **Memorize that**.

You can see how this might help law schools to identify potentially great legal minds. Laws are written to use sets of rules to limit possible outcomes. If you can do it with tools and carpenters, people in bus lines etc, you can probably do it with statutes, municipal codes, administrative regulations etc.

HERE IS ONE FINAL AND VERY IMPORTANT, NOTE BEFORE BEGINNING THE METHODOLOGY. We begin with the easiest of games, and with the easiest of rules. This is by design. We want most of your energy going into ***learning the steps of the method and learning how to use them well.*** MANY times throughout the next chapter you may see "obvious" deductions and "obvious" answers even before you begin applying the strategies you are learning. This will be because it is an easy game by design, in order to better help you learn and master the methods. DO EVERY STEP, EVERY TIME. That is a fundamental rule of law school and lawyering. The lawyer who gets lazy while handling a simple drunk driving case and fails to go down the check list might miss important Constitutional issues. That is called malpractice. That is not cool.

DO NOT DELUDE YOURSELF INTO THINKING THAT YOU DO NOT NEED TO LEARN ALL OF THE METHODS WE TEACH! When the games get tougher (and they will) you will NOT maximize your potential unless you have mastered ALL of the steps on the easier games. Think of it thusly: when a person is learning to hit a baseball for the first time, they practice the fundamental skill of swinging the bat. Next, a ball is put upon a tee-stand for them to practice using their fundamental swing to make contact with the ball and not the tee-stand. Once that is perfected, the ball gets pitched slowly so the batter can practice the ***additional*** skill of keeping their eyes on the ball in flight to make contact while adjusting to variations in position and speed. Then, when those skills meld, the pitches get faster and the kinds of pitches (knuckle balls, curves, sliders etc.) are varied. The batter cannot hope to become a top-level hitter if he or she is not doing ALL of the acquired skills simultaneously. They can become a bench warmer or get cut from the team all together. We sincerely hope that these are not your intentions. We assume that you want to play in the big leagues. Here is how you do it.

III. The Five Step Method

Here is where we get down to the nitty-gritty.

The single most important key to LSAT success is to know the answers to the questions before you look at the answer choices[9]. **MEMORIZE** that and make it part of your being.

BAD HABIT #1

The reason that the average test taker is "average" (153-ish) is because they lack the discipline to stick to an absolute methodology. These people use "ad hoc" methods (i.e. they wing it). That cannot be you. Memorize this method and practice it until you begin to have nightmares about it.

This is not just an LSAT truism, it is a rule for being a great law student and for being a great lawyer: law school and the practice of law are *NOT* multiple-choice (although part of the bar examination is...go figure). On *any multiple choice test* (including the bar exam), if you know the correct answer before you look at the choices, your only task is to identify the answer choice that is the same as the answer you know to be true. This is much safer and far more wise than reading every choice and considering them all.

The Five Step Method is:
1) GET A GRIP
2) Re-write the FORMAL RULES
3) Make a DRAWING
4) Draw INFERENCES
5) DESTROY the questions

Our study of the logic games method will initially focus on the fact pattern for the following game we discussed previously:

> *"Each of six people, Adam, Bobby, Cindy, David, Edward and Francine are waiting in line for a bus, and are the only people in line. They are standing in a line, one person per spot, with the person at the front of the line being first and the person at the end being sixth. The order in which they stand is consistent with the following rules."*

STEP ONE: Get a Grip

The first step involved in doing *any* logic game is to get a grip on the game itself. "Get a grip," means that you need to identify the relevant information for game solving

---

[9] There will be occasions when you will be forced to look at the choices first, because of how the question is phrased. For example, you might have a question that reads, *"Which of the following must be true?"* You can hardly be expected to answer that question without looking at the answer choices. HOWEVER, as you will see, if you are doing everything that you paid heap-big-dollars to learn from this book, you will already have the answer anyway!

located in the **FACT PATTERN**. This does **not** include looking at the list of formal rules that follows the fact pattern: we will get to them in step two. Just remember that every game has a fact pattern paragraph at the beginning that contains critical GRIP information.

Here is the list of the relevant things you must identify every single time, without fail. **Memorize them**.

A) What is the NATURE of the game: what kind of game is it?
B) Who are the PLAYERS?
C) What are the HIDDEN RULES?

A) What kind of game is it?
In the first chapter we saw that there are only six kinds of games:
1) Put things in ORDER (Firm or Squishy)
2) Put things into BUCKETS
3) Pick WINNERS and LOSERS
4) Follow PROCEDURES
5) Make a DRAWING
6) COMBINATION

We also saw that each type of game has distinguishing characteristics. We told you to memorize them. **_If you did not, go back right now and do so._** Seriously... go do it now. We will all just wait for you...

> "Each of Adam, Bobby, Cindy, David, Edward and Francine are waiting in line for a bus, and are the only people in line. They are standing in a line, one person per spot, with the person at the front of the line being first and the person at the end being sixth. The order in which they stand is consistent with the following rules."

In this game, we are being asked to figure out which order people are in. That makes it a "put things in order" game, or "ORDERING". If you do not see why, take the time right now to think it through. The last sentence of the fact pattern is our biggest clue: *"The order in which they stand is consistent with the following rules."* That tells us half of what we need to know. We also will have to determine whether this is a "firm" or "squishy" ordering game, which we will pin down momentarily. For right now it is enough to know that it is an ordering game.

> **BAD HABBIT #2: Sloppiness**
> On the actual LSAT, there is NO SCRATCH PAPER ALLOWED. You must work in the test booklet, and space is sometimes limited. There is no shame in losing to the LSAT. There IS shame in throwing away easy points because you were a sloppy spaz.

B) Who are the players?
Next you must identify who *and what* the relevant players are. What is important to know is that "players" are *everything* that might participate in the game. Notice that

we did not say, "everyone." In the present game, there are six people, A,B,C,D,E and F. But there are also six "positions" to which they are assigned, slots one through six.

So off to the side, or at the top or bottom of the page, you are going to write out all of the players and label them appropriately. It should look something like this:

> People- ABCDEF
> Slots 1 - 6

Each of Adam, Bobby, Cindy, David, Edward and Francine are waiting in line for a bus, and are the only people in line. They are standing in a line, one person per spot, with the person at the front of the line being first and the person at the end being sixth. The order in which they stand is consistent with the following rules.

C) What are the Hidden Rules?

As you realize by now, we have the fact pattern paragraph for the game, and then we have a list of *formal rules* right below it. We have deliberately left the list of rules out of the mix in the "Get a Grip," step for good reasons. Most people make two FATAL mistakes early on in doing logic games: they rush through the "Get a Grip" step and/or they put all of their attention on the list of rules. If there are rules hidden in the fact pattern (there usually are), people who are speed freaks are dead on arrival, which is awesome for you, because the speed freaks have to pay for law school, thus financing your scholarship.

> *Hurrying is a sin.*
> **Memorize that.**

The key to figuring things out is to take the time to THINK before we act. The test makers take special care to provide you with lots of opportunities to screw things up…royally. That is mighty decent of them, no? We will always take our time and follow the step-by-step process with merciless, mechanical, Terminator©-esque discipline and precision.

The fact pattern tells us that there are no other players, that all six players participate ("Each of…"), that the front of the line is position number one, and that the back of the line is position number six. If there are six people and six positions, and each person must be in the line, then they must all participate in this little monkeyshine. All of this is critical to the logic!

So now we have to add little notes to our list of players to indicate that these "hidden rules" exist and are not to be overlooked, like so:

> People- ABCDEF   No others
> Slots 1 - 6   All Play
>   1=front, 6=rear

Each of Adam, Bobby, Cindy, David, Edward and Francine are waiting in line for a bus, and are the only people in line. They are standing in a line, one person per spot, with the person at the front of the line being first and the person at the end being sixth. The order in which they stand is consistent with the following rules.

MAJOR, IMPORTANT POINT!
The RULES DEFINE THE ISSUES being tested. Both the hidden rules from Step One and the Formal Rules of Step Two are **not** there to mess with your head. They are there to define exactly what issues are addressed. If a rules says that Adam and Cindy are separated by exactly one space, then one of the *issues* being tested is whether or not you can recognize situations that would force a violation of that rule. ANY run-of-the-mill, mouth-breathing, slack-jawed troglodyte can spot an answer choice that has Adam and Cindy too close together or too far apart. The best test takers can infer from the rest of the rules and the additional information in question calls when such a violation will result later, even though it is not expressly stated in an answer choice.

RULES DEFINE ISSUES

Step 2: Re-write the FORMAL RULES

Below the fact pattern will be a list of *formal rules*. This is where we get most of the logic for solving the questions. This logic ALWAYS leads us to an absolute, 100% clear answer to any question, provided we do not screw it all up, which we will not, because we are going to do as we are told.

Here is our little sample game with its formal rules:

> *Each of six people, Adam, Bobby, Cindy, David, Edward and Francine are waiting in line for a bus, and are the only people in line. They are standing in a line, one person per spot, with the person at the front of the line being first and the person at the end being sixth. The order in which they stand is consistent with the following rules."*
>
> *Adam and Cindy are separated by exactly one space in line.*
> *Francine is the fourth person from the front.*
> *Bobby is in a lower numbered position than David.*

We are going to **re-form every formal rule** into a notation that is usable later on. It **must** be *visually consistent* with the nature of the game (which we will discuss in more detail shortly). But we can already imagine that six people standing in a line going from the front (at the left) to the back (at the right) looks like six spaces lined up left to right.

Begin by putting a little number next to each of the printed formal rules so that you can keep track of them. If you are tempted to *not* get into this habit, FORGET ABOUT IT! Yes, this is an easy game with three simple rules. That does not mean that you can be a lazy slacker and not develop good habits[10]. We are building skills through developing good habits. We are trying to make the initial phases of the process easier by making things straightforward. If you do not develop all of the skills and

---

[10] Many a lawyer, used to handling complex litigation, have gotten their rear-end kicked in small claims battles because they were out of practice with fundamental habits. They miss basic things...all because the small claim was an "easy" case and they slacked off. There is a word for that: *malpractice.*

habits early with the easy games, you will not do well at the challenging games. Then you will try to blame this book for your failings, rather than take personal responsibility for your failure to learn and master what we are teaching. Let us just resolve to avoid that distasteful possibility right now: write in the freakin' numbers please. NOW.

Formal rule number one (which is easy to identify by the "1" you just put next to it) says that Adam and Cindy are separated by exactly one space. Can Adam and Cindy have two spaces between them? Nope. There must be EXACTLY one space between them. Can they be side-by-side? NOPE. There has to be exactly one space between them. When the test makers go to the trouble of handing you an iron-clad, absolute, no-b.s. rule like this one, you must (a) take advantage of it and (b) make sure that you include the "absoluteness" of it in your re-forming of it.

What we are NOT being told in rule number 1? They are separated by exactly one space, but we have no clue as to whether it goes Adam-space-Cindy or Cindy-space-Adam. That means that it could, as of this moment, go either way. So that is how we re-phrase the rule. We write:

1) A/C _ C/A

The slash "/" means, "either - or". MEMORIZE THAT. It indicates that either "A" or "C" goes into a slot, then there is precisely one space, (the "_" indicates one space) then its opposite number goes into the third spot. These three "players" (A, space and C) form a three-player "bundle". As we shall see in a bit, this is AWESOME.

Our second rule says that Francine is fourth. More awesomeness! It is even more definite than the first rule. We re-write it as:

1) A/C _ C/A
2) F=4

Finally, our third rule says that Bobby is in a lower numbered position than David. This tells us a good deal more than we might initially believe. If the "front" of the line is position number one, then Bobby is closer to the front than David. We have no idea whether Bobby is in position 1, 2 etc. Similarly, we have no idea if there are any people standing between Bobby and David: Bobby could be in position 1, and David could be in 2 without violating this rule.

Because we have no idea how many spaces there are (or are not) between them, we rewrite the rule thus:

1) A/C _ C/A
2) F=4
3) B....D

The ellipsis indicates a relationship between B and D (platonic, for sure) where B is always to the left of D. In other words, B is always BEFORE D, and that means BEFORE is always to the LEFT of AFTER.

And now we have all three of our rules written out in a compact form that is *visually* useful. The importance of visual appeal is about to become clear.

STEP 3: Make a DRAWING

Your job in Step 3 is to create a visual picture of what is going on in the game. This is of SUPREME importance; so do not even *think* about skipping this step.

We are going to use our little picture to figure out the hard-core logical guts of the game, all of the tricks and most of the answers *before we ever even look at the questions*! The picture and the work we do with it makes it all happen.

We know that this is an "ordering" game. Remember that

> **Numbering Things in Ordering Games**
> Here are hard and fast rules that you will always follow. MEMORIZE THEM!
> A) Unless otherwise instructed, the first position is on the left, the last is on the right.
> B) Top position is always at the top, bottom position is always at the bottom.
> C) "Higher" is always drawn above "lower".
> D) Sometimes the bottom position is number one, sometimes it is number last (if we are told that the top shelf is shelf #1, the bottom is last).
>
> Yes, these seem pretty, "duh," right now, but if they are not ingrained and absolute in your head, it will slow you down and/or screw you up at some point.

there are two varieties of ordering: "firm ordering" and "squishy ordering". Often times it is hard to tell from the fact pattern which variety the game actually is. Once we have listed out all of the *hidden rules* and the given list of *formal rules* it is obvious which it is.

Firm ordering games have definite positions and lots of definite rules, just like in our present game.

People ABCDEF	1) A/C _ C/A
Slots 1 - 6	2) F=4
No others	3) B....D
All Play	
1= front, 6=rear	

The only squishy rule that we have is rule number three, which says that B is "somewhere" before D, but otherwise the game is looking pretty firm. Let us proceed to draw it as such.

ABCDEF

Front _ _ _ _ _ _ Back
1 2 3 4 5 6

Voila! Here we have a visual representation of the line of positions with "1" at the front and "6" at the back. We have our other players (the people) listed above it. We can imagine this queue at a curb in any city in America, Belize or even Canada. Beauty, eh?

The key to making any drawing is to make sure that the drawing looks like the real-life scenario we are wrestling with. Here, our column of people looks just as we might imagine it in reality...ish.

Because there are a limited number of game types, there will also be a limited number of drawing types. You will memorize all of the drawing types (we will provide a comprehensive list of them, as well as teach you how our methods apply to them all in the coming pages) so that you will know exactly how to proceed automatically. Once you know the drawing that goes with the game, you can get on to the business of step four.

The type of drawing above will work for all firm ordering games. **Memorize it**.

FREE STUFF!

Every now and then the LSAT will provide you with a drawing. They do this because their written description of that game provided too much trouble for test takers when the problem was experimental. So the rule is thus: ***IF THEY GIVE YOU A DRAWING TO USE, USE IT!***

Step 4: DRAWING INFERENCES = ABCDEF

Thus far we have a whole bushel of useful information and it is all very well organized. You may, however, be thinking to yourself, "I still have six freakin' spaces and six freakin' people to put into them, so I am no better off than a monkey at a dartboard!"[11] Here is what separates you from our hairiest of cousins.

The INFERENCES step has rules and checklists. You want to be a lawyer (or else you are a masochist who likes to take the LSAT for no good reason). The law is, in a nutshell, a series of rules and checklists. The LSAT is testing whether or not you have the "goods" to be a lawyer, and one of those "goods" is memorizing and following rules, and then drawing conclusions from them.

For our purposes, "inferring," means applying the rules and drawing *logically valid* conclusions from them. Here are the rules for inferring your way through ***ANY*** type of game.

Memorize them, in order, as "A, B, C, D, E, F". We will march down the list, from A through F, ***every single time*** we do a logic game, so get with the program and memorize them.

---

[11] Any given monkey should be able to score about 125 on any given LSAT. Honest. We are not making that up... that is part of the pre-set curve as well. Also, many actual lawyers are virtually indistinguishable from chimps, which, although technically not monkeys, should reinforce the comforting idea that if those chimps can do it, so can you.

1) Absolutes
2) Bundles
3) Calculators
4) Double-ups
5) Extras
6) Free-rangers

These are the six types of inferences we are going to look for in the game in order to simplify it and to extract the useful inferences before ever seeing a single question.

"Absolutes" are players that absolutely must be in a particular place, or may absolutely **not** be in a particular place or places. Observe that when we are talking about where things **must** be, we used the word "place" rather than "places." There will be times when you will have a rule that says that a player must be in one of two places. That is indefinite though limited: it is not absolute. We will deal with that later. When it comes to where things cannot be, multiple locations *are* definite: if "A" cannot be in spot 1 or three, then it is impossible for it to be in 1 or 3, those things are absolute.

Absolutes, if they exist, need to be considered carefully, and whenever possible, stuffed into our picture. Do we have any absolutes? Yes we do! Rule number two says that "F" is always in spot number four. Let's jam that bad boy into 4 and circle it to indicate that it is 100% anchored there. After that, we will cross the "F" off of our list of players, because we no longer need to worry about "F", as it is ALWAYS going to be right there, absolutely:

People ABCDEF
Slots 1-6   1) A/C _ C/A
No others   2) F=4
All Play   3) B....D
1=front, 6=rear

A B C D E ~~F~~

Front _ _ _ Ⓕ _ _ Back
       1̄ 2̄ 3̄ 4 5̄ 6̄

Are there any other things that fit the definition of an *absolute*? YES there are...if you remember the definition. If B must always come before D, which slot can B **never** go into? Slot 6, because if B were to be in 6, how could D possibly go after it, when the kind test makers told us that 6 is the last spot? So B can never go in 6, and by the same type of reasoning, D can never go into slot 1. So **below** slots 1 and 6 we are going to indicate the things that cannot go into them, like so:

People ABCDEF
Slots 1-6
No others
All Play
1=front, 6=rear

1) A/C _ C/A
2) F=4
3) B....D

A B C D E̶F̶

Front _ _ (F) _ _   Back
       1 2   3   4 5 6
      -D   -B

"Bundles" are groups of players that are always together in a clump. Do we have any of those? YES! "A/C _ C/A" is a bundle of three. Even though we do not know exactly where they go or which comes first, we do know, for example, if "C" is in slot 1, "A" has to be in slot 3, or if "A" is in slot 1, "C" is in slot 3.

The magic of bundles is that they can only go into *available* slots. They can never go into non-existent (positions zero and 7) slots, nor slots which are occupied by "absolutes" (like slot #4 where F *must* be)!

So where can we stuff our bundle? We know it will go into 1 and 3. Can either A or C go into slot 2? If A is in #2, where does C have to go? Slot 4, which is where F is. So the bundle cannot go into 2 or 4. What about slot 3? We already saw that A/C can go into 3, and its opposite can go into 1. Can its opposite go anywhere else? Look at the picture. If A or C is in 3, its opposite can also go into 5!

Find, Bubble, Move

For EVERY question on the LSAT there is *exactly one correct answer*. If you find an answer in any logic game that both fits your picture and complies will the rules that are not in the picture, it MUST be the correct answer, and all of the other choices **must be incorrect!**

Ergo, if you deem "C" to be the correct answer, NEVER, EVER, EVER read "D" or "E", as they cannot be correct. "Just checking to be sure," translates to, "I don't want to go to law school all that badly, and a career at Wal-Mart is on my horizon." You can work at Wal-Mart without taking the LSAT, so logically, if you are going to waste time, stop studying right now, buy a blue vest and apply for the job.

MEMORIZE THAT.

So here is what we do: we put the "A/C _ C/A" bundle into the 1 and 3 slots, then we re-draw the picture with the bundle in the 3 and 5 slots. Those are the only two places that the bundle is allowed to go because F is clogging up the works. If you do not see what we mean, take a moment and try to jam the A/C _ C/A bundle into any other slot combination other than the 1-3 and 3-5 pairs. Go ahead...do it, just to be sure.

Thus, we have taken a game that appeared to have *720* possible outcomes at the start to a game with only TWO POSSIBLE SOLUTIONS! Let us label them P1 for "possibility 1" and P2 (if you cannot figure out what P2 stands for, perhaps a career in law is not for you). Once the A/C _ C/A bundle is placed in the only two places that it can go, we can check them off of the list of things we need to pay attention to as well.

People ABCDEF
Slots 1-6
No others
All Play
1=front, 6=rear

1) A/C _ C/A
2) F=4
3) B....D **

P1   A B C D E F

Front ᴬ/ᶜ   ᶜ/ᴬ Ⓕ _ _ Back
       1̄ 2̄ 3̄ 4̄ 5̄ 6̄
       -D   -B

P2   A B C D E F

Front _ ᴬ/ᶜ Ⓕ ᶜ/ᴬ _ Back
       1̄ 2̄ 3̄ 4̄ 5̄ 6̄
       -D   -B

Notice how we added a pair of asterisks after rule #3. Rules 1 and 2 are both stuffed into our drawing, and they are absolutely the only ways that the players involved may be arranged. So it serves no purpose whatsoever for us to waste time looking back at those rules. The asterisks indicate that rule 3 is the only rule we will ALWAYS need to keep an eye on because it is not in the drawing!

REMEMBER: Just because an answer choice to a question might fit one or both of your pictures, that does not mean that the answer choice is the correct one. In order to be correct, an answer has to comply with the picture(s) **and** whichever rules *are not incorporated into the picture(s)* EVERY TIME! **Memorize that!**

If you do not understand what was just said, the following example should clarify matters completely.

1) *Which of the following is an accurate possible listing of the people in line, in order, from first to last?*

A) *Francine, Bobby, David, Cindy, Adam, Edward*
B) *Adam, Edward, Cindy, Francine, David, Bobby*
C) *Edward, Bobby, Cindy, Francine, Adam, David*
D) *Adam, Bobby, Cindy, David, Edward, Francine*
E) *Cindy, David, Adam, Francine, Edward, Bobby*

When we compare answer choice (A) to our pictures it is obvious that it is incorrect in both P1 and P2: F can never be in slot 1. So we would draw a line through "A" and move on to choice (B): *A, E, C, F, D, B*. When we compare it to P1, it works perfectly, so we get spastic, bubble in "B" on the answer grid and move on to the next question, because you followed the rule in the last call-out box on page 26. The problem is that "B" is incorrect even though it fits into a drawing. Rule number 3 says that B must always come before D, and in answer choice B, the order is reversed. We should have cross off B and move on to "C".

If we look at answer choice (C), *E, B, C, F, A, D*, we compare it to P1. P1 has A or C in slot 1, so answer "C" does not fit into P1. How about P2? C is in 3 and A is in 5, which is precisely what P2 requires (along with F in slot 4). We only have to check to make certain rule 3 is complied with. B comes before D, so answer choice "C" MUST BE correct... HEY! This is just like law! There are rules, and if you comply with the rules you are "valid." Bubble that bad boy in on the answer form and move to the next question without wasting time looking at D or E.

Thus far we have addressed the "A" and the "B" of the ABCDEF steps of drawing inferences. The "Calculators" "Double-ups" "Extras" and "Free ranger" steps are not critical to this game. However, we ALWAYS want to make certain that we check all six steps **EVERY SINGLE TIME**: this is a battle, and success in battle depends upon discipline just as much as it does skill. Combined, skill and discipline create speed. Speed, discipline and skill add up to a full scholarship to law school.

"Calculators" means that we are looking over the rules for any indication that there might be some mathematical implications to the game, either in the form of numerical combinations, ratios or permutations. DON'T PANIC![12] The math-like concepts are super easy. Allow us to illustrate with an example.

Let us pretend that there is an additional rule that reads, "Bobby's space number in line is half of that of David's." That would tell us a whole bunch. First, it means that David cannot be in an odd-numbered slot, such as 5. That is because there is no slot 2½ for Bobby to go into. It also means that if Bobby is in slot 1, David is in slot 2, or if David is in slot 6, Bobby is in slot 3. I do hope that this clarifies matters. We will see games later that require us to spot *calculators*.

There are four calculators that we always want to look for.
   a) Ratios (the requirement of so many "X" for every "Y")
   b) Combinations (things that can and cannot go together)
   c) Permutations (number of different possible arrangements)
   d) 2/3 Scenarios (two spots available for three things)

We will flesh all of these out later on.

"Double-ups" refers to the hunt for *two or more rules that apply to the same player(s)*. If there are two or more rules that constrain the actions of the same player, there are usually logical inferences we can draw from them by merging the individual rules into "über-rules".

For example, let us pretend for a moment that we have a different additional rule, which states that, "D always comes before F."
                1) A/C _ C/A
                2) F=4
                3) B...D ***
                4) D...F

Rule 3 says that B always comes before D, and rule 2 says F is always in slot 4. Rules 3 and 4 both talk about D, and rules 2 and 3 both talk about F. There are two "double-ups," (2 & 4 talking about "F" and 3 & 4 talking about "D") so we think about putting them together, like so:

                    B...D...F
                        4

---

[12] The test makers know that almost all LSAT takers fear math. If you were really comfortable with math, you wouldn't have gone from pre-med or pre-engineering to pre-law, right? So sometimes they throw in math-like stuff just to mess with your head. It's all good if you remember the guiding principle, "What one fool can do, so can another," because although it is math like, it is simple.

If B must be in front of D, and D must be in front of F, and F is in 4 at all times, that would tell us that D would have to go into slots 2 or 3. Our two drawings:

```
                    People ABCDEF
                    Slots 1-6        1) A/C _ C/A
                    No others        2) F=4
                    All Play         3) B....D **
                    1=front, 6=rear
        P1                                   P2
            A B C D E F                          A B C D E F

     Front A/C   C/A (F)     Back     Front         A/C (F) C/A     Back
           1  2  3  4  5  6                    1  2  3  4  5  6
           -D             -B                   -D             -B
```

would tell us that slot 3 can only have A or C, so B would have to go into 1, D into slot 2, A or C in 3, and F into slot 4. But we know even more! If B is in 1, then we cannot be looking at Picture 1, because A or C have to be in Picture 1. So we have to be in Picture 2. That means that C or A have to be in slot 5, and that just leaves E for slot 6.

If we had this imaginary "D...F" rule, there would be exactly *one* solution, and this would not be a very challenging logic game...that's why it is not there in the first place. HOWEVER, this is precisely how the game makers form questions! They give you the three rules and then they ask, "If D comes before F, which of the following must be true?" We can figure that out, easy as pie.

We will work with double-ups and merging rules together later. Do not try too hard to wrap your brain around it yet. We only introduced it now so that you don't spend the next fifty pages wondering what they are. We will vigorously employ double-ups later and learn the nitty-gritty thereof.

"Extras" are yummy-delicious, hard-core logical inferences planted within the rules, whether they be in a hidden rules (from step one) or the formal rules (step two). We will cover hard-core LSAT logic rules in painless detail after we cover the basics of firm and squishy ordering as well as *bucket* games. *Winner-loser* games are built on conditional logic, so we cover those games right after we do the logic chapter. NOTE however that conditional logic is not exclusive to *winner-loser* games: it can rear it's fugly face **_anywhere_** on the LSAT, and in *any* type of game.

There will be six "Extras" to be on the lookout for:
   a) Bi-conditionals
   b) Forced dichotomies
   c) Affirmative duties
   d) The right-side rule
   e) Contradictions
   f) Lone conditionals

Don't worry about what they are. We will reiterate and illuminate later. For now, try to memorize them in order, because that is how we will be using them, and there will be a "quiz" in the next segment on Squishy Ordering games.

"Free-Ranger(s)" are all of the players that have large degrees of freedom because there are no rules which *directly* address them. Our slots, which are also players, have no freedom at all. They are all locked into an absolute order (and THAT fact is crucial: any time we are in doubt about how to construct a drawing in step 3 of the process, we will hunt for the most *absolute* player, because if something cannot move, it is easier to kill...just ask a lion).

Are there any other players that have rules limiting their freedom? F is totally limited. A and C are locked in a three-slot-bundle. B and D are trapped in an abusive relationship where B always comes first. That leaves E. E has no rules or other restrictions on it. "E" is our one and only free-ranger.

Please bear in mind that when we say, "free ranger," we do not mean that literally. The logic of the game and the other rules obviously constrain E. For example, E cannot ever go into slot number 3, because our picture shows us that there are only two ways that the game can be played (P1 and P2), and in both of those pictures either A or C must stand in slot 3. The same goes for slot number 4: "F" must be there, so "E" cannot go there, no matter how badly it wishes to do so. In sum, what we really mean is that:

- A free ranger can go anywhere we want, so long as the placement does not force a violation of the rules, and
- Once all of the other players are situated in a manner that does not break any rules, the free ranger can fill in any open spot(s).

We know that every other player has to follow some rule, whereas E just has to fill in whatever slot remains once everyone else is in compliance with the law. The corollary to that is also true. Once E has a home, the rest of the players must work around it. It is critical to identify the free-rangers because they are very frequently the easiest player to deal with in answering questions: they can boss around the other rule-bound players. Also, when the LSAT weasels ask us:

"If Edward is in position 1, which of the following must be true?"

We take a look back at P1 and P2.

People ABCDEF
Slots 1-6
No others
All Play
1=front, 6=rear

1) A/C _ C/A
2) F=4
3) B....D **

P1   A B C D E F

Front A/C _ C/A (F) _ _ Back
       1 2 3 4 5 6
      -D   -B

P2   A B C D E F

Front _ _ A/C (F) C/A _ Back
       1 2 3 4 5 6
      -D   -B

E cannot go into slot one in P1, as A or C must. So we are in P2. Once our lone-free-ranger is stuffed into slot 1, we know that E has to be in 1, F has to be in 4, the A/C _ C/A bundle has to be in 3 and 5 (but we do not know which MUST be where, so they will have nothing to do with our correct answer choice, which is something that MUST be true), and "B" MUST come before "D", and that fills up slots 2 and 6. Yippie-ki-yay!

Knowing who is free to roam about the cabin is powerful when question time rolls around.

STEP FIVE: DESTROY THE QUESTIONS ●

GO WITH WHAT YOU ALREADY KNOW

Destroying the questions is another great place for you, the highly trained logic game player to screw up. After doing all of the work in the first four steps, there is a real temptation to get both a sense of urgency (because you spent a good chunk of time figuring stuff out) and of overconfidence (because you own the game by the time you get to step five).

You must practice answering and destroying questions in a very systematic way. There is an actual process to doing it, and it is only by rigidly sticking to the methodology that you will maximize efficiency and thus, your score. Here are the steps.

MEMORIZE THEM:
 a) Read and translate the _call of the question_ into what it means logically.
 b) Check what we already know and GO WITH IT.
 c) Only if necessary: Pencil Protocols
  1) Re-picture
  2) Apply new information from the question call (the "if")
   Go to the rules and see what the rules indicate must happen.
      *If the rules tell you that something else must occur, apply that change to your re-picture and repeat step 3.
      *If the rules do not indicate that anything else is to occur (i.e. no further changes need to happen to your re-picture) then you have the answer.

We will explain how these steps work as we plow through questions together in just a page or two.

As if those were not enough to contend with, there are other considerations as well. First, you have to pick your victims carefully. What that means is that you have to learn to recognize which games are the easiest and which are the most difficult **for you**. We emphasize "for you," because not every problem is equally easy or difficult for every person. For some people the questions that ask you for the "complete and accurate list," of the players who can do certain things are difficult, whereas others find those to be simple. It will almost always vary from person to person[13].

---

[13] Most of the companies that sell LSAT material go to the effort of rating the "difficulty" of the problems. This is a completely loaded diaper. First, it plants seeds in your mind, and they are weed

Don't let that get you down, especially if you are studying with a "Rain Man"[14] who just glances at a problem and says, "Definitely 'C.' Time for *Wapner*." Learn which games to do first and which questions within a game to kill immediately, and which to skip and come back to later. Frequently, answering some of the other questions will help us to answer the ones that we personally find problematic. We will try to give you guidance on such matters as we go, with most of it coming later in the book, after we have learned and mastered more of the fundamentals.

Second, by the time you get to the questions, you *have* done a lot of work. Why, in the name of all that is holy, would you do all of that work and then just leave it all behind, or worse, mess it all up? Lots of people do, and it is almost always because they worry about time and thus rushing, or they get too cocky (easy to do when you are a wicked-bad-awesome LSAT Jedi) or both. Rationally however, this means that such people *wasted* all of the time they spent working through the first part of the game. WE NEVER WASTE TIME. We are always looking at everything that we have already done and we are NEVER touching our pictures once completed: if we need to pencil something in for a problem, we have the pencil protocols outlined above.

If you do happen to find yourself having wasted time, consider punishing yourself. I recommend viewing the movies, *Buffalo '66* and/or *The Last Winter.* If they don't teach you a lesson about wasting time, nothing will.

We will walk through every type of game, step-by-step and emphasize the importance of using all of the work you did in the first four steps. Doing those four steps perfectly is critical, and it is a gigantic investment of time. If you do not maximize your use of that work, the time, or a portion of it, was essentially wasted. That is naughty.

AN IMPORTANT NOTE ABOUT DOING PRACTICE PROBLEMS

In order to convince you of the power of that which you have just learned, we are going to do a few additional questions from the bus line game. Get out your pencil and notepad, because we will explain some of the question types you will encounter, strategies for crushing them, patterns that habitually show up on the test and reiterate many of the principles covered thus far.

---

seeds, not valuable crops: if you *think* they are difficult, for any reason, they become more so. Think about it. You might be able to do something that I think is hugely difficult: play a wicked guitar solo, crochet a poncho, stomach a Matthew McConaughey movie, etc. To you it may be as easy as breathing. Second, their "difficulty ratings" are based on either statistics (if 75% of their slack-jawed students miss it, the problem is "difficult") or the "considered judgment" of a bunch of their in-house LSAT monkeys. What does any of that have to do with whether or not <u>you</u> can crack the problem? JACK SQUAT.

[14] "Rain Man" is the copyrighted property of Metro-Goldwyn-Mayer Studios, Inc. If you have not seen it, do so, but rent it *legally.* You are going to be a lawyer for crying out loud. It is a great movie. It also proves that Tom Cruise can act, and that Dustin Hoffman is, *Mr. Magoriam's Magic Emporium* notwithstanding, amazing.

There is a proper way to do practice problems. We are about to tell you how. There is our way and then there is the incorrect way. Take your pick. Our people have earned jillions of dollars in scholarship money based off of their LSAT scores, if that helps you to decide.

Always work the steps for destroying the problems completely and in order. You do not have to do the questions in order though. As we get deeper into the course, you will notice that doing the problems in the order in which they are presented is not necessarily the most helpful strategy. We will give you tips for each individual problem type as we address them. HERE IS THE MOST IMPORTANT PART.

Math is logic, and so logic games have much in common with math. Most people who are not strong at math are also not very strong at games. We believe that there is a simple explanation in most peoples' cases: math is taught poorly, so students become frustrated or bored or both. Thus most "poor" math students do not practice applying the rules of math, they become more frustrated, they practice less and the entire sweater becomes un-knitted.

We are trying to avoid these pitfalls on our end: We explain every step in laborious detail, (often times overdoing it), tell you to memorize things, draw pictures etc. **Your job is NOT to get correct answers. *Your job is to learn the techniques we are teaching and learn how to apply them well and consistently. If you do this, you will NEVER get an incorrect answer on the logic games section.*** Just like in math class, if you do problems and then rush to check your answer to see whether you are correct or not, you are wasting time and energy. Focus on making sure that you know every step of the process by heart AND how to use them; we are teaching you how to fish so as to enable you to eat for a lifetime.

The greatest progress comes from making certain, each and every time, that you understand why the incorrect answers were incorrect and that you found the proper answer _by way of the correct means_. Practicing the steps over and over is the key, just like in math. Master the process and the correct answers will follow.

Finally, if you do not learn all of the rules, steps and process like the back of your hand, that is not our problem, it is yours. The LSAT is brutally unforgiving of people who slack off and half-ass anything. We will do everything we can to help you, but the LSAT gods help those who help themselves. Why? Because YOU WANT TO BE A LAWYER, and lawyers who are lackadaisical (lazy, indolent etc.) not only get sued, they are an embarrassment to the profession and they ruin the lives of their clients. Again, very naughty.

KNOW EVERY STEP OF THE PROCESS. KNOW HOW THEY WORK IN PRACTICE.

IV. APPLYING THE METHOD TO GAMES

How to Answer the Questions

Remember how the problem has an "anatomy"? There is the *fact pattern* and there are *formal rules*? The questions have parts also: the *"call"* of the question is the part that asks us for an answer. The *"choices"* are the possible answers themselves. The first, obvious thing about the relationship between the call of the question and the choices is this: *there will always be exactly one correct answer and four incorrect answers.* In the event that you are doing a problem and you are convinced that there are two or more possible correct answers, it is virtually guaranteed that you screwed something up: you did some portion of the Five Step Method incorrectly or you have misinterpreted the call of the question, or you did both. Any way you slice it, if you believe that there are more than one correct answer, you need to go back and figure out where you screwed up.

This obvious (and easy to overlook) fact is super-helpful: sometimes, we might not have to take the time to figure out what the correct answer *is.* Rather, we can kill all of the answers that are incorrect. There are problems on the LSAT that are a bugger to solve, but if we can easily get rid of three choices, there will be two left, only one of which we actually have to test out (because if it is a good answer, we bubble it, and if it is a bad answer, the other remaining choice must be correct).

Recall that we said that there are some questions that we may want to skip and come back to later? That almost certainly does not apply to the first question in any given game. The first question in almost every game has something about it that, whether intentional or otherwise, we need to take advantage of. Typically the first question and the answer choices that come with it are arranged in a way that helps one to see whether or not they have screwed up or overlooked something.

For example, if we have a rule in the game that we are looking at presently that says that F is in slot 4. Some people might start looking for all of the answers that have F in some other slot and then crossing them off. Any bloody chimp can do that, and the people who do that score just like every other LSAT chimp: 153. So in almost all cases, we will *not* skip the first question, nor will we approach them as we do the rest of the problems. Rather, the rule for the first question in a game set is:

APPLY THE METHOD FOR DESTROYING THE QUESTION, BUT DO THE ANSWER CHOICES IN ORDER FROM (A) THROUGH (E), PAYING ATTENTION TO PRECISELY WHAT MAKES EACH INCORRECT ANSWER INCORRECT. WE STOP WHEN AND ONLY WHEN WE HAVE FOUND THE CORRECT ANSWER.

The rationality, practicality and usefulness of this approach will become apparent later. For now, you just have to trust us on this one. We are experts. Honest.

When it comes to Step 5, we have a process, and we never want to deviate from that process.

    a) Read and translate the *call of the question* into what it means logically.
    d) Check what we already know and GO WITH IT.
    e) Only if necessary: Pencil Protocols
        1) Re-picture
        2) Apply new information from the question call (the "if")
            Go to the rules and see what the rules indicate must happen.

                If the rules tell you that something else must occur, apply that change to your re-picture and repeat step 3.

                If the rules do not indicate that anything else is to occur (i.e. no further changes need to happen to your re-picture) then you have the answer.

YOU HAD BETTER HAVE MEMORIZED THIS! If not, do it. NOW.

(a) says that you must read *and* you must *translate* the call of the question *completely*. Sometimes it is simple:

> *Which one of the following must be false?*

We do not have much interpreting to do. These questions are for the simple folk: people who can only hope to do an average job (and borrow tons of money in order to finance *your* scholarship). The "tougher" questions (which separate the good from the great) have more complex calls, such as,

> If Roberto does not have pasta and Angela
> does have the falafel, which one of the following
> cannot be amongst the foods eaten by Julio?

WHISKEY-TANGO-FOXTROT? We have to slow down and interpret what we are being asked. We would probably make a note:

$$R = -P, A=F, J \text{ CANNOT HAVE?}$$

Then we would apply the rest of the steps as necessary.

(b) says that we have to check what we already know and GO WITH IT. This is a biggie....HUGE. Giganticus.

Remember the SAT? In particular, do you remember the *math* section of the SAT? Most people, when confronted with anything that is intimidating in the least, grab their security blanket. On the SAT math section, that was the calculator. Most of the math on the SAT is not about solving problems, but is about knowing and following rules and principles. People who grab their security calculator-blankets are wasting time and missing the point (and losing actual points on the test) more often than not. On the LSAT, your *pencil* is the only security blanket you have, and you should not use it unless it is absolutely necessary (which is less than half of the time, if you did steps 1-4 of the Test Mentors Method correctly). When you *need* to use your pencil, it is no longer a security blanket-pencil, it is a *sword*, because it will be destroying questions and getting you points that most other people (the non-above-average) will miss, thus driving you toward the scholarship zone.

DO NOT USE YOUR PENCIL UNNECESSARILY!

(c) says that we are to "re-picture." We already have a picture (from step 3) and we may have two (as a result of step 4's inferences). WE **NEVER** TOUCH THOSE ORIGINAL PICTURES ONCE WE ARE DONE WITH STEP 4!

> You will NOT "lightly" pencil hypothetical information into
> P1 or P2 and then erase it later.
> You will NEVER add to them or erase from them after step 4.
> After step 4, every touch of your P1 and/or P2 is a **BAD TOUCH**.

Why? Because you invested a ton of time into making the picture in the first place. If you screw it up in any way in order to save a few seconds, you have essentially wasted all of the time prior to answering the questions. Say good bye to law school.

So rather than messing with the pictures we have, *if* we need to mark one of them up, we will re-draw the picture and mess with it. For example, returning to our bus stop game, if we have a question call that says,

> If Cindy is the fifth person in line, which
> one of the following must be false?

We would (a) read and interpret, then (b) figure out what we know already and GO WITH IT. Our two pictures

People ABCDEF
Slots 1-6
No others
All Play
1=front, 6=rear

1) A/C _ C/A
2) F=4
3) B....D **

P1   A B C D E F   P2   A B C D E F

Front   A/C   C/A (F)   _ _   Back   Front   _ _ A/C (F) C/A _   Back
     1 2 3 4 5 6   1 2 3 4 5 6
    -D   -B   -D   -B

tell us that if Cindy is in fifth, we can *only* be in P2. WE ALREADY KNOW, without drawing a single other thing, that in P2, C=5 means that A=3 and F=4 and B=1 or 2 and D=2 or 6. We can scan the answer choices for any answer that puts the wrong people in the wrong places (i.e. the answer choice, "D is third" cannot be true and so is the correct answer, just as "B is sixth," would be.

Not everyone is so good at working things like that out without seeing it in pencil. We get that. It is no big deal. If you need to pencil it out, do. BUT YOU SHOULD WORK ON GETTING BETTER AT REDUCING THE AMOUNT OF TIME YOU SPEND DRAWING UNNECESSARILY.

If, based upon all that we know, we cannot find the correct answer, then we can go to our pencil protocols. We would re-picture P2 as physically close as possible to the question, or if there is not enough room, somewhere where there is[15]. As always, we re-picture neatly, compactly and exactly. We would re-picture P2 only, and put C in slot 5 (because they told us that for this question, that is where she is), circle the C, and put A in slot 3, circling it:

P2　　　A B C D E F

Front　　⎡A⎤⎡F⎤⎡C⎤　Back
　　　　 ‾ ‾ 1 2 3 4 5 6
　　　-D　　　　　　 -B

We can see from this re-picture that the things that *must be false* (which is what the call asked for) are: D in 1, B in 6, anyone other than A in 3, F in 4 and C in 5, and A anywhere other than 3, F anywhere other than 4, C anywhere other than 5. If they get "cute" with an answer choice such as,

> Bobby is immediately after Cindy
> Or
> David is immediately in front of Francine

We can see, as clear as day, that they cannot be true. Once we have our re-picture and have applied the new information from the call,

The Pencil Protocols say that we have to check the rules, which we will do. The only one that is not in the drawing is rule 3: B...D. This tells us that B has to be in 1 or 2, and that D has to go into 2 or 6. No big whoop, because we knew that, BUT we are being thorough and developing good habits. They also tell us that if the rules changed anything in the re-picture (made you add or subtract anything), go back to see it the rules apply to the newly modified picture to force further changes. In this case, they did not, so we are done.

---

[15] In olden times, many of the logic games had very little room for scratch work. So if you get your hands on old, "official" LSATs, there may be very little room to work. No worries. Just re-picture neatly and compactly right next to the answer choices for that question. Recently the LSAC started providing tons of extra room for scratch work. Yay.

ORDERING - FIRM

People ABCDEF
Slots 1-6
No others
All Play
1=front, 6=rear

1) A/C _ C/A
2) F=4
3) B....D **

P1

A B C D E F

Front A/C   C/A (F) _ _ Back
       ‾1 ‾2 ‾3 ‾4 ‾5 ‾6
       -D   -B

P2

A B C D E F

Front _ A/C (F) C/A _ Back
       ‾1 ‾2 ‾3 ‾4 ‾5 ‾6
       -D   -B

1) Which of the following is an allowable arrangement of the people, in order from first to last?

   A) *Francine, Bobby, David, Cindy, Adam, Edward*
   B) *Adam, Edward, Cindy, Francine, David, Bobby*
   C) *Edward, Bobby, Cindy, Francine, Adam, David*
   D) *Adam, Bobby, Cindy, David, Edward, Francine*
   E) *Cindy, David, Adam, Francine, Edward, Bobby*

Remember how we told you to focus upon what you already know? Now would be a good time to do that.

Answer "A" is incorrect because in both P1 and P2, F is not allowed in slot 1.
Answer "B" is incorrect because, even though it fits into P1, rule 3 is violated, with David coming before Bobby.
Answer "C" is correct because it fits into P2, and rule 3 (the only rule not in the drawing) is not violated.

WE DO NOT LOOK AT D or E! THAT WOULD BE A WASTE OF TIME!
FIND THE ANSWER, CIRCLE IT, BUBBLE IT IN, MOVE ON!

2) Which of the following is a complete and accurate list of any of the positions in which Cindy may stand?

   A) 1
   B) 1,2
   C) 1,3
   D) 1,3,5
   E) 1,2,3,5,6

Do we already know where Cindy may stand? Yes! P1 and P2 are the ONLY two ways the game can be played. In P1, Cindy can go into slots 1 or 3. In P2 she can go into 3 or 5. All of the time you spent doing the work at the beginning has answered this question ahead of time! The correct answer has to be 1,3,5. That is choice "D" and we are on to the next problem.

NOTE: "C" is incorrect because, though *accurate,* it is not *complete,* and that is what we were asked to find by the call of the question, which we read and translated completely, per Step 5 of the Test Mentors Method.

3) *If Adam is the fifth person in line, which of the following must be true?*
    A) David is second.
    B) Bobby is second.
    C) Edward is fourth.
    D) Edward is before Francine
    E) Bobby is before Francine

NOTE: This **_is_** nearly the same problem we talked through just a few pages back, but you should feel free to use this as a review. Here is our first actual encounter with a "*hypothetical.*" In law school, you will learn rules and study their origins and evolution. Then your professors will ask you hypothetical questions to force you to understand how the rules actually work. That is what the hypothetical questions do on the LSAT as well.

Here, we are being asked what **_MUST_** happen if Adam is in position 5 (which is the same as if Cindy was, just flipped). What do we already know? In P1, Adam is in either slot 1 or 3, so we cannot use that picture. In P2, Adam can be in 3 or 5. So if Adam is in 5, Cindy is in slot 3 and Frank is in 4.

When we are presented with a hypothetical, we do just what we always do: **first** check to see whether or not we have answered the problem in our original work, i.e. "Go with what you already know." This includes ALL OF THE WORK WE HAVE DONE in all of the other questions. Frequently the work on one problem will answer multiple questions (on one LSAT logic games section, *five of the six* questions were answered once one of them was solved).

If we have not (technically, we have not) already discovered the answer AND we cannot logic it out otherwise, then we find the picture that works (P2), and we **_re-picture_** it PUTTING A in 5, F in 4, C in 3 along with all of the other information from P2.

IMPORTANT! You may be thinking, "It is obvious what happens, so why do I need to re-draw the picture?" Well bravo for you. If you do not need to draw it again, do it anyway. Later on we will see that we can skip the re-picture when things are obvious (which is a great way for you to discover whether your sense of "obvious" is correct). HOWEVER, do not skip the re-picture just to save time and/or be lazy. You re-draw WHEN YOU NEED TO because that is the **_habit_** you **_must_** develop: find the answer for yourself, know it to be correct and live or die by your decision. If you do not develop sound habits with the easy games, you will not have the skills and habits for the harder ones. As stated previously, we are simply teaching techniques to you with easy questions so you can focus on *learning the methods.* So pretty please with sugar on top, don't be a prat. Do what we are teaching and re-draw the freakin' picture.[16]

P2   A B C D E F

Front   _ _ Ⓒ Ⓕ Ⓐ _ _   Back
      1   2   3   4   5   6
     -D   -B

Bobby cannot go into slot 6, so he is stuck in 1 or 2. D cannot go into slot 1, so he has to go to 2 or 6. E is our free-ranger, so he goes in any left over spot. We know that there is still a little fluidity to this game, but it is so limited that we can answer this question with very little sweat.

Finally, we need to check the rules. Rule 3 is the "B...D" rule, and that does not force a change to our re-picture, so according to 5(e) we have the answer...

(A) MUST it be true that D goes into slot 2? Uh, NO! He could go to 6.
(B) MUST it be true that B goes into slot 2? No, he could go to 1, just so long as D is in 2 or 6.
(C) MUST it be true that E goes into slot 5? DUH NO! "A" is there. Besides, "E" is our free-ranger! He does not HAVE to do anything except fill in the left over slot!
(D) MUST E come before F? If B is in 1 and D is in 2, then E can fill 6.
(E) MUST BE THE ANSWER because the other four are ABSOLUTELY INCORRECT. We can bubble it in without even checking it, because it MUST BE CORRECT! If we look at it, B DOES have to come before F because F is in 4, A is in 5 and 6 says "-B" below it, as in "B can never go into slot 6."

"Naked" questions - Getting Naked with the LSAT

4) Which one of the following must be false?
     A) Edward stands in a lower numbered position than Francine
     B) David and Bobby are both in front of Francine
     C) Adam, Cindy and Bobby are all in front of Francine
     D) David, Bobby and Cindy are all in front of Francine
     E) Bobby, David and Edward are all in front of Francine

Notice how this question, unlike the last, does not give us **any** additional information to work with. We call this a "naked question" because it does not

---

[16] Besides, if you are just going to do whatever you want, why did you bother to get this book at all? Go take the LSAT. Harvard's a callin'.

provide us with anything extra, such as a hypothetical, a new rule (applicable only to that question) or a change to an existing rule (also applicable only to the question at hand and not to any others). Naked questions are directly asking you, "What do you already know?" But we knew that it was coming and you are ready to destroy it.

If you think about it for a second, there are four ways the LSAT games can get naked.

What *must* be true? (NMT: The "N" is for *naked*)
What *must* be false? (NMF)
What *could* be true? (NCT)
What *could* be false? (NCF)

"Naked-must," means that we are looking for things that are absolutely true or false, depending upon the call of the question. These are easier to answer because ***everything that is optional is incorrect***. For example, an answer choice to a NMT call in the bus line game might say, "A is in position 3." We already *know* that "A" can go into slots 1 or 3 or 5, so this *could be true,* but does not *have to be true,* i.e. it is *possibly false.* A different NMT answer choice might read, "Either A or C is in 3." We *already know* from P1 and P2 that slot 3 is *always* either A or C, so that would be a correct answer.

The NCT/NCF calls are a bit more challenging, because we have to figure out if something *not necessarily in the picture* is possible/impossible. BUT we already know three amazingly helpful things:

(a) that the ***incorrect*** answer choices to NCT questions are things that *cannot possibly be true* (absolutely false things),
(b) that the ***incorrect*** answer choices to NCF questions are things that *cannot possibly be* false (absolutely true things) and
(c) that the drawing contains some of the rules, and that the only rule(s) *not* in the drawing are marked with an asterisk (and they limit what is and what is not possible).

Most of the time the NCT/NCF questions turn on the rules that are not in the drawing. For example, if we are asked a NCT question (Which of the following could be true?), the correct answer must depend entirely upon an understanding of the original rules and inferences from our drawing(s) AND the rule(s) not incorporated into the drawing(s). In our bus line game, an NCT that has an answer choice of, "B is in the sixth position," is incorrect, because our drawing shows that it cannot possibly be true. Likewise, an answer choice that says, "B is in a slot immediately after A," *could* be true, as A can go into slot 1, 3 or 5, and if A is in 1, B can go into 2 and the B...D rule *can possibly* be complied with by putting D into 5 or 6.

But there is a catch (Isn't there always?)

A question can LOOK like a naked question but in actuality be a total non-naked question. The difference is found in the answer choices. We saw a moment ago what true naked questions and answers look like. At their heart is the fact that no additional work should be required by you *if* you did all of the steps of the Test Mentors Method™. But consider this:

Which of the following must be true?
    A) If Adam is in slot three, Bobby is in slot 2.
    B) If Bobby is in slot 5, David is in slot 6.
    .
    .
    .

They put the additional, hypothetical "*if*" information in the flippin' answer choices! So there would be additional work to do, and almost all of it will have to do with the *incorrect* answer choices. The correct one (B, in case you missed it), requires nothing beyond what we know already. Ergo, these kinds of "*faux-nakeds*" can be regarded as a feeble attempt by the test makers to rattle your cage. This again highlights a point we made many pages ago: they are testing more that just logic; they test mental steel, composure, maturity, thoroughness etc.

If you are paying attention to all of this and *actually learning it,* then the average test taker has a far inferior grasp of the entire game than you do... always. They are typically in such a hurry to get to the questions and start bubbling answers that they do little actual *thinking* before diving in. Do not laugh at them, pity them and thank them for bumping themselves to the low side of the curve. YOU will be getting the scholarship that they will be borrowing money to pay for.

Getting back to Question 4 above, notice that the call of the question is NMF, i.e. what can never, ever be true under any circumstances? If something COULD POSSIBLY be true, then it is the incorrect answer. And now, even though this is a naked question, we have **additional information** about the game; we have answered three other questions and thus have increased, "What we already know."

(A) Could E possibly come before F? We saw that in question 3, and we know that the answer is affirmative. In P1 E can go into 2, with B before D in 5 and 6. We do not have to check both pictures because if it could be true in either, it is the wrong answer to a "must be false" question.

(B) May D and B come before F? Again, we saw this before. In P2, with B in 1 and D in 2, A or C in 3, F in 4, C or A in 5 and free-ranger E in 6.

(C) May A, B and C come before F? P1 allows us to put B in 2 with D after F, A and C in 1 and 3 and free-ranger E going wherever D is not.

(D) May D, B and C come before F? Isn't that the same as answer choice (B)? If it was the wrong answer then, it is still the wrong one.

(E) B, D and E cannot all be in front of F. How do we know? Because A through D were incorrect. But for the sake of completeness, if B, D and E fill slots 1-3, neither A nor C can be in space 3. P1 and P2 both require either A or C to be in 3 at all times. Nobody else can be there!

5) Which of the following is a position to which Edward may never be assigned?
      A) 1
      B) 2
      C) 3
      D) 5
      E) 6

Again, we can see that if a person has not taken the time to understand the game before diving into the questions, this one may be unnecessarily challenging. We know it cold. The average test taker is looking for an answer choice saying slot 4, because F always has to be there. The average test taker is an idiot.

We *already know* (from all of our work on P1 and P2, and from the previous questions) that there is an additional spot into which E may never go: **_slot 3!_** For us, this answer was a slam-dunk, just like three of the other answers were. We only had to do a little work on one question, and therein resides one of the biggest test secrets you are learning:

If you spend time at the beginning of a game doing the Five Step Method, the last step, destroying the questions, is usually quick and always brutally accurate. Any time you have to slow down to solve an individual question, you will do it, sticking to the Test Mentors Method™ every step of the way.

If you invest your time backwards (i.e. skipping all of the thinking and using your time to brute-force the answers), you are far more likely to get incorrect answers and you are far more apt to waste huge amounts of time (thus being far more likely to NOT get into law school and NOT get scholarship money).

THE TIME BALANCE

Notice one last important point about what we just saw. There was one question that we had to actually break a sweat on and several that we were able to nearly kill on sight. Every logic game section follows this pattern, and there is a great reason for it. If ten per-cent of the test takers (including you) can do all of the intellectual and mechanical work perfectly, what distinguishes the great from the greatest (i.e. the 165 from the 180 LSAT score)?

The answer is, "*coolness.*" If you can methodically work through the more labor-intensive questions and *not* get your underpants into a wad about how much time that they takes, you will be rewarded with quick, easy answers in other places to balance out the time factor. The best test takers know that if they run into "grinders" (questions you have no choice but to grind out with your pencil), they will soon be visited by quick-and-easy pay-back questions. Sometimes an LSAT games section (which always has four games and a total of about 23 questions) will have three easy games and a single game containing five or six grinders. However, more often than not, there are one or two grinders in each game as a test of your coolness. Be cool baby. Be cool.

FRONT-SIDE / BACK SIDE

The other time balance issue that you are going to have to acclimate yourself to is that some games have lots of work to do in the first four steps of the Test Mentors Method whereas other games do not. There are games that simply do not give you a lot of juicy nuggets of yummy goodness on the front-side (steps one through four). Rather, they force you to do lots of thinking and work on the back-side (step five, Destroy the Questions).

The reason for this is simple: back-side games are poking at your psyche to see if you can take the heat of solving one problem at a time. These games take about the same amount of total time, but the anxiety, frustration and cognitive dissonance (look it up) you experience will dictate how well you handle the heat in the kitchen, so to speak. When there are very few inferences to make, you are going to complete steps one through four quickly. Take a second to remind yourself that you have to take your time and do the problems as well as you possibly can.

Ordering – Squishy

> **We have covered a LOT of ground thus far. If you do not know all of the steps and all of the things we have told you to memorize, GO BACK NOW and do so.**

Let us examine another fact pattern.

> A polling company has been asked to determine which laundry detergent customers prefer. Six detergents, Fresh, Good Smellin', Happy Clothes, Ivy Soft, Juniper and Koala Dew, are the only detergents involved in the survey, and there are no ties. The survey results are consistent with the following rules.

STEP ONE: GET A GRIP

WHAT KIND OF A GAME IS IT? Clearly it is an ordering game of some sort, as we are being asked to do one thing only: *determine the highest-to-lowest ranking of things.* Once your brain says, "ordering," your very next question should be, "firm or squishy?" It is hard to tell from just the fact pattern (this is, of course, a deliberate maneuver by the test makers, who are also testing whether or not you assume too much). We, being good test takers, do not assume JACK. We make sure, every time. How? By glancing at the formal rules of the game! If they are squishy, it is a squishy game. If the rules are absolute, i.e. definitive and declaratory, it is a firm ordering game[17]. Let's peek, shall we?

> **WHAT KIND OF GAME?**
> A real momentum stopper for many people occurs when it is time to decide the game type, or the *nature of the game.* They tell themselves that they can't figure it out. They have forgotten the fundamental question: "What do I already know?"
>
> You know that there are only six kinds of games, and that the game you are looking at *must* be one of them. Just walk down the list, asking, "Is it an ordering game? Firm or squishy? Is it a buckets game?" etc. IT HAS TO BE ON THE LIST!

> Ivy Soft is less popular than Good Smellin' yet more popular than Juniper.
> Both Happy Clothes and Ivy Soft are less popular than Koala Dew.
> Good Smellin' is more popular than Fresh.

Each of my three rules tells me about some vague, *relative* relationship detergents have with each other, but none of them tell me anything *absolute.* This indicates perfectly that we are dealing with a squishy ordering game: relative positions and nothing absolute.

WHO ARE THE PLAYERS? Look at what these cheeky chumps have done to mess with us! They have created six players some of which are blessed with complex,

---

[17] There are games that, believe it or not, have firm and squishy rules *at the same time!* Why would they do that? To see whether or not you can be cool and roll with it. These squishy-firm, or "Squirm" are just as easy as squishy or firm individually JUST SO LONG AS YOU FOLLOW ALL OF THE STEPS!

two-word names. WHY would they do that? After all, it would be easier to call "Ivy Soft," "Ivy," or to call "Good Smellin'," "Generic," or some other one-word "G" name, would it not? OF COURSE! Remember that they are simultaneously testing your ability to do logic and remain careful under pressure. They do this by constantly offering you the opportunity to be a disorganized spazmo who abbreviates "Good Smellin' " as "S" and then later on confuses it with, "Ivy Soft." Even better, they offer you the opportunity to list "Ivy" and "Soft" as two different players, I and S. Can you think of a reason that they might do such a dastardly thing?[18]

So we see (because we are careful) that our players are F, G, H, I, J, K. We are ready to bang out the last part of Getting a Grip: *hidden rules.*

WHAT ARE THE HIDDEN RULES? Are there any rules hiding in the fact pattern? Go back and look. It says that there are no other detergents in the survey and that there can be no ties. We need to write those down in the same place we wrote out our list of players and make sure that they are part of our list of re-written rules in step 2. DO NOT give in to the temptation to say, "I'll just remember that there are no other detergents." And skip writing it down. That is a sloppy habit, and we are all about hard-core good habits.

STEP TWO: RE-WRITE THE RULES
What do we do first in step 2? WE PUT NUMBERS NEXT TO EVERY FORMAL RULE IN THE PROBLEM! Please do so now.

Rule number 1 says that I is *less* popular than G, but *more* popular than J. As you had BETTER recall from before, things that are "higher" in value are drawn *above* things that are "lower". Being more popular puts a player higher on the list (higher ranked), and being less popular puts it lower. Here is how we re-write rule 1:

I is less popular than G but more than J, just as the rule requires.
Rule 2 says that both H and I are less popular than K. In a similar fashion, we re-write it with K *higher* :

---

[18] These kinds of errors on the test point to a certain lack of organization and/or maturity. When you make such an error on the test, you lose points and you do not get into law school, which is GREAT because when you make such errors in real life as a lawyer, it is called *malpractice*. That can hurt your career, which we suspect the test makers do not give a rip about. Rather, we believe that law schools *are* concerned about protecting innocent *clients* from incompetent people, because said clients often have their lives ruined by such malpractice.

Rule 3 says that G is more popular than F, which is simple:

```
G
:
:
F
```

And now we have our three formal rules, re-written in a *hugely* useful form that is *visually consistent* with what we are being asked to do; rank things high to low. If we are ahead of the curve, we can see how these different rules will combine together in step 4. If you do not see it, don't sweat it. REMEMBER, we don't want to get ahead of ourselves. Doing things in *disciplined*, step-by-step order is the key to LSAT success.

STEP 3: DRAWING

In squishy ordering games we have a unique circumstance. We do not have any foundation upon which to draw our picture. In firm ordering games, the slots provide an absolute framework for a picture. What are poor, frightened lads and lasses to do? *We do the drawing step and the "D" (double-ups) inference step at the same bloody time!* So we do step 3 and the "D" part of Step 4 at the same time, thus making Squishy Ordering games 3-D!

Drawing the picture is as easy as pie once all of our rules are drawn out. When we look at them as a group, we can see that there is some commonality amongst them: G is above I in rule 1, and G has to be above F in rule 3 (G is in two rules, hence a double-up). So G has to be above both of them. So we start our drawing by putting rules 1 and 3 together:

Notice that there is no information in the rules nor in the picture about any relationship between I and F other than that they are both below G. Now G is above both I and F, and J is below I.

Do we have another double-up? YES! Rules 1 and 2 both talk about "I". It is also fairly clear how we can work rule 2 into our combined picture we just drew of rules 2 and 3. If K has to be above H and I, and I is already in the picture, we can just work our re-write of rule 2 into our picture on the left-hand side like so:

Let us take a second to think about how to interpret out picture, along the way figuring out what it means *and what it does not mean.*

The obvious visuals we notice are that the K and G line up horizontally, that the H, I and F line up horizontally, and that H, I and F are all "above" J. *This is just a happenstance and has **NOTHING** to do with the logic of the game.* When inferring from the drawing in a squishy ordering game, we must remember this important rule:

THE DOTTED LINES DEFINE THE RELATIONSHIPS.

MEMORIZE THAT! The ONLY things that mean ANYTHING in a squishy ordering game are the **players** and the dotted **lines between the players**. Let us show you what we mean.

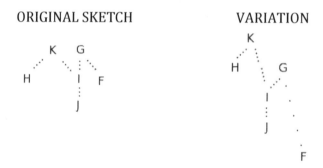

ORIGINAL SKETCH · VARIATION

Both the original sketch and the variation *mean* the same thing even though they are visually dissimilar. In the variation, F is visually lower than every other player. This leads some people to misinterpret the drawing to mean that F has to come after every other player because it appears lower on the page than them. This is incorrect: **both drawings are, logic-wise, *identical.***

In both drawings, the dotted line from K to H tells us that those two have a relationship. K also has a relationship with I. K has no relationship with F though, as there is no line connecting them, either directly or through another player. F only has a relationship with G, and so long as that relationship obeyed (F comes after G), no matter what else is going on, all is well. The same goes for all other relationships defined by the lines. G and K must *both* come before I, because they are connected by lines, and in those **connections**, K and G are above I. In the variation, "I" is below H visually, but because there is no line connecting them, thus the "visual cue" is meaningless, if not misleading to the uninitiated.

So in the squishy game, the golden rule is thus: **THE DOTTED LINES DEFINE THE RELATIONSHIPS** (Yes, we are repeating it: it is *that* important). There are no lines connecting K and G, either directly or through others. This means that they have NO relationship at all. H and J have no relationship either. H can come before or after J because of this lack of lines. So long as H comes after K, and J comes after K, G and I, it matters not whether H is before or after J. Again, to reiterate, the fact that H appears "higher" in the picture than J is irrelevant. **THE LINES DEFINE** THE RELATIONSHIPS!

STEP FOUR: INFERENCES = ABCDEF

ABSOLUTES: Do we have any? It does not appear so at first glance. In a squishy ordering game you have to look a little harder. No soap is required to be in a particular position, to be sure. But remember that "rankings" or "spaces" are also players. Rank #1 must have something true about it. Let us see.

Which detergent could possibly be ranked first? The easiest way to tell is to figure out which ones can never be #1. We won't go so far as to say, "it should be obvious that..." because to some of you, it might not be. But it will be in a moment.

H, I, F and J all have dotted lines coming out of the tops of them. That defines their relationship with others as being "after" them. How can a player be first if they must come after someone else? They cannot, duh. K and G, however, have no lines coming out of the tops of them, which means that they do not **have** to come after any others. They *can* come after others, but it is not *required of them* as it is for all of the others. Thus, H, F, I and J *absolutely cannot be* first. If this is still unclear, ask yourself this: if "I" was the top-rated detergent, how could K and G be higher ranked, as is required by our rules and the dotted lines in the picture? We could write all of that down, or we could just say that K or J must be first, which is what we are going to note below our one and only drawing.

> **The "ABSOLUTE" Trap**
>
> When you are determining the absolutes in a squishy ordering game, something will become clear and potentially tempting. If we can figure out who can never be first and last, (thus telling us who can possibly be first and last) we can also figure out who can never be second through fourth and who might be second through fourth and.... THIS IS A TOTAL WASTE OF TIME!
>
> Any time that we are *forced* to answer such questions, we can do them individually. There is **never** justification for figuring out anything other than the first and last positions in a squishy ordering game.

Which soap is allowed to be ranked sixth (i.e. *last*)? Again, it is easier to figure out who can absolutely never be last. K, G and I all have to come before some other detergent, as is designated by the dotted lines coming out of their respective "bottoms." H, F and J have no lines coming out of their bottoms, which means that no detergent is *required* to come after them. Thus any one of them could, and exactly one of them *must* be sixth. If this is still not clear, ask yourself this: if "I" were in sixth place, how could J be lower-ranked, when there are only six positions? Again, we could write all of that down, or we could just say that H or F or J must be sixth, which is what we are going to note below our one and only drawing:

51

```
            K   G
         .'  `. : '.
      .'      `.:  `.
   H             I   F
                 :
                 J

        1 = K/G
        6 = H/J/F
```

This notation has the same meaning as, "Position 1 can never be H, I, J nor F." It is just cleaner and more positive sounding.

One last thing about calculating in a squishy game. There is a real temptation on the part of students to look at this picture and say, "Let's calculate out all of the people who can be in every position, first through sixth." That's a huge waste of time. The truth of the matter is that most of the time there are only five questions in a squishy game, and most of the questions are easily resolved knowing about who can be first and last...even the questions that ask about the middle. We will conclusively demonstrate this point in question #2 below.

BUNDLES: We have ourselves one gigantic bundle. Hurrah. Sometimes in a squishy game you will have a rule that requires two or more people to be bundled together, such as, *Q and Z always perform together.* Later on you will get a question call that mentions only one of them. If you failed to bundle them into your picture and you failed to note that they are a bundle (meaning that a reference to Q is a reference to Z and vice-versa), you can lose easy points.

CALCULATORS: There are six detergents and each must be ranked, so there are no "ratio" or numerical issues at all.

DOUBLE-UPS: We took advantage of the double-ups earlier. Do you remember when and where? It was when we constructed our drawing by connecting players that were mentioned in different rules! Squishy ordering games are the perfect place to use and abuse the double-ups!

EXTRAS: There are no *obvious* extras (as there is no conditional logic), which is really not that big of a deal, because the picture shows us everything we need to be aware of. Please keep in mind that "extras" will come into play soon enough. They will be explained thoroughly and they will be some of the most important inferences we draw. However we always want to run down the list of extras every time because, as intimated above, there are no *obvious* extras but there could be some not-so-obvious ones. Also, and of much greater importance, HITTING EVERY ITEM ON YOUR LIST OF PROCEDURES EVERY TIME IS ONE OF THE GREATEST HABITS OF EVERY GREAT LAW STUDENT AND LAWYER... but you remember that from before, correct?

So here is what we look for. Bi-conditionals (we have not explained what they are, but there are none here). Forced dichotomies (this is where player(s) *must* play and they can only do one of two things). We have that situation here with the highest or "first" position. It has to be either K or G but it cannot be both.[19] The same cannot be said about the sixth position, because there are three players that can go there. Next we look for Affirmative Duties (none here, and we will get to them), Right Side Rule™ (again, none and later), Contradictions (none) and Lone Conditionals, which there are none of.

FREE-RANGERS: We have six detergents, and there is at least one rule referencing each. Hence there are no free-rangers. All which remains is for step five, DESTROY THE QUESTIONS!

Let's try some problems now.

YOU MUST REMEMBER THAT WHEN YOU ARE DOING THE PROBLEMS, THERE ARE STEPS TO FOLLOW!

---

[19] Okay! We know! This is in fact a bi-conditional, ya flippin' brainiacs. If you see that this is a bi-conditional, then you probably are way ahead of the game. Buy yourself a beer. For those who did not, which we assume to be most of you, DON'T PANIC, and for the love of Q do not feel even the slightest bit insecure about your present state of ignorance. You **_will_** learn all about them later and you will be in the same position as the smarty pants who know what they are already. There are going to be **LOADS** of times throughout this process and law school where people are talking about things that you do not know anything about. Again, DON'T PANIC. Nod your head and pretend that you know what the hell is going on and extricate yourself from the conversation with all deliberate speed. Then LEARN ABOUT whatever it was that you were pretending to understand. Temporary ignorance is a given: you cannot know everything. Allowing your ignorance to continue is inexcusable, and if you do then you should feel bad and you ought to punish yourself. (Just do not make a video of you punishing yourself and post it on line... law schools see that stuff!). One of the BEST comments we have ever received from a former student was this: "Thanks to what Test Mentors taught me, I realized today that I am as smart or smarter than all of my classmates and probably even my professors. Some of them just know more _facts_ than me. When I learn the facts, I always come out on top!" True that. Double true, like Google Maps.
http://www.hulu.com/watch/1397

STEP FIVE: DESTROY THE QUESTIONS –

Problem Set #2 – Squishy Ordering

(Answers and explanations in Appendix "B")

```
        K    G
  H         I   F

            J
  1= K/G
  6= H/J/F
```

1) Which one of the following is an accurate possible ranking of the detergents, from highest to lowest?
   A) Fresh, Good Smellin', Ivy Soft, Juniper, Koala Dew, Happy Clothes
   B) Koala Dew, Good Smellin', Juniper, Ivy Soft, Fresh, Happy Clothes
   C) Good Smellin', Ivy Soft, Juniper, Koala Dew, Happy Clothes, Fresh
   D) Good Smellin', Koala Dew, Fresh, Ivy Soft, Juniper, Happy Clothes
   E) Koala Dew, Ivy Soft, Juniper, Good Smellin', Fresh, Happy Clothes

HARDCORE RULE: When the first problem of an LSAT logic game asks you for the "complete and accurate list," and it does not have any conditions attached to it (i.e. it does not say something like, "If Fresh is third, what is the complete and accurate list of all of the detergents that could be fourth) START WITH "A" AND WORK YOUR WAY FROM "A" THROUGH "E", STOPPING ONLY WHEN YOU HAVE FOUND THE CORRECT ANSWER.

You do **NOT** want to be one of those *Simple Jacks*[20] who says, "One of the rules says that G has to be higher than F, so I'm going to scan the answers for any choice that has F before G and cross it off." THIS IS A HUGELY BAD HABIT because it denies you something that we know and that you do not, to wit, starting with "A" and checking it against the picture and the rules *reinforces the rules and the subtleties of the inferences* and it gives you an opportunity to recognize how and where you may have made an error in steps 1 through 4. Frequently over the years we have had students report that as they are using our method, they see, clearly, that more than one answer choice appears to be correct. This means that they re-wrote a rule incorrectly in step 2, or that they botched an inference in step 4, or both. CATCHING IT EARLY on the first question is an unintentional gift from the test makers.

REMEMBER THE STEPS!
   a) Read and interpret the *call of the question completely*.
   b) Check what we already know.
   c) IF you do not have the answer already, *Apply the Pencil Protocols.* (If you do not remember what they are, go back to page 37 and MEMORIZE THEM like we told you to seventeen pages ago!)

---

[20] *Simple Jack* is a character in the movie, *Tropic Thunder*, which is the copyrighted work of DreamWorks SKG. "Never go full…"

```
          K     G
       ⋰    ⋱  ⋮ ⋰ ⋱
   H           I      F
                ⋮
                J

   1= K/G
   6= H/J/F
```

So the call of the question is for the complete and accurate ordering of the detergents. What do we already know? We have a drawing that tells us that K or G has to be first. (A) has to be incorrect because it has F first.
(B) lists K, G, J.... which makes (B) incorrect because J has to also come after I.
(C) has G, I as first and second, but I has to come after *both* K and G, so it cannot be second.
(D) lists G, K, F, I, J, H. According to what we already know, this works. K or G is first, I is after G, J is after I, F is after G and H is after K. BUBBLE IT AND MOVE!
Just in case you are wondering why (E) is incorrect, I still cannot be second, just like it could not be second a moment ago when we were looking at (C).

2) If Koala Dew is the second-highest ranked detergent, which of the following must be true?
   A) Happy Clothes is ranked third.
   B) Ivy Soft is ranked third.
   C) Fresh is ranked third.
   D) Good Smellin' is ranked first.
   E) Juniper is ranked sixth.

If K is second highest, *what do we already know?* G has to be the highest ranked. That is (D). BUBBLE AND MOVE!

3) Which of the following is a complete and accurate list of all of the detergents which cannot be ranked second?
   A) Juniper
   B) Ivy Soft
   C) Ivy Soft, Juniper
   D) Ivy Soft, Juniper, Good Smellin'
   E) Juniper, Ivy Soft, Good Smellin', Koala Dew

Oooo! A complex NMF (Naked must be false) question. We can smoke this ham. FIRST OFF, we already know that K or G could be first. THAT ALSO MEANS that either one of them could be second. Think about that. K first, G second and vice versa. So (D) and (E) are incorrect. If we look at our drawing, we can see that I has to come after K and G, so it cannot be ranked any higher than third, and J, which has to come *after* I has to be ranked lower still. Thus, the correct answer has to have both of them. (C) is the only one left with both. BUBBLE IT AND MOVE!

```
                    K     G
              ⋰        ⋱  ⋮  ⋱
         H              I    F
                        ⋮
                        J

              1 = K/G
              6 = H/J/F
```

4) If Fresh is ranked second, what cannot be true?
   A) Koala Dew is ranked third.
   B) Juniper is ranked fifth.
   C) Happy Clothes is ranked last.
   D) Koala Dew is ranked fourth.
   E) Ivy Soft is ranked fifth.

Here is a tricky-ish one! What do we know for sure already? Look at the picture! If F is second, G is first. NOBODY ELSE can then be ranked until K goes, so K is third. Does that answer our question? Yes it does. (D) says that K is 4th. Oops.

NOTICE what was done to mess with you! Answer choice (A) says that K is third. HA! That is what *must be true*, not what cannot be true. This is a constant, relentless way that they can see whether or not you are a malpractice threat. They can test you early, they can test you late. They can see whether you fall for it when you are fresh, or whether you fall for it after you have been working for three solid hours. WHY? Because, dear reader, if you are going to be a lawyer, the *lightest* day of law school will be twice the work of the LSAT. If you make those kinds of mistakes on the test after two or three hours, you will be a lesser law student than someone who can think straight and be careful for three and a half hours.

5) Which of the following is a complete and accurate list of all of the detergents which cannot be ranked third?
   A) Juniper
   B) Ivy Soft
   C) Juniper, Ivy Soft
   D) Juniper, Ivy Soft, Good Smellin'
   E) Juniper, Ivy Soft, Good Smellin', Happy Clothes

Same song, different verse. We already know the answer. K, G, H, F and I can all be third. How do we know? COUNT THE LINES! The dotted lines define the relationships. K and G can be first or second...or third. K, H, G works (as there is one line between K and H), as does G, F, K (as there is only one line between G and F). F has one line before it, so K, G, F works. By the same reasoning, K, G, H works. Finally, I just has to come after K and G (two lines above I). J however, has three lines above it: J to I, I to both G and K. Three lines means that J can come in fourth at best. (A) has to be the answer.

56

6) Which of the following, if known, would allow all of the rankings of the detergents to be determined?
    A) Juniper is ranked fourth
    B) Ivy Soft is ranked fourth
    C) Ivy Soft is ranked fourth and Fresh is ranked third
    D) Happy Clothes is ranked second and Fresh is ranked fourth
    E) Good Smellin' is ranked first and Happy Clothes is ranked fourth

THINK LIKE STALIN

We just *had* to hit you with this. This is one of the most intimidating kinds of questions on the LSAT, and we want you to *not* be frightened by it. This is really a question of how to restrict everyone or "eliminate their freedoms." In other words, think like Joseph Stalin.

We know that either K or G could be first, so we need to take their freedom away. We know that H, J and F could be last, so we need to remove that freedom as well.

The key to all of this is the idea that *any answer choice that allows any freedom is incorrect.* For example, (A) says that J is 4th. If J is 4th, do K and G still have freedom? Yes. K or G could be first. (A) is incorrect. (B) has I ranked 4th. Does that take away freedom from K and G? Nope. The same problem plaguing (A) exists in (B), making it equally incorrect. (C) says that I is 4th and F is 3rd. Do K and G still have the freedom to be first and/or second? Yes! K, G, F, I or G, K, F, I both work. (C) is incorrect.

(D) has H 2nd and F 4th. If H is 2nd, K has no freedom: it has to have been 1st. If F is 4th, G has to have been ranked 3rd: G has no freedom. If we know that the first four are K, H, G, F, we also know that I and J have no freedom: they must be 5th and 6th respectively. No freedom exists. (D) is correct.

(E) says that G is 1st and H is 4th. Does that take away the freedom of K? NO! K could be 2nd or 3rd, as could F. (E) is incorrect.

Ordering – The Goldberg Variations[21]

There are two minor variants of the ordering game, one of which we referenced previously and will now illuminate.

Squirm is the name that we give to a game that is part Firm and part Squishy. Get out your scratch pad and try to map out the first two steps of the Test Mentors Method™ on the following example. NO CHEATING! You can look back if you need to refresh your memory, but DO NOT look ahead unless you are absolutely stuck or you believe that you are done.

> The new H.R. director at BigJob Co. is trying to determine the seniority, from most to least, of the shipping division's seven employees, T, U, V, W, X, Y and Z. Every employee was hired at a different time. Her determination is based upon the following additional known conditions:
> T was hired before Z.
> Exactly one person was hired between Z and V.
> No employee was hired between X and Z.
> W was hired after Z.
> X was hired fifth.

STEP ONE: Get a Grip. The nature of the game is clearly Ordering. But we have three rules that are Firm (2, 3 and 5) and two that are Squishy (1 and 4). Scary? Pshaw! We call it Squirm, we isolate out the Players (Hiring order 1-7 and the seven shipping employees), find the Hidden Rules (all hired at different times) and move on.

STEP TWO: Formal Rules – Remember that we are supposed to number them on the actual list and then re-write them in a manner that is visually consistent with the nature of the game. It ought to look a little something like this (actually, exactly like this):

1) T....Z

2) Z/V _ V/Z

3) X Z or Z X

4) Z....W

5) X = 5

---

[21] The Goldberg Variations are a set of tunes for the harpsichord (or piano if you prefer) written by J.S. Bach and then re-worked about a million times (okay, more like thirty) by a dude named Goldberg, who really is not famous for any other reason. The section title is a reference to the fact that there are minor variations on the main theme (firm and squishy) but they are trivial, and nobody should get a medal or even a cookie for having come up with them.

NOTE that this is the point at which we should begin to be *keenly aware* of the **issues** being tested in this game. Step four, Inferences, is where we pin them down precisely, but we should smell, right now, where they are poking: T has to come before Z, but *could* fall between V and Z if V comes before Z. The same goes for X: it can always go between V and Z regardless of their order. If Z comes before V, then W could go between the V space Z bundle.

STEP 3: DRAW A PICTURE
When there is a Squirm, we will do both a firm and a squishy picture below it. So first we do the firm:

$$\overline{}\ \overline{}\ \overline{}\ \overline{}\ \overline{}\ \overline{}\ \overline{}$$
1 2 3 4 5 6 7

Next we add the squishy parts by connecting all of the squishy rules together:

$$\overline{}\ \overline{}\ \overline{}\ \overline{}\ \overline{}\ \overline{}\ \overline{}$$
1 2 3 4 5 6 7

T.....Z.....W

Do not forget that you should put check-marks next to rules #1 and #4: they are in the drawing.

STEP FOUR: INFERENCES
Absolutes? Recall that we are first looking for things that *must be in a particular place all of the time.* After that we look for places that players can *never go.* So do we have any of that first kind of action? Heck ya! Rule #5. Put X into space 5 and put a check next to rule #5.

√1) T....Z

2) Z/V _ V/Z

3) X Z or Z X

√4) Z....W

√5) X = 5

$$\overline{}\ \overline{}\ \overline{}\ \overline{}\ \overset{\text{ⓧ}}{\overline{}}\ \overline{}\ \overline{}$$
1   2   3   4   5   6   7

T.....Z.....W

How about the other type? Is there any place that some player(s) can never go? HECK YA! We can see that T cannot go into 6 or 7 (if T were in 6, there would not be room for Z in 7 and W after. By the same reasoning, Z can never be in 7. So we can mark that in our drawing as well.

```
 __  __  __  __  Ⓧ  __  __
 1   2   3   4   5   6   7
                    -T  -T
          T.....Z.....W    -Z
```

What we also can see, by the same kind of reasoning, is that W cannot go into #2 (that would put Z in #1 with no place for T before it) nor can we put W or Z into #1.

```
 __  __  __  __  Ⓧ  __  __
 1   2   3   4   5   6   7
 -W  -W              -T  -T
 -Z        T.....Z.....W    -Z
```

Now we have a really clear picture of what is going on *and* we can see that there are two rules remaining to deal with. They also happen to be the ones that we smelled as being the problem children we are going to have to deal with as major issues, *and* we can see that rules 2, 3 and 5 will all Double-up later.

Are there Bundles? YA! There are two, both contained in the two remaining rules. Do not allow this to overwhelm you. Simply note that the bundles both talk about Z so they will Double Up, and that they will connect to the X cemented into space #5.

Calculators? None. There are seven people, each having one of seven spots.

Are there any Double-ups? If you said, "No," please go punish yourself. Recall that a Double-up is two or more rules that talk about the same player. They are like a rash here! Z is mentioned in 80% of the rules! Let us take advantage of this logical smorgasbord we have been served.

Per rule three, Z *must* be either immediately before or immediately after the X glued into spot 5. This means that there are only two ways to play this game: Z in 4 or Z in 6. PWNed!

Per rule 4, W must be *after* Z. So if Z is after X in space 6, W *must* be in space 7 and that would, per rule #2, force V into space 4. Let us draw this out and call it P1:

P1

```
 __  __  __  Ⓥ  Ⓧ  Ⓩ  Ⓦ
 1   2   3   4   5   6   7
 -W  -W              -T  -T
 -Z        T.....Z.....W    -Z
```

If Z is *before* X in space 4, then V could be in either space 2 or in space 6. W will still be confined to 6 or 7. Let us draw this as P2, making certain that we do it in a way that shows all that we know clearly.

P1

P2

$$\underline{\quad}\ \underline{\quad}\ \underline{\quad}\ \underline{ⓥ}\ \underline{ⓧ}\ \underline{ⓩ}\ \underline{ⓦ}$$
```
  1   2   3  4  5  6   7
 -W  -W            -T  -T
 -Z                         -Z
         T.....Z.....W
```

$$\underline{\quad}\ \underline{ⱽ/}\ \underline{\quad}\ \underline{ⓩ}\ \underline{ⓧ}\ \underline{ⱽ/}\ \underline{W}$$
```
  1   2   3  4  5  6   7
 -W  -W            -T  -T
 -Z                         -Z
         T.....Z.....W
```

WAHOOOOO!!!!! We can see just how home-free we are, and just how easy it would be to destroy any question they may ask us...and we are not even done yet! We can see that T is stuck in 1, 2 or 3, that Z is stuck in 4 or 6, that W is stuck in 6 or 7... how flippin' easy is this?

EXTRAS – Again, we have to run through them out of habit: Bi-conditionals, Forced dichotomies, Affirmative duties, Right-side rules, Contradictions and Lone conditionals. None.

Any FREE RANGERS? You bet your boots! U and Y are rule-free, though they are far from free to do whatever they want. We can now see that they can use these two players to test how well we did drawing inferences by sticking them various places to gum up the works.

At his point, we are ready to DESTROY THE QUESTIONS! Remember that there is a process to destroying the questions, so let us not run off all spastic ad disorganized. Here are a few choice questions:

Which one of the following could be a complete and accurate listing of
the seniority of the employees from most to least senior?
- A) Z, U, Y, T, V, X, W
- B) V, T, Z, X, U, Y, W
- C) U, T, V, Y, X, Z, W
- D) T, Y, U, Z, X, W, V
- E) T, V, U, Z, X, W, Y

We know that the first question is handled A – E, stopping only when we have hit the correct answer. (A) has to be incorrect because Z is in 4 or 6 only. (B) has Z in third but after T to trick the people who do not know better...in other words, not you. (C) has V in position 3, which can never happen. (D) Z in position 4, so we are in P2. In P2, V must be in position 2 or 6, not in 7 as in (D). CIRCLE (E) AND MOVE ON! Notice however how (E) has W in position 6? If you did not pick up on that possibility by now (some people might think that W has to be the least senior) you learned it from the answer choice.

P1

P2

(V) (X) (Z) (W)   V/   (Z) (X) V/   W

$$\underline{\ }\ \ \underline{\ }\ \ \underline{\ }\ \ \underline{\ }\ \ \underline{\ }\ \ \underline{\ }\ \ \underline{\ }\qquad \underline{\ }\ \ \underline{\ }\ \ \underline{\ }\ \ \underline{\ }\ \ \underline{\ }\ \ \underline{\ }\ \ \underline{\ }$$

```
1   2   3   4   5   6   7     1   2   3   4   5   6   7
-W  -W                 -T  -T   -W  -W                 -T  -T
-Z          T.....Z.....W      -Z  -Z          T.....Z.....W      -Z
```

If Y is the sixth most senior employee, which of the following could be true?
A) W is the fourth most senior employee
B) V is the most senior employee
C) Y is the fourth most senior employee
D) U is the second most senior employee
E) T is the third most senior employee

DO NOT GO STAMPEDING TO YOUR PENCILS! What do we know already? If Y is in position 6, where do we have to be? P2! That means that we know that V=2, Z=4, X=5, Y=6 and W=7. That leaves U and T to fight it out for positions 1 and 3, either of which will work. Guess what? We know the answer. (A) through (D) are all incorrect. Circle (E), bubble it in on your answer form and move along.

Which of the following is a complete and accurate list of all of the possible rankings of V?
A) 4th
B) 4th, 5th
C) 4th, 6th
D) 2nd, 4th, 6th
E) 2nd, 4th, 6th, 7th

What do we already know? DUH! That the answer has to be (D).

You can see just how simple and powerful this method is.

Zig-Zag Firm is a minor variation on the firm order. Rather than put things into a set order that is a straight line, the order does a zig-zag. Allow us to demonstrate.

Rube must complete six tasks working Monday, Tuesday and Wednesday of one week. His tasks are cartooning, doodling, editing, filing, grinding and inventing. He performs exactly two tasks each day, one in the morning and one in the afternoon according to the following constraints:
Filing must be done before cartooning.
Inventing and editing cannot be done on the same day.
If Cartooning is done on Tuesday, doodling must be done on Wednesday.

There is a temptation to draw this like so:

$$\overline{Ma}\ \ \overline{Mp}\ \ \overline{Ta}\ \ \overline{Tp}\ \ \overline{Wa}\ \ \overline{Wp}$$

We do not recommend that you do it like this, and here is why. If you draw it this way,

	M	Tu	W
AM			
PM			

it is much clearer as to what is actually being tested: Monday has two events with the A.M. coming before the P.M. which is followed by Tuesday A.M. etc. The "flow" of the order is not visually linear. Rather, it is "zig-zag," which is precisely how it works in reality. We are always trying to make things as close to reality as we can because that is what is bing tested: real world concepts, just under fabricated circumstances.

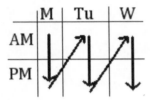

"What difference does it make?" I hear you asking. Good question! Look at the rules again and you will see the answer, but do not freak out over rule #3: we have not covered it yet.

1) F....C
2) Never I and E same day
3) CT ⊃ DW
   -DW ⊃ -CT

Rule 3 is written in a simple, symbolic way of saying that if cartooning is on Tuesday, doodling is on Wednesday AND that if doodling is not being done on Wednesday, cartooning cannot be done on Tuesday. We will cover that in just a bit. What is important for the purposes of the present conversation is that we can see, visually, much more clearly the distinction between the days, and we can see that F....C really does not mean that F and C are necessarily on separate days. Also, if C is on Tuesday, D is on Wednesday, A.M. or P.M. and F can be on Monday or Tuesday A.M. with C on Tuesday P.M. So when they sub-divide the order by breaking days into mornings and evenings, or months into weeks, zig-zag it!

Let's do the drill, just for the extra practice.

STEP ONE: Get a Grip – Nature of the game is Firm Ordering (with a zig-zag). Players are C, D, E, F G, I = Tasks along with M, Tu and Wed as the days, and A.M. and P.M. being the sub-divisions of the days. Hidden rules are that there is exactly one task in the A.M. and one in the P.M. of every day, and that All of the Tasks must be done (all play).

STEP TWO: Formal Rules:
4) F....C
5) Never I and E same day
6) CT ⊃ DW
    -DW ⊃ -CT

STEP THREE: DRAW A PICTURE

	M	Tu	W
AM			
PM			

STEP FOUR: INFERENCES

ABSOLUTES – YES! C can never go in the A.M. on Monday and F can never go in the P.M. on Wednesday.

	M	Tu	W
AM	-C		
PM			-F

BUNDLES – There is a *negative bundle* in that I and E can never be on the same day. We should mark that directly below our drawing so it is in our field of vision:

	M	Tu	W
AM	-C		
PM			-F

I/E diff. days

CALCULATORS – Six tasks, six days... nothing mathy-looking in the formal rules or the hidden rules.

DOUBLE-UPS – Rules #1 and #3 talk about C. If C is on Tuesday, then D is on Wednesday and that means F is before C... BUT THAT DOES NOT MEAN THAT F HAS TO GO ON MONDAY! If C is Tuesday P.M. then F can go Tuesday A.M.

AND NOW WE CAN SMELL THE MAGIC AND SIMPLICITY of what we have gotten ourselves into! C and F can be on the same day, A.M. and P.M. respectively, and because of rule #2, I and E will get split up between the two remaining days. We own this game!

EXTRAS – Bi-conditionals (none). Forced Dichotomies (none). Affirmative duties (none). Right Side Rules - (There is one, but we do not know what it is yet. Rule #3 tells us that D can be on Wednesday even if C is on Monday or Wednesday. Again, hold tight. We will get to it. It's magicalness. Contradictions (none). Lone Conditional – There is a single conditional (if/then) rule (#3). We do not need to deal with it as a lone conditional. As we shall learn, we only pursue the lone conditional if it would prove to be highly beneficial. Here, we know that it would be a waste of time.

FREE RANGERS – There is one, and we need to indicate it next to the drawing.

STEP FIVE – DESTROY the questions, always Going with what you already know.

1) F....C

2) Never I and E same day

3) CT ⊃ DW
   -DW ⊃ -CT

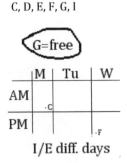

C, D, E, F, G, I

G=free

I/E diff. days

Let's play a few rounds with this one, seeing as how we have already done the heavy lifting.

1) Which of the following list the order in which Rube may complete his tasks?
   A) cartooning, doodling, filing, editing, grinding, inventing
   B) inventing, editing, filing, cartooning, doodling, grinding
   C) editing, filing, cartooning, inventing, doodling, grinding
   D) filing, editing, cartooning, doodling, inventing, grinding
   E) grinding, filing, editing, inventing, cartooning, doodling.

REMEMBER! Top to bottom, just in case we missed something. Again we wish to reiterate the importance of sticking with the pedagogy. It seems pretty clear that we did not miss anything along the way, but the BEST HABIT is to ALWAYS BE THOROUGH.

(A) has C first. KILL IT.
(B) has F before C. It also has I and E on the same day. NEXT!
(C) has F before C, I and E on different days, C on Tuesday and D on Wednesday. It complies with all of the rules, thus it MUST be correct. Circle it and go!
Just to be thorough:
(D) has C on Tuesday and D on Tuesday in violation of rule 3.
(E) has E and I together on Tuesday. Naughty.

1) F....C

4) Never I and E same day

5) CT ⊃ DW

    -DW ⊃ -CT

C, D, E, F, G, I

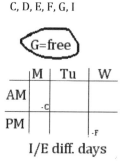

I/E diff. days

2) If Rube's schedule for the mornings, Monday through Wednesday is editing, filing, cartooning respectively, then which one of the following must be true?

   A) Grinding is done on Monday

   B) Grinding is not done on Monday

   C) Doodling is done on Monday

   D) Inventing is done on Monday

   E) Inventing is not done on Monday.

Ha ha! They have tried to make us think that there is something tricky going on here...but there is nothing of the sort. ***LOOK AT WHAT WE ALREADY KNOW AND DO NOT GO TO THE PENCIL!*** They told us that the Monday through Wednesday morning line-up is E, F, C. So F and C are on different days, and C is NOT on Tuesday. That means that rule #1 is complied with and rule #3 does not apply at all because it only is meaningful ***IF*** C is on Tuesday, which it is not. So the ONLY thing that MUST be true is.... Rule #2: E and I have to be on different days. That is (E). Move along. There is nothing to see here.

3) Which of the following could be true?

   A) Editing is done Monday morning and cartooning is done Monday afternoon.

   B) Filing is done Tuesday morning and cartooning is done Tuesday afternoon.

   C) Filing is done Wednesday morning and doodling is done Wednesday afternoon.

   D) Doodling is done Monday morning and cartooning is done Tuesday afternoon.

   E) Cartooning is done Monday morning and doodling is done Tuesday afternoon.

Bwahaha! Another easy one, if we stick to our game plan. Remember that there are only three rules to comply with and we have pulled out all of the useful inferences. (A) has E and C respectively on Monday. C cannot come before F. Cross it off. (B) HERE IT IS! This is the question where all of the people who incorrectly "surmised" that F and C had to be on different *days* get their clocks cleaned..because none of the other answers are correct and this one is so they cross off (B) and then (C), (D) and (E) and then... IMPLODE! Not us. Circle it.

Just to get your ya-yas out, figure out why the remaining answers stink. It's good practice. Just remember that this is for practice only. In a real test situation you would move on to question 4.

4) Which of the following, if true, would allow the days on which the tasks are completed to be completely determined?
    A) Editing is done Monday morning and filing and grinding are done on Tuesday.
    B) Cartooning is done on Tuesday afternoon and doodling is done on Wednesday.
    C) Cartooning is done on Tuesday morning.
    D) Grinding is done before cartooning but after editing.
    E) Filing is done first and cartooning is done last.

This looks spooky... but it is not. Remember that the CALL OF THE QUESTION defines what we are supposed to determine. Here we are only being asked to determine which answer choice locks down every activity's *day*, not it's A.M. or P.M. status. So really we are just being asked to evaluate each answer to see whether it logically squeezes things before and after other things in a two-per-day manner. Easy as cake.

(A) has E on Monday morning with F and G filling Tuesday. What does that "squeeze"? If F and G are Tuesday, C has to be on Wednesday. E on Monday squeezes I to another day, but Tuesday is full so I goes to Wednesday. This is the answer. Circle it.

(B) does not squeeze E, I and F. (C) squeezes F back to Monday, but E and I are still free to roam. (D) just says that E...G....C is the order of those three, but not any particular day for any of them. E and G Monday leaves F and C for Tuesday or Wednesday together or allows for F on Tuesday and C on Wednesday. (E) is just... bad. Filing Monday morning and cartooning Wednesday afternoon leaves a wide-open free-for-all with our left overs. Rule #3 no longer applies and rule #2 allows E and I to be on any days, just not together.

5) If the condition were added that grinding cannot be done on the same day as neither inventing nor editing, but if all other conditions remained in effect, then which of the following must be false?
    A) Cartooning and editing are done on Tuesday.
    B) Doodling and editing are done on Tuesday.
    C) Filing and grinding are done on Tuesday.
    D) Doodling and editing are done on Wednesday.
    E) Cartooning and Filing are done on Monday.

It is the last question! They always save a little bit of the special sauce for the last! We must remember: DON'T PANIC! We have to translate the call of the question into what it *means*. And this is where we see how simple this Rubik's® cube really is to crack. We already know that I and E cannot go on the same day. If G cannot go on the same day as either of them, then they have to be spread across three days and in no particular order. So each of Monday, Tuesday and Wednesday will have exactly one of G, I or E, and nobody cares about the A.M./P.M. thing (which seems to have only been included to mess with people baffled by rule #1).

What does all of that tell us? F, C and D also have to be distributed across the three days with F before C. So F is on Monday or Tuesday, C is on Tuesday or Wednesday,

D goes wherever F and C are not. F, C and D can never pair up on a day, and neither can E, I and G.

(A) has C and E on Tuesday. Fine.
(B) has D and E on Tuesday. Same thing.
(C) has F and G on Tuesday. Fine.
(D) has D and E on Wednesday. No problem again.
(E) must be correct, and it is: C and F can no longer be on the same day. Duh.

FINAL NOTES ON ORDERING GAMES

As we have seen, ordering games present us issues involving two simple relationships: before and after. This is inherently a forced dichotomy: if X is not before Y, then X is after Y. This "binary" logic is hugely beneficial for us to be aware of. We will dive into "forced dichotomies" in greater detail in just a bit.

Occasionally there will be rules in a game that look like this:

Either X is before Y and Z or X is after Y and Z.

Are there any other possible relationships that X can have with Y and Z? Don't strain yourself. X could come between them. So this rule pins down X, Y and Z precisely. This means that there will be exactly two drawings for the game, one representing the two possible relationships and then fleshed out through the inference process.

On the whole, these ordering games will probably be the ones that you get good at (i.e. really fast and accurate) first. This is great because there is a very high probability that you will see an ordering game on the day you sit for the actual LSAT.

You will crush it.

BUCKETS – "Better Get a Bucket…"

Let's take a look at our fact pattern for a "Buckets" game, and walk through all of the steps.

> *Two chisels, two drills, two planes and one saw, are the only tools being distributed amongst four carpenters, Willis, Xenophilius, Yancy and Zunfufu. Each carpenter receives at least one tool, and all of the tools are distributed. The following conditions determine the assignment of tools to carpenters.*

STEP ONE: **GET A GRIP**
WHAT KIND OF A GAME IS IT? Obviously, because of the heading at the top of the section, we realize that this is a "buckets" game. As you ought to recall from before, a

"buckets" game is defined as a game in which we have some "stuff" and we have a **set** number of "buckets" or repositories for said "stuff". In a Bucket game, the order in which the buckets are listed does not matter, so we tend to arrange them in their "natural" order. In this case, that would be the alphabetical order. If the order of the players is in any way important or changed by any of the conditions of the game, it is not a Bucket game, it is a Combo game, where you are being asked to put things into buckets and to put them into an order based upon the conditions.

WHO ARE THE PLAYERS?
Here, our "buckets" are really just the four people, W, X, Y and Z, and we are going to put our tools into our "buckets". We have a set number of "things" to put into the "buckets," and they are the items on the list: two chisels (CC), the two drills (DD), the two planes (PP), and the one saw (S). Remember that the only "flavors" that there are for Bucket games are the "we know exactly how many of each thing we have," versus when we do not. Regardless, they play exactly the same way, and no additional labels or steps are required.

WHAT ARE THE HIDDEN RULES? Are there any? YES! C C D D P P S, are the only tools. Also, because each carpenter receives at least one tool and all of the tools must be distributed., every player must participate. ALL PLAY!

> carps = W,X,Y,Z
> tools = CCDDPPS
> -No others
> -All Play

STEP TWO: RE-WRITE THE FORMAL RULES
First, we slap a number on each one of the rules. Here they are.

> 1) Yancy receives more tools than Zunfufu.
> 2) No carpenter receives more tools than Xenophilius.
> 3) Whichever carpenter receives the drill also receives a chisel.
> 4) If a carpenter has more than one tool, none of them are the same.

The first rule says that Y has more than Z, which we can easily re-write into:

> 1) Y>Z

If you do not like this "mathy" looking re-write, you might try this:

> 1) Y more than Z

Either will work. The only thing you need to keep in mind is this: **the re-write must mean exactly what the original rule means** and you have to be

---

BAD HABIT #3
Bad test takers accept rules at face value. SUCKERS!

As we saw in rule #2, all rules (both formal and hidden) can *mean* one thing while *not meaning* something else. The average test taker fails to take this into account.

You must ask of every rule, "What do you mean, and *what do you **not** mean?*"

able to interpret it the way the test makers originally meant it, without error, every time you see it. So, in whichever form you re-write a rule into, make sure that these conditions are met.

The second rule says that nobody has more tools than X. What does that mean? People often misinterpret it to mean that X has the most tools. But is that what it really *means*? Not in the least! It means that if X has three tools, nobody else has FOUR or MORE! Another carpenter may have the *same* number as X, just not *more*. So we re-write the rule:

2) Nobody MORE than X but possibly equal

The third rule says that whoever receives the saw also gets a chisel. Does that mean that if we know that X has a chisel, he also must have a saw? NO! If X has a saw he has to have a chisel, but NOT the other way around[22]. If we were to write "SC together," we could easily misinterpret it to mean that saws and chisels must always go together, which would be incorrect. As the call-out box says, we have to think about what the rule *does not* mean as much as we have to focus on what it *does means*. This is a **huge** source of errors, confusion, delay and loss of valuable time for many. We must be very clear and careful. *What we do know* is that there are two chisels and only one saw, that one of the chisels has to go to whoever ends up with the saw and that the other chisel will go to someone who does not have a saw.

3) Carp w/ S must get C

Later, we will learn to re-write rules like this in an even more useful way. For right now, we can leave it in this form without penalty.

Our fourth rule says that if a carpenter has more than one tool, none of them can be the same. What does that mean? It means that if Z has two tools, they have to be two unique, i.e. different, tools. No carpenter can have two chisels or two planes etc. It also means that at most, any one carpenter can have four tools, C, P, D, S. Thinking it through like this helps us to think of a good way to re-write it.

6)   Each carp all diff. tools

So now our work looks like this:

```
carps = W,X,Y,Z
tools = CCDDPPS
-No others
-All Play

1) Y > Z
2) Nobody more than X, possibly =
3) carp. w/S must get C
4) Each carp all diff tools
```

---

[22] If this is freaking you out, FEAR NOT! A few pages down the road we will do a healthy review of conditional logic and you WILL feel like you own it.

STEP THREE: DRAWING

This is a "Buckets" game: we are throwing *stuff* into *buckets*.

What are our buckets? THE MOST ABSOLUTE THINGS, AND/OR THE THING THAT IS HAVING THE "STUFF" THROWN AT/INTO IT. Here, we have tools being distributed amongst the carpenters: tools (stuff) being thrown at Carpenters (buckets). W, X, Y, and Z are the most absolute (one only of each) AND they are having tools thrown at them). Let's draw them like this:

Now all of our buckets look sort of boxy, and all of the tools we are throwing into the buckets are listed out above them so we can cross them off as we put them into buckets. That will allow us to see what is left to throw into other buckets as we go.

STEP FOUR: INFERENCES

ABSOLUTES

Do we have any absolutes? Not really. There is no rule stating that "X has a chisel" or the like. That's a mild let down, but not a big deal. Is there any carpenter that *cannot* have a certain tool? Not as far as we can tell right now. How about the hidden rule that says that each carpenter *must* have at least one tool? Is that *absolute*? ABSOLUTELY! We can add 1 "space" to each carpenter.

BUNDLES

Do we have stuff that bundles together? YES! Whoever gets the saw has a chisel bundled with it. All of the tools have to play, and so someone *will* get a saw, thus a chisel, thus a bundle. We can change our picture a tad to put those two together and segregate out the other chisel. We MUST REMEMBER to cross off the chisel that is being moved (so we do not mistakenly believe there is a third chisel) *and* circle the SC bundle so as to never forget that they *must* be together, like so:

We do not appear to have any other bundles, so we move along.

CALCULATORS

Finally we have some calculators. We have exactly four carpenters and exactly seven tools. There is an SC bundle, so there are really only six things to put into our four buckets. We also have rules that talk about numerical sounding stuff. Rule 1 says that Y has more than Z, and rule 2 says that nobody has more than X and every person has to have at least one tool. JEEZ! Where to begin?

What do we already know? Y has to have more than Z. This means that Y must have two or more, because Z has to have at least one (just look at the picture!). If Z has one and Y has two, X must have at least two, because NOBODY can have more than X. So Z can have one, Y can have two, X has two and that leaves two for W, and 2+2+2+1=7.

Can Z have 2 tools? If he does, then Y has to have at least 3, which would mean that X would have to have at least 3... but that would be 8 tools and W is still needing at least one. Can Z have 1 and Y have 3? Nope. X would have to have three, and that would be 3+3+1 = 7 before W gets any. As sure as the sun will rise in the east, Z *must have one and Y must have 2*.

Z has one and Y has two and X could have three, leaving one for W as well. 1+2+3+1=7 as well. MATHEMATICAL! So Z can ONLY have one, Y must have two, and X can have 2 or 3, which leaves W with either one (if X has three) or two (if X has two). So our "calculator" tells us that there are only TWO WAYS that this game can be played:

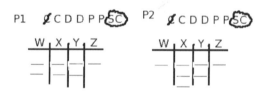

Our first two rules are now incorporated into the picture, and our other two rules may still be amenable to calculator analysis. Rule three says that the person with the saw has to take a chisel too. There are two exclusive ways to play this game and we have drawn them. Do they help us?

In P2, W and Z are only allowed one tool. Our calculation is that S and C cannot go to either of them...but that's just us. Try the math yourself. I can add a notation to P2 to the effect that the SC bundle has to go to either X or Y. In P1, Z can't have the bundle. I could indicate that S cannot go under Z. The better practice is to show where the bundle SC *can go*, like so:

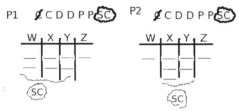

(We're trying really hard to make it look like pencil work)

DOUBLE-UPS

Do we have multiple rules that mention the same players? Not really. Although we do have rules 3 and 4 both mentioning "C", there isn't any sort of logical relationship, so they are pretty un-helpful as double-ups.

EXTRAS

There are no conditional logic statements, so *Extras* are off of the table (and again, we will deal with more specifics about "extras" soon). But we want to walk through them, just for practice and to be developing good habits. Bi-conditionals, forced dichotomies, affirmative duties, Right Side rule, contradictions and lone conditionals.

FREE RANGERS

Do we have any players that are rule-free (i.e. can do whatever they want-ish)? "W" has no rules, but W is also, by the logical implications of the rules, highly constrained (one or two tools, and that is included in our drawings). P and D are free rangers without rules placing restrictions directly upon them. They can fill in anywhere there is an available space, so long as they are not the second of their type for that bucket (because rule four says that a carpenter cannot have two of the same tools).

QUICK CHECK: Which of our rules are *not* in the drawing?

Just #4! That tells us that this game is going to hinge on the drawings and special attention to rule 4. Notice how rule 4 is also the one that makes us have to be cautious with the Free Rangers? Rule 4 is where the money is, and we need to put asterisks next to it as a visual cue to never overlook the bad boy.

Now that we have done all of our inferring it is time for step 5: DESTROY THE QUESTIONS!

This time, we will give you the questions and walk you through them step by step. PAY CLOSE ATTENTION! Doing the steps of the process is magical, but only if you learn to do them precisely. We will show you how to extract the maximum advantage from your hard work on every problem.

We also want to remind you that the game we are about to go over is *not* the most difficult "buckets" game that you are ever going to come across. It is typical of a "basic" game by design, in order to highlight the rules and processes being taught, and to give you practice at seeing said rules in action in a clear, mostly uncomplicated environment. What this means, of course, is that you will probably NOT be actually doing the steps for yourself, but rather you will follow my lead. This leads to the, "It is so easy when we do them together, but when I do them alone, I get confused," syndrome.

There is an elegantly simple solution to this common and devilish conundrum: re-do the game WITHOUT our guidance after we have gone through it together. Then do it again...and again until the steps are familiar, natural and darned near annoying. As the games get tougher, the EXACT same methods will work with the exact same devastating efficacy. If you don't get all of the steps down now, there is **_NO HOPE_** for you later.

Do not be tempted to skive off of learning and practicing each and every step or I will frown at you from afar and feel no sympathy for your lack of progress.

Problem Set #3: Buckets

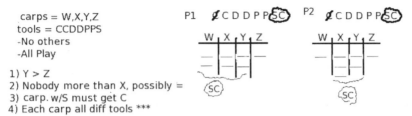

carps = W,X,Y,Z
tools = CCDDPPS
-No others
-All Play

1) Y > Z
2) Nobody more than X, possibly =
3) carp. w/S must get C
4) Each carp all diff tools ***

18) Which of the following could be a complete and accurate distribution of tools to carpenters?
   A) Wilson: plane, Xenophilius: chisel, Yancy: chisel, plane, drill, Zunfufu: plane, saw
   B) Wilson: plane, drill, Xenophilius: chisel, drill, Yancy: chisel, plane, saw, Zunfufu: plane
   C) Wilson: chisel, saw, Xenophilius: chisel, drill, Yancy: plane, Zunfufu: plane, saw
   D) Wilson: chisel, Xenophilius: chisel, drill, saw, Yancy: plane, drill, Zunfufu: plane
   E) Wilson: chisel, plane, Xenophilius: chisel, drill, Yancy: plane, saw, Zunfufu: plane

Many people will try to solve this problem by brute force. What we mean by "brute force" is that such people will use the least efficient (though effective) method of finding the correct answer. There are two main ways that they make this error. Let us examine both of these less correct approaches and make sure that we beat them out of our own thinking.

The first brute force method goes like this. The test taker will begin with answer (A) and say, "Can Wilson have a plane?" The answer is yes, of course, so then they go on and say, "Can X have a chisel?" Some people will screw this up and say that X cannot, because the chisel has to go with the saw, which is incorrect: the one and only saw has to go with a chisel, but not every chisel has to have a saw. Even if they do not make that error, they are still wasting time.

The second errant brute-force attack is one we discussed previously and it looks like this: "I will start with rule number one, 'Y has to have more than Z' and eliminate all of the answers where Y has the same or less than Z." Again, this approach will work, and it can get you correct answers...sometimes. This is the methodology of the *average* test taker, the one who is frustrated by the fact that they cannot score above 153. It is grossly inefficient, and it ignores one of our fundamental rules: "Always ask, '*What do I already know?*'" Here is how you will do it, because it is how we do it, and it is awesome, and our students are the best test takers and law students on the planet.

We start with what we already know: we begin with choice (A) and we use what we inferred from all of the rules in our "INFERENCE = ABCDEF" step to our advantage. "A" has Wilson with one tool and Xenophilius with one tool. Our two pictures show the only two ways that this game can be played. P2 says that if Wilson has one tool, Xenophilius must have three. (A) is incorrect, period.

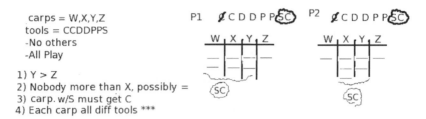

carps = W,X,Y,Z
tools = CCDDPPS
-No others
-All Play

1) Y > Z
2) Nobody more than X, possibly =
3) carp. w/S must get C
4) Each carp all diff tools ***

We look at (B). Wilson has two tools. P1 says that if W has two, then so must X and Y, with Z having exactly one. But (B) has Y with three tools. It is incorrect, absolutely. (C) has W, X, Y and Z with two, two, one and two respectively, which is also severely incorrect. (D) has W with one, X with three, Y with two and Z with one. That is P2 exactly, which shows where the SC bundle has to go. Does the person with the saw have a chisel, and, per P2, is that person either X or Y? YES!. NOW we take the time to apply the rule that did not get put into the drawing, rule four. Does anybody have two identical tools? Nope. That is our answer. Circle it and walk away. "E" cannot be correct.

That was much more efficient because it was faster, 100% accurate and it forced us to learn about the subtleties of the rules. Now we are moving to the right side of the LSAT curve into the high 150's and low 160's, or as we prefer to refer to it, "scholarship country."

19) If Xenophilius receives exactly three tools, which one of the following must be true?
A) Yancy does not receive the saw
B) Wilson receives the saw
C) Zunfufu receives the saw
D) Either Wilson or Zunfufu receives the saw
E) Wilson and Zunfufu receive the same number of tools

Here we are confronted with another question that KILLS the mental health of the average test taker, because that average person will not have done the work that we did in advance and thus will not have the answer right in front of her.

We know that if X receives three tools, W can only have one, Y must have two and Z has to have exactly one: that is P2! We therefore know that (A) does not have to be true (and remember, we are being asked what MUST be true) because anybody who can have two tools can have a saw (and its bundle buddy the chisel). By the same reasoning, Wilson cannot have the saw, so (B) is incorrect, as are (C) and (D).

(E) **_must_** be correct, and on the day of the test you will simply bubble it in and run for the next question without hesitation. **Remember, "Just checking to be sure" means, "I like wasting time."**

Just to put your mind at ease, go ahead and consider (E). According to P2 The "X has three tools" picture), W and Z must each have one tool. There. Now you are certain of the correctness of (E) and you have wasted time. Were we correct *before* we wasted the time? Yep. We always are. Don't let it happen again or I will frown at you and possibly have a curse of some kind place on your grandchildren.

20) Which of the following is a complete and accurate list of the carpenter or carpenters who may never receive a saw?
A) Zunfufu
B) Wilson, Zunfufu
C) Wilson, Yancy
D) Wilson, Xenophilius, Yancy
E) Yancy, Zunfufu

Average test taker: "OMG! I have to figure out who can never have it? How can I be sure?" They proceed to waste time, gain anxiety and psych themselves out.

YOU say, "This is so freakin' easy! *What do I already know?*" In order to be able to have a saw, you have to have the chisel, which means you have to be able to have at least two tools. Who can never have two or more tools? Hmmm... this is a toughie.... (you are not sweating; you are busy contemplating how to sound humble when you tell people that Stanford is actually a realistic school for you to apply to). P2 has both W and Z with one only, but in P1, W is allowed to have two but Z can only have one, so Zunfufu is the only one who can never have the saw. You circle (A) and run away.

21) If Xenophilius has both a drill and a chisel, which of the following must be true?
A) Either Wilson or Yancy has the saw
B) Xenophilius has the saw
C) Neither Wilson nor Zunfufu has the saw
D) Either Wilson, Xenophilius or Yancy has the saw
E) Either Wilson, Yancy or Zunfufu has the saw

X has D and C. What do I know? In P1, X has two spaces, so it is full with D and C. In P2, D and C can go in and there is a third space for either S (to complete the SC bundle) or P (because all three tools have to be different). This *might be tough* for you to keep track of in your skull. DO NOT, UNDER ANY CIRCUMSTANCE, EVEN *PRETEND TO THINK ABOUT* LIGHTLY DRAWING D and C INTO YOUR TWO PICTURES. If 5b (What do I know already?) does not get us the answer, 5c says RE-PICTURE. Do a small, neat re-picture of both P1 and P2 and then put the D and C under Xenophilius.

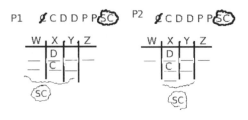

carps = W,X,Y,Z
tools = CCDDPPS
-No others
-All Play

1) Y > Z
2) Nobody more than X, possibly =
3) carp. w/S must get C
4) Each carp all diff tools ***

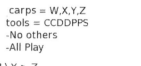
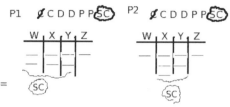

Here is where the real test is. Some people (we will call them "slightly above average but way below you") will have figured out P2, the easier of the two pictures to figure out. The test makers know that there is a range of intellects attacking the test, and so they have built in questions like this one in order to ferret out the truly capable students.

Let us examine this question in the context of the two pictures, first from the perspective of someone who, being too smart for their own good, assumed that P2 was the be-all, end-all of this game.

If X has both the drill and the chisel, does that pin anything down absolutely? If we are just using P2 (because we failed to do all of the steps), we believe incorrectly that it does:

If this poor sap were correct, then either W or Y would have to have the saw, being the only carpenters capable of having two tools. NOTICE that answer choice (A) is designed to trap this poor sod dead in his or her tracks.

We however, see it like this:

78

To us, this means that W, X or Y could have the saw and that Z cannot. That is answer choice (D), and that's MONEY!

22) Suppose the rule that says that Yancy has more tools than Zunfufu is changed to say that Zunfufu must always have more tools than Yancy. If all of the other conditions remain the same, which of the following must be true?
   A) Yancy does not receive the saw
   B) Wilson receives the saw
   C) Zunfufu receives the saw
   D) Either Wilson or Zunfufu receives the saw
   E) Wilson and Zunfufu receive the same number of tools

Arrrgh! They have changed the game on us! Those evil Curs! Not really.

This is another psychological trick they are playing on you. They know that when you are taking a test, you are almost certainly experiencing stress. They know that by the time you get to the last question in the game you are very probably worried about time (even though **YOU** are not worried about time because you are doing what we told you to). So the last question is often one of these, "rattle your cage," problems. Don't be a sucker and fall for it. DESTROY THE QUESTION!

If, instead of Y>Z we now have Z>Y, and all of the other rules (and logical inferences based upon them) remain in effect: nobody can have more than X, a chisel goes with the saw, and no carpenter can have two of the same kinds of tool. So what *actually* changes? Think about it for a second, and go back and look at our original two pictures before going on.

We *could* take the time to re-figure the entire game and incorporate the new condition for problem 22 into the mix: THIS is exactly what they are testing – whether you incorrectly believe that it is necessary to re-figure everything. What we already know from Step 4 is that the Y-Z relationship does not "Double-Up" with anything. It has logical implications, but it does not directly connect to any other rule. So when we invert the relationship between Y and Z form

$$Y>Z \text{ to } Y<Z$$

are we not just changing their positions on the top of the drawing, like so?

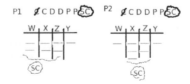

Yes, that is all we did, and so NOTHING really changed logically. Two carpenters changed positions. That makes things infinitely easy. Y is the one who cannot have the saw now, because in both pictures Y is allowed to have but one tool. So which answer choice must be correct? (A)! DO NOT LOOK AT THE OTHER ANSWERS, EVEN WHEN YOU ARE PRACTICING! We are trying to develop top-drawer LSAT **_habits_**, one of which is NOT WASTING TIME. There can only be one correct answer. Once you have found it, get the hell out of there!

A final note before we look at a variation of the buckets game. There are certain *recurring patterns* and themes within games and they need to be recognized by you, the test taker.

In the carpenter "buckets" game, we saw that there was a very critical set of inference we had to make in step four of our processes involving *calculators*. Most of the questions turned on those inferences. The test makers then asked us several questions that, although *sounding* unique, really were not. They focused upon our basic understanding of the fact that there are only two ways that the game could have possibly been played: that "X" could possibly have three, and that W can have either one or two tools. This recurring pattern is a godsend for you. Any time you are doing a new game and you encounter a similar pattern, you will know how to deal with it and you will know that you are about to DESTROY EVERY QUESTION!

Other games will have major inferences that emerge from other parts of step four. Begin to develop your own personal list of patterns that you observe in games. We will point out all of the ones that are vital to your success, but that does not mean that you will not find things that strike you as being unique or important. We are always surprised by the number of new ideas we get from readers, students and test takers after every new release of an LSAT.

If you see a pattern (or anything else interesting) not mentioned in this book, feel free to point it out to us. We will give you full credit if we use it, because that is how we roll. My email address is back on the dedication page at the front.

A NOTE ABOUT RE-PICTURING

You may have noticed and/or thought that it was not necessary to re-draw the picture(s) in some of the problems. You are absolutely correct, from a certain point of view. As each of us becomes more skilled with the material and the methods, the need to re-picture diminishes. If you do not **_need_** to redraw a picture and you can do it in your head, feel free. HOWEVER, do not skip redrawing just to save time. If you make a mistake because you failed to be thorough, that is on you, not us. DO WHAT YOU NEED TO DO IN ORDER TO BE CORRECT.

BUCKETS, REDUX
Consider the following set up for a logic game:

> Five bakers, Gina, Henry, Ida, Jason and Kelly are going to be assigned ingredients, butter, cocoa and flour as their only ingredients. The ingredients are given to the bakers according to the following rules.

It does look a lot like a "buckets" game, huh? There are people in the form of bakers who are clearly defined as our "buckets," into which we will deposit ingredients. There is a big difference however between this set up and the "carpenters" game we just worked on. Do you recognize what it is?

At the outset, it looks as though all five bakers could have all three ingredients, or that they could all have nothing. What are the odds that the LSAT will allow something like that to actually happen? "Substantially less than zero," is the correct answer.

What "*supposably*"[23] raises the difficulty level here is that we were not told *how many* of each type of ingredient we have. We are supposed to be intimidated by the *absence of information* in the set up. WE, however, don't give a rip. We do the steps and know that, as always, the test **must** give us enough information to solve every question...duh.

STEP ONE: GET A GRIP
What is the nature of the game? We know that you know this one, so say it out loud. GET IN THE HABIT of mumbling the steps! Buckets. *Who are the players?* We have five bakers, G, H, I, J and K. We also have three ingredients, B, C and F. Are there any others? NADA! Are there any *hidden rules*? NOPE! The fact pattern does not indicate that any or all of the bakers have to receive any ingredients, and the set up does not indicate that all of the ingredients must be used. We have jack squat to work with, which actually makes us happy, because it allows us to go onto step two.

STEP TWO: FORMAL RULES
REMEMBER that you are supposed to NUMBER the rules and then re-write each one, with the corresponding number by your re-writes.

---

[23] "Supposably" is NOT a real word. If, after today, you **ever** say that word out loud, you had better either be: (a) joking, and making the deliberateness of the joke obvious like we just did, or (b) prepared to be labeled an idiot. The correct word is, "supposedly." Look it up in a real dictionary (urban dictionaries do NOT count). While you are purging things that will make you look dumb, hit the eject button on "expresso" (it's espresso, with no "x" sound) and "quote-unquote" (it is "quote - end quote," because you are not "un-quoting" something, you are *ending the freakin' quote*). You are going to be a lawyer and part of the elite class of society (whatever that is), like it or not. Try not to sound like you just fell off of the turnip truck. Better to be thought of as an elitist snob than an idiot, because most other lawyers, judges and law professors are *supposably* elitist snobs, and you do not want to be disadvantaged by their perception of you. More to the point, you do not want your *clients* to be disadvantaged by it.

Ida is given cocoa.
Gina receives more ingredients than Henry.
Kelly and Gina have exactly two ingredients in common.
Each baker receives at least one ingredient.

Rule number 1 is an "absolute" and it is simple looking enough, but remember what you are supposed to ask of every rule: "What does it tell us, and what does it NOT tell us?" Rule 1 says that Ida gets cocoa. It does not say that Ida receives *only* cocoa. It does not tell us whether or not she is allowed to receive anything else. As of this point, she could receive all three as far as we can tell. So the re-write looks like this:

$$1) \; I = C...$$

The ellipsis indicates that "I" is not limited to only "C". We could also have written:

$$1) \; I = C \text{ and possibly others}$$

as we did before in the carpenters game.

The second rule says that G has more than H and nothing more. We can smell the yummy goodness wafting off of this one, because when we get to "calculators" in step four, this will almost certainly make our day a little brighter.

$$2) \; G > H$$

The third rule says that K and G have exactly two of the same ingredients. What does it NOT say? It does not say whether or not they both have exactly two or not. G could have three and K could have two (or vice-verse), and so long as two are the same, the rule would be complied with. Again, we can smell the victory over the horizon because we have spotted in advance an issue being tested.

$$3) \; K\&G \; 2 \text{ same EX.}$$

Rule number four is almost an absolute. We say *almost* because it provides a minimum number of ingredients each baker is to receive, but that tells us little absolutely other than that there will be absolutely nobody without ingredients. That's a big help. So we write:

$$4) \; 1 \text{ MIN/BAKER}$$

STEP THREE: DRAWING
We draw this exactly the same way we would draw any other "Buckets" game. The "stuff" being assigned to each baker goes above the buckets just like before. The only difference is that we don't know how many B, C and F there are... yet.

STEP FOUR: INFERENCES
ABSOLUTES - We have TWO! What are they?

Rule 1 is an absolute, as is rule 4. We can stuff in one slot under each baker for their minimum ingredient (noting below the drawing that one is a minimum). We can shove C into Bucket I and circle it to indicate that it is absolutely, always there.

BCF

G H I J K

Ⓒ

1 MIN/BAKER

BUNDLES
Are there any bundles of things that always have to be together? Nope.

CALCULATORS
Are there any "mathy" looking rules here? You'd better believe it! G must have more ingredients than H. Does that help us at all? Look at the picture up above and try to think this one out for yourself BEFORE you turn the page. Use a pencil and scratch paper to draw it out if you need to... and THINK. We will resolve this on the next page, just to keep you from peeking.

If they all must have at least one, and G>H, then if H has one, G has two or three, and if H has two, G must have three! That seems to give us a way to break our picture into three separate ones, as such:

> **The Multiple-Picture Rules**
> a) Draw two pictures when there are ONLY two ways for the game to be played AND the two drawings provide valuable additional information.
> b) You had better have a damn good reason for making three pictures.
> c) **NEVER** make more than three pictures.

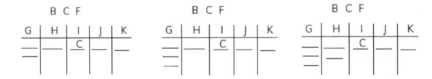

Rule 4 says that K and G have exactly two in common, which also means something, calculator-wise. If G has three ingredients, then K must have two, because if K had three, it would have three in common with G and if K had one ingredient it would not have two in common with G. But if G has TWO ingredients, K could have two or three ingredients. We could draw out those possibilities as well, BUT WE ARE NOT GOING TO!

Did we actually get anything *useful* out of the three drawings above? All that they really represent is rule two, and they do not provide us with anything valuable beyond that. If we had drawn out the K and G scenarios as well, we would have three more drawings for a total of SIX FREAKIN' PICTURES! None of them would tell us anything useful about G, H and K and they would not pin down any additional ingredients for any baker.

We will NOT draw out multiple pictures for any game unless doing so nets us something more than mere numerical clarity. REMEMBER THE RULE that you were supposed to have memorized: We do NOT make multiple pictures if we do not definitively gain greater information from them. If the only thing we would gain from drawing two pictures is a simple fact (such as, "Larry has to have either pie or ice cream) then we make a note of the fact but we do not make more pictures. There will be a single exception to this "only two pictures," rule, and we will learn about it much later when we discuss conditional logic.

It is an exceptionally rare day when we draw out more than two pictures for a game. We had better net a steaming pile of insight if we do so. If you think about it, this makes sense. As we see in the present game, we *could* draw out six different versions of the picture and fill in lots of information about the numbers of ingredients. The time required to do those drawings is not being efficiently used, however. If we can go into the questions understanding that there are only a few ways to work the problem and then get cracking on said questions, our time is much more effectively used doing that, rather than hashing out combinations and permutations. Just like we see above with our three drawings, it really is not worth 90 seconds of precious time on the day of the test to draw them all out. Just make a note of the numerical combinations and move on.

So we are back to our single original drawing with an added note as to the numerical combinations. Based upon rule 2 (G>H), we see two things clearly. First, if H has 2, G must have 3 and K has to have 2 (in order to have two in common with G per rule 3) and those are slam-dunk, absolute truths. Second, all other combinations have H with one, and G and K with 2/3. We will add those to our picture as follows:

DOUBLE-UPS - We already hit upon the one double-up in calculators. That was a function of the fact that two of our rules talked about the same player, G, and that both of those rules were calculator-related.

This points to an important idea I have been saving until just this moment. The reason it is imperative to memorize and know how to use all of these rules and to practice them, step-by-step, every time is at least in part because of what we are seeing here: sometimes the various steps or processes we employ get rolled together. We have to know the rules and processes so well and so completely that we can see when the different factors are interrelated. We have to be agile in our use and application of them, recognizing them when they pop up in other contexts. If you are not 100% savvy with them, you will miss important inferences, thus losing time, points, acceptance letters and big piles of scholarship money.

We cannot encourage you enough to become a master of the rules and the steps of the system.

EXTRAS - We still have not learned what they are (though it has been challenging enough without them). It is still imperative that we think in an orderly fashion and mention them. They are coming, with full force, in the section on Winner/Loser games. BUT, we have to walk through the steps: Bi-conditionals, Forced dichotomies, Affirmative duties, Right side rules,™ Contradictions and Lone conditionals.

FREE RANGERS - Do we have any free-rangers? J does not have any rules aside from the fact that J must receive at least one ingredient like everyone else. J can do whatever J wants at this point. Again, this is important why? Because when the questions ask us, "What could be true," we know that anything involving J could be true (except having zero ingredients). We also know that there is nothing about J that *must* be true (other than having at least one ingredient), so if we are asked a hypothetical such as:

"If Jason is given both cocoa and flour, which of the following could be true?"

we know that this is a scam question that is only testing whether or not we know that J's actions do not have any consequences to any of the others.

So now we have completely processed the game for inferences and we have ended up with one simple picture, four numerical combinations and a free ranger. We need to be 100% clear within the confines of our own brains that if we have done all of the steps completely and accurately, there is **nothing** more that we need to do in order to efficiently lay waste to the questions.

That may not seem very satisfying to you at the moment, but it should be. We began with over one thousand possible combinations of entities and reduced it dramatically. Once we look at how the rules work within the context of a given problem, we will ALWAYS get precise results.

REMEMBER: When you have worked through all of the steps and you come out with a picture that does not look very well developed, THAT IS BY THE TEST MAKER'S DESIGN! The test makers are attempting to intimidate you and prey upon your insecurities. They know that many people will look at their final picture and think, "I MUST HAVE MISSED SOMETHING!" If you did the first four steps of the process, step 5 will be as easy as it can possibly be.

Are you beginning to see why logic games are such an important factor in determining ability to matriculate law school? Organizing information, drawing inferences from rules, knowing what can and what must be true etc. Games are a highly accurate measure of your ability to perform fundamental lawyer skills.

STEP 5: DESTROY THE QUESTIONS - Let's do some problems based upon this game. As you do them, remember to GO WITH WHAT YOU ALREADY KNOW, and re-draw your picture for individual problems **ONLY** as needed. Answers and explanations are in the back.

PROBLEM SET #4: BUCKETS, PART 2

Answers and explanations in Appendix "B" pg 245

Five bakers are going to be assigned ingredients to make their recipes. The bakers, Gina, Henry, Ida, Jason and Kelly will be working with butter, cocoa and flour as their only ingredients. The ingredients are given to the bakers according to the following rules.

1. Ida is given cocoa.
2. Gina receives more ingredients than Henry.
3. Kelly and Gina have exactly two ingredients in common.
4. Each baker receives at least one ingredient.

6) Which one of the following could be a complete and accurate assignment of ingredients to bakers?
A) Gina: butter, cocoa, flour
  Henry: butter, cocoa
  Ida: butter, cocoa, flour
  Jason: flour
  Kelly: butter, cocoa, flour
B) Gina: butter, cocoa, flour
  Henry: butter, cocoa, flour
  Ida: butter, cocoa, flour
  Jason: flour
  Kelly: butter, cocoa
C) Gina: butter, cocoa
  Henry: butter, cocoa
  Ida: butter, cocoa, flour
  Jason: flour
  Kelly: butter, cocoa, flour
D) Gina: butter, cocoa
  Henry: butter
  Ida: butter, cocoa, flour
  Jason: flour
  Kelly: butter, cocoa, flour
E) Gina: flour
  Henry: butter, flour
  Ida: butter, cocoa, flour
  Jason: flour
  Kelly: butter, cocoa, flour

7) If Jason has more ingredients than Gina, which of the following must be false?
A) Kelly has three ingredients
B) Kelly has two ingredients
C) Henry has one ingredient
D) Henry has two ingredients
E) Jason has three ingredients

8) Which of the following, if known, would allow us to completely determine how many ingredients each baker has?
A) Kelly has three ingredients
B) Kelly has two ingredients and Henry has one
C) Jason has two ingredients and Ida has only cocoa
D) Jason has only flour, Ida has cocoa and butter only and Kelly has cocoa, butter and flour
E) Jason has only butter, Ida has only cocoa and Henry has cocoa only

9) Which of the following must be true?
A) If Henry has butter, Jason must have flour
B) If Ida has cocoa and butter, Henry must have butter
C) If Gina has cocoa and flour, Kelly must have butter
D) If Henry has cocoa, Gina must have butter and flour
E) If Henry has cocoa and flour, Gina must have butter

10) If the condition is added that nobody may have more ingredients than Jason, which of the following must be false?
A) Jason has Flour and cocoa only while Henry has flour
B) Jason has Flour and cocoa only while Kelly has flour and cocoa
C) Jason has Flour and cocoa only while Gina has flour and cocoa
D) Jason has Flour and cocoa only while Ida has flour only and Henry has butter and cocoa
E) Jason has Flour and cocoa only while Ida has flour and cocoa and Henry has butter.

V. LOGIC

Author's Note

If logic is new, hazy or unfamiliar to you, it is *imperative* that you be very patient in learning the material in this chapter. Take it slowly, be careful and be methodical. This stuff turns up in **EVERY SECTION of the LSAT.**

Impatience will ruin you in logic, so plan on spending several days or even a week or two getting this stuff down *perfectly*.

It is virtually guaranteed that there will be at least fifteen questions involving conditional logic on the LSAT. If you do not know it cold, you are killing your score before you ever set foot in the test center, because fifteen questions is the difference between 155 (mediocre) and 165 (93rd percentile), and that is the difference between borrowing $100,000.00 for law school and going for free.

Thus far we have seen how to put things into order, both Firm Ordering and Squishy Ordering, and how to put things into buckets. Before we can learn how to pick winners and losers, we need to take an official time-out and learn something a bit … well … intimidating.

Picking winners and losers requires that we be rather adept at doing propositional or "conditional" logic.[1] The application of this flavor of logic extends beyond the "picking winners and losers" logic game: every type of game on the LSAT has incorporated at least one type of rule employing propositional logic at some time or another. These issues will crop up in the other sections of the LSAT (logical reasoning and reading) as well. So to maximize your score, you **_must learn and master this stuff._**

The good news is that it is fairly easy to learn IF you do not psych yourself out, stick to what we teach you, practice diligently and do not give up. Even better, when you recognize a conditional logic problem and you use the techniques we teach, you will always get an exact, absolutely correct answer.

CATEGORICAL vs. CONDITIONAL LANGUAGE

The LSAT employs two kinds of logical language. Luckily for us, they are used in only one way in the games section(s). A critical step in the process of applying it adroitly is **_recognizing_** when you need to use it. If the magic language is there and you fail to pick up on it, you miss out on using the logic tools we are about to give you, and thus you lose points that should be guaranteed freebies.

---

[1] Okay, we admit it up front: the "conditional logic" we cover in this section is **not** pure, "according to Hoyle," propositional logic. It is not necessary to have an Einstein-like grasp of logic in order to blow away the LSAT. We will teach you *everything* that you **must** know for the exam (even as it applies to other sections), as well as to be a top-drawer law student and supreme-court-capable attorney, no more, no less. That is what we do: teach you how to be awesome. Anything that we left out is unnecessary for being #1 in your class at Harvard or Stanford or Chula Vista College of Law and Play Station Repair or anywhere else.

"Categories" = groups

If someone were to say to you,

"All of the goats in the herd have beards."

They would be making a categorical statement. This statement speaks of two different *categories* or "groups" of things: (1) goats that are part of the herd and (2) things that have beards. This is a "categorical" statement because it refers to groups or *categories* of things, even though it does so in two very different ways.

"Goats," are referred to in what is called a *distributed* manner: I know something about every goat in the herd. All of them. Each and every last one. If there is a goat in that herd, we can all be certain based upon the above statement that said goat will have a beard, without fail.

"Bearded things," on the other hand, is not referred to universally: if there is an animal in the herd that has a beard, it might not necessarily be a goat. For example, if Sanajlih has a beard and is in the herd, is Sanajlih a goat? Sanajlih may be the goat herder, and not a goat at all. If Sanajlih is a goat in the herd, then we know for certain that Sanajlih has a beard.

When we see "universal" statements that refer to every member of some category of stuff, we immediately make such inferences about them (if it is a goat in the herd, it has a beard). We may also immediately recognize the things that we cannot infer from them: if it has a beard, it does not necessarily have to be a goat, or in the herd, but it could be in the herd and have a beard but not be a goat.

MUY IMPORTANTE! VERY IMPORTANT! TRES IMPORTANT! SEHR WICHTIG!
On the LSAT, we are interested in what logical statements tell us *for certain*. Logical statements are VERY LIMITED in what they tell us, and most people think that they tell us more things for certain than they actually do. Take the example above,

"All of the goats in the herd have beards."

That tells us one useful thing for certain: every goat in the herd has a beard. It also tells us other things, such as that some things (but not necessarily all things) that have beards are goats in the herd, and that anything that does not have a beard cannot be a goat in the herd. It does not tell us that if I have a goat, that it must have a beard (only goats *from the herd* must have beards) and it does not tell me whether or not goats are the only animals in the herd. If there are other animals in the herd (let's say, amphibious rodents kept within city limits) we would have no idea as to their state of beardedness based upon the available information because it is only the goats in the herd that we have any information about.

The test is trying, in several places, to test whether or not we understand the limits of the information before us as well as the maximum inferential value thereof. The good news is that in logic games, the logic is the most simple and the most absolute.

Universal Truth

If we were to assert that, "Falafel is tasty," would that be a universal statement? We did not say, "all," did we? On the flip-side, we did not say, "most," or "many," or "several," or yadda yadda yadda. Admittedly, this may sound like a trivial schoolyard-argument distinction, but it is important, particularly when you are a lawyer, which you very nearly are.

The hard and fast rule is so: If a statement does not qualify the size of the category, limiting it to less than "all," we treat it as if the speaker had said, "all." Thus, such statements are treated as universal. If the speaker intended to say something different, they probably ought to have. So if presented with a statement such as, "Bankers are criminals." We take it on its face as meaning, "All bankers are criminals." Someone who intended to convey the thought that, "Most bankers are criminals," needs to select their words with more prudence.

Complements to the Logician

The same can be said if a statement is universally *negative*, as in the following:

Bankers are not honest.

This statement **means** that if you were to scour the entire universe looking for just one honest banker, your results would be null. In other words,

No bankers are honest.

If we had a gigantic bucket, and in that bucket were all of the honest things in the universe (monks, puppies, newborns...), where would the bankers be? *Outside of the bucket.* The bankers would be non-honest things.

"Non" can be added to any category to make it a *complement* of that category. For example, there are only two kinds of sweaters in the entire universe: striped sweaters and non-striped sweaters (and only one "best time" to wear the striped sweater[2]). There are only two types of people in the universe: earthlings and non-earthlings. In other words, things are either *in* the bucket or they are out of the bucket and are *non-whatevers.* You will be a lawyer, distinct from non-lawyers.

Complementary categories set up what are called *dichotomies*: there are only two choices available (we will talk about them more in a bit). This can simplify our thinking dramatically.

---

[2] "The best time to wear a striped sweater is all the time." *SpongeBob SquarePants, speedboat legend.*

Sadly, sometimes the thinking is not so simple and yet people misconstrue it to be so. As we are well aware, most things in reality do not fall neatly into complementary categories, even though some people will try really hard (and invalidly) to make us believe it to be so. For example, a President might say, "*You either support the war on terrorism, or you support the terrorists.*" A non-war-supporter is not the same as a terrorist supporter, because a person can be both non-war-supporting and non-terrorism-supporting quite easily. So people who create these *false dichotomies,* by assuming that two categories complement each other when they really do not, are at best committing a logical error and at worst acting like the Luchador *Ramses*[3].

Finally, knowing that something is a *non-whatever* is not particularly informative. For example, if you became aware of the fact that Tony is a non-racecar driver, what do you actually know? Very little. Is he a good driver? We do not know. Can he safely drive a car at speeds in excess of one-hundred miles per hour? We do not know. We do not know what Tony *is* when we only know what he is not. We will be challenged to use the limited information provided in the appropriate manner. That means we must **never mistake what information does tell us for something that it does not.** If Bonnie has an I.Q. that is non-average, we cannot leap to the conclusion that her I.Q. is above or below average. She may be hugely deficient intellectually, or she may be hugely brilliant, or she may be just slightly above or below average or.... She is **anything other than average**, but that is every possibility in the universe, minus average. In sum, by knowing that X is non-Y, we know just one tiny bit more than Jack squat.

Conditional Statements

Contrast the above categorical information with **conditional** statements. These are really "*hypothetical*" in nature. Take the statement,

> "If it is a goat in the herd, then it will have a beard."

This says even less that the categorical statement before. It does not say that there is a herd, or that there are any goats or beards. It merely *conjectures* that *if* there were to be a goat, and *if* that goat were to be in the herd, it would have a beard. If there is no goat, this rule is meaningless. If there is a goat and it is hanging out in a bar in Scotland and not in the herd, the conditional rule is equally meaningless. It is only when there actually *is* a goat and it definitely *is* in the herd that the rule has applicability and *requires* us to conclude that there is a beard involved. Otherwise, all bets are off.

LSAT Conditionals usually come in the form of "if – then," statements. "If it is a goat in the herd, then it will have a beard," is a conditional statement. The universal categorical statement, "All goats in the herd have beards," allows us to properly

---

[3] *Nacho Libre, Nickelodeon Movies and HH Films,* 2006. Quoting Jack Black as Nacho, "I used to really like Ramses. I wanted to become him! But it turns out, he's a real douche."

make a logical translation into a conditional without fear, so long as we translate it with fidelity. This makes sense in the context of the law. "Vehicle operators with a blood alcohol level at or above .08% are guilty of driving while intoxicated." That is a very universal statement. The conditional translation, "If a person is an operator of a vehicle and has a blood alcohol level above .08% then that person is guilty of driving while intoxicated." If a person is not "operating" something (for example, they are sleeping on the hood of the car), this conditional does not apply to them. If they are operating something that is not a vehicle, for example, they are operating a KitchenAid® Mixer, this conditional does not apply to them. If they are operating something and that something is a vehicle but their blood alcohol level is below .08% the conditional does not apply to them. That is why people like us do not worry about receiving the death penalty: we are never going to do anything that remotely resembles the conditions required to receive it.

If the original statement had not been universal we could not work such magic. For example, if the original categorical statement had been, "*Some* of the goats in the herd have beards," we could not turn it into any sort of a *useful* conditional statement; "If there are goats in the herd, then there is at least one with a beard," does not help us to definitively determine how much Goat Chow® to buy, how many beard trimmers to employ or how much spot remover will be needed for our carpets. Think about why that is so: if we had an animal from the herd and that animal was a goat, this new, non-universal statement only says that it *might* have a beard, because some goats in the herd have beards, but apparently not all of them and probably less than half of them, because if it was more than half they would have said that *most* of the goats have beards. That the animal *might* have a beard is pretty worthless when trying to solve a Scooby Doo[4] mystery, which is what LSAT logic games are.

So whenever the LSAT uses absolute, universal language in a statement, i.e. "all," "every," "each," "any," "no," "none," etc., AND whenever the LSAT uses language that is universal but does not employ such words (photographers are artists, chickens can't bowl) we can turn them into a conditional statement, and that will lead to much goodness, rejoicing and yummy points.

CATEGORICAL	CONDITIONAL
1. Cats are dumb.	1. If it is a cat, then it is dumb.
2. Everyone on my team has B.O.	2. If a person is on my team, they have B.O.
	3. If it is a dog, it is a non-felon.
3. No dogs are felons.	
	4. If a person is a Yankee, then they are non-good at ballet.
4. N.Y. Yankees are not good at ballet.	

[4] *Scooby Doo* is the copyrighted property of Hanna-Barbera studios and/or Warner Bros. studios. The name is used herein without anyone's permission, but they ought to be glad that anybody remembers that tragically awful franchise. Seriously... Freddie Prinze Jr. had his entire career torpedoed by it.

IT IS WHAT IT IS... AND NOTHING ELSE

We reiterate. Conditional statements are extremely narrow in their meaning and you cannot construe them to mean ANYTHING more or less than what they mean. Take our statement,

"If it is a goat in the herd, then it will have a beard."

This tells me ONLY about what I can infer IF there is a goat and IF that goat is in the herd. It does *not* tell me anything about non-goats (it does not say, If there is a non-goat....). It does not tell me about animals that are not in the herd, even if they are goats. There are non-goats with beards (Sigmund Freud, Socrates, MME. Clofullia, and George Lucas, to name a few). There may also be animals that are not in the herd that are bearded (same list of fuzzy peeps).

This requires you, dear reader, to be a complete, hard-core, no compromise word interpreter. "If it is a gull, then it flies." This tells us NOTHING about anything other than gulls and what they do. Other things that fly and other non-gull animals: we do not know JACK SQUAT about them.

WE WANT CONDITIONAL STATEMENTS WHENEVER POSSIBLE

Conditional statements are extremely useful in logic games due in large part to their absolute nature. We always know several things for certain whenever we have them. This is why whenever we are presented with an opportunity to interpret something as a conditional statement we jump all over it and whenever we see a universal categorical statement we convert it into a conditional statement and jump upon it just as vigorously.

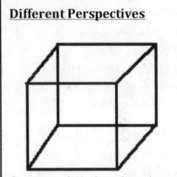

Different Perspectives

Some people look at the cube and see it as going back and to the upper-right. Others see it as going down and to the lower-left. It all depends upon which of the top two horizontal lines you think of as being front most. Obviously, both interpretations are correct, because it is the same flippin' cube!

You Say Poe-tay-toe, I say Tay-ters...

Let us pretend that we have a universal statement that reads, "All cats are non dogs." That sounds pretty universal, simple and definitive, does it not? But different people see this statement in different ways. One person might say that this statement's conditional form is, "If it is a cat then it is a non-dog." Another person might say, "If I have a dog then I know it is not a cat."

Do they not mean the exact same thing? YES! They are *logically* the same statement viewed from two different perspectives. We can see this if we draw a picture to represent the relationship between the two categories of things (see below).

If we had a giant bucket that contained all of the cats in the universe, there would not be ANY dogs in it: they would be outside of the cat bucket in a separate "dog" bucket, like so:

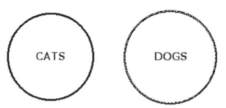

If it is a cat then it is non-dog.
If it is a dog then it is non cat.
They mean the same danged thing!

As we will confirm in a few minutes, there are at least two ways to see *every* conditional statement. It is easier to see this in a simple example such the cat scenario above. After we take a short break to be certain that we are getting this, we will teach you how to easily see every conditional statement from both perspectives. Then we will teach you how to extract all sorts of genius-like superpower from them to crush logic games.

It would be very helpful if you were to take a few moments and convert the following categorical statements into conditional statements. We will leave out the tricky ones for the time being: DON'T PANIC! We will cover them soon enough. For now, we want you to focus on three things: recognizing when a statement is categorical, recognizing whether or not it is universal and converting the universal categorical into the conditional.

BEFORE YOU BEGIN, it is important to reiterate a major pedagogical point: people who do things exclusively in their heads usually *think* that they understand problems and they usually do not. There is a vast difference between the two, and "thinking" that you know how to do it is much different than actually being able to do it. Law schools do not give two hoots about whether or not you are smart on the inside of your head. They only care about your score, and that means that you MUST be able to execute on paper. SO DO IT.

Get out a sheet of scratch paper and WRITE THESE OUT, then check the answers in the back of the book AFTER you have tried your dead-level best to do them on your own.

IF YOU CANNOT DO IT HERE IN PRACTICE, YOU WILL NOT BE ABLE TO DO IT ON THE LSAT, AND THAT MEANS THAT YOU WILL NOT BE ABLE TO GO TO LAW SCHOOL. So, pretty please, do the flippin' practice.

PROBLEM SET #5: Converting Universal Categorical Statements to Conditionals

For each of the following, determine whether or not it is categorical in nature, then whether or not it is a universal statement (telling us about every member of **_one_** of the categories). If it is both, convert it into a conditional statement.

1) Everybody at the park has on red pants.

2) There are not any people in my class with halitosis.

3) The only things Hyundai makes are high quality cars.

4) Many fast foods give one gout.

5) None of the people in the top ten-percent of the class are non-speed readers.

6) Each child is special.

7) Catastrophes never strike Delaware.

8) Leprechauns are mostly benign.

9) Chickens make lousy house pets.

10) There are no Vogons who are unencumbered by administrative inertia.

And & Or

The words "and," and "or," have particular meanings that you must be aware of. You have to think in terms of their technical meaning. After all, that is what lawyers do.

"**And**" is the *conjunction*: it "joins" things together. This means that each of the terms in a statement that are joined together by an "and" must occur for the statement to be true. Take for example, "Scotch and soda." If you do not have both Scotch AND soda, you do not have a Scotch and soda. This same concept applies to conditional statements. Take for example, "If you eat beans and broccoli, you will get gas." This statement really means that you have to eat both beans and broccoli in order to be sure you will get gas. If you just eat beans, the *conjunctive condition* is not met, so you do not know for certain whether or not you will get gas. The same thing goes for just having broccoli. Both of the conjuncts must be known to be true in order for the "if" to have been met, thus informing us that the "then" has to be true.

"**Or**," (the *disjunctive*) functions to mean that we have to have one or the other in order for the statement to be true. Take for example, "Coke or Pepsi." If we have Coke, the statement is true. If we have Pepsi, the statement is true. If we have *neither* then the statement is false. But what if we have *both* Coke and Pepsi?

"Or" is slightly more agile because it has two meanings. Let's look at an example. The cabin attendant on your flight to Rio comes by your aisle seat and says,

"You can have steak or chicken."

Yum! Which can you have? It turns out that the answer depends. The cabin crew, highly trained in the art of extracting extra revenue from "guests," interprets "or" to mean, "Steak or chicken, but not both steak and chicken." Most of us will roll with this interpretation because that is what most people mean when they make such statements. This is called the *exclusive* use of "or": one, the other, but not both.

In the law world (and especially the LSAT world), "or" is used in the *inclusive* manner. This means that you can tell the attendant that you want both steak and chicken, because "steak or chicken," means, "steak or chicken or both steak and chicken." Good luck trying to logic your way past the rapier-like mind of the sky butlers.

MEMORIZE THIS: Unless otherwise indicated, "or" is used *inclusively* (steak, chicken or both steak and chicken) on the LSAT. If "or" is intended to be used *exclusively* on the LSAT, the statement will clearly indicate, "steak or chicken, but not both."

This helps us tremendously. If there are disjunctive (or) conditional statements on the LSAT, we can always treat them the same way AND we can ignore the test makers' silly attempts to mess with our heads. "If Tommy has Coke or Pepsi, he will belch." If Tommy has Coke, he burps. If Tommy has Pepsi, he burps. If Tommy has both Coke and Pepsi, he will burp offensively.

The most common head games the test makers will play are as follows. First, they will say, "Bill can have a Chevy or a Ford or both a Chevy and a Ford." That's the *inclusive* "or" that we always use anyway, so we do nothing special with it, and we do not get fooled into thinking that there is more to the meaning of the words, "Chevy or Ford, inclusive." We know that "or" is inclusive and we will not be a pack of insecure ninnies who are tricked into thinking that there might be some hidden meaning in their messed-up verbiage.

The second is what is called the **disjunctive syllogism.** In their most rudimentary form, these look like this:

Q or P.
Not Q.
Therefore P.

There are two choices, Q or P or both. The next piece of information says that Q is not selected. Logically, if a person has Q or P and we know that they do not have Q, they must have P. This may seem like a completely obvious, almost tautological argument to many. It is very easy to overlook in the heat of battle. These little gems get buried in any conditional logic based problem (such as Winner/Loser games).

The third is to say, "Chuck has a truck or a sedan, but not both a truck and a sedan." In a few more pages, we will see that this is just a mean spirited attempt to get the other test takers in the room to pay for your scholarship. It sucks being them.

Logic Symbols

In order to see just how much these conditional rules tell us and to see where the hidden tricks and traps are within them, we are best served by turning our conditional statements into symbols for easier manipulation. DON'T FREAK OUT! It looks like math, but you can handle it.

There are just four symbols you need to know, each one representing a logical concept. They are:

"X ⊃ Y" means "if X then Y"
"X · Y" means "X and Y" (the " · " is the "***conjunction***" symbol)
"X v Y" means "X or Y" (the "v" is the "***disjunction***" symbol)
"- X" means "not X" (the "-" is the "***negation***" symbol)

MEMORIZE THAT! While you are at it, memorize this too:

> The terms on the left side of a conditional are called the
> **antecedents** and the terms on the right side are called
> the **consequents**.[5]

The statement, "If Charley pulls pork, David cuts cheese." Looks like this:

$$CP \supset DC$$

IF Charley pulls pork (the antecedent), **then** we know for sure that David will cut cheese (the consequent will occur) because the hypothetical, conditional logic says so. Is Charley pulling pork the only way to get David to cut cheese? Not according to the statement given. It does **not** say, "The only way David will cut cheese is if Charley pulls pork." That is an entirely different proposition, is it not?

If David cuts cheese, does that mean that Charley pulls pork? NO! The statement does not say anything about what happens "if" David cuts cheese, so we have no basis for saying anything other than, "If we know that David is cutting cheese, we only know that David is cutting cheese. Maybe Charley pulled pork, maybe not."

Left side vs. Right side

Use this last example and the one that follows to anchor within your grey matter the following absolute, black letter rule (in other words, **MEMORIZE IT**):

Knowing that the LEFT, antecedent side is true proves SOMETHING ELSE absolutely. Knowing that the RIGHT, consequent side is true tells us NOTHING[6] else absolute.

Use the following example to crystallize this rule in your brain:

If I shoot you, then you will die.

$$S \supset D$$

Yes, it is a bit rash, but it makes the point. The rule says that **IF** the antecedent of shooting you happens, **THEN** we know the consequent of your death absolutely will

---

[5] We have elected to use the grown-up terms, *conjunctive, disjunctive, antecedents* and *consequents.* Many people use other simpler words such as "trigger" for the antecedent and "response" for the consequent. The problem with that approach, in our humble estimation, is that it sets you, the learner, up to look like a truck-stop ambulance chaser who attended cut rate academic institutions and cannot use the proper, intellectually rigorous terminology. Use *antecedent* and *consequent,* because that is what the judges will use. Think about it: If you graduated at the top of your class from Harvard Law School, people would still think you are an idiot if you used the term, *"supposably"* in conversation, which is why we told you previously to NEVER say that awful pseudo-word.

[6] As we saw in the last example, if we know that David cuts cheese, we do know, absolutely, that David cut cheese. So what we really mean is that the consequent side tells us nothing *non-tautological.* "Tautology" is Greek for "duh".

result. Shooting, on the left, tells me something absolute, i.e. that the thing on the right will be known to be true. Here is how to say it, both out loud and in your head, EVERY TIME:

> Knowing that the antecedent (left side) is true is **sufficient** to establish that the consequent (right side) **necessarily** happened.

The consequent of dying, on the right, tells me nothing other than that you are dead (though you are still going to have to study for the LSAT, as death is no justification for skiving off). But there are millions of ways you could end up dead, and the original statement did not indicate that your deadness was *sufficient* to establish any other fact definitively. Perhaps I pulled out a gun to shoot you, you saw it, had a heart attack and dropped like a stone.

There is an important lesson to be learned from all of this, and it is a biggie, so MEMORIZE IT!

> If you have a conditional statement, and then you are told that the *consequent* (right side) did in-fact happen, that does not mean that the *antecedent* (thing(s) on the left) happened.

Modifying our example into a basic argument, we can see how this all plays out together in action:

> If Billy shoots David, David will die.
> David is dead.
> Thus, Billy shot David.

In symbols:

> BS ⊃ DD
> DD
> Thus, BS

Why Should I Care?

The LSAT is riddled with conditional logic for a reason: laws are almost entirely crafted in exactly such a manner... ALL laws, whether statutes, administrative rules, municipal codes, county by-laws, judicial opinions or otherwise. If you cannot deal with such logic on a simple test, what is to make law schools believe that you can handle them in complex legal discussions at law school or as an attorney?

This is not even close to a logically valid argument. This logical error is called, *affirming the consequent*: affirming (saying that it is true) that the consequent happened and then drawing a faulty conclusion from that established fact. Real live lawyers make this mistake all of the time, and the results can be horrific.[7] The LSAT test makers are hoping to trick you into falling for this error all over the test, especially in logic games (but also in logical reasoning). Do not get sucked in! The right side tells us SQUAT! Some of you might have noticed something about the argument above: if DD is known, the argument *could* be valid if, and only if, we assume that BS is the *only thing* that can cause DD. If *that additional fact were true* then we would know that DD proves BS. This little assumption point is not important for logic games, but it is in terms of logical reasoning and reading comprehension.

What happens if Billy *never* shoots David? Will David live forever? Again, this is silliness, but it highlights another important point. MEMORIZE IT:

> You cannot say that if the *antecedent* (thing on the left) fails to occur that the consequent (thing on the right) does not happen.

That is because of what we discussed earlier: conditional statements tell us very little, and what they tell us is narrowly defined and limited to just the circumstances described. In words then in symbols:

> If Billy shoots David, David will die.
> Billy did not shoot David.
> Ergo, David will not die.

$$BS \supset DD$$
$$-BS$$
$$Thus$$
$$-DD$$

---

[7] You may have heard of the famous trial of Casey Anthony, the sweet, misunderstood little lady in Florida accused of killing her baby and then going on a sex and party spree. The prosecutors said, "If she killed the baby, then she would lie about the baby's whereabouts and party like she doesn't care." In symbols, $K \supset L \cdot P$. They then proceeded to prove conclusively that L and P happened, expecting that the jury would infer K. The jury did not fall for it: knowing the consequent to be true only proves that the consequent is true. So another killer walks free among us...maybe she can date O.J. Simpson when he gets out...

This says nothing about what happens when –BS (Billy not shooting) is known to occur. So this is not a logically valid argument (NOTE how we used the "minus" symbol to show "NOT"). It commits the logical error called, *denying the antecedent*. That is just fancy talk for, "Just because the *antecedent* did not happen, that does not mean that the *consequent* did not still occur, because Billy might not have shot, but a Russian meteor could have fallen on David's head making him equally dead, if not more so."

Some of you might have noticed something about the argument above: if we know for sure that Billy did not shoot and the conclusion of the argument is that David is not dead, the argument *could* be valid if we were to **_assume_** that Billy shooting is the *only thing* that can cause David to die. If *that additional fact were true* then we would know that -BS proves -DD. If the only way for David to die is for Billy to shoot him, and Billy shooting will definitely kill David, then BS proves DD, and –BS proves –DD, because there is not other way that David could be dead. If it is not fully clicking in your brain, do not worry. We are going to come back to this again later when we talk about bi-conditionals.

Of importance on the subject of fancy talk, law professors and judges speak in terms of antecedents and consequences all of the time. You should learn the fancy-talk way of saying things now, as it gives you legitimacy (street cred) in conversations with peers and others you may hope to be impressing, intimidating or romancing.

Let us reinforce these concepts with a few more examples. Try to say the answers out loud, like a crazy person in the park talking on an old-school telephone that has no cord.

Is this a good argument and why?

> All Carpathians are blood drinkers.
> Telly is a blood drinker.
> So Telly is a Carpathian.

In symbols:

$$C \supset B$$
$$T \supset B$$
$$\text{So } T \supset C$$

Is it logical? NO! Every C is a B, so if we are looking at a C, then we are looking at a B. "B" is on the right side however, so knowing that T is a B proves nothing other than that T is a B. Maybe Telly is Carpathian, maybe he is a Cullen, or maybe he is just a scamp that just likes drinking blood. Thou shall not affirm the consequent!

Try another.

Things with fiber are good for you.
Chicken has no fiber in it.
So chicken is not good for you.

In symbols:

$$F \supset G$$
$$C \supset -F$$
So C is $-G$

Is it logical? NO! Knowing that C is $-F$ tells me nothing certain: the first statement tells us that having fiber proves goodness, and tells us nothing about things that have no fiber. If C had been F (chock-full of fiber), then we *would* know something for sure (that it's G), because if chicken has fiber and all fiber things are good, then chicken would have to be good. Knowing that C is $-F$ and then trying to conclude something about its goodness *denies the antecedent* and does not help us because C could still be good for us in some other way. Thou shall not deny the antecedent!

Unlike Politics, In Logic the Left and Right Work Together

This symbolic relationship works for any "if – then" relationship we find, and for any universal categorical statements we turn into conditionals (i.e. "All cats are stupid," means "If it is a cat, then it is a stupid animal"). To beat the point into your head,

> **If we know that the antecedent is true, that is sufficient to prove that the consequent is necessarily true also.**

As luck would have it, the same notation and logical tricks work for two other important types of relationships on the LSAT.

Causal[8] Relationships

What if I told you that, "Tornadoes cause some form of destruction." From our recent discussion you might think of this statement as a categorical and universal: it means that *every* tornado causes some kind of destruction. You would be absolutely correct.

---

[8] It is pronounced causal (kaw-zal) NOT casual (kazh-yoo-all). The first says that X caused Y. The second says that X and Y hooked up, but that it wasn't serious. Do not call a *causal* argument a *casual* one...it's another way to make yourself sound as if you are stupid in front of others when you might not be... or at least do not want them to know it.

Whenever "A causes B" is asserted, we can convert it into symbols just like before, with the cause on the antecedent (left) side and the effect on the consequent (right) side. We could convert the above statement into:

$$T \supset D$$

Meaning, "If I know there is a tornado, that is *sufficient* to establish that it will *necessarily* cause some type of destruction." If there is destruction, it does not mean that the destruction was caused by a tornado, and if there are no tornados, it does not mean that other things will not cause destruction (think earthquakes or a Josh Groban concert).

Causal relationships work precisely like conditionals when the assertion is made that X *causes* Y. The causal relationship must be asserted to be absolute. If X *may* cause Y, or if X *sometimes* causes Y, we are not able to use our conditional logic conversion. GOOD NEWS! In games, the relationships are absolute.

Sufficient and Necessary

Have you noticed how we have been using "sufficient" and "necessary" when describing antecedents and consequents, respectively? We have done it that way to help anchor in that thick skull of yours the idea that antecedents (things on the left) are sufficient to prove consequents (right side), and that things on the right side (consequents) are necessary BUT NOT sufficient to prove anything. Of all of the logical relationships, this one is the easiest to overlook, so *BE SHARP!* Here is another example:

In order to make fresh cookies, we must have flour, brown sugar and eggs.

This statement establishes that there is a relationship between having fresh cookies and having the *necessary ingredients for making them*. The flour and eggs are *requirements* for the snack. This is precisely how we have to think about these sorts of statements. They assert that in order to get an end product, we *must* have the necessary ingredients. In symbols we write:

$$C \supset F \cdot B \cdot E$$

Having an end product (cookies) is *sufficient to establish that you had the necessary ingredients.* So the *sufficient* end product goes on the left side (because *if* you have a batch of fresh cookies, that is *sufficient* to prove that you had the *necessary* ingredients, flour, brown sugar and eggs).

If we know that a person has flour, brown sugar and eggs, does that mean that they made cookies? NO! For all we know they got drunk, passed out and made no cookies at all[9]. So *necessary* ingredients prove *nothing*, whereas end products *prove* that we had the ingredients. Symbolically, this means:

Sufficient ⊃ Necessary
OR
End Product ⊃ Ingredients

When we hear a situation described where there are requirement for some end result, we know how to put them into logical symbols!

Let us condense the yummy goodness. As you look these over, we encourage you to substitute in your own tangible subject matter to replace X and Y in order to make them more concrete in your head:

<u>X ⊃ Y MEANS;</u>
"If X then Y"
"All X are Y"
"End product X is sufficient to prove ingredients Y etc."
"X caused Y" or any other terminology that means the same,
i.e. "X is responsible for Y" or "Y is brought on by X," etc.

The Rule Does Not Apply to Me!
For those of you who missed it... Are you aware that there is a rule in every state that says that if you intentionally kill another person, you will go to prison? You probably are. If not, we are glad to have enlightened you. Now tell us, how much time do you actually spend each year worrying about going to jail for murder? Our psychic senses tell us that your answer is, "None," (except possibly for the one guy in Kentucky who needs to turn himself in...you now who you are).

Why do you *not* worry about going to jail for murder? Probably because you do not commit intentional killings of other persons... I said "probably." Just like you, the fictitious players in our games are subject to arbitrary rules. *If* they do the thing(s) then we have to worry about the consequent on the right side. If they do not fulfill the antecedent condition on the left side, *the rule does not apply to them.* MEMORIZE THAT!

Smooth Operation
Every conditional statement can be turned into another *logically equivalent* statement. Logicians know many of them: converting, obverting, contra-position etc.

---

[9] In fact, that is a perfect way to think about the difference between the left antecedent side and the right consequent side: EVERYONE on the right side is drunk, so we don't know for sure what they did!

We only need to know one: contra-position. Rather than get you bogged down in the ugly details of how this works, we are going to teach you precisely how to do it and then give you a cogent explanation as to why it works. Then we will explain why it is so damned powerful, thus requiring you to do it with every conditional statement you come across: **_EVERY_** conditional statement.

NOTE: It is very helpful to avoid thinking about what is going on, and what things mean in our three-step logical operation until *after* we have finished all of the steps. To be honest, even professional logicians still get confused when they think about the meaning of a statement half way through the contra-positioning process, and we have been doing this for quite a long time. Learn the steps, (they are easy and simple) and do them mechanically, like the LSAT Terminator[10] that you are.

The Contra-position Three-step

Contra-posing involves a three-step process, to wit:

1) Flip everything (converse)
2) Negate everything
3) Swap all " · " and "v" symbols with each other.

MEMORIZE THAT! EVERY TIME we have a conditional logic statement in symbols we want to *immediately* contra-pose it by doing these three steps. Many of the questions on the LSAT are designed to test whether you get this deeper meaning (and more) from the logic.

Here it is in action: In order to do very well on the LSAT (W), you must learn the contra-positive steps (L). Hey! That sounds like a conditional logic statement!

$$W \supset L$$

So to contra-pose it, first, we want to flip everything around the "⊃" symbol.

$$L \supset W$$

Now we need to "negate" everything: we have to "switch signs" by turning everything which is positive into a negative, and everything that is negative into a positive (if you are a math lover, think of it as multiplying everything by -1).

---

[10] "Terminator" is the copyrighted product of MGM Studios of the United States. It's the heartwarming tale of robots taking over the world and trying to exterminate humanity. When said robo-jerks discover a flaw in their own plan, they then figure out how to go back in time to kill the mother of the one person who will eventually unplug them, pour water on their keyboards or otherwise thwart their wicked robotness. It's very uplifting stuff. If you think about it though, why would the robots go back in time to kill the *mother* of the once an future robo-slayer? Why not just go back to the time 10 minutes before he unplugged the robot high command computer and kill the dude then? Probably that would be a less interesting movie.

In our present example, L ⊃ W, both the L and the W are positive. We need to add a "-" to each:

$$-L \supset -W$$

Lastly we need to "swap" every "and" with "or" and vice-verse. But there are not any in our example, so we are done with all three steps. See how easy that was! Now we have the original rule and its contra-positive.

$$W \supset L$$
$$-L \supset -W$$

What does it mean? "In order to do very well on the LSAT, you must learn the contra-positive steps." And, "If you do not learn the contra-positive steps, you will not do very well on the LSAT." This makes complete sense and it perfectly illustrates the relationship between the original proposition and its contra-positive.

If you do not learn the steps, you will not do well. Why? Because the original rule says that if you had done well, it would prove that you learned the steps. After all, if X always brings about Y, we know for certain that if Y did not occur, X did not happen, because if X had occurred, Y would have had to.

This circular reasoning is the result of one simple fact: both statements are logically equivalent statements looked at from different perspectives. By contra-posing[11], we are simply turning the statement inside out. This is similar to what happens with a sock: you can turn it inside out and it will look very different, but it is still the same sock. A very tiny bug crawling on the surface can go down the length of the sock, inside the opening, around the interior to the toe, then circle back out and around to the outside surface where it began its epic quest. We have merely, "inverted a logic sock."

Let's try another one just to be sure we have the idea clearly ensconced in our brains.

If I shoot you, you will die.

In symbols:

$$S \supset D$$

Now we contra-pose it. Step one, FLIP IT

$$D \supset S$$

---

[11] In all honesty, the term "*modus tollens*," is more proper for the given example. We are just going to give it the more general and useful label *contra-positive*. I mention it here only for completeness, and so we do not lose any street cred: it is not something you need to know.

Then we negate everything:

$$-D \supset -S$$

Then we swap our "and" and "or" symbols... but again, there aren't any, so we are done.

$$S \supset D$$
$$-D \supset -S$$

The original rule and its contra-posed form tell us that if I shoot you, you will die, but if you are not dead, that proves that I did not shoot you. How do you know this to be true? Because if I had shot you, you would absolutely be dead, so not being dead proves that I did not shoot you. Again, we have inverted the logic sock.

Let us try another one, this time with a bit of a challenge:

> **The Underlying Truth**
> All that a contra-positive tells us is that when we have a conditional rule (if X is known to happen, then Y will also be known to happen) we can be sure that if the consequent Y is known not to have happened, then the antecedent X must not have occurred, because if it had, the original consequent Y would have.
>
> This is purely circular reasoning, but there is an important purpose that you shall see soon.

If there is a tornado or an earthquake, there will be famine but not pestilence.

In symbols this rule looks so:

$$T \lor E \supset F \cdot -P$$

Now we contra-pose. First we flip everything:

$$F \cdot -P \supset T \lor E$$

Next, we negate everything, turning negatives to positives, positives to negatives:

$$-F \cdot P \supset -T \lor -E$$

Finally, we have to swap by turning ands into ors, and ors into ands:

$$-F \lor P \supset -T \cdot -E$$

Now we have our original rule and our contra-positive.

$$T \lor E \supset F \cdot -P$$
$$-F \lor P \supset -T \cdot -E$$

The original rule says that if there is a tornado or an earthquake, there will be famine and no pestilence. The contra-positive tells us that if there is no famine or there is pestilence then there was no tornado and there was no earthquake. How do we know that the contra-positive is correct? We *check for circular reasoning, beginning with the contra-positive.* How do we know for sure that if there is no famine or there is pestilence that there was no tornado and there was no earthquake? Because (original rule) if EITHER a tornado or an earthquake had happened, there would have been *both* famine and no pestilence. The contra-positive tells us that if either one of the original rule's consequents *fails to happen,* then we know that the antecedents which would have proved that they did happen, *did not.*

Let's look at a less complex example. In it we will find even more useful and helpful information.

If Tom goes to the gym, Bobby will eat pie.

TG ⊃ BP

Contra-pose: FLIP EVERYTHING and NEGATE EVERYTHING all in one move:

-BP ⊃ -TG

Now we have one rule stated two different ways:

TG ⊃ BP
-BP ⊃ -TG

RIGHT SIDE RULE ™
The consequent of a rule and its contra positive (the right side) can both occur at the same time. Knowing that something on the right side did in-fact occur tells us only one thing for certain: that the thing on the right side happened. It implies/proves NOTHING MORE. ***MEMORIZE THAT!*** So why do we put so much emphasis on it?

The LSAT will mercilessly work to do two things: (1) dupe you into thinking that *something* from the consequent side proves a point of some kind and (2) fool you into thinking that the consequent side cannot happen because the antecedent side did not.

These are the critical points that the average test taker blows and you ***WILL*** get!

If Tom goes to the gym, that is *sufficient* to prove that Bobby has pie. If Bobby does not have pie, that is *sufficient* to prove that Tom did not go to the gym BECAUSE if Tom had gone to the gym, Bobby would be eating pie, but he isn't eating pie, so Tom could not go to the gym, because if Tom had gone to the gym...

If Tom goes to the gym, Bobby has pie. Correct? So if we go to Tom's apartment, knock on the door and Bobby opens the door sporting a face covered in cherry pie, where is Tom? *We do not know!* Bobby eating pie is on the right side. Bobby can eat pie any time the pastry-eating mother-snacker wants. For sure, Bobby will have pie if Tom is at the gym, but Bobby can have pie any other time he chooses.

We already know that the left side is the side that is sufficient to tell us something absolutely, i.e. that the consequent did happen. We also know that the consequent side proves nothing other than itself absolutely. Look at the right side of both the rule and the contra-positive. They say that Bobby can have pie and Tom cannot go to the gym *at the same time*.

This "Right Side Rule™," keeps us from getting sucked into the errors of either affirming the consequent or denying the antecedent. The right side rule says that we know three things: the rule, the contra-positive and the right side as a possibility. **MEMORIZE THAT!**

There is *one* exception to the right side rule, and we will cover it shortly.

So, *IN YOUR TEST BOOKLET*, a rule like the one above should look like this:

$$TG \supset \boxed{BP}$$
$$-BP \supset \boxed{-TG}$$

Let us practice a couple more just to be sure that everything is working for you. Get out the scratch paper and be thorough.

Translate each of the following rules into symbols, contra-pose them and then circle the right side.

PROBLEM SET #6   Pg 25 \

1) If Jerry wears pants, Delores wears a hat.

2) If Bill does not have roast beef, Nancy has pie or ice cream.

3) Janet skydives and swims if Raoul knits.

4) Esteban will not play guitar if Celine is hit by a meteor.

5) If Siegfried buys steak sauce, Roy has meat but not potatoes.

6) Ronnie eats jelly beans whenever Nancy skinny dips.

7) Alan Scott will have a ring and a lantern if Bill drinks whiskey or Martin does not.
8) Rain will cause the ball game to be cancelled.

9) Licensed dogs have vaccinations.

10) Non-citizens and convicted felons are not allowed to vote.

Steak or Chicken, *Redux*?

We are revisiting the concepts of inclusive and exclusive "or" because most people do not take the time to really get it the first time. It is so important that a redundant review and explication cannot hurt. Nor can one more look.

"Or" has two usages in logic, one "inclusive" and the other "exclusive." "Inclusive," means that both are allowed. The statement, "You may have steak or chicken," really means, "You may have steak or chicken or both steak and chicken." THAT is how "or" is used on the LSAT logic games. If the logic games section wants to use "or" *exclusively*, the statement will read, "You may have steak or chicken, but not both."

Inclusive "or" should make perfect sense when you think about it. If a rule says,

> If Guy wears plaid or paisley, Hilda will leave him,

We can see that if Guy wears both, the antecedent is still satisfied, just in a turbo-charged, garish way and Hilda is *really* going to take a hike (and will probably take her mattress with her).

If the rule says,

> If Jill has Tequila or Scotch, she will have a hangover,

is Jill *not* going to have a hangover by having both? DUH, because "or" is inclusive in logic games.[12] "Or" is *inclusive* unless specifically stated otherwise. So **MEMORIZE THAT if you have not!**

Exclusivity

The *exclusive "or"* is sporadically employed, which is why it is so dangerous. When it crops up, most people are ill prepared to deal with it. You will be, which is why the non-hackers in law school are going to have to buck-up to fund your scholarship. Here is how to deal with it.

On the LSAT, *exclusive "or"* comes up in rules like this:

> Terry goes to law school or business school but not both.

In symbols and contra-posed it looks like this[13]:

---

[12] In theory, non-games sections could leave you guessing as to the use of "or" as either inclusive or exclusive, especially the logical reasoning section. For example: "If Edna eats vinegar or milk, she will get sick." Might be a premise in an argument. If she ingests both, their sickening effects might cancel each other out, so in order to infer that she gets sick off of both, we have to assume that the "or" is inclusive in some phraseology.

$$T \supset L \vee B \cdot -(L \cdot B)$$
$$(L \cdot B) \vee -L \cdot -B \supset -T$$

The original rule says that if we know that Terry is involved in any way, then he *will* go to law school or business school, *and* he will not go to both law and business school. We have to slap "grouping symbols" (brackets) around the "L · B" in order to make sure that we treat the negation as working on them together. That cluster inside the grouping symbols will function as ONE WHOLE UNIT in the logic, i.e. doing both at the same time is forbidden as far as Terry is concerned, which is why, when we contra-pose the original rule, we do not change the "and" (·) to an "or" (v) *inside of the grouping symbols*. We can see why this is so in the contra-positive. If a person either does both programs *or* that person fails to go to law school and also fails to go to business school, then that person is *not* Terry, because the original rule says that if it is Terry, he must do one or the other and not both.

If that last example left your head spinning, go back over it again and again. DO NOT get frustrated and gloss over it. We will do more of them, so chillax. You MUST know this stuff inside and out in order to crush the logic games.

If you are feeling more comfortable with the above, let us try another one.

If Abigail goes to Greece, Vince goes to France or Luxembourg but not both.

In symbols, it looks like this, with its contra-positive:

$$AG \supset VF \vee VL \cdot - (VF \cdot VL)$$
$$(VF \cdot VL) \vee -VF \cdot -VL \supset -AG$$

Ugly, no? The mechanics are a tad confusing. Let us sort them out and then simplify.

First, the symbolic representation of the original rule employs spooky "grouping symbols," i.e. parentheses. In plain English, parentheses are used to represent the word, "together" or the phrase "at the same time." If we read the original rule from left to right in English,

$$AG \supset VF \vee VL \cdot - (VF \cdot VL)$$

---

[13] If you are a logic person, you know that this is a hand-waving shortcut. We are not going to employ XOR or J or ⊗, so think of this as the "training-wheels" version. You will see that it is actually very useful to do it this way on the LSAT anyway. If you have no idea what any of this means, GOOD FOR YOU! It's not important to anyone but computer programmers, logicians and geeks. Live long and prosper. Engage.

It says, "If Abigail goes to Greece, then Vince goes to France or Vince goes to Luxembourg and Vince does not do both "together" or "at the same time." The contra-positive,

$$(VF \cdot VL) \vee {-}VF \cdot {-}VL \supset {-}AG$$

reads, "If Vince going to both France and Luxembourg at the same time, or if Vince does not go to France and Vince does not go to Luxembourg, then we know for sure that Abigail does not go to Greece." To many readers this will make slightly more sense of things. The grouping symbols clarify matters quite a bit.

"Nor" = "And Also Not"

If your significant other says, "We will not see any movie with Sylvester Stallone, nor any movie with Jennifer Aniston." What does that person mean? In a nutshell, "No Stalone *and also not* any Aniston." Always translate "nor" into "and also not".

Sometimes, Separation is Good

There is something else that we can do that will make the disjunction "or" even more simple to understand when it shows up on the left hand, antecedent, side. Take a look at the following rule:

If Coke® is purchased or Pepsi® is purchased,
tortilla chips must also be purchased.

In symbols,

$$C \vee P \supset T$$
$$-T \supset -C \cdot -P$$

What happens if Coke is purchased? Tortilla chips are too.
What happens Pepsi is acquired? Tortilla chips are too.
What happens if both Coke and Pepsi purchased? Chips.

Coke and Pepsi are *independent disjunctive antecedents* (they are on the left side and "or" is employed between them): either of them, is sufficient to prove the necessary consequent. So when there is an "or" (i.e. disjunctive) antecedent, each disjunct is independent, so we can break them apart like so:

$$C \supset T$$
$$-T \supset C$$
and
$$P \supset T$$
$$T \supset -P$$

CAUTION!

WE CAN _ONLY_ SEPARATE OUT DISJUNCTIVE (or) ANTECEDENTS and CONJUNCTIVE CONSEQUENTS!

Think about it: "If I wear genie pants, then I will be ridiculed or get called Hammer." If we break it into two, the _**meaning**_ will be changed.

$$G \supset R \vee H$$

Is different than

$$G \supset R$$
$$G \supset H$$

Because the "split" means that G is sufficient to prove that both R and H will be known, but the original conditional means that either R or H or both must result.

We can separate conjunctive (and) consequents because the antecedent is sufficient to prove that both conjuncts necessarily must occur:

If I wear a kilt, I will get laughed at and punched.

$$K \supset L \cdot P$$

So

$$K \supset L$$
$$K \supset P$$

Means the same thing (but as we will see, is very counter-productive).

Is this overkill? _Perhaps_ it is. But if it leads you to a better understanding of the rules and how they work, _do it!_ If you truly grasp it in its original form, then do not bother. However this separation of independent disjunctive antecedents can significantly simplify complex rules and/or complex contra-positives.

Returning to our intrepid world travelers Abigail and Vince, our rules were,

$$AG \supset VF \vee VL \cdot -(VF \cdot VL)$$
$$(VF \cdot VL) \vee -VF \cdot -VL \supset -AG$$

The contra-positive can be broken up into independent conditions, the separate condition VF at the same time as VL, or –VF and –VL occurring.

$$a) \; VF \cdot \; VL \supset -AG$$
$$b) \; -VF \cdot -VL \supset -AG$$

Notice how we were able to get rid of the grouping symbols! They are used to denote, "the separate condition," but now they are unnecessary because we separated the independent disjunctive antecedents: we isolated them into separate rules. (a) says that VL and VF _both_ happening is sufficient to establish –AG. (b) says that if there are –VF and –VL at the same time, that is sufficient to prove –AG as well. Theses two statements _together_ represent the logical equivalent of the original, scary looking contra-positive, and they are much easier for many people to wrap their brains around. They also help us to clarify the meaning of the contra-positive: if Vince does _both_ or if Vince does _neither_, we know that –AG is true.

Let's try another pair of examples and then do a few practice problems just to be sure we are getting this.

> If Marcia paints a landscape or a still life, Jan paints a unicorn.

In symbols:

$$ML \vee MS \supset JU$$
$$-JU \supset -ML \cdot -MS$$

The original rule has two independent antecedents: ML gets us JU. MS also gets us JU. We can split it into two rules if we so desire.

$$ML \supset JU$$
$$-JU \supset -ML$$
$$MS \supset JU$$
$$-JU \supset -MS$$

The right-side rule tells us that we can have JU even if we do not have MS and/or ML.

The contra-positive, $-JU \supset - ML \cdot -MS$, has only one antecedent: -JL. It cannot be broken apart, *but it does not need to be!* When we broke the original rule apart and contra-posed each piece, it was logically equivalent to contra-posing the original rule (it just looks different, but we promise to fix that shortly).

Here is another.

Every frog and each lizard has either scales or warts but not both.

NOTE: Think about what this *means* before you try to write it out in symbols. If there is a frog, what must be true? If there is a lizard, what must be true? Do not let the presence of the word, "*and*," fool you into thinking that there has to be a frog and a lizard at the same time to meet the conditional. That is not what the words actually mean. Frogs or lizards are sufficient.

In symbols and contra-posed:

$$F \lor L \supset S \lor W \cdot -(S \cdot W)$$
$$-S \cdot -W \lor (S \cdot W) \supset -F \cdot -L$$

The original rule has two independent disjunctive antecedents, as F or L are both independently sufficient to establish scales or warts. So we can separate them and contra-pose both:

$$F \supset S \lor W \cdot -(S \cdot W)$$
$$-S \cdot -W \lor (S \cdot W) \supset -F$$

If we translate the contra-positive into words and test it against the original rule, we read, "If there are no scales and there are no warts, or if the separate condition that scales and warts are both present occurs, that is sufficient to prove that we are not dealing with frogs." How do we know that? Because the original rule says that if there is a frog, then there has to be scales or warts, but both cannot be present together.

The separated lizard rule:

$$L \supset S \lor W \cdot -(S \cdot W)$$
$$-S \cdot -W \lor (S \cdot W) \supset -L$$

This is almost exactly the same as the last rule, which makes sense because it is just lizards doing the exact same thing as the frogs did: each independent conditional is sufficient to establish the same necessary outcome.

The original contra-positive looked like this:

$$-S \cdot -W \lor (S \cdot W) \supset -F \cdot -L$$

It has two independent disjuncts on the left (denoted by the "v"), so we can separate it into two rules:

$$-S \cdot -W \supset -F \cdot -L$$
$$S \cdot W \supset -F \cdot -L$$

In other words, if we have *both*, or if we have *neither*, then we are not dealing with frogs and we are not dealing with lizards. That makes sense because a frog cannot (per the original rule) have both but must have one.

Here are a few more examples to put into symbols, contra-pose and split apart. The detailed answers to the exercises are in the back of the book.

PROBLEM SET #7   pg 253

1) If Veronica lays carpet, Robert installs drywall or does framing.
2) If Jill wins the high jump or the pole vault, Xavier runs the triple jump and the long jump.
3) If Steven waits tables and busses them, Anthony vacuums or polishes silverware but does not polish the silverware and vacuum.
4) If Donovan is assigned to Tuesdays or Thursdays, Miles is not assigned to Wednesday.
5) If Fred fails to pay child support or does not show up for visitation, Gail gets custody of the children.

"Only" = "Then"

The words "only" and "unless" are used on the LSAT to confuse and intimidate students. Let us put that to rest right now. Look at this rule.

Fred will go for a walk only if Dino needs to go out.

Which thing goes on the left side, Fred going for a walk or Dino needing to go out? This can be a tricky little *sufficiency / necessity* problem until it is clarified thus: *What is the end product?* Remember the cookies and ingredients example? This is the same sort of issue. The end product is Fred going out for a walk, so it goes on the left. This makes perfect sense if you think about it thus: *If Fred is out walking, the ONLY way we know it could happen is if Dino needed to go out, so Fred walking is sufficient to prove that it was necessary for Dino to go out.*

Still confused? Let us simplify matters even further by giving those of you who need it a black-letter rule of law. "Only" = "then", and words that come after "then" go on the consequent (right) side. **MEMORIZE THAT** and make the substitution EVERY TIME you see the word "only." I recommend that you physically write the word, "then," directly above the, "only."

Fred will go for a walk *then* Dino needs to go out.

This means:
FW ⊃ DG
-DG ⊃ -FW

This *always applies to the word "only."* If we were to tell you that, "Only Aquaman buys Topo's eight-leg-hole underwear." That means, "If a person is buying Topo's eigh-holed-underwear, then it is Aquaman." To reiterate, this is because "only" means "then". The same goes for, "Bill is the only one in line." If I know it is Bill, that is sufficient to prove that he is in line.

"When/Whenever" = "If"

What the what? You read that correctly. Remember back to the hypothetical nature of "if"? "If" simply means, "in the event that..." Does not "when" mean the same thing? Looketh at thiseth:

We shall all partake of his flesh, when the Flying Spaghetti Monster returns.

Is the Flying Spaghetti Monster going to return? Does it even exist? The "when," seems to imply that the speaker *believes* that it will return... but there is a great deal of real estate between belief and reality sometimes. The speaker's belief actually means "when," and that means "if". Try another example:

Whenever Adam has beer, Brittney runs away.

Does this mean that Adam *will definitely* have beer? Nope. It just means that IF, hypothetically, Adam has a beer, Brittney will run away. I know that if Brittney has not run away, Adam is on the wagon because *whenever he does have a beer...*

So for LSAT logic games, "when" will always mean "if".[14]

"Unless" = "If not..."

The same kind of substitution applies to the use of, "unless." With it, we will substitute the phrase, "If not."

> Cartman cannot have pot pie unless Kenny dies.

Becomes,
> Cartman cannot have pot pie if not Kenny dies.

We know that the "if" goes on the antecedent (left) side, meaning that knowing it to be true is *sufficient* to prove something. If Kenny is not dead, Cartman *cannot* have pot pie[15]. Contra-pose: if Cartman is eating pie, what has to be true? Kenny must be dead, because Cartman cannot be eating the pot pie if Kenny is not dead.

$$-KD \supset -CP$$
$$CP \supset KD$$

To simplify matters, "unless" = "if not". **MEMORIZE THAT** and make the substitution whenever you see the word "unless," not just in logic games on the LSAT, but *everywhere you see it or hear it for the rest of your natural life.* We recommend that you physically write the words, "if not," directly above the, "unless."

This works regardless of where in the sentence the "*unless*" falls. So long as you remember that the "*if*" always moves to the antecedent side, you will have no problems with it. For example,

> Unless Roger eats Pecan Sandies, Francine will not get on the treadmill.

Substituting, "if not,"

> If not Roger eats Pecan Sandies, Francine will not get on the treadmill.

---

[14] Again, we know this is a dubious treatment. If it is used in reference to the past, such as, "When Oswald shot Kennedy, the world changed." It is obviously not intended to be conditional... BUT IT WILL NEVER BE USED THAT WAY ON THE LOGIC GAMES SECTION, so put those thoughts out of your pretty little heads.

[15] Let's not quibble over the fact that Kenny McCormick, a.k.a. *Mysterion*, never really dies.

So if Roger does not eat Pecan Sandies, Francine is not on the treadmill.

$$-RP \supset -FT$$
$$FT \supset RP$$

You will never fall into these types of the test maker's traps if you *automatically* make the substitutions every time you see, "only," and "unless."

Bi-Conditionals: "If and only if..."

Many people (including test prep tutors) treat this big beastie as if it were a Gordian knot (if they bother dealing with it at all, which they should but usually do not). For LSAT purposes (and for almost all others), "if but only if," "if and only if," "when and only when," and "when but only when," work the same way as described above: they are each **two things in one**. There is the "if" part and there is the "only if" (then) part. That means "if and only if" means "if and then."

Consider the following example.

Jackson cha-cha's if and only if Kim Tangos.

First, we do what we told you to do a moment ago, turning the "only if" into a "then".

Jackson cha-cha's if and then Kim tangos.

Now we have, "if and then," in the middle. This means precisely what it so ineloquently says: "Jackson cha-cha's if Kim tangos," **and** "If Jackson cha-cha's then Kim tangos..." That is TWO RULES IN ONE and they both play at the same time because it is all one überfugly compound rule. *JC is the antecedent and consequent of KT!*

To say it another way, we know what both of these parts mean, because now the rule tells us two things at once: IF Kim tangos, then Jackson cha-cha's, and If Jackson cha-cha's *then* Kim tangos. *In other words, the phrase, "if and only if," turns Kim doing the tango into both a sufficient (left-side antecedent) and necessary (right-side consequent).* This is called a **bi-conditional.** MEMORIZE THAT!

We write them both out, one at a time, and contra-pose them *as we write each one,* in turn. In symbols, they look like this:

$$JC \supset KT$$
$$-KT \supset -JC$$
$$KT \supset JC$$
$$-JC \supset -KT$$

The super simplified way to deal with it *and understand* it is first to recognize that *every* antecedent-consequent relationship is found elsewhere in the "quartet," just *conversed*, or flipped around. Go ahead and look above to verify this. JC is an antecedent of KT and JC is a consequent of KT. –JC is also an antecedent of –KT and –JC is a consequent of –KT. **RECOGNIZING THIS PATTERN IN THE LOGIC IS VERY IMPORTANT!** We will see why in just a bit, when we talk about the difference between latent and overt bi-ness.

The first part of the rule says JC ⊃ KT. Its contra-positive says that –KT ⊃ -JC. SO we have KT and –JC on the consequent (right side) of the first two pieces, which, if the right side rule applied, would mean that we could have *both* KT and –JC at the same time. **However** the second half of our bi-conditional says that KT ⊃ JC, which completely destroys the idea that KT and –JC might happen at the same time. We did NOT circle the right side because there is no point to doing so: the second half of the bi-conditional constrains the right side of the first half, and the first half constrains the right side of the second half... poop...but not really[16].

There is a silver lining. Bi-conditionals lay out all of the possible relationships between the things on either side of the conditional symbol ⊃. In the example above, we ended up with four "hypotheticals" that told us what happens if any of the four possible antecedents, JC, -JC, KT and –KT occur.

When we have an "if and only if," rule, we **bracket** the whole thing and mark it as "bi" to avoid screwing up and thinking that the right side rule applies, and to remind us that all four of these bad boys play as a team: we know about every possible combination of JC and KT, both when they are known to have happened and when they are known not to have happened. Remember how we told you a while back that the "right-side rule" has an exception? BI-CONDITIONALS ARE THE EXCEPTION TO THE RIGHT-SIDE RULE. *When you have bi-conditionals, the right side rule does not apply to any rule in the game.* MEMORIZE THAT!

$$\text{Bi}\begin{cases} \text{JC} \supset \text{KT} \\ \text{-KT} \supset \text{-JC} \\ \text{KT} \supset \text{JC} \\ \text{-JC} \supset \text{-KT} \end{cases}$$

---

[16] If you are somewhat confused, that is perfectly understandable. As a practical matter, the super simplified way to deal with a bi-conditional without actually wrapping your brain around the logic is to say that when you see "if and only if," (or "when and only when, etc.) you identify the two terms or categories in the premise (Kim doing tango, Jackson doing the cha-cha) and you put either one of them on the antecedent side, the other one on the consequent side. Then you "converse" the rule (re-write that rule by swapping the sides around so that you end up with the original statement and the new, "flipped" statement). Then contra-pose ***both of them***. You get the exact result required.

The Importance of Being Bi

In our last example, we were not allowed to have JC without KT, and we cannot have KT without JC: if one is there, so must be the other and if one is gone, so must be the other. So in this example the, "if and only if," means that it is an all or nothing scenario: we must have both or we must have neither. You may be thinking, "What an awesome rule!" Stop. That is not a universally generalizable rule, it is just the case in this particular example. We would be rash to leap to the conclusion that this is a general rule of bi-conditional rules. We should test other scenarios to get to the truth.

Let us try another example. Turn the following rule into symbols as two rules, contra-posing each. Bracket the entire rule to denote how everything works together.

Rory leaves the TARDIS if and only if Amy does not.

So here we have an "if Amy does not," and we have a "then Amy does not." We will use LT for "leave the TARDIS." So the "if Amy does not leave the TARDIS" and its contra-posed form look like this:

$$-ALT \supset RLT$$
$$-RLT \supset ALT$$

and the "then Amy does not leave the TARDIS" looks like this:

$$RLT \supset -ALT$$
$$ALT \supset -RLT$$

-ALT is both the antecedent and the consequent of RLT. Also, -RLT is both the antecedent and the consequent of ALT. If we look at the consequents (right sides) of both pairs, we can see that in the first it appears that we can have both RLT and ALT at the same time. However the second pair shows us that we cannot. RLT is sufficient to establish –ALT and ALT is sufficient to establish –RLT.

The right side of the second pair seems to tell us that we can have –ALT and –RLT at the same time. However the first pair says that –ALT is sufficient to prove that RLT is so, and that –RLT is sufficient to prove that ALT is so.

What all of this means is that when one of them is known to leave the TARDIS, the other one cannot AND when one of them is known to have *not* left the TARDIS, the other one *must leave it.* Can they both leave it? NO! Can neither of them leave it? NO! EXACTLY ONE OF THEM MUST!

We previously saw a bi-conditional that required us to have both or neither. Now we see a bi-conditional that requires us to have "exactly one." This is a curiosity of the bi-conditional's nature, or just "bi-curious." If we put the two of them side by side we can easily see what is going on.

Example 1	Example 2
JC ⊃ KT	-ALT ⊃ RLT
-KT ⊃ -JC	-RLT ⊃ ALT
KT ⊃ JC	RLT ⊃ -ALT
-JC ⊃ -KT	ALT ⊃ -RLT

Notice the difference between the two? In example 1 each conditional has the same sign on both sides of the if-then horseshoe. In example 2 each conditional has opposite signs on either side of the if-then horseshoe. So if a bi-conditional has the same signs on opposite sides, it is an all-or-nothing rule. If it has opposite signs, it is an "exactly one" bi-conditional. As Pirate Lawyer would say, *"Thar be a good thing t'be knowin'."* So you should **MEMORIZE THAT**, and here is why.

Frequently on the LSAT (and in the law) there are bi-conditional rules that are expressed as follows:

(a) Either Bobby or Hank wipes the propane tanks, but not both.
(b) Romeo and Juliet both go to the apothecary or neither does.

Example (a) *means* that exactly one of B or H wipes the tanks. *EXACTLY ONE* means opposite-sign bi-conditional. Example (b) means *BOTH OR NEITHER*. That means same-sign bi-conditional.

Worst Case Scenario
The ugliest possible scenario we may find ourselves in would involve a bi-conditional with conjunctions or disjunctions or both in the original rule.
NOTE: If this were to actually show up on the LSAT, it would be the rarest of rare occurrences, and you should consider yourself supremely lucky: NOBODY else in the room is going to have a clue as to how to deal with it. Also, once you have a bi-conditional as a rule in a game and you have written it out, the inferences you draw (connection other rules to it, and it to other rules) will almost certainly raise these issues.

We are going over it here in order to further illuminate the "deeper" meaning of bi-conditional relationships. THE BIG POINT we want you to get from this is how to look at the symbolic notation and understand the *issues* that they raise in real, practical terms.

Bobo juggles and unicycles if and only if Shakes taunts the bear.

The two rules in this bi-conditional rule are,

>   1) If Shakes taunts the bear, then Bobo juggles and unicycles.

AND

>   2) If Bobo juggles and unicycles, then Shakes taunts the bear.

In symbols, the rules and their contra-positives look like this:

$$B\begin{cases} 1a)\ ST \supset BJ \cdot BU \\ \quad -BJ \vee -BU \supset -ST \\ 1b)\ BJ \cdot BU \supset ST \\ \quad -ST \supset -BJ \vee -BU \end{cases}$$

Everything on the left is also on the right in a different rule, and they are antecedents and consequents of each other (ST is an antecedent of consequent BJ and BU, and BJ and BU are antecedents of consequent ST, etc.). The *right side rule* does not apply (1a's RSR says I can have BJ and BU and -ST at the same time, but 1b says that BJ and BU are sufficient to prove that ST is necessarily there!).

However the lingering question from the last section is, does the bi-conditional create an all-or-nothing scenario? Hmmmm. Put on your, "I want a Jedi LSAT score," hat and sort this out. TAKE YOUR TIME, THINK IT THROUGH AND DO THE WORK! The answer is in Appendix "C", and you should check it out and TAKE NOTES! There are some very important, juicy things to be learnt in Appendix C, so work it baby, work it.

So, What Does it Mean (and what does it *not* mean)?
Look back at the last rule. 1a shows that ST proves BJ and BU. 1b says that BJ and BU together proves ST. The contra-positive of 1a says that if either BJ or BU does not happen, ST cannot happen. The contra-positive of 1b says that if ST does not happen, then either BJ did not happen or BU did not happen, or *neither* happened, because "or" is inclusive.

Can we have a situation where there is *only* BJ, where ST and BU do not happen? If we only have BJ, then there is no BU. The contra-positive of 1a says that if BU is missing, ST must also be missing, and the contra-positive of 1b says that if ST is missing, BJ or BU must be missing... and BU is! So we *can* have BJ by itself, so long as we have -ST.

This same reasoning applies to the situation where we only have BU. That means BJ is missing, and if BJ or BU is not there, ST is not, and if ST is not, BU or BJ is missing (and BJ is gone).

Do not allow yourself to get sucked into the misperception that, "if and only if," means that ST, BJ and BU must all occur together, or that none of them can occur. "If and only if," is NOT an all or nothing situation in most cases. MEMORIZE THAT! When you see such a rule, break it into two and symbolize and contra-pose each. If you like, split the "or" antecedent conditionals into separate rules, and treat them with great caution. Then FOLLOW THE MEANING OF EACH PRECISELY!

Here are a few more problems for you to chew on, just to make certain that you are getting it. Do them all on a separate sheet of paper and check your answers in the back of the book (Appendix "B") to make sure that you understand things properly.

PROBLEM SET #8

1) Quincy gets the twelve-gauge if and only if Janet has a forty-four caliber.
2) Peter runs the marathon if and only if Tanya swims or bikes.
3) Uma stocks shelves and dusts when, but only when Yvette is the manager.
4) Eve buys a Ferrari if but only if Kim does not buy a Porsche.

"It ain't always obvious when something is bi."

Thus far the bi-conditionals we have seen have been *"overt."* We have been presented with, "if and only," rules that throw the bi-ness in our collective faces. Some above-average test takers (you, for example) will recognize those bad boys and deal with them appropriately. The best test taker will recognize the *latent bi-conditional*, which is, just as the name indicates, hidden from us.

The first latent bi-conditional is easier to spot. Take a look at the following:

Johnny sees both *Rocky Horror Picture Show* and *Evil Dead* or he sees neither.

This is telling us that Johnny sees both or he sees neither. So if we know that he sees *Evil Dead,* he has to also see *Rocky Horror* because we know he did not do the, "...sees neither," option. In other words, if we know that he sees one, we know that he sees both, and if we know that he does not see one, then he cannot see the other. Ergo, we write it just like a bi-conditional because that is what it truly is, just gussied up.

$$JR \supset JE$$
$$-JE \supset -JR$$
$$JE \supset JR$$
$$-JR \supset -JE$$

"But WHY do I have to all of that extra work, LSAT experts?" We hear some of you asking. Because average people write, "J = R and E or neither," AND THEN THEY FAIL TO SEE THE LOGICAL INFERENCES DRAWN FROM HAVING DONE IT THOROUGHLY AND APPROPRIATELY, THUS MISSING THE POINTS THAT 95% OF TEST TAKERS DO NOT GET! Sorry about yelling... we get on-edge when people question our authori-tah.

That is a lot of delicious and nutritious logic! THE TRAP we do NOT want to fall into is thinking that other similar statements are bi-conditional when they are not. For example:

If Jackson does not read Nietzsche then he does not read Kierkegaard.

In symbols:

$$-JN \supset -JK$$
$$JK \supset JN$$

He can read Nietzsche and not read Kierkegaard per the right side rule. THE KEY DIFFERENCE is that the Evil Dead example told us "both or neither," whereas the Nietzsche example said nothing about both.

The toughest to spot (but really they are not that difficult to see) bi-conditionals are teams of different statements that work together to function as bi-conditionals. Allow us to demonstrate.

Consider the following three rules:

    1) If Clark has pie, Lois has ice cream.
    2) If Jimmy has sky cake, Mr. White has baklava.
    3) If Clark does not have pie, Lois does not have ice cream.

In symbols:

$$1) \quad CP \supset LI$$
$$1a) \ -LI \supset -CP$$
$$2) \quad JS \supset WB$$
$$2a) \ -WB \supset -JS$$
$$3) \quad -CP \supset -LI$$
$$3a) \quad LI \supset CP$$

There are no "if and only" rules. But rules 1, 1a, 3 and 3a form a bi-conditional! How do we know? Because our definition of the bi-conditional was that the original rule appears somewhere else, just "flipped" around. Here,

1) CP ⊃ LI
1a) –LI ⊃ -CP
2) JS ⊃ WB
2a) –WB ⊃ -JS
3) –CP ⊃ -LI
3a) LI ⊃ CP

rules 1 and 3a fit the definition. That means that their contra-positives (1a and 3) will do the same thing. CHECK IT OUT! They do. We must remember to be on the look out for the latent bi-conditional because WHEN WE HAVE A BI-CONDITIONAL, WE WILL NOT USE THE RIGHT SIDE RULE, and we will make inferences that get us the toughest points in the least amount of time.

Fortunately, when we are working on games, one of the A, B, C, D, E, F *inference* steps (step "E" for *extras)* will tell us to look for each of the logic issues, one at a time and in order. So if you are following the procedures you are learning in this book *exactly*, you will not overlook the overt or the latent bi-conditionals... or any other important score-enhancing issues.

Forced Dichotomies and Bi-conditionals

Recall what logic games really are: they test whether you can spot the *issues* that arise within the context of certain logical scenarios and deal with them by applying the rules of reasoning. Bi-conditionals create their own issue (namely, they pin down all four relationships between antecedents and consequences). The more subtle the LSAC can make the relationship look, the more apt we are to miss it and the more valuable that issue becomes (i.e. 97% of test takers will miss it, so only the best of the best will need these questions to boost their already wicked-bad scores from the 97th percentile to the 98th or 99th). So don't cop an attitude and think that you already know enough to get a good score, so you do not need this next part. You do. Maybe not today. Maybe not even on the LSAT. But at some point you will.

As if there has not been enough technical nonsense, here is one more thing to wrap your brain around.

Forced dichotomies can give rise to bi-conditionals. Consider the following example:

> Each of six students, Alain, Babette, Cherri, Dulac, Etien and Fred will enroll in exactly one of two classes offered this term at University of Paris, on-line: Taunting 101 and Snobbery 103. Their enrollments are consistent with the following conditions.

Voila! A, B, C, D, E and F must play and they each must do exactly one of two things, S or T. Now let us further suppose that we have a rule that says:

> Alain and Babette cannot enroll in the same class.

Ordinarily we would write:

$$AS \supset \text{-}BS$$
$$BS \supset \text{-}AS$$

Alain has to enroll in one of the two classes. Whichever class Alain is in, Babette is not. Babette has to enroll in one of the two classes. If Babette is not in the class Alain is in, Babette is in the only other class offered. If Babette is known to be in one of the classes, Alain cannot be in it and must be in the only other class offered. Are you reading our mail here? Are you smelling the potato salad? You getting the drift of things?

Because there are only two choices, and because everyone is forced to play, we have a unique logical situation. "Not being in Snobbery" is the same as "Being in Taunting." Also, "Not being in Taunting" is the same thing as "Being in Snobbery." Again, just for certitude, if someone is not in Taunting class, and they have to be in one of two classes, that forces them into Snobbery. *Ca va?*

The magical situation that arises in the forced dichotomy is that rather than writing "-S" for "not in the Snobbery class" we can write "T" for "is in the taunting class. So our condition looks like this:

$$AS \supset \text{-}BS = AS \supset BT$$
$$BS \supset \text{-}AS = BS \supset AT$$

We want to use the right side, positive equivalents $AS \supset BT$ and $BS \supset AT$.
But notice how the first conditional, $AS \supset BT$ has a converse $BT \supset AS$ that is also true. If Babette is in Taunting, Alain cannot be in taunting and so must be in Snobbery. *Zut alors, enfant!*[17] That one simple condition that they cannot be in the same course, coupled with the forced dichotomy is a bi-conditional!

$$AS \supset BT$$
$$BS \supset AT$$
$$BT \supset AS$$
$$AT \supset BS$$

DO NOT BE A SUCKER! This does not mean that if you have a rule such as:

If Alain is in Taunting, Babette is in Snobbery,

that you have a bi-conditional. Au contraire! This condition only means that:

---

[17] TRANSLATION: *"Damn, baby!"*

$$AT \supset BS$$
$$BT \supset AS$$

This condition does not say anything about what happens if Alain is in Snobbery, so the Right Side Rule™ tells us that both A and B can be in Snobbery together.

The CRITICAL DISTINCTION is that the bi-conditional creates four rules whereas the conditional creates two. For our purposes, the more rules that we have to work with, the more connections (inferences) we can make.

BUT YOU MAY BE ASKING…

"Really? Why can't I just write, 'A and B never same team'?" That is an excellent question, Timmy. If we were yo' mama, we'd say, "Because I said so, and because I am the expert, you should just do what I say."

The real answer is this. As always, the rules say things in words that have logical implications that are not always obvious. Your job as a law student and lawyer are to read those words and interpret what they really mean and how they really function logically, especially in regards to how they logically connect to other conditions. If you do write, "A and B never same team," you will miss all of the double-ups based upon all four of the bi-conditional elements. THE WHOLE DAMN TEST IS ABOUT HOW GOOD YOU ARE AT FINDING AND USING INFERENCES. If you fail to see the bi-conditional nature of the Alain-Babette rule, you will probably only miss one or two question based upon that mistake. But little mistakes here and there add up and drive your score toward mediocrity.

AFFIRMATIVE DUTIES: You're Not the Boss of Me?

Let us pretend that Liz is at the grocery store. While we are busy imagining, let us also suppose that the store in which she is shopping has some rigorously enforced rules. Amongst them is a rule that looks like this;

If you do not buy Trix, you buy Cap'n Crunch.

In symbols and contra-posed,

$$-T \supset C$$
$$-C \supset T$$

Simple enough, no? The danger of rules like this lays in their *meaning* when taken in the context of a set of other rules. This rule, by itself, seems clear enough. Yet it is so fundamentally misunderstood that most people overlook its most important feature.

Suppose that Liz walks around the store for a while and decides that she really does not like the looks of anything in the store. She returns her cart to the return area and says to the friendly security guard, "I don't think I'll buy anything today, so I'm going home empty handed." What is the guard going to say in response?

"You cannot leave without buying something, so get your pretty little butt back in there and shop!"

Liz will undoubtedly be offended, but ultimately she will have to go back inside, because she cannot leave the store having purchased nothing. Why? (THINK! WHY?)

Because if she leaves with nothing, she has no Trix, and that means she has to buy Cap'n Crunch. She also has no Cap'n Crunch, so she will have to buy Trix. Those are the rules. She does not have to buy both though, because as soon as she buys Trix the –T rule does not apply to her and the contra-positive says –C ⊃ T, which she is in compliance with. The same goes for a situation in which she just buys Cap'n Crunch. The *right side rule* tells us that she *can also* have both at the same time, and you can bet your seat in law school that there will be a question somewhere in the mix that tests whether or not you understand these vital concepts.

> Negative antecedents that have affirmative consequents are called, "*affirmative duty rules:*" You *must* do something.

In sum: *Whenever there is a negative antecedent with an affirmative consequent, there is an __affirmative duty__ to do something.* **MEMORIZE THAT!** Rules like this come up in the context of logic games all of the time, especially in "picking winners and losers" games. The average test taker thinks that anybody can walk out of the store without buying anything (like in real life). Not at this store and not in logic games with *affirmative duty* rules, because we are not in real life, we are in law life, which is a mixed up, topsy-turvy, *Through the Looking Glass* place indeed, where the written rules control all, even when they make no sense or are offensive to our brains. In real life there are rules like this all around us. If you do not pay taxes, you will go to jail. In most states, if you see a child drowning and you fail to help her, you will be charged with a crime. It is a highly relevant concept to test on the LSAT.

Problem Set #9

Write out the following rules in symbols, contra-pose them and then circle the right side to note what you are allowed to have at the same time.

1) If there are no bananas there must be cherries.
2) If she selects disco and she does not select funk, she must also select classical.
3) If she buys nothing from Blerg, she buys chairs from Ikea.
4) Tom inherits no decorative plates unless Becky inherits the silver service.
5) Unless Gaius is a republican, Cicero is.

Double-Ups = MONEY

Remember our process for doing logic games? We have steps that we go through:

1) Get a GRIP
2) Re-write the FORMAL RULES
3) Make a DRAWING
4) Draw INFERENCES
5) DESTROY the questions

Step four, *INFERENCES*, requires us to do the "A, B, C, D, E, F." We saw earlier how the D step (double-ups) can be very powerful, as it allows us to take two or more rules concerning the same player(s) and combine them into super rules. Nowhere on the LSAT is this more powerful and useful than in a game with several conditional logical statements that have all been contra-posed.

IMPORTANT REMINDER!

This is NOT intended to be a complete course in logic. It is a utilitarian approach to the law and the LSAT's logic requirements only. As such, there are many other advanced and esoteric things we could teach in the name of completeness, none of which we teach here, mainly because *you don't need to know them* in order to smoke the LSAT, be a top-flight law student, be a great lawyer, etc.

If you do know additional and advanced logic, have yourself a jolly time employing it. Just remember this: we are the experts and it is our position that if you do additional logic, you are wasting valuable time and costing yourself points. Just like in life, time is money. Don't lose a scholarship just to prove to yourself that you still have kick-ass logic skills.

The average test taker can read the individual rules (not contra-posed) and use them to eliminate a few incorrect answers. This usually results in the test taker getting two or three answers correct. They also miss three or four answers because they do not understand the deeper meaning of the logic. If we put rules into symbols, contra-pose them, identify the possible on the right side and merge the double-up rules whenever we can, we will NEVER miss an answer, provided we stick to our methods, do not choke, freak out, go spastic or otherwise self-destruct. You know whether or not we are talking about you.

These super rules we create are the things that the average test taker does not grasp, which is why they are going to have to pay to go to law school and you are not.

DOUBLING UP CONDITIONAL LOGIC: Combining Identical Terms

There are two steps to doubling up the conditional logic. We will break them down into the individual steps, showing you how to do each individually. Then we will show you how to implement them both in one swift and powerfully efficient motion.

Part A – Harriet buys a car

Harriet purchased a new car. In her state there are rules that attach to buying a new car, just as there are in all states. First, if she buys a car, she has to get insurance for it. Second, if she buys a new car she must register it. Third, if she buys a new car she must pay the tax on it.

In symbols:

$$1) \; C \supset I$$
$$\text{-}I \supset \text{-}C$$
$$2) \; C \supset R$$
$$\text{-}R \supset \text{-}C$$
$$3) \; C \supset T$$
$$\text{-}T \supset \text{-}C$$

This seems like a ridiculous number of rules for car ownership (and, as you are probably aware, real life has about a jillion more). If we look down the left antecedent side of the list of rules and contra-positives, we see that the three original rules tell us what happens if she *does* buy a car.

$$\textbf{1) } \mathbf{C \supset I}$$
$$\text{-}I \supset \text{-}C$$
$$\textbf{2) } \mathbf{C \supset R}$$
$$\text{-}R \supset \text{-}C$$
$$\textbf{3) } \mathbf{C \supset T}$$
$$\text{-}T \supset \text{-}C$$

Rule 1 says, "If she buys a car, she must buy insurance." Rule 2 says, "If she buy a car, she must register it." Does that not mean that if she buys a car, she must buy insurance *and* register it? Yes! That is a valid inference we can draw (though admittedly not Einstein-caliber): when one antecedent causes two independent consequents, we can *merge* them thus.

$$1) \; C \supset I \cdot R$$
$$\text{-}I \supset \text{-}C$$
$$2) \; C \supset R$$
$$\text{-}R \supset \text{-}C$$
$$3) \; C \supset T$$
$$\text{-}T \supset \text{-}C$$

Rule 3 says that if she buys a car she must pay taxes on it. Because the same antecedent is sufficient to establish that a different consequent will necessarily result, we can merge that consequent of rule three into the consequent of the first rule as well.

$$
\begin{aligned}
&1) \quad C \supset I \cdot R \cdot T \\
&1a) \; \text{-}I \supset \text{-}C \\
&2) \quad C \supset R \\
&2a) \; \text{-}R \supset \text{-}C \\
&3) \quad\; C \supset T \\
&3a) \; \text{-}T \supset \text{-}C
\end{aligned}
$$

The just completed example demonstrates the first step in the conditional double-up: *look at the (antecedent) of a rule (we'll call it "rule 1") and find all other rules with an __identical__ antecedent. Combine the consequents of those other rules into "rule 1" by employing a conjunction (·) symbol between the consequents.*

If there are no other rules with the same antecedent, or once you have combined all of the rules with the identical antecedent into the rule you are working on (still Rule 1), look at the contra-positive of rule 1 and see if there are other rules or contra-positives with the same antecedents, then rule 2, 2a, ... see the pattern? When you are done combining the common antecedents for the first rule, you are not done with the first rule by any means. To see why, let us examine a *slightly* more complicated example.

Part B: The Domino Theory

For reasons not understandable to the rational person, Dorothy really wants to buy a pet lion[18]. The only lion dealer in Oz has two simple rules:

> If you buy a lion, you must also buy a tiger.
> If you buy a tiger, you must also buy a bear.

Dorothy, an attorney at the firm of Jello, Brique and Rhodes, puts the rules into symbols and contra-poses them immediately, because she is a good lawyer, not a bad, *malpractice claims fall on her like a house from the sky,* lawyer:

---

[18] This happens all of the time, and you may want to consider thinking about it now, well ahead of time. Many people, having spent the last seven years of their lives going to college and law school, supping on ramen and sleeping on futons, get jobs (you will, because you will be a legal Chuck Norris). These jobs pay well. Then they lose all perspective, rationality, morality etc. They buy (or worse, lease) cars that are overpriced in order to impress others, they buy homes or possessions that are gauche (lions qualify here). Who they "really are" becomes subsumed by the money, ego and pride. We are not judging. We are just saying that you may want to think NOW about who you really are and what you are going to do with all of that lawyer cash/prestige and whether or not you want to have a plan for keeping them from defining you, rather than the other way around. It's a long road to competence and success and it is a short path to douchebaggery.

1)   L ⊃ T
1a) –T ⊃ -L
2)   T ⊃ B
2a) –B ⊃ -T

Because she knows the Test Mentors Method™ she immediately looks at the first condition and checks to see whether or not the antecedent, "L," is an antecedent in any other rule(s). What does she find? Antecedents -T, T and –B. There are none that match. She then thinks to herself, "The first condition says that, in the event that I buy a lion, I will consequently have to also buy a tiger, because buying a lion is sufficient to establish that I necessarily have a tiger. Rule 2 says that if I buy the tiger, I will also have to buy the bear. So if I buy a lion, I will have to buy a tiger and thus having a tiger, I shall be forced to buy a bear, so I will end up with lions and tigers and bears, oh my!" Her logic is impeccable, and, being on a tight budget (because she is a junior associate at the firm), she decides against buying a lion, as the cost of lion, tiger and bear chow would eat her alive, much like the lion, tiger and bear would.

Many people find this confusing because in rule 1,

1)   L ⊃ T
1a) –T ⊃ -L
2)   T ⊃ B
2a) –B ⊃ -T

El Tigre is on the right side, making it a meaningless consequent.

The clarification comes when we remember the fundamental principle of conditional logic. Each rule is a *hypothetical* when we read it. *If* we know for sure that she buys a lion, that is sufficient to prove that she *necessarily* buys a tiger. If she does not buy a lion then the rule does not apply to her. But *if* she buys the lion, she *must* get a tiger, and in that circumstance, she buys a lion and a tiger. That creates the connection between rule 1 and rule 2, because she also is buying a tiger now, and rule two says what must happen if she buys a tiger: buy a bear. It is a domino effect, because lions beget tigers, which beget bears. Now that we have to get a bear, does having a bear force us to do anything (i.e. is it an antecedent in any other rule(s)? Nope. So now we are officially done with rule 1.

After we have checked the antecedent of a rule to see if there are other identical antecedents in other rules, we have check whether any of the <u>consequents</u> of that rule are <u>antecedents</u> in any other rule(s). If they are, we merge those consequents with a conjunction (and) as well.

$$1) \quad L \supset T \cdot B$$
$$1a) \; -T \supset -L$$
$$2) \quad T \supset B$$
$$2a) \; -B \supset -T$$

We already did it for rule 1. Moving on, 1a says that if she does not buy a tiger then she cannot get a lion. There is only one –T antecedent, so our first step is covered. Is the consequent, *not buying a lion,* an antecedent in any other rule? No. We are done with it and are fully aware of all of the logical implications of *not buying a tiger.*

Condition 2 says that if she buys a tiger, then she must also buy a bear. There is only one "T" antecedent, so our first step is covered. Is buying a bear an antecedent in any other rule? No. We are done with rule 2.

Rule 2a says that if she does not buy a bear, she cannot buy a tiger. There are no other –B antecedents, so our first step is covered. Is the consequent of *not* buying a tiger an antecedent in any other rule? *Yes!* Rule 1a says that if she does not buy a tiger then she cannot get a lion. So we add that consequent (not buying a lion) onto rule 2a, appending it with a conjunction:

$$1) \quad L \supset T \cdot B$$
$$1a) \; -T \supset -L$$
$$2) \quad T \supset B$$
$$2a) \; -B \supset -T \cdot -L$$

Now we have tacked on another consequent (-L) to the antecedent, *not buying a bear.* Because we know that whenever she does not buy a bear, she cannot get a lion, we have to see whether there are implications from her non-lion-buying-ness. Does *not* having a lion force us to do something (is -L an antecedent in other rules)? No. We are done. 2a now says that if she does not buy a bear, then she cannot buy a tiger and she cannot buy a lion.

The Right Side rule informs us that (1 and 1a) she can have a tiger and a bear *without* having a lion and (2 and 2a) a bear can be had without a tiger or a lion. Those are valid inferences, which makes them possible answers to questions that we will answer quickly and accurately.

Our original two conditional statements turned into four rules. Those four rules now inform us that knowing Dorothy bought a lion, bought a tiger, did not buy a bear or did not buy a tiger are all sufficient to prove other things. If we know that she bought a bear, that is not sufficient to establish anything else. If we know that she did not buy a lion, that is insufficient to prove anything else. Knowing what we *cannot* prove is often more important than knowing what we can.

We see something play out in the last example that bears (no pun intended) emphasis. Just because a certain rule will merge with another, that does not mean that its contra-positive will, and vice-versa. Sometimes a rule will have no logical implications beyond what it says on its face, while it's contra-positive will combine with many other rules, and vice-versa. THAT IS PRECISELY WHY YOU MUST CONTRA-POSE EVERY RULE, EVERY TIME! THIS IS WHERE THE SCHOLARSHIP MONEY IS! Understanding that simple, straight-forward looking rules can have hidden implications is a big part of what makes a superior law student and a non-malpractice-committing attorney.

So the "Black Letter Rule[19]" is thus: EVERY time there are conditional rules, we write them out in symbols and immediately contra-pose them. When we get to the "Double-ups" step in the inference process (AND NOT BEFORE), we begin with the first rule and (a) see if the antecedent is an antecedent in any other rule and then (b) seeing if ANY of the consequents are also antecedent in any other rule(s). *We must ALWAYS check every rule and its contra-positive for every merger possibility with all other rules.* MEMORIZE THAT!

In the previous example, rule 1 merged with rule 2, but rule 1's contra-positive did not. Rule 2 did not merge with any other rules, yet its contra-positive did. We must be thorough, we must be mechanical and we must be precise *every single time*.

Let's do one more together, this time applying all that we have learned.

DO THESE ON YOUR OWN! IF YOU DO NOT DO THEM PROPERLY, REVIEW WHAT WE HAVE COVERED! DO NOT BE A GIMP AND JUST READ ALONG AND SEE HOW EASY WE MAKE IT LOOK. WE MAKE IT LOOK EASY BECAUSE *WE KNOW WHAT IN THE HELL WE ARE DOING.* YOU NEED TO KNOW WHAT YOU ARE DOING OR YOU WILL END UP AT TACO BELL, BUT NOT AS THEIR LEGAL COUNSEL, IF YOU KNOW WHAT WE MEAN.

Foo Fighters are figuring out who will play solos at tonight's concert. Dave's rules are:

> 1) If Dave solos, Taylor does not.
> 2) Unless Chris solos, Taylor does not.
> 3) Nate does not solo if Chris does not.
> 4) Pat solos only if Taylor does.

---

[19] A "Black Letter Rule," is a hard, fast, etched-in-stone, no bullshit, absolute law. Law professors, lawyers and judges say that phrase all of the time. Now you know what they are prattling on about.

Holy crud! We hit you with a smattering of everything. If you do not recall what "unless" means, LEARN IT. If you do not recall what "only" means, GET YOUR ACT TOGETHER.

So we put them into symbols and contra-pose each as we go.

$$1) \quad D \supset -T$$
$$1a) \ T \supset -D$$
$$2) \quad -C \supset -T$$
$$2a) \ T \supset C$$
$$3) \quad -C \supset -N$$
$$3a) \ N \supset C$$
$$4) \quad P \supset T$$
$$4a) -T \supset -P$$

Now we need to begin combining them into super rules by using our two-step process. We begin with conditional 1 which has D (Dave soloing) as an antecedent. Are there any other rules with D as an antecedent? NO! But the consequent of D is -T (Taylor does not solo). Is -T an antecedent in any other rule? Contra-positive 4a! -T $\supset$ -P. So *IF* D, we know that -T happens, and when the -T happens, -P happens as well. We merge:

$$1) D \supset -T \cdot -P$$

-T is not an antecedent in any other rule. Now there is an additional consequent whenever we know D, namely -P. Is -P an antecedent in any other rule? No, so we are done with rule 1.

1a has T as the antecedent. Is T an antecedent in any other rule? YES! 2a has it, so we merge the consequents into 1a:

$$T \supset -D \cdot C$$

No other rules have T as an antecedent. Now we check to see if the -D is an antecedent in any rules. It is not, so we check to see if the C is an *antecedent* in any rule. Nada. We are done with 1a and now we know that if Taylor does a solo, Dave does not and Chris does.

Rule 2 has -C as an antecedent. Does any other rule? #3! So we merge consequents into rule 2:

$$-C \supset -T \cdot -N$$

No other rules have -C as an antecedent, so we check the consequents. Is -T an antecedent anywhere? YES, 4a. So we merge 4a's consequent in as well:

$$-C \supset -T \cdot -N \cdot -P$$

No other rules have -T as an antecedent, so we check -N. Any antecedents? Nope. How about -P? Zilch. So we are done with rule 2. We now know that if Chris does not solo, Taylor, Nate and Pat also do not. Does this mean that Dave does a solo? NO! This rule says NOTHING about Dave, so maybe he does solo, and maybe he does not.

2a has T as an antecedent. Do any other rules? YES! 1a does, and we already drew ALL of the inferences from it, so we can just copy them into 2a and then go on to rule 3, because they will be exactly the same!

$$T \supset C \cdot -D$$

Rule 3 has the same antecedent as rule 2, which has already been merged out. Just copy it into rule 3 and move on.

3a has N as the antecedent. Do any other rules? No. Its consequent is C. Is C an antecedent in any other rule? No. So we are done with 3a: it has no additional consequences.

Rule 4 has P as an antecedent. Are there other P antecedents? Not a one. Rule 4 has T as a consequent. Are there any rules with T as an antecedent? 1a! We merge all of 1a's consequents into rule 4:

$$P \supset T \cdot -D \cdot C$$

We know, because that merger came from above, that it is complete, accurate and DONE. -D and C were hashed out long ago, so we need not waste time re-doing them.

4a has -T as an antecedent. No other rules do. Check the consequent: -P. No rules have it as an antecedent, so we are, at long last, *finito*. Our new list of super-rules says:

1) $D \supset -T \cdot -P$
1a) $T \supset -D \cdot C$
2) $-C \supset -T \cdot -N \cdot -P$
2a) $T \supset C \cdot -D$
3) $-C \supset -N$
3a) $N \supset C$
4) $P \supset T \cdot -D \cdot C$
4a) $-T \supset -P$

Just *look* at all of the yummy goodness we have extracted! Our original rules told us four simple facts. Our super rules tell us one helluva lot more! The original rule 2

137

told us that if Chris does not solo, Taylor doesn't either. That is the level of understanding that will get you a 152 on the LSAT. Super-rule 2 says that if Chris does not solo, Taylor does not, Nate does not and Pat does not! Guess what the correct answers to questions about Chris *not soloing* are going to have to do with? Probably nothing to do with Taylor, I'll tell you what! And if Pat does solo (rule 4), the original rule just said that Taylor does too. Super rule 4 tells us this, *plus* the additional facts that Dave cannot, and that Chris must! ***This is GOLD, we tell ya!
Pure, actual GOLD!***

Let's practice using these "money rules" on another pair of scenarios. If you need to review the rules, do so. Do not rely upon the answers in Appendix "B". Only use them if you get totally stumped, but don't be a wuss and say you are stumped when you are really just too lazy to do the work. The LSAT will punish you for being a slacker and law school will too by taking away your scholarship or worse, booting your happy butt out.

PROBLEM SET #10 – Merging Conditional Logic

A) Sponge Bob and Patrick are going to the movies.

> If Sponge Bob sees *Jaws*, Patrick sees *Free Willy*.
> If Patrick Does not see *Free Willy*, he sees *The Abyss*.
> If Sponge Bob sees *The Little Mermaid* he also sees *Jaws*.

   i)   Patrick wants to see both *Free Willy* and *The Abyss.* Is he allowed to?
   ii)   What do we know FOR ABSOLUTE CERTAIN if Sponge Bob does *not* see *The Little Mermaid*?
   iii) If Patrick does not see *Free Willy*, what must be true?

B) Tony, Christopher and Paulie are, "doin' family business."

> If Christopher hijacks a truckload of Blu-Ray players, Tony gets paid.
> If Paulie robs a bank, Christopher does not hijack a truckload of Blu-Ray players.
> If Paulie does not rob a bank, Tony fixes a fight.
> If Tony does not fix a fight, Tony does not get paid.

   i)   What must be true if Tony does not fix the fight?
   ii)   If Tony does get paid, what is the only thing that must be true?
   iii) Can it be true that Paulie did not rob the bank and that Christopher did not hijack the Blu-Ray player truck?
   iv)   Is it possible for Tony to *not* fix the fight and for Christopher to hijack a load of Blu-Ray players?

Disjunctive Consequents: Choices Are Not Always Equal

Picture yourself in a boat on a river. If you are in that boat then there are, invariably, rules.

1) If you are in the boat, then there are marmalade skies or there are tangerine trees.
2) If there are marmalade skies, then the cellophane flowers are green.
3) If there are tangerine trees, the cellophane flowers are yellow.
4) If the cellophane flowers are green, the rocking horse people eat marshmallow pies.
5) If the rocking horse people are eating marshmallow pies, the plasticine porters have looking glass ties.

Condition #1 says that if you are in the boat, then there are marmalade skies or tangerine trees (or both, because "or" is still inclusive). From there, it gets ugly. So let us take a moment to turn these rules into symbols and contra-pose them.

$$1) \quad B \supset MS \lor TT$$
$$-MS \cdot -TT \supset -B$$
$$2) \quad MS \supset C \cdot CFG$$
$$-C \lor -CFG \supset -MS$$
$$3) \quad TT \supset CFY$$
$$-TT \supset -CFY$$
$$4) \quad CFG \supset RHPEMP$$
$$-RHPEMP \supset -CFG$$
$$5) \quad RHPEMP \supset PPLT$$
$$-PPLT \supset -RHPEMP$$

Take a look at condition number one. B is sufficient to establish MS or TT or both. But if we look down the antecedent side, we can see that there are separate antecedent conditions for MS and for TT. Furthermore, we can see that the outcomes of MS and TT are very different. Below, we have simply taken the two different disjuncts on the consequent side of condition one and separated them out. This allows us to see the differences between the choices (if we do not have both MS and TT) by doing the Double-up to each separately:

$$1) \quad B \supset MS \cdot C \cdot CFG \cdot RHPEMP \cdot PPLT$$
$$B \supset TT \cdot CFY$$
$$-MS \cdot -TT \supset -B$$
$$2) \quad MS \supset C \cdot CFG$$
$$-C \lor -CFG \supset -MS$$
$$3) \quad TT \supset CFY$$
$$-TT \supset -CFY$$
$$4) \quad CFG \supset RHPEMP$$
$$-RHPEMP \supset -CFG$$
$$5) \quad RHPEMP \supset PPLT$$
$$-PPLT \supset -RHPEMP$$

Now it is clear that IF you are in the boat, the consequences of having the marmalade skies (MS) are far more weighty than those of having the tangerine trees (TT). This is important to know if, for example, you do not have a lot of LSD available to help you cope. You really want to do something aquatic, but if your tolerance for coping with insanity is limited, you either pick the tangerine trees option or you pass on the boat on a river and hop on the yellow submarine to the octopus's garden in the shade.

The key point is that when you have a disjunctive consequent, each of them may have further consequents attendant to them, and that means you had better know the differences. The easiest way to achieve this is to separate them out as well. YOU DO NOT HAVE TO, but you can. There is an alternate way to do it, and it looks a little something like this:

$$1) \quad B \supset \underset{\underset{\displaystyle C \cdot CFG \cdot RHPEMP \cdot PPLT}{\llcorner}}{MS \underset{\displaystyle \llcorner CFY}{\vee} TT}$$

-MS · -TT $\supset$ -B
2) MS $\supset$ C·CFG
-C v -CFG $\supset$ -MS
3) TT $\supset$ CFY
-TT $\supset$ -CFY
4) CFG $\supset$ RHPEMP
-RHPEMP $\supset$ -CFG
5) RHPEMP $\supset$ PPLT
-PPLT $\supset$ -RHPEMP

This is the way we suggest that you try doing it. It is crystal clear that the "or" did not go away, and it puts it all right there in a compact set of notations that are difficult to confuse or lose.

When this issue is tested on the LSAT it should be pretty transparent to you. There will probably only be one disjunctive consequent, which is your biggest clue. You ought to be able to anticipate a question such as, "If Ringo only has two hits of acid, and each one allows him to cope with one weird event, then which of the following must be true?" You know that the answer must be that if he rides the boat on the river, he must see cellophane flowers of yellow and tangerine trees: he lacks enough supplies for all of the chaos that come with marmalade skies.

To be fair, we can only think of two times in the history of the LSAT that this issue has been tested. BUT IT HAS, which means that it could be tested again at any moment. It will be the one point that 2% of the test takers get correct. Besides, that is not really the point of the exercise at all, is it? Real lawyer stuff is actually LOADED with these monkeyshines. The best students and lawyers see the differences in the consequences (i.e. find the loopholes), exploit them and then earn the best grades, paychecks, etc.

CONTRADICTIONS: The Rarest of Gifts

Occasionally there may be a situation in which the rules of a game lead to a *contradiction*. The word *contradiction* has a very specific meaning that most people are unaware of or unclear about[20]. It means that if one thing (X) is true, the other (Y) *must be false*, and that if Y is true, X must be false. For example, if it is true that Virgil is Dante's only guide through Hell, then it must be false that Charon is. If Charon is Dante's only guide through Hell, then it must be false that Virgil is.

In all things legal, contradictions are verboten (look it up!). A person cannot be guilty of something and not guilty of the same thing at the same time. You cannot be required to put a restroom in your café and be required to not have a restroom in it at the same time. Are you reading our mail? So the LSAT will occasionally throw in a contradictory set of rules. The contradiction will NOT be blatant; you are going to have to gin it out.

Let us paint a picture for you using three simple rules:

> If Luke gets x-rays, he visits Yoda.
> If Luke goes to the zoo, he does not visit Yoda.
> If Luke gets x-rays, he goes to the zoo.

In symbols:

> 1) $X \supset Y$
> 1a) $-Y \supset -X$
> 2) $Z \supset -Y$
> 2a) $Y \supset -Z$
> 3) $X \supset Z$
> 3a) $-Z \supset -X$

By this point you ought to be pretty good at working the magic on these. Briefly; Rule 1 has X as an antecedent. Are there any other X antecedents? Yes, in rule 3. So we tack the consequent of rule 3 onto the consequent of rule 1 with a conjunction.

$$X \supset Y \cdot Z$$

---

[20] This is owing to the fact that when most people hear a word used, they think that, based upon the context of its use, they understand what it means. YOU are going to be a lawyer. Words have *precise* meanings. You can no longer afford to stumble through life incorrectly believing that you know what words mean when you really do not. Ergo, if you are one of these "misinterpreting" people, get in the habit of *knowing for certain* what words mean: look stuff up, and not in phony on-line dictionaries.

The first consequent of rule 1 is Y. Is Y an antecedent in any rules? Y is the antecedent of 2a, so we have to tack its consequent, –Z, onto the consequent of rule 1.

$$X \supset Y \cdot Z \cdot -Z$$

What the deuce? The logic allows us to infer that if we know for sure that Luke gets an X-ray, that fact alone is sufficient to prove that he visits Yoda, goes to the zoo and does not go to the zoo. HOW can he go to the zoo and not go to the zoo?

The answer is, quite simply, he cannot. Getting an X-ray leads to a contradiction: if "Luke goes to the zoo" is true, then "Luke does not go to the zoo" must be false. If we know that Luke does not go to the zoo, then Luke goes to the zoo must be false. It is not our job to figure it out. It is our job to figure out the mere fact that getting an x-ray is sufficient to prove that there will necessarily be a contradictory consequence. What are ya gonna do? We shall tell you momentarily.

Take a few minutes and practice your merging skills by drawing Double-ups for all of the rules, top to bottom. DO THEM ON YOUR OWN ON A SEPARATE SHEET OF PAPER! DO NOT CHEAT!

The rules merge thus:

1) $X \supset Y \cdot Z \cdot -Z \cdot -Y \cdot -X$
   $-Y \supset -X$
2) $Z \supset -Y \cdot -X$
   $Y \supset -Z \cdot -X$
3) $X \supset Z \cdot Y \cdot -Z \cdot -Y \cdot -X$
   $-Z \supset -X$

Beginning with rule 1, HOW can it *possibly* be that if Luke gets an x-ray, he visits Yoda AND goes to the zoo AND does not go to the zoo AND does not visit Yoda AND does not get an x-ray? Remember, as a hypothetical-conditional, we read it, "If we know for sure that Luke gets an x-ray, that is sufficient to prove that, amongst other things, he did not get an x-ray." That, ladies and germs, is another huge, flaming contradiction.

As a practical matter, what that means is that Luke can NEVER get an x-ray, because every incidence of him hypothetically getting an x-ray leads to the necessary conclusion that he did and did not go to the zoo, and that he did not get an x-ray (even though getting the x-ray is the sufficient condition). If it is true that he did get an x-ray, then the conclusion that he did not get one must be false[21].

---

[21] This does not apply to quantum particles. Quantum particles are what scientists like to call, "Very, very small." They are so small, in fact, that they CAN be many things at once, like being here and there *at the same freakin' time*. We, however, live in the world of the not-so-tiny, so these rules do not

When the logic of an individual rule leads to a logical contradiction, the antecedent that brought about the contradiction can NEVER occur. THIS DOES NOT mean that the antecedent of the contra-positive cannot happen! MEMORIZE THAT!

The original rule may lead to an absurd result, but that is because of how it interacted logically with the rest of the conditions. The contra-positive interacts differently, and may or may not lead to another contradiction: that is precisely why we have to thoroughly and methodically work ourselves through all of the logic, every time. This is very powerful information, particularly if it comes up in a complex logic game (the kind that you need for a wicked-high score).

Pretend, for example, an artist named Deann has to choose five colors of paint for a mural, and she has nine colors to chose from: blue, chartreuse, ebony, green, indigo, orange, red, violet, and yellow (C, B, E, G, I, O, R, V, Y). Her rules for picking colors are:

1) If she picks red or violet, then she must also pick blue.
2) If she picks green, she also picks indigo, blue or both.
3) If she picks yellow, she selects neither ebony nor blue.
4) If she selects blue, she cannot select red, nor can she select violet.

Take a few minutes and put this into symbols, contra-pose and merge the rules. When you do it, SPLIT the disjunctive antecedents in rule 1, 3a and 4a into separate conditionals... DO IT! NOW!!!! NO CHEATING OR PEEKING AHEAD!

Here is what it should look like:

$$1)\ R \supset B \cdot -B \cdot -Y \cdot -R \cdot -V$$
$$-B \supset -R \cdot -V$$
$$V \supset B \cdot -B \cdot -Y \cdot -R \cdot -V$$
$$-B \supset -V \cdot -R$$
$$2)\ G \supset I \lor B$$
$$-I \cdot -B \supset -G \cdot -V \cdot -R$$
$$3)\ Y \supset -E \cdot -B \cdot -R \cdot -V$$
$$E \supset -Y$$
$$B \supset -Y \cdot -R \cdot -V$$
$$4)\ B \supset -R \cdot -V \cdot -Y$$
$$V \supset -B \cdot -R \cdot -V$$
$$R \supset -B \cdot B \cdot -Y \cdot -R \cdot -V$$

---

apply to us. If you would like to learn more, grab a copy of, _The Search for Schrodinger's Cat,_ by John Gribbon, and a large bottle of Scotch. We recommend Johnny Walker Double-Black. You will thank us and curse us simultaneously.

DON'T PANIC! There is a whole lot of fantastic stuff to glean from all of this, so let us all take a deep breath, maybe a stiff drink, and look at it nice and calm like.

First, we hope that you noticed that condition 1 is **riddled** with contradictions! It says that if Deann is known to select red, violet or both, that is sufficient to prove that she does not have red and that she does not have violet AND that she has and does not have blue. "*Inconceivable!*[22]" So rule #1 tells us that Deann can NEVER select red nor can she ever select violet.

Note also that condition three tells us that any time yellow is selected, ebony, blue, red and violet cannot be selected, which eliminates four colors, which makes the complete selection of five colors(the remaining colors) easy to determine!

It is VERY helpful to know that contradictions in the rules tell us that red and violet can never be selected: ANY question that asks us about what can or might be possible that has an answer choice with red and/or violet in it HAS TO BE AN INCORRECT CHOICE! We can *automatically kill them all!* That makes step 5 of our process, DESTROY THE PROBLEMS, much more easierer!

And in conclusion...

And now, dear reader, you are more knowledgeable about the logic necessary to be a top-flight law student and lawyer than 99.9% of all of the people alive on planet earth today... actually probably ever. You must practice it and you MUST use *everything* we have taught you *every chance you get.* With what you now know, nobody should ever get the better of you in a battle of wits (even if you are going against a Sicilian). Also, you should be able to answer EVERY logic game question correctly.

From here on out, your job is to get better at using all of the things you have just learned more quickly and efficiently. This is about spotting and understanding the issues raised by the various types of games. This is about reading a situation and being able to anticipate all of the tricky logical issues that will arise. This is about knowing the answers to questions before they are asked. It is NOT about getting a great score. If you understand, the score will follow, guaranteed.

NEVER sacrifice accuracy in the name of speed. Solid performance can be sped up. So can lousy performance. Guess which one gets you a better score, more scholarship money, fame, glory and fancy creams and lotions?

---

[22] Must be said in the voice of Wallace Shawn, portraying Vizzini in *The Princess Bride,* Act III Communications, Buttercup Films Ltd., et. seq. 1987. Watch it if you have not. It is severely cute and charming.

There are a few tiny additional, though not irrelevant, points of logic that you can add to your skill set in Appendix "C", none of which are worth a bag of spit to you if you do not have this logic section down colder than the butt of a wild polar bear in January. So practice, practice, practice. After that, practice some more. The competition is.

VI. Applying the Method, Act II

Picking Winners and Losers

Now that we are all super-charged logicians, we can turn all of that hard work and effort into points, which happen to turn into money. "Winner-Loser" games are exercises in which we are presented with a pool of players and asked to determine (based upon a set of rules) which players "play" and which players "ride the bench." In a way, these work a lot like *Bucket* games, where there are but two buckets, a "winner" bucket and a "losers" bucket. Some of you might be saying to yourselves right now, "If there are only two choices and all of the players have to be in or out, isn't that just a forced dichotomy? If a player is not out, they must be in. If they are not in, they must be out." That pretty much sums it up right there my friends. In their most basic form, that is all that we are doing...ish.

The slightly more encompassing truth of the matter is that there really is not a need to draw a distinction between Bucket Games and Winner/Loser games. It is made because of this simple fact: Winner/Loser games always focus on a specific sub-set of issues that involve the advanced application of conditional logic, whereas Bucket games do not. Where a Bucket game is apt to have a "Lone Conditional" in the "Extras" portion of Step Four, Winner/Loser games are not, because they are made up almost exclusively of conditional logic. Bucket games often have "absolutes" where Winner/Loser games rarely do, and even then, we ferreted them out from combining conditional statements. So the "Winner/Loser" label is there to alert you to the fact that the bulk of the issues we will deal with are conditional logic based.

Flavors of Winner/Loser

There are two variations on Winner/Loser games, just like we saw in the Bucket games. Guess what? The variations turn on the exact same issue: calculators. Recall that some bucket games tell you exactly how many items you have to put into a set number of buckets: seven items to go into three buckets, etc. Others do not tell you exactly how many items you have to put into a set number of buckets: There are brownies, cakes, donuts and pies available for Quincy, Robert and Susan to buy. Maybe all three have pie, maybe none of them do...who knows?

In Winner/Loser games we face the same distinction. Sometimes we are just given a large group of players and we have to pick which ones win and which lose. Other times we are given a large group of players and are told that a set number of them win. For example, there are seven pilots to be slotted for four missions. We now know that there are four winners... and that there are three losers. If we know who the three losers are, we also know who the four winners must be, and vice-versa. That is *mucho useful-o*.

We can also be given a more "complicated" set of information. For example, the test may give us three "groups" of players (three OBGYNs, A, B and C, three oncologists, G, H and I, and four proctologists, W, X, Y and Z) and make us pick two winners from each group, or a total of five etc. This is just trickery that we can deal with.

THE MOST IMPORTANT POINT to remember about this distinction is that _when we have a set number of winners, losers or both, we will make a drawing (step 3) and if we do not have a set number of winners or losers we will not make a drawing._ **MEMORIZE THAT!**

When we have no idea how many must win or lose, we will simply work with our list of players and apply the rules to them in the inference steps and in every problem. When there is a set number, we can use that "calculator" to draw more inferences. Because that is what logic games are all about, we will maximize our outcome with a drawing.

NOTE: They can also try to trick us by making a game _look like_ a Winner/Loser game when it is in fact a buckets game. Usually this is done by having a third place to put our players. For example, there are seven players to choose from to make a pair of 3-person basketball teams: three go to team A, three go to team B and the seventh person "rides the pine." That's buckets, not winner-loser... Those also tend to be very taxing on the CPU.

FEAR NOT! This is all just psychological warfare! Logic is logic is logic, and what one fool can do, so can another. Let's start with a simple problem and gradually build our way toward staring down the _terror Cimbricus._

BEFORE WE BEGIN, review the steps for doing a logic game if you need to. It may have been a while since last you reviewed all of the steps as we just spent a lot of time on logic, so it would be understandable though not forgivable. Go back, get it all straight in your head, and then move forward.

Try to do these problems on your own before you look at the explanations, please. We cannot come to your house and hit you in the forehead with a tack hammer every time you cheat. That is just a limitation of the format. We trust that you will engage in some form self-flagellation whenever necessary... unless you are totally into that sort of thing. In that case, _deny_ yourself the pleasure as a punishment.

Problem Set 11 – Winners and Losers

The manager of a football team has to decide what to put into the team's supply room. She has six possible items to choose from: footballs, helmets, knee pads, muscle rub, shoulder pads and weights. What she puts in the supply room depends upon the following conditions:

> If she puts in weights, she must also put in footballs.
> If she does not put in any knee pads, then she does put in shoulder pads.
> If she puts helmets in the room, she does not put in footballs.
> If there are knee pads or if there is muscle rub or if there are both, she also includes helmets.

1) If she decides not to put any knee pads in the room, what CANNOT be true?
   a) Muscle rub is in the room.
   b) Helmets are in the room.
   c) Neither muscle rub nor helmets are in the room.
   d) Neither muscle rub nor shoulder pads are in the room.
   e) Helmets and shoulder pads are the only items in the room.

2) If she decides to put footballs into the storage room, what MUST be true?
   a) She also puts in shoulder Pads.
   b) She also puts in weights.
   c) She puts in both weights and shoulder pads.
   d) At most, there are two different items in the supply room.
   e) There are at least three items in the room.

3) Which two things can never be together in the supply room?
   a) Shoulder pads and weights
   b) Shoulder pads and muscle rub
   c) Knee pads and muscle rub
   d) Knee pads and shoulder pads
   e) Knee pads and weights

4) If there are both helmets and muscle rub in the room, which of the following must be true?
   a) There are at least two other kinds of equipment in the room.
   b) At most, there are two other kinds of equipment in the room.
   c) The room has neither knee pads nor shoulder pads.
   d) Knee pads are the only other equipment in the room.
   e) Shoulder pads are the only other kind of equipment in the room .

5) Which of the following is a complete and accurate list of all of the equipment that might NOT be in the supply room?
   a) Knee pads and shoulder pads
   b) Helmets and goal markers
   c) Footballs, knee pads and muscle rub
   d) Footballs, muscle rub, shoulder pads and weights.
   e) Muscle rub and shoulder pads.

6) The minimum and maximum number of items in the supply room, respectively are:
   a) 0, 6
   b) 0, 5
   c) 1,4
   d) 1,5
   e) 2,6

STEP ONE: Get a Grip – The nature of the game is Winner/Loser **_without_** numbers. That is important why? Because our picture will just be a list of all of the players and we will circle and cross off players as they win and lose respectively. The players are F, H, K, M, S and W. Hidden rules: none. Zip. Nada.

STEP TWO: Formal Rules – There are four rules and four contra-positives. For the most part, there is nothing tricky going on. The fourth condition has one of those phony "or both" things going on. Recall that it is meaningless because "or" always means "or both."

$$F, H, K, M, S, W$$
$$1) \ W \supset F$$
$$-F \supset -W$$
$$2) \ -K \supset S$$
$$-S \supset K$$
$$3) \ H \supset -F$$
$$F \supset -H$$
$$4) \ K \lor M \supset H$$
$$-H \supset -K \cdot -M$$

STEP THREE: DRAW A PICTURE – F, H, K, M, S, W. That was easy. REMEMBER that the only reason that we are not making a drawing is because there are no NUMBERS requirements (exactly four items will be in the closet, or other such nonsense). Had there been, we _would_ draw something.

STEP FOUR: INFERENCES
This is where we have to do something slightly different. In a moment, you will come to understand the brilliance of what we are about to explain. There is a NEW RULE to _memorize_: WHEN DOING INFERENCES IN WINNER/LOSER GAMES, WE DO THE DOUBLE-UP STEP FIRST, THEN WE GO BACK TO THE TOP OF THE A, B, C, D, E, F LIST.

There are a boatload of reasons that this adjustment makes sense in the context of these games. The first and most obvious is that all of the issues arising in Winner/Loser games derive not from the rules themselves, but from how they connect together (just like with real laws). The second reason is that the other things that we look for (absolutes, affirmative duties etc.) yield more complete information for us when we have already doubled-up. For example, a rule that has a negative antecedent and a negative consequent might combine with other rules to add an affirmative consequent as well. That makes the rule into an affirmative duty, something we are more apt to notice after combining the double-ups. That makes "absolute" spotting more complete. So let's do Step Four in the modified, Winner/Loser order.

DOUBLE-UPS – Rather than walk you through them line by line, we are simply going to point out the highlights and let you try to get them on your own. DON'T BE A SISSY! You can do it. If you need to review the process, then do so.

Condition 1 has W sufficient to prove F. There are no other W antecedents, but the F is an antecedent in the contra-positive of rule 3. That brings in –H. The –H is an antecedent in the contra-positive of rule 4, so we added the consequents –K and –M. The –K is the antecedent of rule 2, so we have to tack on the S. So rule 1 (and the rest of the rules)end(s) up looking like this:

$$1)\ W \supset F \cdot -H \cdot -K \cdot -M \cdot S$$
$$-F \supset -W$$
$$2)\ -K \supset S$$
$$-S \supset K \cdot H \cdot -F \cdot -W$$
$$3)\ H \supset -F \cdot -W$$
$$F \supset -H \cdot -K \cdot -M \cdot S$$
$$4)\ K \vee M \supset H \cdot -F \cdot -W$$
$$-H \supset -K \cdot -M \cdot S$$

There are a few interesting things to point out before we trundle off. Six of the eight rules combined with other rules to yield more information on the consequent side. The most common mistake that gets made in doubling these up is where people overlook the rules that have no additional "add-ons" from the process. What we mean is that rule 2 does not combine with anything and retains its original consequent. That rule does however factor into every other rule that has –K in the consequent (such as rules 1, contra 3 and contra 4). That requires us to add the "S" and that is frequently missed. When it does, the affirmative duty that springs forth from the contra-positive of rule 4 is missed. Oops.

Also important (and a very real part of the LSAT) is that condition 4 has a disjunctive antecedent that we did not separate out into two distinct rules. That decision is one that has to be made on the fly, and the rational way to make it is thus: are either of the disjuncts, K or M, antecedents in any other rules? If not, then there is no real point to separating them (other than personal comfort, which is not illegitimate). We said that it is a real part of the LSAT because, as stated earlier, the LSAC is not in the habit of testing whether or not we separated disjunctive antecedents: we can find no example where it was necessary to separate a disjunctive antecedent on those grounds.

Finally, there is the fact that condition 1 includes all six of the players. In other words, when we know that W is in the closet, we know about ALL of the items in and out of the closet. That is what we call a "smiley face" rule: it gives us a complete answer, and "W" tells all.

NOW we have to go back and do the A, B, C, E, F of the Inference step.

1) $W \supset F \cdot -H \cdot -K \cdot -M \cdot S$
   $-F \supset -W$
2) $-K \supset S$
   $-S \supset K \cdot H \cdot -F \cdot -W$
3) $H \supset -F \cdot -W$
   $F \supset -H \cdot -K \cdot -M \cdot S$
4) $K \vee M \supset H \cdot -F \cdot -W$
   $-H \supset -K \cdot -M \cdot S$

ABSOLUTES – Are there any players that must play or who must not play? As far as we can tell right now the answer is what? Look long and hard and think about everything we have covered. Rule 2 has a negative antecedent and an affirmative consequent. That is called what? An *affirmative duty rule.* This means that either S must be a winner or that K and H are both winners. Per the Right Side Rule, they can all be winners (i.e. in the storage closet). K and S cannot both be absent from the closet however. So we know for sure that S or K or both will be in the closet at all times, which is sort of absolute. What IS absolute is this: the closet has to have at least one item in it.

BUNDLES – Are there any players that always have to be together? This is a trap set for the average mouth breather. Condition 1 makes it look like W and F always go together, but that is not true. W proves F, but F does not prove W (i.e. F is nowhere on the list as an antecedent with W as its consequent. If it were, then we would have a rule with W as an antecedent and F as a consequent, and another with F as an antecedent and W as the consequent. That would make a latent bi-conditional. Thank goodness we don't have to mess with that.

CALCULATORS – We know that there are six items that are eligible to go into the closet. We can also sniff out a few things, and in a Winner/Loser game, the thing we want to *try* to get our brains around are the minimum and maximum number of items that can win.

We know that the closet cannot be empty because of the affirmative duty rules in 2 and contra 2. Rule 2 allows us to have –K with S winning. S *could* be the only item in the closet. The contra of rule 4 is also an affirmative duty, but it also requires S to be in. So we can get by with just one item in the closet.

Can all six of the items actually be in the closet? Not even close. Rule 1 shows that knowing that W is a winner automatically includes two others and excludes three items. If we want to put more than three items in the closet, we have to throw W out of the closet. BUT NOTE that there is no "-W" antecedent, so we do not actually have a basis for thinking that merely getting rid of it means anything. The contrapositive of 1 gets rid of F and W but says nothing about the other four (H, K, M, S), so they *could* be in the closet because the H antecedent in rule 3 gets rid of the F and W again, the K or M antecedents from condition 4 drag in H and get rid of F and W again, and S is not an antecedent. Four items winning is possible. Finally, we KNOW, to a certainty, that there cannot be five items in the closet. How do we know that factoid, geniuses? Look at rule 3. It is a *mutual exclusion*. H excludes F and W, and in the contra-positive, F excludes H, K and M. There just are not enough players left to get a fifth item in.

One item minimum (S) and four items is the maximum (H, K, M, S).

EXTRAS – NOW, finally, at long last, you get to learn the "extras". These are the technical, logic-based considerations you need to be aware of, in the exact order you need to look for them. ***MEMORIZE THEM!*** They are:

i)   **Bi-conditionals** – If there are any bi-conditionals, we need to be aware of them because they vitiate the *right-side rule.* In our present game, we do not appear to have any.

ii) **Forced dichotomies** – If a player is forced into playing (which is easiest to determine in an "all-play" game) and there are only two ways that said player can play, that is a *forced dichotomy.* That means that everything is binary. For instance, if everyone in the game has to eat either steak or chicken, -S means CHICKEN, and –C means STEAK, because ... we don't want to insult your intelligence, so forgive us, if you must eat something and the only two choices are S and C, not doing one forces you into the other. Recognizing that you have a forced dichotomy allows you to write things such as –C as S.

In our present game, we DO have a forced dichotomy. It is subtle because the game is trying to hide it from us.

Sometimes people think that they are doing a Winner/Loser game that has a very interesting property: there is a third choice. For example, let's pretend there is a logic game that has seven people to choose from for a basketball team. Five will be on the team, one will be a sub on the bench, and one will be the referee. THAT IS NOT A WINNER/LOSER GAME! It is a "Buckets" game with three buckets: Play, no-play, referee. Don't make that mistake.

iii) **Right side rule** – If there are no bi-conditionals, we look at the right side of every rule and its contra-positive and note that they are allowed to happen at the same time.

iv) **Affirmative Duties** – We want to know whether or not there are any affirmative duty rules. Remember what they are? Broadly stated, they are rules that *require us to do something under all circumstances.* Rules with negative antecedents and affirmative consequents are the easy-to-spot versions of affirmative duty rules.

v) **Contradictions** – Do you remember what they are from the logic section? We hunt for whether or not there are any conditions under which you are required to both do and not do the same thing. Any antecedent that results in a contradiction cannot happen.

vi) **Lone Conditionals** – The last extra is the "lone conditional," which is precisely what it sounds like. Some games (not winner/loser games) have just one conditional rule. When that happens, we (a) know that there will be at least two questions that turn on our understanding of it, and (b) have to make a decision as to whether or not it is worth our time to draw out the lone conditional scenario. It may be that if we make a special drawing just for the lone conditional, it solves everything having to do with that conditional scenario. In such a case, we are answering every question about that scenario in advance (and it will take us less than 30 seconds to get the correct answer).

So now we want to run down the list in order.
Bi-conditionals: as pointed out earlier, there are none.

Forced dichotomies – Are there any situations in which player(s) MUST play and they only have two options? The answer is "definitely." Every player has to either be in the closet or out of the closet. There is no third choice.

Affirmative Duties – We have spotted all three previously. We are good.

Right-Side rule – For those of you who did not catch it earlier (or did not really understand it when we hit it) we can use the Right Side Rule to determine valuable stuff, like the fact that S can be the only winner. Look at the right side of condition 3 and its contra-positive. They tell us that we can have S with all of the other five players losing. If we did not see it before, it is crystal clear now. The Right Side of rule 2 and its contra-positive says that we can have S, K and H without F and without W. It is silent as to M, so we *could* throw it in, because per rule 4, K and M function identically. You can CIRCLE the right side of each rule and contra, as we did back when we were learning the Right-Side rule, if that makes it easier for you to see.

We can also see that rule 4 and contra 4 allow for H and S in the closet (winners) while F, K, M and W are out (losers).

So HERE is the magic of the Right Side Rule: they give us *combinations of winners and losers that are complete, correct answers!* We have EIGHT COMPLETE ANSWERS:

1) Rule 1 alone says that W, F and S in, with H, K and M out is a valid answer.
2) 1 and contra 1 say that F and S in with W, H, K and M out is valid.
3) 2 and Contra 2 say that S, K, H and M in with F and W out is valid.
4) 2 and Contra 2 say that S, K, H in with F, M and W out is valid.
5) 3 and contra 3 says that S alone in the closet is valid.

6) Rule 4 says that K, M and H in with F, W and S out is valid.
7) Rule 4 says that K, M, S and H in with F and W out is valid.
8) 4 and contra 4 tell us that H and S in with the rest out is valid.

Contradictions – Do we have any contradictions? No, we do not.

Lone conditionals – Is there a single conditional rule that has not been incorporated into our drawing? Well, because this is a "no numbers" Winner/Loser game, there is no drawing. Also, there are eight total conditional statements, so the answer is clearly "NO!"

FREE RANGERS – Are there any players that do not have any rules associate with them? Nope. They are all sucked into the mix, which should be obvious given our cornucopia of complete answers.

STEP FIVE – DESTROY THE QUESTIONS! Remember that there are TWO sub-parts to this step. First, we always have to go with what we already know. THIS IS THE PLACE WHERE YOU ARE LIKELY TO REALLY SCREW UP!

"Go with what you already know," is an admonition to NOT waste time drawing things out and reinventing things that you have already done. That would be a complete waste of time, and for us, time is at a premium. So we have to avoid, at all costs, unnecessarily doing any additional work. Please recall that, "what you already know" grows and changes with every question, and that you cannot forget to take what you learn from earlier problems in the set with you to the later ones.

1) $W \supset F \cdot -H \cdot -K \cdot -M \cdot S$
   $-F \supset -W$
2) $-K \supset S$
   $-S \supset K \cdot H \cdot -F \cdot -W$
3) $H \supset -F \cdot -W$
   $F \supset -H \cdot -K \cdot -M \cdot S$
4) $K \vee M \supset H \cdot -F \cdot -W$
   $-H \supset -K \cdot -M \cdot S$

1) If she decides not to put any knee pads in the room, what CANNOT be true?
   a) Muscle rub is in the room.
   b) Helmets are in the room.
   c) Neither muscle rub nor helmets are in the room.
   d) Neither muscle rub nor shoulder pads are in the room.
   e) Helmets and shoulder pads are the only items in the room.

Here is a nice, straight-forward one to start out with. We knew going into the questions that affirmative duties were going to be on the menu. What do we already know about –K? Rule number two says that shoulder pads have to be in the closet. That is the ONLY thing that we know. So our first course of action is to look for an answer choice that mentions shoulder pads NOT being in the supply room. That would be answer choice D.

We heard that! Somebody said, "What? How do you know the other choices are wrong?" We know that you meant "incorrect," and the answer to your question is pretty simple. The *LOGIC* told us that shoulder pads ___must___ be in the storage room. Any answer that says that they are not ___must___ be incorrect. There is only ONE correct answer per question. D says no shoulder pads in the storage room. D must be that one. Ergo, the others must logically be incorrect. Q.E.D. (look it up).

2) If she decides to put footballs into the storage room, what MUST be true?
    a. She also puts in shoulder Pads.
    b. She also puts in weights.
    c. She puts in both weights and shoulder pads.
    d. At most, there are two different items in the supply room.
    e. There are at least three items in the room.

Oh, my, God, Becky! Would you look at that, question. Another super-sweet and easy one. Rule three's contra says that F is sufficient to establish –H and –K and –M and S. Answer choice A says that shoulder pads are in the storage room. That is our winner. Circle it in your test booklet, bubble it in on the answer sheet and get moving. NO WASTING TIME "just checking" THE OTHER ANSWERS!

3) Which two things can never be together in the supply room?
    a. Shoulder pads and weights
    b. Shoulder pads and muscle rub
    c. Knee pads and muscle rub
    d. Knee pads and shoulder pads
    e. Knee pads and weights

ANOTHER EASY ONE! We have to determine which two listed items cannot be in the storage room at the same time. How easy is that?

(A) says S and W. Rule one says that if W are in, S must be. Incorrect. Next!

(B) Has S and M. There are no rules for either of them. Incorrect. NEXT!

(C) K and M. Fascinating choice. They are testing whether or not you recognize that "or" is inclusive. You had better. Incorrect. NEXT!

(D) K and S. Guess what they are checking here? RIGHT SIDE RULE! The right side of rule two allows it. Incorrect. CIRCLE "E" without wasting your time.[1]

---

[1] A special note ___ONLY___ for those who "checked" E - YOU BLOODY WANKER! WE TOLD YOU NOT TO CHECK "E" because it has to be the correct answer. You wasted valuable time and that will cost you money! This is as much about discipline as it is about anything else. DISCIPLINE YOUR HAPPY BUTT TO DO THINGS PROPERLY! Of course W and K cannot be in the storage room together! Rule one says so. SMALL COMFORT to you, that satisfaction, when you have to work as a peon (look it up) at some fender-bender ambulance chasing law firm to pay off the $100,000.00 in student loans you had to take out because you missed scholarship money by one freakin' point. Now get serious about doing things properly.

4) If there are both helmets and muscle rub in the room, which of the following must be true?
   a. There are at least two other kinds of equipment in the room.
   b. At most, there are two other kinds of equipment in the room.
   c. The room has neither knee pads nor shoulder pads.
   d. Knee pads are the only other equipment in the room.
   e. Shoulder pads are the only other kind of equipment in the room.

H and M are both in the room. Oh my! This is an intimidation question. Rule three talks about H being in the room and rule four talks about M. You can do this in any of three ways. Figure out which works best for you and stick with it.

METHOD #1: Sketch it up. In the space adjacent to the question, list out all of the objects that are available:

> 1) W ⊃ F · -H · -K · -M · S
>   -F ⊃ -W
> 2) -K ⊃ S
>   -S ⊃ K · H · -F · -W
> 3) H ⊃ -F · -W
>   F ⊃ -H · -K · -M · S
> 4) K v M ⊃ H · -F · -W
>   -H ⊃ -K · -M · S

F H K M S W

Now apply the conditions that were stated in the call of the question to the list: mark H and M as "in" either by circling or drawing a box around them:

F (H) K (M) S W

Then go to the rules and see what they tell you. Condition three says that if H is in the closet, F and W are not. Cross them off NEATLY.

F̶ (H) K (M) S W̶

And there you have it. Rule four says that K or M being "in" proves that H is in (we knew that) and that F and W are not (ditto). But what about K and S? EXACTLY! And we KNEW this was coming! They set up some sort of phony-baloney hypothetical to poke at the K and S affirmative duty rules! We know that ONE of them MUST be in, and it matters not which. We also know that both *can* be in. Another one bites the dust.

A) Incorrect. There are not "at least" two more, there are "at most" two more.
B) Oh, wow…. That's what we just said. Two more at most. Done deal daddy-o. Circle, bubble and run.

METHOD #2 – Give it the Finger(s). Way back at Step One of our process, we listed out all of the players. Barring some catastrophe, they should still be there. The call of the question says H and M are in the store room. Take one of your hands and from the top-side of the list place one finger directly above the H and a different finger directly above the M. The top-side is the "winner" side. Look at your rules. They tell you that F and W are out. So with the *other* hand, place one finger directly below the F and a different finger directly below the W. The bottom side is the "loser" side.

We can see that K and S did not get fingered. We see the affirmative duty issue and we end up at the exact same place we did in method #1.

METHOD #3 – "Steal From the Russian Mob." Do either method #1 or #2 *in your head*. In other words, simply *look* at the list of players that you made in Step One and *visualize* circling and crossing off or *visualize* putting your fingers above and below. This name derives from the fact that you really do not want to do this even though it is oh-so tempting. Yes, we are all very impressed by your Steven Hawking-like intellectual prowess, but that is beside the point. When you are taking a test and you are working on a problem that requires the use of the pencil protocols, USE THEM. It is immaturity of the highest order to take a course of action that has a significantly higher chance of ending badly. Be a big kid and do it correctly. DO NOT USE METHOD #3.

5) Which of the following is a complete and accurate list of all of the equipment that might NOT be in the supply room?
   a. Knee pads and shoulder pads
   b. Helmets and footballs
   c. Footballs, knee pads and muscle rub
   d. Footballs, muscle rub, shoulder pads and weights.
   e. Muscle rub and shoulder pads.

Recall that we mentioned once or ten times that there is always a question or two that are designed to make you slow down and work in order to get you to freak out about time? Heeeerrrrrr's Johnny! They want us to identify a *complete and accurate* list of stuff NOT in the storage room. If, for example, we had an answer choice that just said, "Footballs," what would that actually mean? Footballs out, *everything else in.* Can that happen? NO! Because H being in means W is out. So we are "challenged" here, but it's not so bad.

Unlike the last question, we *can* eyeball a number of these answer choices. For example, (A) says that K and S are out. We can look for −K and −S rules and see that, once again, they are beating that poor, dead horse, affirmative duty. They cannot both be out, so we can kill (A).

(B) has H and F out, and we can see that the contra-positive of rule four says that −H proves that we also have −K and −M. Ergo, (B) sucks.

(C) has -F, -K and −M. We can see from contra one that −F proves −W which proves that (C) is incomplete and incorrect.

(D) however has −F, -M, -S and −W. There are no −F or −M antecedents. −S requires that we have −F and −W and that K and H be in the storage room. Our job is done here.

6)   The minimum and maximum number of items in the supply room, respectively are:
        a) 0, 6
        b) 0, 5
        c) 1,4
        d) 1,5
        e) 2,6

In keeping with the traditions of the test format, there is always a balance between the "easy" and the "difficult" questions. We know this one from way the heck back at Calculators. We could have S alone as our only item in the room, and we can have four items maximum. Circle C, pour yourself a cold one and dream of the day when these skills net you a paycheck.

Problem Set 12 – Winners and Losers (Numbers)

A Major League Eating team captain must pick exactly four types of food for his team's training table. The choices available to him are burritos, donuts, hot dogs, pies, ribs, sandwiches and tacos. The food selection is based upon the following conditions.
 Tacos or burritos must be selected, but not both.
 Either hot dogs and tacos are both selected or neither are.
 If donuts are selected, then ribs are also selected.
 If pie is not selected, burritos must be.

1) Which one of the following could be a complete and accurate list of the foods selected?
        a) burritos, pie, sandwiches, tacos
        b) burritos, donuts, hot dogs, ribs
        c) burritos, pie, ribs, sandwiches
        d) donuts, hot dogs, pie, tacos
        e) hot dogs, pie, ribs, sandwiches.

2) Which of the following must be true of the selection of foods?
        a) either pies or ribs must be selected
        b) either hot dogs or tacos must be selected
        c) either pies or tacos must be selected
        d) either burritos or donuts must be selected
        e) either burritos or ribs must be selected.

3) If sandwiches are not chosen for the training table, which of the following must be false?
     a) pie is selected
     b) donuts are selected
     c) burritos are not selected
     d) tacos are not selected
     e) ribs are not selected

4) Which one of the following is a pair of foods that cannot both be selected for the training table?
     a) burritos and pie
     b) burritos and hot dogs
     c) ribs and sandwiches
     d) donuts and ribs
     e) hot dogs and tacos

5) Which of the following items, if not selected, would establish the complete list of items selected for the training table?
     a) burritos
     b) donuts
     c) hot dogs
     d) ribs
     e) tacos

6) If burritos are not chosen, which one of the following must be false?
     a) donuts are not chosen
     b) pies are chosen
     c) ribs are not chosen
     d) sandwiches are not chosen
     e) neither ribs nor sandwiches are chosen

7) Which one of the following, if true, would allow for more than one possible combination of items that could be selected?
     a) pies are not selected
     b) ribs are not selected
     c) neither hot dogs nor tacos are selected
     d) neither sandwiches nor tacos are selected
     e) neither burritos nor ribs are selected

8) If hot dogs are not selected for the training table, how many different possible combinations of food might the manager create?
     a) 1
     b) 3
     c) 5
     d) 7
     e) 9

STEP ONE: Get a Grip – What is the nature of the game? Obviously it is a Winner/Loser game. What *flavor* is it? In other words, are there numbers involved? Yes there are. There is a hidden rule that says that the captain must pick four foods. That means there will be four winners. It also means that we can determine the number of losers based upon the total number of players. Which raises the question, who/what are the players? B, D, H, P, R S and T. That is seven. So there will be four winners and three losers. Yea.

STEP TWO: Formal Rules – Holy mackerel, Amos! Do you see what we see? Look at rule number one. What does it say? "Both or neither." Sound familiar? If you did not emphatically say "YES!" then you need to review your logic. This is a "same-sign bi-conditional." Look at condition number two. Does *that* look familiar? Of course it does. It is an "exactly one bi-conditional." Rules three and four look pretty pedestrian. Put them all into symbols and then compare them to the list below.

B, D, H, P, R S, T

1) T ⊃ -B
  B ⊃ -T
 -T ⊃ B
 -B ⊃ T
2) H ⊃ T
 -T ⊃ -H
  T ⊃ H
 -H ⊃ -T
3) D ⊃ R
 -R ⊃ -D
4) -P ⊃ B
 -B ⊃ P

Voila! And now we are ready for...

STEP THREE: Draw a Picture – We know that there are going to be four winers and three losers. The order of the winners and losers does not matter, so we can create a picture that looks just like a Buckets game with two buckets:

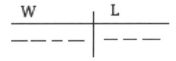

Now we can clearly visualize the numerical requirements. That is going to be very useful. Please continue to see just why that is.

STEP FOUR: Inferences – Recall that we "called an audible" and adjusted the order of the inferences for the Winner/Loser game. We are going to do the Double-ups first. Take a moment or two to do them and then compare your work to the job done below. NO CHEATING!

B, D, H, P, R S, T

1) T ⊃ -B · H · P
   B ⊃ -T · -H
  -T ⊃ B · -H
  -B ⊃ T · P · H
2) H ⊃ T · -B · P
  -T ⊃ -H · B
   T ⊃ H · -B · P
  -H ⊃ -T · B
3) D ⊃ R
  -R ⊃ -D
4) -P ⊃ B · -T · -H
  -B ⊃ P · T · H

Hmmmm. Something very interesting has happened. Let us take a look at what all of this means in relation to our drawing and the next part of the process.

ABSOLUTES – Do we have anything that always has to be in a particular place? If we are not thinking too lucidly, we might say, "no." We would be incorrect. Our first condition tells us that the first spot on the winner side has to be filled by either T or B. It also tells us that our first spot on the loser side has to be filled by whichever one is not the winner. So we know that one winner must be T or B and that the same thing can be said about one loser.

W	L
T/B _ _ _	B/T _ _ _

We only have one of those kinds of rules. The other bi-conditional is a both-or-neither AND it doubled-up with rule one. THERE ARE ONLY TWO WAYS that this game can be played! Either T wins and B loses or B wins and T loses. In both cases, we have a ton of additional information that we can fill in. Let's do that by creating two pictures, one with T winning and one with B winning.

P1
```
      W              L
   _____    |_____
   T  H  P  __   | B  __  __  __
```

P2
```
      W              L
   _____    |_____
   B  __ __ __   | T  H  __
```

This looks very promising indeed! P1 tells us that there is only one winner spot left! P2 tells us that there is only one loser spot left! We can see that the taco-burrito distinction is going to be HUGE. We can anticipate questions like, "If burritos are not selected but donuts are…." We are totally in control, and we are not even close to being done with the inferences. In P1 we noted that there is only one winner left. Is that helpful? Look at the other rules and THINK. **HINT – rule three.**

Rule three says that if donuts are selected, then ribs must be also. But in P1 there is only one space left on the winner side. That means that in P1, D must lose. That means that the last winner space in P1 and the last loser space is going to be a toss-up between sandwiches and ribs!

P1
```
      W                L
   _____    |_____
   T  H  P  S/R   | B  D  R/S
```

P2
```
      W                L
   _____    |_____
   B  __ __ __    | T  H  __
```

The same sort of Festivus miracle happens when we look at the loser side on P2. It says that if ribs lose then so do donuts. That is not possible in P2. Thus, ribs cannot lose in P2, they must win.

P1
```
      W                L
   _____    |_____
   T  H  P  S/R   | B  D  R/S
```

P2
```
      W                L
   _____    |_____
   B  R  __ __    | T  H  __
```

And that means that if we know who the third loser (out of D, P and S) is in P2, we have a complete answer.

This creates what we like to call a 2/3 scenario: two out of three have to win in P2, so one out of three loses. We can fill that in right below P2:

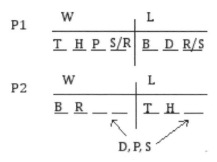

PWND! But there is more thinkification required, and the one thing we do not want to do is get all stupid-giddy about what is happening and lose our focus. STICK TO THE PLAN! BE DISCIPLINED!

BUNDLES – Are there players that always have to go together? If we just looked at the rules we might be of the opinion that T, H and P are a bundle. But the pictures paint a different... um.... picture. T and H definitely go together. But P2 shows us that P can cleave itself free. Also, D and R are NOT a bundle, even thought the rules might trick some people into thinking that they are. If we do not see that now, we will when we do the Extras later.

CALCULATORS – We killed that pig and roasted it long ago. Four plus three equals seven.

DOUBLE-UPS – Done.

EXTRAS – There are two bi-conditionals. The right side rule should be ignored.[2] Are there any forced dichotomies? HELLS YEAH! The entire game is a forced dichotomy. Items win or lose and all must play. But we have already hashed out the significance in the drawing. ***THIS IS PRECISELY WHY WE MUST USE AND ABUSE DRAWINGS IN WINNER/LOSER GAMES WITH NUMBERS REQUIREMENTS.***

Are there affirmative duty rules? Yes. Every rule save for one that has a negative antecedent has an affirmative consequence. In the context of a forced dichotomy, that is how we really end up with two pictures much of the time. How about contradictions? Are there any? No there are not. Lastly, there is not a "lone conditional." Rules three and four are not in our drawings per-se, but we understand them and how they will work. We also understand that drawing them out would be a complete waste of precious time.

---

[2] Please see Appendix C for a little additional insight on this matter. Remember, it is NOT that the right side rule is not in-fact useful here. Rather, it is far more simple and far more safe to just say that the right side rule is inapplicable.

FREE RANGERS – Sandwiches do not have any rules associated with them. They also have the luxury, in both pictures, of going either way. We can anticipate that there will be at least one question based upon this chicanery.

STEP FIVE – Destroy the Questions! Remember to use EVERYTHING you know!

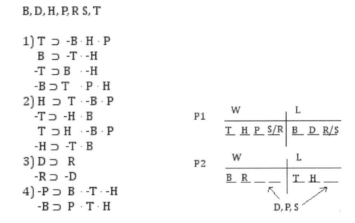

1) Which one of the following could be a complete and accurate list of the foods selected?
    a) burritos, pie, sandwiches, tacos
    b) burritos, donuts, hot dogs, ribs
    c) burritos, pie, ribs, sandwiches
    d) donuts, hot dogs, pie, tacos
    e) hot dogs, pie, ribs, sandwiches.

Are you ready for the bloodbath?
A) INCORRECT. Cannot get B AND T together.
B) INCORRECT. Cannot get B and H on the same side.
C) That is P2 and it works. Circle it, bubble it in on the answer form and run.
D) WHY ARE YOU LOOKING AT "D"? "C" WAS CORRECT!
E) See "D".

2) Which of the following must be true of the selection of foods?
    a) either pies or ribs must be selected
    b) either hot dogs or tacos must be selected
    c) either pies or tacos must be selected
    d) either burritos or donuts must be selected
    e) either burritos or ribs must be selected.

The call is asking you to determine what has to be true, and the answer choices are making you pick between two foods being winners. In other words, "Must it be true that either X or Y is a winner?" If we think about it for a second, all this is really asking us is, "Which is a pair both of which cannot lose at the same time?" If X and Y cannot both lose at the same time, then one or the other (or both... *inclusive)* must play. Ha ha ha!

B, D, H, P, R S, T

1) T ⊃ -B · H · P
   B ⊃ -T · -H
   -T ⊃ B · -H
   -B ⊃ T · P · H
2) H ⊃ T · -B · P
   -T ⊃ -H · B
   T ⊃ H · -B · P
   -H ⊃ -T · B
3) D ⊃ R
   -R ⊃ -D
4) -P ⊃ B · -T · -H
   -B ⊃ P · T · H

P1	W		L	
	T H P S/R		B D R/S	

P2	W		L	
	B R __ __		T H __	

D, P, S

A) P1 requires pie and P2 requires ribs. There are NO OTHER WAYS for this deal to go down, so this is correct. Circle, bubble, move.

3) If sandwiches are not chosen for the training table, which of the following must be false?
    a) pie is selected
    b) donuts are selected
    c) burritos are not selected
    d) tacos are not selected
    e) ribs are not selected

Didn't see that coming. S is the free ranger. If it loses in P1, T, H, P and R win. If it loses in P2, B, R, D and P win. Both pictures require P and R to win. Neither picture has a common loser. This should be easy money...unless you screw up. We are asked to find the thing that must be *false*.
A) Pie always wins. INCORRECT. (BUT it does clue us in to the fact that the "ribs" answer is probably going to be correct).
B) May be true (P2), may be false (P1). INCORRECT.
C) May be true (P1), may be false (P2). INCORRECT.
D) That is a freebie. Tacos go both ways. INCORRECT.
E) Circle it, bubble it, MOVE. Ribs.

4) Which one of the following is a pair of foods that cannot both be selected for the training table?
    a) burritos and pie
    b) burritos and hot dogs
    c) ribs and sandwiches
    d) donuts and ribs
    e) hot dogs and tacos

Wow. Another slam dunk, home run, bicycle-kick...
A) Can B and P both win? P2 says yes. INCORRECT.
B) Can B and H both win? P1 has them on opposite sides. So does P2. Circle it, bubble it. Run.

B, D, H, P, R S, T

1) T ⊃ -B · H · P
    B ⊃ -T · -H
   -T ⊃ B · -H
   -B ⊃ T · P · H
2) H ⊃ T · -B · P
   -T ⊃ -H · B
    T ⊃ H · -B · P
   -H ⊃ -T · B
3) D ⊃ R
   -R ⊃ -D
4) -P ⊃ B · -T · -H
   -B ⊃ P · T · H

P1

W				L		
T	H	P	S/R	B	D	R/S

P2

W			L		
B	R	_ _	T	H	_

↖   ↗
D, P, S

5) Which of the following items, if not selected, would establish the complete list of items selected for the training table?
    a) burritos
    b) donuts
    c) hot dogs
    d) ribs
    e) tacos

Here is a great opportunity to screw up. On item on the list, if not selected, will completely fill in all of the winners and all of the losers. The thing that they are poking at here is that whatever that item is, it has to do it in **both** P1 and P2.
A) If B loses in P1, we do not know about R or S. Incorrect.
B) Same as (A).
C) Hot dogs only lose in P2, and when they do, we do not know jack about our 2/3 problem. INCORRECT.
D) Ribs can only lose in P1 and that forces S to the winner side with T, H and P. Circle it. Bubble it. Move.
E) How many more times are you going to make us say it. STOP CHECKING ANSWERS THAT CANNOT POSSIBLY BE CORRECT!

6) If burritos are not chosen, which one of the following must be false?
    a) donuts are not chosen
    b) pies are chosen
    c) ribs are not chosen
    d) sandwiches are not chosen
    e) neither ribs nor sandwiches are chosen

Too easy! We are in P1. The only way we can mess this up is if we forget that we are being asked to determine that which cannot be true. No mistakes, please.
A) Perfectly true, ergo incorrect.
B) Ditto.
C) Could be true or false. HA! Incorrect.
D) Ditto.
CIRCLE "E" WITHOUT EVEN READING IT! It must be the correct answer.

7) Which one of the following, if true, would allow for more than one possible combination of items that could be selected?
   a) pies are not selected
   b) ribs are not selected
   c) neither hot dogs nor tacos are selected
   d) neither sandwiches nor tacos are selected
   e) neither burritos nor ribs are selected

Once again we need to make certain that we are answering the correct question. We are being told that four answer choices will lock down the exact winners and losers,

whereas one will allow for more than one combination. WE KNOW WHERE THE ANSWER LIES! It is in the P1 S vs. R thang and in the P2 D, P, S "2/3 issue."

A) P losing happens in P2 and it locks everything down. INCORRECT.
B) R losing is P1 only, and it locks everything down. INCORRECT.
C) H and T both losing happens only in P2 and leaves the 2/3 problem unresolved. Circle it. Bubble it.

8) If hot dogs are not selected for the training table, how many different possible combinations of food might the manager create?
   a) 1
   b) 3
   c) 5
   d) 7
   e) 9

This one has *got* to be making most people uncomfortable. It is so... *mathy.* HA! We laugh in the face of such cowing. (It's a word. Look it up).
What do we already know, team brilliant? Hot dogs are out in P2. In P2 there are only THREE possible ways for the winners to go, because there are three players for the one loser spot! D lose, P and S win. P lose, D and S win. S out, D and P win.
(B) wins.

Problem Set 13 – Winners and Losers (Answers on the following page)

Julio is going to the South by Southwest (SXSW) music festival and will attend exactly five shows. The acts he has to chose from are: Alabama Shakes, BettySoo, Candy Claws, Dwellers, Eve 6, Foo Fighters, G$Baby, Holy Grail and Japanther. His selection must conform to the following conditions:

        If he attends BettySoo, he also attends Dwellers or Candy Claws.

        If Julio attends G$Baby or Eve 6 he will not go to BettySoo.

        If he attends Holy Grail then he will also go to Eve 6.

        If Julio does not see BettySoo, he will see Foo Fighters.

1) Which one of the following could be a complete and accurate list of the shows Julio attends?
    a) BettySoo, Candy Claws, Dwellers, Foo Fighters, Holy Grail
    b) Alabama Shakes, Candy Claws, Dwellers, G$Baby, Japanther
    c) Alabama Shakes, BettySoo, Eve 6, Holy Grail, Japanther
    d) Alabama Shakes, BettySoo, Candy Claws, Dwellers, Japanther
    e) Eve 6, Foo Fighters, G$Baby, Holy Grail, Japanther

2) Which one of the following must be false about the acts Julio sees?
    a) BettySoo, Dwellers and Candy Claws are seen
    b) He sees both BettySoo and Foo Fighters
    c) He sees neither Holy Grail nor Eve 6
    d) He sees neither BettySoo nor Foo Fighters
    e) He does not see BettySoo but does see Holy Grail

3) If Julio does not see the Foo Fighters, then what must be true?
    a) He sees Eve 6
    b) He sees G$Baby
    c) He sees both BettySoo and Holy Grail
    d) He sees both Alabama Shakes and G$Baby
    e) He sees both Alabama Shakes and Japanther

4) If Julio does not see Candy Claws, which of the following must be false?
    a) He sees Dwellers
    b) He sees BettySoo
    c) He does not see Foo Fighters
    d) He sees Foo Fighters
    e) He does not see Dwelers

5) Which three acts cannot be amongst the ones Julio sees?
    a) Alabama Shakes, BettySoo and Japanther
    b) Alabama Shakes, BettySoo and Holy Grail
    c) Eve 6, Holy Grail and Foo Fighters
    d) G$Baby, Eve 6 and Foo Fighters
    e) BettySoo, Candy Claws and Dwellers

6) If a new condition is added that says that if BettySoo is seen Dwelers cannot be seen, and if all other rules remain in effect, then which of the following acts must Julio see?
    a) BettySoo
    b) Eve 6
    c) Foo Fighters
    d) G$Baby
    e) Holy Grail

Problem Set 13 EXPLANATION

Here we have another Winner/Loser game with numbers, but *without* the bi-conditionals. The logic should have been a little bit easier for you. Of course we realize that what we just said was completely subjective. Take a walk through the explanation that follows, learn from your mistakes and get a little bit better every day.

STEP ONE: GET A GRIP - What is the nature of the game, who are the players and what are the hidden rules?

We would have to be pretty dim to miss the fact that this is a Winner/Loser game (because it said so at the top of the page). The "flavor" is "numbers". Our players are A, B, C, D, E, F, G, H and J. The hidden rule is that Julio must attend **exactly five shows**. WRITE THAT DOWN! It is a real, honest to God/Allah/Buddah/Elvis rule and it is integral to solving the game. If we are on top of our business, we can see that this will almost certainly be critical when we get to the "calculators" inference step, as well as the picture we draw later.

STEP TWO: FORMAL RULES.
What are you supposed to do here? NUMBER EACH FORMAL RULE and then re-write each rule, one at a time with a corresponding number next to it. When there are conditional logic rules, we CONTRA-POSE each rule immediately!

PAY CLOSE ATTENTION! CONDITION 1 has a disjunctive consequent. Make sure that you leave sufficient room between it and its contra so you can map out the alterative consequents.

> Julio is going to the South by Southwest (SXSW) music festival and will attend exactly five shows. The acts he has to chose from are Alabama Shakes, BettySoo, Candy Claws, Dwellers, Eve 6, Foo Fighters, G$Baby, Holy Grail and Japanther. His selection must conform to the following conditions:
> 1. If he attends BettySoo, he also attends Dwellers or Candy Claws.
> 2. If Julio attends G$Baby or Eve 6 he will not go to BettySoo.
> 3. If he attends Holy Grail then he will also go to Eve 6.
> 4. If Julio does not see BettySoo, he will see Foo Fighters.

$$* \text{ EX 5 selected}$$
$$1.\ B \supset D \vee C$$

$$-D \cdot -C \supset -B$$
$$2.\ G \vee E \supset -B$$
$$B \supset -G \cdot -E$$
$$3.\ H \supset E$$
$$-E \supset -H$$
$$4.\ -B \supset F$$

$$-F \supset B$$

STEP THREE: DRAW A PICTURE

$$A\ B\ C\ D\ E\ F\ G\ H\ J$$

W		L	
— — — — —		— — — —	

STEP FOUR: INFERENCES

Double-up time (because it is winner/loser). Work through all of the antecedents and consequents! We are going to "hold your hand" on this one, just to help a little. If you already have this under control, feel free to skip to the end of the Double-up step and confirm your awesomeness.

Rule 1 says "If B then D or C." Is B an antecedent in any other rule? The contra-positive of rule 2! So we combine the consequents onto BOTH the D and the C because whatever consequents come from B applies to both:

$$1)\ B \supset \underset{\downarrow}{D} \vee C\ \cdot\ -G\ \cdot\ -E$$
$${\llcorner} -G\ \cdot\ -E$$

We can now look for D and C antecedents in an effort to see whether there are differences between them. Lo, there are neither, so the consequences of B having been seen are identical whether Julio sees D or C or both. But now we know that if B is attended, G cannot be. Is –G an antecedent? Nope. We also know that E cannot be attended. Is -E an antecedent? Rule 3's contra. So we can tack on –H:

$$1)\ B \supset \underset{\downarrow}{D} \vee C\ \cdot\ -G\ \cdot\ -E\ \cdot\ -H$$
$${\llcorner} -G\ \cdot\ -E\ \cdot\ -H$$

Is –H an antecedent in any other rule? Nope. So now we have a complete handle on the first rule.

The contra-positive says that if we know –D and –C, we will end up with –B. We can only merge the antecedent if it is an exact match to the antecedent in another rule. There is no other –D and –C antecedent. The consequent, -B, is also the antecedent in rule 4, so the consequent merges:

$$-D\ \cdot\ -C \supset -B\ \cdot\ F$$

"F" is not an antecedent in any rule, so we know the full consequent any time both D and C are not attended at the same time: -B and F.

Rule 2 has a *disjunctive antecedent*. We do not know which one of these two (or both of them) will be "true" and establish the consequent. Fortunately for us, there are no other "G" or "E" antecedents, so we do not need to "split" this rule. We just have the consequent, -B, and it is the antecedent in rule 4, so we merge in the "F":

$$G \lor E \supset -B \cdot F$$

F is not an antecedent anywhere else, so we are done with rule 2. Its contra, however, is just rule 1 again, with "B" as the antecedent.

NEW TRICK! – Rather than waste a lot of time re-writing all of the same bloody rule information from condition 1, we are going to connect it with an arrow:

```
1) B ⊃ D v C · -G ·  -E · -H
↑           ↳ -G ·  -E · -H
 |      -D · -C ⊃ -B · F
 | 2) G v E ⊃ -B · F
 └──  B ⊃ -G · -E
```

This lets us know, if we are dealing with a known "B" scenario, that rule #1 is the one to go to, not contra 2.

Rule 3 has "H" as the antecedent. Are there any other identical antecedents? No. The consequent, "E" is checked to see whether or not it is an antecedent in any other rule. IT IS! In rule 2, G or E gets us –B · F. We can tack them on.

$$H \supset E \cdot \cdot -B \cdot F$$

We saw before that neither –B nor –F are antecedents in any other rule(s), so we are done with this one.

The contra-positive of 3 has –E as the antecedent, and there are no other rules with the same antecedent. The consequent, -H, is not an antecedent anywhere else either.

Rule 4 says that –B is sufficient to establish F. Are either of these terms antecedents anywhere else? They are not. So we can look at the contra.

If we know –F, that is sufficient to establish B. DON'T GET AHEAD OF YOURSELF and go rushing off to merge in rule #1. You have to check "-F" first. It is not an antecedent in any other rule. NOW we can merge in the "B" rule from above, exactly as we did before by using our new trick employing an arrow.

1) B ⊃ D v C · -G · -E · -H
   ⤒   ↳ -G · -E · -H
   -D · -C ⊃ -B · F
2) G v E ⊃ -B · F
   — B ⊃ -G · -E
3) H ⊃ E · -B · F
   -E ⊃ -H
4) -B ⊃ F
   -F ⊃ B ⤸

Now we are done, right? NOT EXACTLY! We have another double-up! For the prize of a 1975 AMC Pacer hatch-back[3], WHAT IS IT? Hint: It might just be in plain sight.

Our hidden rule says that there are five winners and four losers. How does that help us? The contra of rule 4 says that if Julio does not go to F, he has to go to B and cannot go to G, E nor H. -F, -G, -E and –H makes 4 losers! So if he does not go to F, he has to go to A, B, C, D and J! Do any of the other rules prevent Julio from seeing A, B, C, D and J? NO! So it is not a contradiction. So every time F is not in an answer choice, there is one, and only one correct combination of winners and losers. We should mark that!

1) B ⊃ D v C · -G · -E · -H
   ⤒   ↳ -G · -E · -H
   -D · -C ⊃ -B · F
2) G v E ⊃ -B · F
   — B ⊃ -G · -E
3) H ⊃ E · -B · F
   -E ⊃ -H
4) -B ⊃ F
   -F ⊃ B ⤸ (A B C D J = WIN!)

Now that we have done that, we are ready to go back to the top of the inference batting order.

ABSOLUTES - Do we have any **absolutes** in our rules? No. On rare occasions there are absolutes in winner/loser games. This is not such an occasion.

BUNDLES - Are there any **bundles**? Nope.

---

[3] HELLS-NO! We are not actually going to give you one. First off, you reaaallllly do not want one. Second, I do not have one to give you because I wouldn't own one, even as a goof or on a dare. They may (as my uber-dweeb neighbor informs me) be a really sweet ride, but we feel similar to the way Jules Winnfield feels about pork: *"Hey, sewer rat may taste like pumpkin pie, but I'd never know 'cause I wouldn't eat the filthy mother..."*

CALCULATORS - Are there any numerical/mathy-looking **calculators**? YES! Our hidden rule tell us that Julio will go to precisely five shows. There are nine to choose from. We want to note that there are 5 winners and four losers exactly, every time, which seems to be the only purpose served by our picture this time around.

$$5 \text{ win, } 4 \text{ Lose}$$

1) $B \supset D \vee C \cdot \cdot -G \cdot \cdot -E \cdot \cdot -H$
   $\qquad \quad \hookleftarrow -G \cdot \cdot -E \cdot \cdot -H$
   $\qquad -D \cdot \cdot -C \supset -B \cdot F$

2) $G \vee E \supset -B \cdot F$
   $\qquad B \supset -G \cdot \cdot -E$

3) $H \supset E \cdot \cdot -B \cdot F$
   $\qquad -E \supset -H$

4) $-B \supset F$
   $\qquad -F \supset B$ $(A \; B \; C \; D \; J = \text{WIN!})$

DOUBLE-UPS? – Did them. Or have you forgotten.
EXTRAS –
Bi-conditionals – None.
Forced Dichotomies – Because it is winner/loser, it is inherently a forced dichotomy. "Not win" = "lose" and "not lose = win." In an earlier game (competitive food eater's training table) we saw that knowing what happens to a player or set of players in **both** instances of winning and losing can be very beneficial. There, we achieved nearly-complete answers once we saw tacos and hot dogs winning and losing as a pair.

Here, rules 1 and 4 tell us about the only two ways that BettySoo can play out. Rule 1 tells us what happens if BettySoo *is* attended, and rule 4 tells us what happens if BettySoo *is not* attended. ONE OF THOSE TWO THINGS *MUST* HAPPEN. It is a true dichotomy, and Julio is *forced* to do one or the other: if he goes, he goes. If he is abducted by aliens, he does not go.

Right Side Rule - In our present game, rule 1 and its contra say:

1) $B \supset D \vee C \cdot \cdot -G \cdot \cdot -E \cdot \cdot -H$
   $\qquad \quad \hookleftarrow -G \cdot \cdot -E \cdot \cdot -H$
   $\qquad -D \cdot \cdot -C \supset -B \cdot F$

Which means F with D or (inclusive) C, and without G, E, H and B is an allowable answer. If those four *are* out, F, D, C, A and J must be the answer. The point is that we know that F, D and C are allowed to be together at the same time and that B, E G and H can all be out without violating the rules. We promise you this: the only other people in the room who will be aware of this gem of knowledge are the ones who have either read this book or are super logical to begin with. In other words, top LSAT game players. **PAY ATTENTION TO, AND MARK THE RIGHT SIDE OF THE RULES IF NEEDED!** It is not always possible to circle the right side (and sometime doing so makes a mess). So practice and make it a habit to pay attention.

Identifying this major issue allows us to anticipate that there will be a question that turns on the issue, and prepare ourselves in advance to destroy it.

Affirmative Duties - The contra-positive of rule 1 is one, but it is an affirmative duty by the inference we drew (i.e. when we merged "F" into it). This raises yet another subtle issue. Recall that every time we contra-pose a conditional statement, we can "re-contra-pose" end get the original rule back out of it. So after we do the double-ups, we could re-contra-pose and see even more chewy, caramel goodness at the heart of this logical candy bar. We do not do it because that is not part of the games section; we do not need it to get a 180. The rule 1 contra, if re-contra-posed, would say:

$$B \vee \text{-}F \supset D \vee C$$

That would now tell us that –F gets us the same thing as B. But we know that already because the contra of rule four tells us that. This is precisely why you can rely 100% upon the Test Mentors Method. We hit all of the good stuff hard.

Rule 4 and its contra are as well. *When a rule and its contra-positive are both affirmative duty rules, we want to make a note of it.* Any time we **begin** with an affirmative duty, this will be the case. It tells us that we MUST have one, the other or both of the affirmative consequents. (Remember back in the logic section we had the example, "If you don't buy Trix, then you do buy Cap'n Crunch"?)

Contradictions – Are there any? No there are not.

Lone conditionals? Hardly. There are a ton of them.

FREE RANGERS? Do we have any free rangers? "A" and "J" do not appear in *any* of the rules. They are our free rangers. They can come and go as they please, so long as the *logic* does not constrain them. What does that mean? We are glad that you asked! A and J have no rules, but, as we saw in the contra to rule 4, if we know that Julio does not see Foo Fighters (-F) A and J logically *must be winners*. SWEET! So they are free-ish.

Now that step 4 is complete, it is time to do step 5, "DESTROY THE QUESTIONS!"

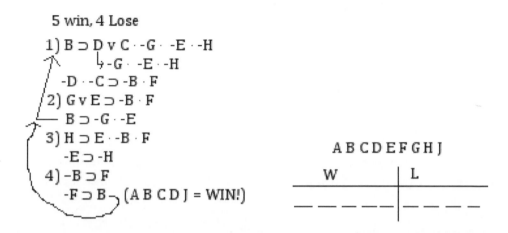

1) $B \supset D \vee C \cdot -G \cdot -E \cdot -H$
  $\hookrightarrow -G \cdot -E \cdot -H$
  $-D \cdot -C \supset -B \cdot F$
2) $G \vee E \supset -B \cdot F$
  $B \supset -G \cdot -E$
3) $H \supset E \cdot -B \cdot F$
  $-E \supset -H$
4) $-B \supset F$
  $-F \supset B$ ⌐ (A B C D J = WIN!)

A B C D E F G H J

W	L

1) Which one of the following could be a complete and accurate list of the shows Julio attends?

    a) BettySoo, Candy Claws, Dwellers, Foo Fighters, Holy Grail
    b) Alabama Shakes, Candy Claws, Dwellers, G$Baby, Japanther
    c) Alabama Shakes, BettySoo, Eve 6, Holy Grail, Japanther
    d) Alabama Shakes, BettySoo, Candy Claws, Dwellers, Japanther
    e) Eve 6, Foo Fighters, G$Baby, Holy Grail, Japanther

All this is asking us is, "Which one of the following does not violate any rules?" As always with these kinds of questions, when they appear first, we start with (a) and we work our way down the list. Do you remember *why* we do it that way, and why we do not spastically start looking at all of the choices, scanning for rule violations? BECAUSE THAT IS WHAT IDIOTS DO! The answers to these kinds of questions are ordered in such a way that we can learn form the work we have done, find errors we may have made, and catch additional inferences we may have missed. We **_lose_** all of that if we start jumping about like undisciplined children.

(a) Can B, C, D, F and H be the shows that Julio sees? Rule 1 says that if he sees B, he cannot see G, E nor H. Wrong answer. Cross it off and move.

(b) Does A, C, D, G, J violate any rules? WE KNOW that A and J are free rangers, so we don't need to check them. C is not an antecedent, so it being there matters not. Same with both D and G. So we are in the clear, correct? NO! Why not? Rule 4. We have an affirmative duty to have either B or F. Oops. INCORRECT answer. THIS IS PRECISELY WHY we check for the affirmative duties. Let that be a lesson to those of you who cut corners on that part of the process.

(c) How about A, B, E, H, J ? It has the same problem as (a) in that it violates rule 1.

(d) Here is where the people who do not know that "or" is inclusive screw up. They think that having both D and C in the answer makes it incorrect. Ha ha ha! A, B, C, D, J complies with rule 1. The contra does not apply because neither C nor D is missing. Rule 2 does not apply, and the contra is just rule 1, and it *still* does not apply. Rule 3 does not apply because there is no H on the list. The contra says that if E is not there (it is not) then H cannot be, and it is not. Rule 4 does not apply and ... THE CONTRA TELLS US THAT IT IS EXACTLY CORRECT! At this point we circle answer choice D and get the heck out of there without reading E (which you can check for yourself, but it has to be incorrect and you are wasting your time when you do, and that is a bad habit, which is something you do not want to develop, unless you want to remain a non-lawyer).

This problem demonstrates what we were talking about before earlier. Answer choices A, B and C forced us to deal with the two most important rules in the game: the "B" rule and the affirmative duty rule. Had we missed them during inferences, the answers would have forced us to acknowledge them. The correct answer also forced us to use the contra of the affirmative duty rule. Had we not noted that it is a "perfect" rule (giving us a complete and perfect answer) we would have seen it then and there.

2) Which one of the following must be false about the acts Julio sees?
      a) BettySoo, Dwellers and Candy Claws are seen
      b) He sees both BettySoo and Foo Fighters
      c) He sees neither Holy Grail nor Eve 6
      d) He sees neither BettySoo nor Foo Fighters
      e) He does not see BettySoo but does see Holy Grail

Here we have a naked must-be-false. No additional information is provided, so we first "Go with what we know." What do we know? "B" is the key player (B is the big shot in rule 1 and –B is the affirmative duty rule with F). Scan the B and –B choices and see if there is a mention of "F". Choice "D" says that She sees neither B nor F, a clear violation of the affirmative duty! That has to be the answer. Circle it and don't bother with the others.

For the most part the LSAT is checking whether or not you know the fundamentals of logic. Because you now do know them, you can easily find answers. When you see a rule that combines with a lot of other rules, you know that there will be questions about those inferences. When you see an affirmative duty rule, there will be at least one question based upon it to see whether or not you recognized it and know how it works. That is why it is so imperative that you learn ALL OF THE THINGS WE TAUGHT in the logic section.

It is entirely possible that you did not get the answer quickly on your own. Speed will come with time and practice. Just keep doing things correctly, as prescribed in this book. Remember that when you are answering questions in step 5, you go with what you know first. If you started with (a) and worked your way down, remember that you only have to do that with the first question when it is a "complete and accurate list" question. Try not to get in the habit of doing that with all of the questions, as it is not super efficient. Remember, we do it on the first one because there is, "Learnification[4]" in the process.

As for the other choices:

---

[4] Man, how we miss former President W.

(a) is incorrect because in rule 1, "or" is inclusive.
(b) Is incorrect by the right-side rule in 4 and contra-positive.
(c) Is incorrect because he can skip E and H according to the contra-positive of rule 3.
(d) Is still correct.
(e) That's just rule 3, so it can be true. Duh.

3) If Julio does not see the Foo Fighters, then what must be true?
     a) He sees Eve 6
     b) He sees G$Baby
     c) He sees both BettySoo and Holy Grail
     d) He sees both Alabama Shakes and G$Baby
     e) He sees both Alabama Shakes and Japanther

PAY DIRT, BABY! We worked out the contra of 4 about a year ago! We know all that there is to know! It has to be (e), SLAM DUNK! "In your face, Flanders!"

BUT WHAT IF I DID NOT GET ALL OF THE INFERENCES?

Let's be honest, shall we? There is always a chance that you missed something in the inferences, and questions such as #3 here are not so obvious based upon what you already know...mostly because you do not already know it. It turns out that the only thing you lose is a spot of time. You will still get the correct answer. Pinky-swears.

The question asks what *must* be true if Julio skips the Foo's. We are going to use what we shall refer to from now on as the *Pencil Protocols*. ALWAYS follow the pencil protocols whenever you are using your pencil to solve logic games problems! MEMORIZE IT!

The steps in using the pencil protocols are:
1) Re-picture whatever it is that you are using for a picture. In the case of winner/loser games, there is no picture, there are just players. So you write them all out.
2) Apply the new "if" that the call of the question provides **_to your re-picture_**. Remember to NEVER touch an original picture with all of the work that you did to it.
    Go to the rules and see what the rules indicate must happen.
    - If the rules tell you that something else must occur, apply that change to your re-picture and repeat step 3.
    - If the rules do not indicate that anything else is to occur (i.e. no further changes need to happen to your re-picture) then you have the answer.

So for problem #3, let's *pretend* that we did not get ANY of the inferences, and we only wrote out the rules and contra-posed them.

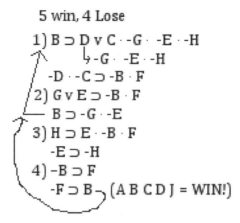

5 win, 4 Lose
1) B ⊃ D v C · · -G · · -E · · -H
       ↳ -G · · -E · · -H
   -D · · -C ⊃ -B · F
2) G v E ⊃ -B · F
    B ⊃ -G · · -E
3) H ⊃ E · · -B · F
   -E ⊃ -H
4) -B ⊃ F
   -F ⊃ B → (A B C D J = WIN!)

Our first pencil protocol tells us to re-picture by listing out all of our players:

ABCDEFGHJ

W	L
— — — — —	— — — —

Second we, "apply the if":

ABCDEⱯGHJ

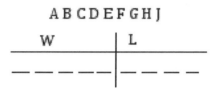

W	
— — — — —	F — — —

Third, we go to the rules and see what they say. The contra of rule 4 says –F proves B. B is a winner:

AⱮCDEⱯGHJ

W	
B — — — —	F — — —

Because the rules told us that something in our picture changed, we have to repeat pencil protocol 3 again. B is a winner. We check to see whether or not the rules force anything else to happen. Rule 1 says that if B wins, we have to have either D or C, and the contra of 2 says that we cannot have G and we cannot have E as winners. So we add those to our re-picture:

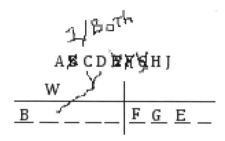

Because we made a change, we repeat rule 3...again. "C v D" is not an antecedent, and neither is –G. However –E is, and it tells us that H is also a loser. So we have to apply that change to our re-picture:

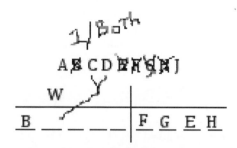

And now, Robert is your mom's brother (Google it). A, B, C, D and J win because the loser side is full up.

3) If Julio does not see the Foo Fighters, then what must be true?
 a) He sees Eve 6
 b) He sees G$Baby
 c) He sees both BettySoo and Holy Grail
 d) He sees both Alabama Shakes and G$Baby
 e) He sees both Alabama Shakes and Japanther

Look at (a): Must Julio see E? NO! HE CANNOT!
Look at (b): Must Julio see G? NO! HE CANNOT!
Look at (c): Must Julio see B and H? NO! He cannot see H.
Look at (d) Must Julio see A and G? NO! He still cannot see G!
THE CORRECT ANSWER MUST BE (e), so you circle that little piggy and you move on without wasting a second, because you wasted a ton of seconds solving this bad boy inefficiently. (e) is correct, by the way.

JUST TO BE PERFECTLY CLEAR: We use our pencils and the pencil protocols **_ONLY_** **_WHEN_** we have exhausted everything we already know. Just because you have to go to the pencil, that does not necessarily mean that you messed up (i.e. missed inferences). Sometimes the game and the questions are designed to force you to do things by brute pencil force. So don't worry about time when you have to go to the pencil protocols. JUST DO THEM CORRECTLY AND YOU WILL DESTROY THE QUESTION!

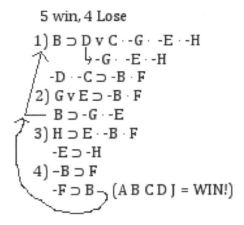

5 win, 4 Lose

1) B ⊃ D v C ·· -G · -E ·· -H
         ⌐-G · -E · -H
   -D ·· -C ⊃ -B · F
2) G v E ⊃ -B · F
    B ⊃ -G ·· -E
3) H ⊃ E ·· -B · F
   -E ⊃ -H
4) -B ⊃ F
   -F ⊃ B ⌐ (A B C D J = WIN!)

4) If Julio does not see Candy Claws, which of the following must be false?
   a) He sees Dwellers
   b) He sees BettySoo
   c) He does not see Foo Fighters
   d) He sees Foo Fighters
   e) He does not see Dwellers

Alas, we care confronted with what *appears to be* an actual challenge. First, it is asking what can NEVER be true when Julio skips C, i.e. –C is the antecedent. –C by itself tells us naught... if we are only partly competent with our logic and are only looking for –C as an antecedent (remember that in contra of rule 1, we have a conjunctive: we have to have –D AND –C for it to be sufficient to establish the consequent). But what else do we **ALREADY** know *for sure* about C? We just learned in problem #3 that if F is a loser, A, B, C, D and J MUST BE WINNERS! So if Julio skips C, we know that he cannot also skip F, because skipping F forces him to go to C, but the problem says that he definitely does not go to C.

The first step in Destroying the Questions is *Go With What You Know*. The correct answers to the questions you have already destroyed are things that you already know. YOU HAVE TO REMEMBER THAT THEY ARE NOT JUST ANSWERS, THEY ARE LOGICALLY VALID INFERENCES AND ARE THEREFORE VALUABLE TOOLS!

Are you seeing why it is so bloody important to learn ALL of this stuff, and well?

5) Which three acts cannot be amongst the ones Julio sees?
   a) Alabama Shakes, BettySoo and Japanther
   b) Alabama Shakes, BettySoo and Holy Grail
   c) Eve 6, Holy Grail and Foo Fighters
   d) G$Baby, Eve 6 and Foo Fighters
   e) BettySoo, Candy Claws and Dwellers

Go with what you know! You know that A and J are free rangers, and that rules 1 and 4 are the hot rules (as well as the complete answer from contra 4). Choice (a) is right out of the complete answer from contra 4. INCORRET. Choice (b) talks about A and B both, so rule 1 applies (because of B). B eliminates G, E, and H. Choice (b) has B and H together, which is not possible, so that has to be the answer. Yea team.

6) If a new condition is added that says that if BettySoo is seen, then Dwellers cannot be seen, and if all other rules remain in effect, then which of the following acts must Julio see?
   a) BettySoo
   b) Eve 6
   c) Foo Fighters
   d) G$Baby
   e) Holy Grail

"DON'T PANIC!" This is the classic, "Let's see if they will panic," questions. Read the call of the question carefully. It says that all of the rules are still in effect, we are just adding an additional one for the purposes of this question. What is this new, spooky condition? $B \supset -D$.

Some people may think to themselves, "CONTRADICTION! Condition 1 says that B is sufficient to prove D or C." That is exactly what is being tested... only not. This question is designed to test whether or not you can see that it is **not** a contradiction, but rather a **disjunctive syllogism**. That is one of those things that we told you a long time ago to be on the lookout for because they are easy to miss.

On top of that, the question is designed to test your ability to look beyond the most superficial aspect of the question. It gives us a new B antecedent, but that B is thoroughly *hypothetical*. It says that if B wins then four acts lose: D, G, E and H. WHAT DOES THAT MEANS, SPORTS FANS? The other five acts win: A, B, C, F and J. But all of that is contingent upon B winning. What if it doesn't? Aha!!! That's rule 4 again, and F has to win. Are you reading our mail here, sunshine? If B wins, F wins. If B loses, F wins. B can only win and lose, but in either case F wins. That makes "C" the correct answer.

REMEMBER that whenever they introduce a new rule, it (a) is usually the last question in the set, (b) is an addition to all of the other rules and (c) is just there to throw panic into the equation. In this question, we calmly looked at what the new condition added to the mix, looked at how that augmented all of our other hard work, and inferred that the Foo Fighters were always going to have to be seen. That is a heck of a lot easier than doing everything in a piecemeal fashion.

Procedure Games – Medium Rare

Following the procedure used to be a much bigger deal in the land of LSAT. It is a less-tested concept, and is under-emphasized by most of the people who teach games. What you do *not* want is to have one of these bad boys rear its ugly head on test day and allow yourself to freak out because you did not practice them enough. We are going to show you how the methods we have already taught you apply to these games, and we are going to give you plenty of practice. Remember that just because they are not tested often, that does not mean that you are unlikely to see them. The LSAC could, without notice, give you nothing but Procedure games on your LSAT[1], and "Chance favors the prepared mind.[2]"

These games are rare because they tend to *not* be testing the type of logic that is the dominant kinds used in law, i.e. the categorical and propositional/conditional. These games challenge you to be able to apply a set procedure to a factual scenario and (a) predict future outcomes based upon a set of hypothetical circumstances and applying the rules (Simon Says to do...), and (b) retrodict from a given state of affairs and the procedural rules a past state of affairs (what Simon Said). Here are examples of each, just so we are certain that we are all on the same page. PLEASE BEAR IN MIND that the following example is not, in any way, meant to exemplify what an actual game looks like. It is here to demonstrate and clarify principles. It is overly-simple by design.

> Three silver coins are sitting on a table. Each coin has a picture of the Titanic on one face and a garden digging tool on the other[3]. Only one side of each coin faces up at any given time. Determining which side of each coin faces up is determined by the following rules:
> A "cycle" is a process in which every coin is turned so its opposite side faces up.
> The three coins cannot have the same side facing up.

PREDICT – If the coins begin with the sides T, G, G facing up, what will the coins have facing up after two cycles?

---

[1] This is almost certainly not going to happen because of the pre-set curve. Think about it: if there were four Procedure games on the LSAT, that would give people who are Jedi at them a huge advantage, and it would skew badly the scores of people who suck at them but are otherwise great at games. So, although there is a *chance* you could see four of these games on the LSAT, there is also a chance that a whale will materialize out of thin air and begin falling to earth next to a bowl of petunias.

[2] Quoting Louis Pasteur, genius and giver of commercially available chocolate milk, from a lecture delivered in 1854 at the University of Lille. Sure he came up with cures for rabies and other diseases as well as a vaccine for anthrax. But it all pales in comparison to a tall, cold glass of chocolate milk on demand.

[3] "Ships and garden digging tools. Ships and garden digging tools. Gotta get me some more ships and garden digging tools."

If you flip coin 1 twice, you would switch it to G then back to T.... Then you would realize that every even number of cycles returns the coin to its original face up, and that odd numbers of cycles change them.

RETRODICT – If the three coins read G, T, G then which of the following must have been their position three cycles ago?

Going "back in time" applies the same rules in reverse. Because we have "binary" circumstances (i.e. only two choices) the rules apply exactly the same way forwards and backwards. Three cycles back is odd, so G, T, G had to be T, G, T.

As you can see, the basic idea is that you are going to be tested on whether you can follow a "thread" of reasoning in either direction chronologically. This is a great way to test whether or not you have another critical set of inference skills. As a law student and as a lawyer, you are constantly required to think both ahead and backwards in time, applying the law to factual circumstances.

PROBLEM SET 14 – Procedure (Answers and explanations on next page)

There are four circular knobs arranged in a row from left to right on a panel, numbered 1 through 4 from left to right. In a "cycle," each knob turns either clockwise or counter-clockwise and can turn an unlimited number of rotations in either direction. Each knob has etched upon it five letters, A, B, C, D, and E, in that clockwise order around its edge, with "E" considered the highest letter and A the lowest. The reading of each knob is indicated by the letter that is at the top of the knob. The knobs readings change according to the following conditions:

Odd numbered knobs spin clockwise, even numbered knobs spin counter-clockwise.

Every knob is rotated one letter increment more than the knob to its immediate left.

In any cycle, every knob turns at least one position.

1) If knobs 1 through 4 read D, C, A, E respectively and knob two is moved three positions, the new knob positions must have which of the following readings?

A) A, E, E, A
B) A, A, E, C
C) B, B A, E
D) B, A, B, E
E) C, A, C, D

2) If the knobs read D,A,A,D and we know that knob 4 was moved four from its last position, then the previous reading of the knobs must have been which of the following?

A) D, E, E, D
B) A, D, D, A
C) E, D, D, E
D) D, A, D, A
E) C, C, D, C

3) After one cycle, if the knobs read A, A, A, A then their respective readings immediately prior to the cycle could have been:

A) C, C E, A
B) D, D, D, D
C) D, C, E, A
D) C, C, C, D
E) C, C, C, C

4) If three of the knobs all read the same letter, how many different possible letter combinations could be made on the next cycle?

A) 5
B) 10
C) 25
D) 50
E) infinite

5) If, after a given cycle, knob 2 reads the same as it did before the cycle, then knob 1 must read:

A) One position higher than it previously did
B) Two position higher than it previously did
C) Three position higher than it previously did
D) Five position higher than it previously did
E) The same as it did previously.

184

STEP ONE- Get a Grip: the nature of the game, the players and the hidden rules.
Nature: "Procedure" game.
Players: four identical knobs, 1-4, having letters arranged in a circle from A through E: A=low, E=High
Hidden rules are: (a) the knobs turn either clockwise or counter-clockwise, (b) a "cycle" is one set of turns, (c) the knobs can spin an unlimited number of times, (d) that the reading of the knob is the "top" letter's position.

Next we have to number and re-write our three formal rules, which are:

1) Odd = Clockwise, Even = Counter-clockwise.
2) Each knob turns 1 more than knob to its left.
3) Each cycle, every knob must move.

Step Three: Draw a Picture. Well... this does not fit into one of our basic pictures exactly. We know that there will be four knobs, 1 through 4, left to right. We ALWAYS make our drawing around the most definite information we have. There are two solid things: the 1-4 and the letters around the knob. So we picture both:

```
        A
   E        B
     D    C        ___  ___  ___  ___
                    1    2    3    4
```

That was hardly any trouble at all. We have all of the positions for all four of the switches available in the one knob. Think about it for a second. The "reading" of the knob is at the top... they are trying to trick you into thinking that the "top" matters... but it does not. Look at our picture of the knob. If "C" is the reading, we put our pencil on "C" and that becomes the "top". In other words, the "top" is wherever we say it is, or wherever they say the "reading" is. If we spin the knob three positions clockwise, then the turning knob "spins" B under our "top", then "A", then E. HA HA! We win.

STEP FOUR- Inferences
ABSOLUTES: Are there any? YES! There are several.
Knobs 1 and 3 spin clockwise. Knobs 2 and 4 spin counter-clockwise. Each knob moves one more than the knob to its left. Each of these can be put into our drawing:

```
  2,4           A      1,3
     \  E           B   \        ___  ___  ___  ___
                              1    2    3    4
         D    C        # turns = +1 L to R !
```

Ta da! All three things that we know are in the drawing!

BUNDLES: None

CALCULATORS: Hmmm... Here is an interesting proposition for sure. We have a rule that looks very math-like. Each knob turns 1 more than the one to its immediate left. That means that if knob 1 turns two positions, knob 2 turns three, knob 3 turns four and knob 4 turns five. What if, instead, we know that knob 4 turns six spaces? Do we know how many 1, 2 and 3 turned? DUH! If 4 turned six letters, then 3 turned five, knob 2 turned four and knob 1 turned three. In other words, going from right to left we subtract one number of spaces each time we move down a knob, which is the opposite of going from left to right on the list.

And then there are the knobs themselves, which turn in alternating directions. 1 and 3 turn clockwise. If knob 1 reads "A" and it turns clockwise one space, then "E" rotates into the top spot. The letters in the picture, if they could move, would march around in a circle clockwise...but they cannot move. So we either have to imagine it (not so easy for many people) or realize that if we know where 1 or 3 begin, we can put our pencil on them and move the pencil in the opposite direction, representing the "read" position moving. Try it! Put your pencil point on the "A" and pretend that you are on knob 1. If the letters were to spin clockwise three spaces, the "E" would rotate up on the first move (move your pencil to "E") then "D" would pop up (Move pencil) then "C" would (one more exhausting pencil move). So for 1 and 3 our pencil moves in the opposite direction (counter clockwise) and for 2 and 4 our pencil point moves clockwise! THAT IS IF WE ARE LOOKING FOR THE PREDICTIVE, FUTURE OUTCOME. We also know that we will be asked to retrodict, so we know that for the past positions, we start from the known, present position and we do the opposite, i.e. we FOLLOW THE ARROWS FOR PAST EVENTS! We should add that to our drawing!

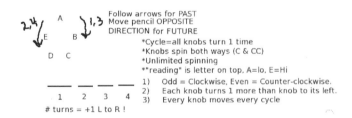

One last calculation we can see is that any time a knob moves 5 spaces, it ends up ON THE SAME LETTER! So if a knob is turned 10 spaces, it ends up on the same letter as well. Hmmmmmm.

DOUBLE-UPS: You may have found this in the Absolutes or Calculator step, but if you did not, hopefully you got it on the Double-ups. If all of the knobs have to move, then the fewest number of spaces each knob can turn are one for knob one, two for knob 2 etc. There is no maximum (that is the hidden rule that Doubles-up with rule 3) BUT, there really is, because every 5 positions is putting the knob right back where it started. If a knob moved, say, 16 positions, the first 15 would be irrelevant because every 5th click would put us back to where we began. So really, 16 positions = 1 position. By the same reasoning, 12 positions = 2 positions because the first 10 mean nothing.

EXTRAS: There are no conditional logic rules, but we want to run through them anyway. There are no Bi-conditionals and there are no forced dichotomies (binary logic). There are also no right side rules. Any Affirmative duty rules? YES! Every knob must move every cycle! Mark rule #3 as an affirmative duty! What about contradictions? None. Obviously there is not a lone conditional.

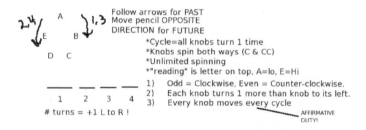

Follow arrows for PAST
Move pencil OPPOSITE
DIRECTION for FUTURE
*Cycle=all knobs turn 1 time
*Knobs spin both ways (C & CC)
*Unlimited spinning
*"reading" is letter on top, A=lo, E=Hi
1)   Odd = Clockwise, Even = Counter-clockwise.
2)   Each knob turns 1 more than knob to its left.
3)   Every knob moves every cycle

turns = +1 L to R !

AFFIRMATIVE DUTY!

FREE RANGERS: Nada. Each knob has a rule and all of the letters are locked into place about the edge of the circular knob. Done deal daddy-o.

You may now be thinking, "Wow. I have a drawing but I have not filled in anything." This is true. These kinds of games are not designed to test your ability to figure things out in advance. They are designed to test your ability to clearly comprehend a set of instructions and follow them. Sure, they leave the average test taker feeling insecure about how little they filled in. That is because the average test taker has no idea what is really going on. Each question will have to provide us with information (some starting or ending point) in order to allow us to figure out an answer.

REMEMBER that Procedure games are testing your ability to follow a set of steps and iterative processes in two directions, forward in time and backwards in time. WE OWN THE **PROCESSES**, so we own the game.

STEP FIVE: DESTROY the questions.

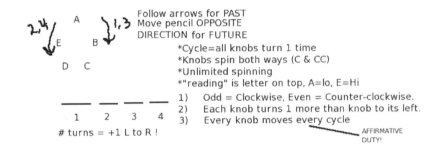

Follow arrows for PAST
Move pencil OPPOSITE
DIRECTION for FUTURE

*Cycle=all knobs turn 1 time
*Knobs spin both ways (C & CC)
*Unlimited spinning
*"reading" is letter on top, A=lo, E=Hi

1)   Odd = Clockwise, Even = Counter-clockwise.
2)   Each knob turns 1 more than knob to its left.
3)   Every knob moves every cycle

AFFIRMATIVE DUTY!

1)   If knobs 1 through 4 read D, C, A, E respectively and knob two is moved three positions, the new knob positions must have which of the following readings?

  A) A, E, E, A
  B) A, A, E, C
  C) B, B A, E
  D) B, A, B, E
  E) C, A, C, D

What do we already know? Knob 2 read C, and it is moved three positions counter-clockwise. Our picture tells us to put our pencil on the C and move it in the opposite direction of the 2,4 arrow three places. We end up on A. Knob 1 read D and was spun clockwise TWO positions. Put your pencil on the D, move it two spaces in the opposite direction of the 1,3 arrow and you end up on B. At this point, we have the answer, because choice D is the only one that has B, A as the first two letters. We should circle it, bubble it in and move on.

Now, **only because** this is our first encounter with this kind of game, we will look at the other answer choices and the *process* of determining the correct positions.

Knob 3 spins one more than knob 2 did, or four spaces, counter-clockwise beginning with A. Put your pencil on the A, move it four letters in the opposite direction of the 1,3 arrow and you should end up on B. Knob four has to spin five positions (one more than knob 3) counter-clockwise beginning with E. Because there are five numbers, five "clicks" of the knob will land us back on E. So the final position has to be B, A, B, E. Thoroughly annoying.

2) If the knobs read D,A,A,D and we know that knob 4 was moved four from its last position, then the previous reading of the knobs must have been which of the following?

  A) D, E, E, D
  B) A, D, D, A
  C) E, D, D, E
  D) D, A, D, A
  E) C, C, D, C

Again, thoroughly obnoxious. For knob 4, put your pencil on D, follow the arrow for knob 4 four spaces and end up on E. That tells us that the correct answer has to be (C). YOU SHOULD CIRCLE IT, bubble it in on your answer form and move on.

Once again, just to be complete: knob 3 had to have been spun three spaces, so put your pencil on A, follow the 3 arrow three spaces and you get D. Knob 2 was spun two spaces, so put your pencil on A and move two spaces in the 2 arrow direction to get to D. Finally, knob 1 was moved one position, so put your pencil on the D and move one position in the direction of the 1 arrow to E. So the previous reading was E, D, D, E. What a horror show.

Here again we see why having an absolute, inviolable set of processes saves our bacon. If we had not taken the time to figure out that the direction of a spinning knob and a moving pencil are *opposite* for future events and the *same* for past events, we could easily miss every question.

3) After one cycle, if the knobs read A, A, A, A then their respective readings immediately prior to the cycle could have been:
A) C, C, E, A
B) D, D, D, D
C) D, C, E, A
D) C, C, C, D
E) C, C, C, C

Well we know something already, don't we? Actually we know a lot of somethings. Going backwards in time, we follow the arrows with our pencil point: that is a biggie. So is the fact that we only care about FIVE moves or less. If knob 4 moved the "maximum" of five, then it would end up on "A" again and knob 3 would have to move four positions to "E". We can check all answer choices that end in "A" and know that knob 3 has to be "E". Answer A has that, C does not so we can cross it off. If 4A and 3E work, then 2 had to read what? "C", which answer (A) has. What about knob 1? It would have to be two positions in the direction of the 1 arrow (clockwise) for the answer of 1C. (A) has to be correct!

4) If three of the knobs all read the same letter, how many different possible letter combinations could be made on the next cycle?
A) 5
B) 10
C) 25
D) 50
E) infinite

This is just a very impolite attempt at seeing something elementary, and which, as a college educated individual, you should know. First there is an attempt to get you to freak out. "They didn't tell me enough to figure it out!" You are supposed to think

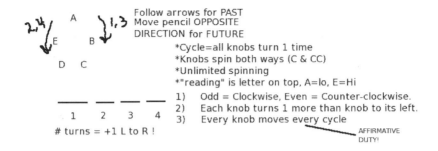

Follow arrows for PAST
Move pencil OPPOSITE
DIRECTION for FUTURE

*Cycle=all knobs turn 1 time
*Knobs spin both ways (C & CC)
*Unlimited spinning
*"reading" is letter on top, A=lo, E=Hi

1) Odd = Clockwise, Even = Counter-clockwise.
2) Each knob turns 1 more than knob to its left.
3) Every knob moves every cycle

AFFIRMATIVE
DUTY!

turns = +1 L to R !

that. Then you are supposed to panic and start acting like someone who really does not belong in law school. CHILLAX! They have to have told you everything you need to know to solve it, and they did.

If three of the knobs read the same thing, then there are exactly how many ways that they can read? Not to be insulting to those of you who are getting it, but the answer to that query is, A, A, A or B, B, B or C, C, C or D, D, D or E, E, E. You might be thinking, "But I don't know which one is number 1 or number 3 or...." IT DOES NOT MATTER! Each knob can only spin to FIVE positions, otherwise, it is just repeating itself, so to speak. The three that are the same all have to be in one of five positions. As for the last knob, it can only be in one of five positions. So we could have four A knobs, or 3 A's and a B, three A's and a C.... We could have three B's and an A, four B's, three B's can a C.... IT'S JUST 5x5=25!

5) If, after a given cycle, knob 2 reads the same as it did before the cycle, then knob 1 must read:
A) One position higher than it previously did
B) Two position higher than it previously did
C) Three position higher than it previously did
D) Five position higher than it previously did
E) The same as it did previously.

What do we know already? If 2 reads the same as before, then it spun some multiple of five, and we don't care what that was. We just treat it as if it were five. So knob 1 moved four positions in the opposite direction of the 1,3 arrow in the drawing, which lands you, no matter where you begin, exactly one position higher than where you started.

Now we want you to notice something about question five. Imagine if you will, that you are a person who got the whole "which direction do I move the pencil when the knob spins," thing bass-ackwards. You could have chopped through the first four questions very quickly and very incorrectly, all the while believing that you nailed them because the test makers included the wrong answers that matched your wrong answers in the first four problems. Then comes number five. If you also did it incorrectly, you would be looking for, "Four positions higher than it previously did," thinking that to be the correct answer. But it was not correct, and it was not there on the list. Suddenly you would have been losing control of your bodily functions. You would realize that you screwed up hard. You would start to panic. You would feel ill, and you would lose your focus on the next game you do and on the next section or two, your confidence crushed.

KNOWING EVERY STEP OF THE METHOD, BEING ABLE TO USE THEM ALL WELL AND NEVER SKIPPING ANY STEP OR CUTTING CORNERS LEADS TO A CRUSHING LOGIC GAMES PERFORMANCE, EVEN IN THE TRICKIEST OF SITUATIONS. Our method saves you from the score killing traps that the test has in store for you. Being regimented, careful, thorough, mature in your thoughts and actions...these are the qualities of a great test taker and a great lawyer.

This method we have taught you is, in all actuality, just a rigid checklist that forces you to *think* about every issue presented in the game you are dealing with and to bring every necessary weapon to bear. YOU can learn. You can adapt. You can get better. The test cannot change. It is about the immutable laws of logic. Once you have the logic down tight, you crush the test and you *deserve* to go to law school for free.

We have set up another procedure game for you on the next page. Work it through by bringing everything you know (which is quite a bit) to bear.

PROBLEM SET 15 (Answers in Appendix "B")

The software company MacroTrugid is creating a security code algorithm. Each "code" consists of four "clusters" arranged A through D, from left to right. Each "cluster" consists of four non-negative numerical digits. Each code must satisfy the following conditions:
No more than two of the clusters can have the same first digit.
No more than two of the clusters can have the same last digit.
Each code is created by having an initial cluster A, and each succeeding cluster is the result of one of three operations performed on the cluster immediately preceding it: replace a single digit with a different one, swapping the first digit and the last digit of the preceding cluster, reversing the order of the digits in the cluster before it.
All three operations must be used in creating a code.

1) Which of the following could be a complete and accurate code?
a) A: 2437 B: 2737 C: 2612 D: 2962
b) A: 3325 B: 3327 C: 7327 D: 7237
c) A: 2112 B: 2119 C: 9112 D: 9212
d) A: 9775 B: 5779 C: 5799 D: 9975
e) A: 6427 B: 7426 C: 8426 D: 9426

2) If cluster B is 2643 and cluster D is 3467, then cluster C must be:
a) 2647
b) 3647
c) 3764
d) 7643
e) 7463

3) If cluster A is 7832 then cluster B can be which one of the following?
a) 2387
b) 9832
c) 7839
d) 8832
e) 9832

4) Each of the following could be cluster A except:
a) 2000
b) 2771
c) 2772
d) 2773
e) 2774

5) If cluster A is 8609 and cluster C is 9678, which of the following must be true?
a) B is an inversion of A.
b) C is an inversion of B.
c) C is a swap of the first and last digits of B.
d) D is a swap of the first and last digits of C.
e) D is an inversion of C.

6) Which of the following must be false?
a) B is an inversion of A.
b) B is a swap of the first and last digits of A.
c) C is an inversion of A.
d) C is a change of one digit form B.
e) D is a swap of the first and last digits of C.

Drawing Games

And so we arrive at the final single-action game, the "Drawing" game. We had a real knock-down, drag-out brawl here at Test Mentors over this one because, to some of us, these games function pretty much like Procedure games: you are told how something is drawn, you follow that procedure and, "Sketch it up... Leonardo Da Vinci![1]" Then you answer questions based on how well you followed the directions. To others among us[2], these are not Procedure games in the least bit. Drawing a picture is just a set of inferences based upon the rules. If you inferred properly, then you can answer the questions. You can think of them either way.

Regardless, when you come across one of these games, you will want to NOT be intimidated by the fact that they look different from every other kind of game. They tend to give you a vague notion of what is going on in the fact pattern, and then they use the formal rules to define how you have to draw things. Typically these games test your ability to follow the instructions and then to determine the most efficient way to do things (though they can also ask you the *least* efficient way to do things as well). In the example that follows, the questions will revolve around the most efficient way to get around in a nature park, with efficiency being defined as the least number of moves one has to make in traveling between places. Here is an example with a walk-through.

> Yolanda is visiting a nature park that has eight exhibits: Aquatics, Bobcats, Chimps, Dingoes, Elephants, Falcons, Giraffes and Hippos. She will "move" between various exhibits, one at a time, throughout the day only on the paths connecting them. Any change of exhibits, whether or not she has visited it previously or not, constitutes a move, and beginning at any exhibit constitutes that exhibit having been visited. The exhibits are arranged in the following manner:
>
> A single circular path connects Aquatics directly to Bobcats, Bobcats directly to Chimps, Chimps directly to Dingoes, Dingoes directly to Elephants and Elephants directly back to Aquatics.
>
> A single straight path connects Dingoes to Bobcats with Hippos in between.
>
> Giraffes are located outside of the circular path, and a single path connects Giraffes to Dingoes, and a different path connects Chimps to Giraffes.
>
> The Falcon exhibit is located outside of the circular path and has two paths leading away from it: one directly to Elephants, a second going directly to Bobcats.

---

[1] Quoting Tony Cox as "Marcus" in *Bad Santa,* Dimension Films et seq. 2003. If you can quote this entire Tony Cox scene, buy yourself a HUGE shot of Pierre Ferrand Cognac. You deserve it.

[2] Congratulations to the astute readers out there who remember us saying, over one hundred-odd pages ago, that there is no "we," just "me." As it turns out, however, I happen to have a significant number of personalities, each of which has a very independent, outspoken nature. This should help reconcile any perceived contradictions, contraries and/or sub-contraries. We all thank you for your patience and indulgence.

There you have it. Does not seem very "logicy," does it? But let us play along, just for yucks and grins.

STEP ONE: GET A GRIP – NATURE: Drawing. PLAYERS: EXHIBITS: A, B, C, D, E, F, G, H. PEOPLE: Yolanda (Y). HIDDEN RULES: Y stays on paths, any change of exhibits = a move, starting Ex = visited, she moves from exhibit to exhibit, one at a time.

MAJOR IMPORTANT ANNOUNCEMENT!
SOMETIMES the description for the "Drawing" will come in the form of Hidden Rules. Roll with it. Rather than re-writing the hidden rules, DRAW THEM. You MUST be extremely careful and make sure that the drawing you make follows the description in the Hidden Rules. We recommend that you mark each one as you add it to the drawing.

Second, we number and rewrite the FORMAL RULES: Here is where things get a little interesting. If we are rewriting the rules, and the rules tell us how to make a drawing, can we not do the drawing and the rules at the same time? YES! We highly recommend that you do. Number them and then draw the picture from the rules.

1)

This should look familiar. Remember our old friend the knob from the Procedure game?

Rule 2 says that a _**single straight path**_ connects D to B with H in between. This is important because this forces H to be on the inside of the circle. If we put H outside, we could connect D to B with H in between, but there would not be a straight path[3].

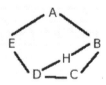

---

[3] Now a few of you semi-smarty-pants out there might be saying, "That depends upon the geometry of the drawing, because on a sphere you could put the H outside of the 2D plane and use a geodesic to connect..." You are not a rocket scientist. If you were, you would not be taking the LSAT, you'd be taking the RSSAT (Rocket Scientist School Admission Test). It's paper. It's 2D. Quit being a smart ass and pay attention to what we are teaching.

Rule 3 says that G is outside of the circle and has two paths on it. One goes to D and the other to C. So we stick G conveniently outside of the circle and make the two connections thus:

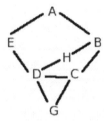

And now we just have to deal with rule #4, telling us to do essentially the same thing we just did, only this time with F connecting to E and B:

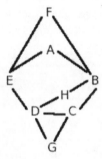

Now ain't that a peach! We have ourselves a modern art masterpiece! The reason we should not care about how pretty it is not has to do with two things: if all of the connections are there and in the correct places, we will answer every question correctly. Also, we are not trying to get into art school.

So steps two and three are complete. Now it is….INFERENCE TIME!

Absolutes? There are all sorts of Absolutes, and they are all in the picture.
Bundles? Same deal.
Calculators? Yes, but they are a bit different than what we have seen. Often times Drawing games ask questions about the number of moves it takes to get between certain places. We can anticipate the answers in the Calculator step by quickly counting how many moves it takes to get from place to place. The SMART way to do this is to start at some place like F and begin with 1 "move". How far can Yolanda get from F in one move, and, more important, can she get to EVERY other exhibit in one move? Obviously she cannot, because she can only get to E or B in one move. The number of lines coming out of F determines how many exhibits can be seen in one move, just like it does for any other exhibit. That means that B and D, both with four lines coming out of them, have the maximum "one move" potential: there are four

possible places Yolanda can go from B in one move (C, H, A or F), and the same goes for D (G, C, H or E).

Now look at two moves. She can go from F to almost everywhere in two moves…everywhere except G, which requires three moves. Do a quick check of all of the other letters for two moves and see whether or not there are any places she can start from where she can get to every other exhibit in two moves. We will wait for you to do that.

B, C, D, E and H can access all other exhibits in two moves. A, F and G require three moves, and that is the maximum number of moves it takes to get between any two points in the game, regardless of where she starts. Make a note of that and move on.

Double-ups? The whole thing is one gigantic bloody Double-up. But what we want to make sure of is that we do not overlook the hidden rules. In Drawing games and Squish Ordering games most if not all of the formal rules will end up in your picture. It will be the hidden rules that get overlooked if you are not careful. Do any of them Double-up with our formal rules? Not really. All we have to do is remember to follow the paths and count each exhibit we go to as a "move".

Extras? There are no conditional logic statements, so there cannot be bi-conditionals or forced dichotomies. There are no right side rules, affirmative duties, contradictions or lone conditionals either.

Free Rangers? There are not any, as all of the exhibits are in the drawing, right? Well actually that is incorrect because Yolanda is not, as far as we know, *required* to see any of the exhibits. There are no affirmative duty rules, so she could go to the nature park and decide to leave without seeing any exhibits. Hmmmm.

Okay, we have beat this horse, postmortem. It is time to DESTROY THE QUESTIONS!

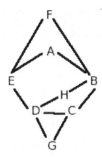

1) Which one of the following, if true, would require Yolanda to go to the Aquatics exhibit?
   a) She visits the Dingoes and the
      Falcons, but not the Bobcats.
   b) She visits the Chimps and the
      Bobcats but not the Giraffes.
   c) She visits the Bobcats and the
      Elephants, but neither the Hippos
      nor Falcons.
   d) She visits the Hippos and the
      Elephants, but neither the Dingoes
      nor the Falcons.
   e) She visits the Giraffes and the and
      the Falcons but neither the
      Dingoes nor the Hippos.

Well now! Don't we have ourselves a "challenging" *looking* problem! TRICKERY! SHEER TRICKERY! All we have to do is trace out paths on our drawing and see what is what. Remember that on the first problem in every game, we want to start with "a" and work our way down the list systematically to make sure that we are learning everything there is to learn about the game.

So (a) says that Yolanda visits the Dingoes and the Falcons, but not the Bobcats. Can we trace a path from D to F without touching the B and without touching the A? DUH! Go from D to E then to F. This is not what we are looking for. KILL IT.
(b) says that she visits the Chimps and the Bobcats but not the Giraffes. We can avoid the Aquatics and the Giraffes, obviously, by going from C to B directly. KILL IT.
(c) says that she visits the Bobcats and the Elephants, but neither the Hippos nor Falcons. Hmmmm. Can we get from B to E without going to A, H and F? SURE! Go from B to C then to G, D then E. KILL IT!
(d) says that she visits the Hippos and the Elephants, but neither the Dingoes nor the Falcons. Can that be done? If she cannot go to D, then the move from H to E requires her to go to B first. She can get to E by going down to C and then G, but that will take her back to D, which is a no-no. She cannot go up to F, so she has to go through A to get to E. CIRCLE IT AND MOVE TO THE NEXT QUESTION!
e) says that she visits the Giraffes and the and the Falcons but neither the Dingoes nor the Hippos. That is easy as cake, because she can go G, C, B then F. Congratulations. You wasted time checking an answer that had to incorrect because (d) was correct. Wasting time costs you points, admissions letters and scholarship

money. STOP CHECKING INCORRECT ANSWERS! Once you have a correct answer, circle that pig, bubble it in on your answer form and MOVE![1]

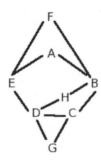

2) If Yolanda begins at the Falcon exhibit, exactly how many other possible exhibits could she possibly see in exactly two moves?
    a) Three
    b) Four
    c) Five
    d) Six
    e) Seven

REMEMBER that the first thing we have to do is make sure that we have our brains around the call of the question. We are being told that she makes EXACTLY two moves, but it asks us how many *other* exhibits she *could possibly* see. We know from our inferences that she needs three moves to get from F to G but that she can get to all of the others in two moves. We cannot count F (it asked for *other* exhibits) so 8 minus F and G makes 6. If you would like you can waste time and verify that which we already know to be true. She can go from F to E then A, or F to E then D. E, A and D make three. She could also go from F to B then H, or F to B then C. That is three more. 3+3=6. SHAZAM!

3) If Yolanda begins at the Dingo exhibit, what is the maximum number of exhibits she can see without repeating any exhibit?
    a) four
    b) five
    c) six
    d) seven
    e) eight

What do we already know? The Dingo exhibit has four paths leading out of it, one to each of E, H, C and G.

D to E forces us to choose between F and A. We cannot have both without ending our trip at a repeat exhibit. So we can go D, E, F or D, E, A, it does not matter which, either gets us three exhibits and moves us to B as the fourth. From B we could go to

---

[1] If you are having trouble with this concept, consider this suggestion from a former student of ours, Ms. Jenapher Lin: "Every time you check an incorrect answer after you have already found the correct one, a kitten dies." DON'T KILL KITTENS!

H and end the trip, or we could go from B to C then to G for six. So D to E gets us six max. Cross off (a) and (b).

If we go from D to H, we have to go to B. At that point we either go from B to C then G for a total of five OR we go D, H, B then A, E, F for 6.

Going from D to C to B (D, C, G is a short trip) forces us to leave H and G out and pick up A, E and F for six again.

D to G to C to B, then A, E, F (or F, E, A, it matters not) gets us seven total. That is the maximum: seven. We cannot get the eight one in under any circumstance because of the "no repeats" condition and the fact that H has only one path in and out.

4) If all of the pathways into and out of the Bobcats exhibit are closed, which one of the exhibits is one that Yolanda cannot visit if she does visit exactly five, and does not visit any exhibit twice?

> a) Aquatics
> b) Chimps
> c) Falcons
> d) Giraffes
> e) Hippos

RULES = ISSUES

Notice how problems 3 and 4 both turn on a similar understanding of the picture. This is never an accident...there are no accidents or coincidences on the LSAT.

The rules of the game tell us what the issues being tested are. In a game such as this, there are very few issues that can be tested (number of pathways, repeat visits, etc.) so we can expect that there will be multiple questions concerning any given issue.

THIS IS WHY IT IS SO IMPERATIVE THAT YOU GO WITH WHAT YOU KNOW FIRST, and that you do not forget that the solutions to problems you have already answered are things that you already know! This test punishes people who are too thick to realize that they do not need to reinvent the wheel every time.

Here they are again (the makers of the test), trying to freak you out. Do not panic. Simply follow the process. The call of the question says that all paths to B are closed, she visits five total, and she goes to no exhibit twice. It asks us to determine which exhibit she **_cannot_** see given those conditions. What do we already know? We have a picture that has all of the paths to B on one side.

We can visualize the solution to this problem in a couple of ways. The easiest is to just take our hand and cover over the right side of our picture so we cannot see any of the paths to or from B. The other way would be to simply re-picture it, which would get the same result but use a lot more time. Either way it will look like this:

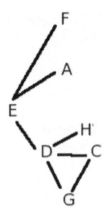

So how can she get five visits in, bearing in mind that wherever we begin counts as a visit? Again we have the problem of the "no re-visit". F, A and H are all hanging out there on solo paths, so if we go out the them (i.e. from E to A, E to F or D to H) our journey ends because we would have to back-track to see more. BUT we have to have one of them in the mix, because if we leave all three of them out, there are only four exhibits left, E, D, C and G. So we either have to begin or end with one of A, F or H.

She can begin with F and work her way through E, D, G and C for five. Thad eliminates answer choices (b), (c) and (d). A works exactly the same way as F, so we can get rid of (a), leaving only (e) Hippos. If she begins at Hippos, her only possible paths are H, D, G, C or H, D, E, A/F. We cannot end on H because A/F, E, D, H is only four, G, C, D, H is only four... Poor, poor sad, lonely Hippos.

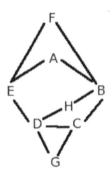

5) If Aquatics is the first exhibit Yolanda visits, and if Giraffes are the eighth, and if she does not visit any exhibit twice, the fourth exhibit she visits must be:
   a) Bobcats
   b) Chimps
   c) Dingoes
   d) Elephants
   e) Falcons

What do we already know? We know that in order to avoid hitting exhibits twice and end up at the bottom at G, she has to clear the top part of the picture first. That means she has to either go A, B, F, E or A, E, F, B. Ergo, (b), (c) and (e) are incorrect.

So which way do we have to go? WE ALREADY KNOW! If we go A, B, F, E then H is left hanging out there because D is the only route to it, but we have to go through D to get to G and/or C. So there is no way to get H without either hitting B twice or D twice. Thus (d) is out and (a) is the winner.

VII. TAKE SOME TIME TO TAKE STOCK

Now that we have seen every single-type game that there is (Ordering, both Firm and Squishy, Buckets, Winner/Loser, Procedure and Drawing) and before we move on to the Combo games, we need to do a few things.

We need to make sure that we know every step of our LSAT Logic Games method. It is imperative that we know how to identify what type of game we are looking at immediately and that we are able to anticipate what kind of picture we are going to draw later. We need to know all of the basic drawing types. We need to know how to re-write all of the formal rules in a way that is visually consistent with the picture we are going to draw. We need to know EVERY step of the Inference Process (step four of the method): NOT JUST saying the names of the steps, but knowing the meanings of the names as well as how every step works. This also means that we have to have the logic section down very well.

REVIEW ALL OF YOUR NOTES!
MAKE CERTAIN THAT YOU KNOW EVERYTHING INSIDE AND OUT!

To that end, we will provide you with additional practice games. It is ABSOLUTELY IMPERATIVE that you DO NOT start working on these in a disorganized, ad-hoc manner. You need to walk through every step, in order, every time. As the games get harder (and they will) the Method will be the difference between failure and success.

Take your time. Do everything correctly and methodically. Get good at the easier, single-action games (where the nature of the game is to do one thing only) so that you know how to slay the tough ones quickly and efficiently.

Problem Set 16 – Practicing the Method Answers in Appendix "B"

For each of the following, complete the first four steps of the method.

A) Seven types of pies will be served, one at a time. The pies are Apple, Blueberry, Cherry, Dewberry, Elderberry, Fig and Gooseberry. A complete pie is served before the next pie is served. The order of the serving of pies is subject to the following limitations:

Cherry pie is served immediately before Dewberry.

The Gooseberry pie must be served before the Cherry pie.

Exactly two pies are served between the serving of the Elderberry pie and the Apple pie.

B) Exactly four people must attend Johnny Sack's funeral. The four are selected from the group of: Artie, Carmela, Furio, Paulie, Silvio, Tony and Vito. Who attends depends upon the following limitations:

Artie attends the funeral if and only if Carmela does not.

Silvio will not attend the funeral unless Furio goes.

Vito does not attend the funeral unless Carmela does.

Either Tony or Silvio, but not both, must go to the funeral.

C) A funky-fresh Hip-Hop artist is creating three new experimental music tracks. He has four kinds of instruments to work with, and he wants each track to have three kinds of instruments on it. His available instruments are: Cow Bells, Marimbas, Piccolos and Xylophones. Each track must be made in accordance with the following limitations:

Track 3 cannot have any Marimba.

Track 1 uses exactly two types of instruments.

All four types of instruments must be used amongst the three tracks at least once.

Cow Bell must appear at least on Track 3.

Piccolo must be on Track 2.

For every Marimba that is used among the three Tracks, there must be at least twice as many Piccolos, whether or not they are on the same Track as the Marimba.

D) Seven proctors, Mary, Nancy, Peter, Quintin, Robert, Steven and Tanya, are each being assigned to supervise exactly one of three exams: the ACT, the GRE or the SAT. The assignment is consistent with the following conditions:

The SAT may not be proctored by Quintin.
If Nancy proctors the ACT then Quintin and Tanya proctor the GRE.
Peter proctors the ACT.
Robert may not be assigned to proctor any test Quintin proctors.
Quintin may not be assigned to proctor any test that Tanya proctors.
The SAT may not be proctored by Robert.
Each test must have at least two proctors.

E) Five candidates for the legislature, Beretta, Colt, Glock, Kimber and Remington, are campaigning in Bakwatir County, which is divided into exactly five overlapping cities: Alcas, Freemont, Leatherman, Mantis and Ontario. The five cities comprise the entirety of Bakwatir County, which can be drawn as follows: Leatherman and Mantis are square cities of equal size and share one border completely. Ontario is a square the same size as Leatherman and Mantis, half of which is inside both Leatherman and mantis in equal parts and half of which is outside of Leatherman and Mantis. Alcas is circular. No part of it is outside of Leatherman, and part of it is also inside of Ontario. No part of Alcas touches any part of Mantis. Freemont is a circular city which partially lies in Mantis and no other city. The five candidates campaign in a manner consistent with the following::
All candidates are within the County.
Colt is in Alcas but not Ontario.
Glock and Remington are never in the same city.
Kimber and Beretta are never in the same city.
Kimber is always in exactly two cities.

F) The magazine, *Reports on Things People Consume* is releasing its most recent rankings of eight bagged snack chips sold in U.S. markets. The chips, Angioplasties, Bipassers, Chlorester-alls, Diabitees, Elegies, Fatboys, G'outaheres and Heart Attackers, will be ranked from most favorable (first) to least favorable (eighth). The ratings are consistent with the following conditions:

Angioplasties are either lower ranked than both Heart Attackers and Bipassers or they are higher ranked than both.
G'outaheres are higher ranked than both Elegies and Angioplasties.
Fatboys and Elegies are both higher ranked than Heart Attackers.
Diabitees are lower ranked than Bipassers

COMBO GAMES –

"The secret of all victory lies in the organization of the non-obvious." Marcus Aurelius[1]

Memorize that quote! Defeating the Combo game is as much about organization as it is about tactics. As we shall see, whenever we are confronted with a combo game, we have to determine how to organize the information and when to do that organizing.

Thus far we have seen examples of the little traps that the single task games set for us, and we know that if we stick to our step-by-step Test Mentor's Method™ we cannot be duped. If you know how to execute the logic of the LSAT and you are practiced at using it within the context of the games, there are very few things that the LSAC can do to ruin your day.[2] There are a wide range of ways that they can up the ante, so to speak: they can allow you to make careless errors (such as treating "Heart Attackers" as two separate players, or creating answer choices based upon denying the antecedent, etc.). They can make inferences based upon contra-posed logic. They can use advanced logic concepts to befuddle (for example, using bi-conditionals to destroy the use of the Right Side Rule™).

The mythical *cima della montagna*[3] in the realm of logic games is the Combo game. Recall that Combos have you doing two or more tasks simultaneously: you may be asked to put things into buckets and then put the buckets into order, pick winners and losers and then put the winners or losers into order, pick winners and then "bucket" them together, etc. Those multi-tasks are just the single tasks we do in other games, only executed at the same time. They look frightening mostly because the fact patterns are typically spooky looking bundles of facts and hidden rules. This is sheer intimidation, nothing more.

The Marcus Aurelius quote above is not some trivial nor cosmetic thing. It is the essence of the Combo game. Combo games look overwhelming because there have to be more players or sub-categories of players in order to provide enough elements to address the two or three tasks assigned. DO NOT allow yourself to get sucked into the pit of despair. Step one of the Test Mentors Method™ requires us to *organize* our

---

[1] We can neither confirm nor disconfirm the authenticity of this attribution, as we cannot locate a primary source. We have been told by teachers, texts and web sites for a very long time that he said this, we just cannot find it in any of his works nor can we locate a primary source. What we can find are lots of people using it as an introduction to some pet project that they are quite proud of and that, ironically, tell us how to organize things in obvious need thereof. "I pity the fools." The primary source for that quote is *Mr. T,* "Rocky III" United Artists, 1982, which is, sadly, far easier to research than anything said by Marcus Aurelius, last of the five great emperors of Rome.

[2] Again, just to be 10,000% clear, the LSAC is **not** setting out to screw you over. They are setting out to test whether you have the fundamental skills required for law school and to gauge the level thereof. Too many students blame the LSAC for their performance when in fact, as near as we can tell, the LSAC has crafted a test perfect for its asserted objectives. All failings are upon the test taker.

[3] Top of the mountain.

information. Once we do that and we see things in their simplest form, the lights come on and the boogey man disappears from the room.[4]

The truth of the matter is this: Combo games are not inherently difficult. As you saw in the last set of practice problems, single task games can be made quite difficult if the logic is twisted up enough. The same is true of the Combo game. Key to defeating them with confidence is realizing that multiple actions means multiple sets of restrictions: each action creates constraints on what can and cannot occur. For us this is fantastic. The more restrictions there are on our players, the fewer possible outcomes there can be.

We are going to take a bit of time to walk you through the two most common types of Combo games. Bear in mind that the skills that we are developing are not unique to the Combo game. In fact, the one and only difference with Combos is that YOU HAVE TO LEARN TO RECOGNIZE THEM. Otherwise, we do precisely the same steps as always. The change will come when we make a slightly modified drawing. As we shall see, the changes are trivial. After we have introduced you to the basic concepts behind each kind of common Combo game, we will give you full examples and walk-through explanations, as always.

NOMENCLATURE ALERT!

"Double-ordering" is used to describe what we are doing: putting one set of things into order and putting another set into the same order. We could "think" of it differently though: We are putting one set of items into an order, thus creating "buckets" and we are putting other things into those buckets. Some people actually teach that...and it is stupid. We will *actually* think about what we are doing, why we are doing it, and name it accordingly.

What are we supposed to know in the end? The order of one set of things and the order of another set of things. In our example below, if Aragon is the first juggler and Orc Heads are the first item juggled, then Aragon juggles the Orc Heads first. There is nothing "buckets" about it.

Double-Ordering

The most common Combo by far is the Double-Order. We are asked to put two separate sets of players into some kind of order. It is important to make sure that we distinguish the Double-Order from a garden variety Ordering game that has both Squishy and Firm elements to it (Squirm). The difference is this, and you have to make sure that you are on the lookout for it: **Double-Ordering games have two different sets of players being put into order, whereas Squirms have just one.** Let us examine the set up for a Double-order:

Six jugglers, Aragon, Frodo, Gandalf, Legolas, Pippin, and Sam are each going to juggle exactly once, one at a time. They will each be juggling exactly one of the following types of items, none of which may be used more than twice: broadswords, Mithril, quarterstaffs, rings and Orc heads. The order in which they juggle and the item each juggles is determined by the following constraints:

---

[4] If you do not believe in the boogey man, think "evil killer clown under the bed" or "Eleanor Roosevelt in the bed."

Do you see what we are talking about? From this fact pattern, we can determine that there will be six juggling spots, 1 through six, that each of our six people will fill exactly one spot and that the items they juggle and/or the order the items appear will be determined by the Formal Rules.

This approach to game making obviously allows LSAC to determine the depth of your ability to logic things out. You may be asked to determine the order of the jugglers based upon the order of the items or vice-versa.

Winner/Loser-Ordering

These are actually really fun games because they tend to turn heavily on the inferences. If we are very adept at Step Four of the Test Mentors Method™ we can beat these into submission easily.

> Exactly four different math classes are being taught, one during each quarter of the school year, at a community college: Algebra, Bayesian Statistics, Calculus, and Discrete Mathematics. At least one and at most two teachers are assigned to each course. Algebra may be taught only by Flanders, Marge, Smithers or Willie. Bayesian Statistics may be taught only by Marge or Smithers. Calculus may be taught only by Homer, Marge or Willie. Discrete Mathematics may be taught only by Flanders, Homer or Smithers. The order in which the classes are taught and the assignment of teacher to them must comply with the following constraints:

We can see that this game is one big attempt at a psych-out. The truth is (and we WILL beat the truth out of it) that once we get done with step four, it is in the bag. We have winners and losers (not every teacher has to play) and we have an ordering of the classes. Notice that all of the classes play, and that all four quarters of the school year play, thus giving us the ordering component.

APPLYING THE TEST MENTORS METHOD

What you are about to see employs almost everything we have covered thus far. That is what Combo games do. The reason is simple: this is how they separate the average applicant form the superior ones (i.e. this is where you get your scholarship money). TRY TO DO THE FIRST FOUR STEPS COMPLETELY, ON YOUR OWN. DO NOT CHEAT AND LOOK FOR HELP. If you get stuck, take a peek, but JUST A PEEK! We will walk you through the first four steps here so you can conveniently check your work AFTER YOU HAVE DONE IT. Then, following the walk-through, the game is re-printed with questions. DO THE ENTIRE FIVE STEP PROCESS AGAIN. Practice makes perfect.

Six jugglers, Aragon, Frodo, Gandalf, Legolas, Pippin, and Sam are each going to juggle exactly once, one at a time. They will each be juggling exactly one of the following types of items, none of which may be used more than twice: Broadswords, Mithril, Quarterstaffs, Rings and Orc heads. The order in which they juggle and the item each juggles is determined by the following constraints:

> Sam juggles either first or second.
> Legolas juggles Mithril unless Gandalf juggles rings.
> Frodo juggles either Mithril or broadswords before Pippin and Gandalf juggle.
> Sam juggles broadswords if and only if Gandalf juggles rings.
> Only the fourth juggler juggles Orc heads.

STEP 1 – GET A GRIP

Nature of game: COMBO.

Players: SIX Jugglers A, F, G, L, P, S, FIVE Objects B, M, Q, R, O and SIX Slots, 1 through 6.

Hidden Rules: All jugglers play EXACTLY once, one at a time. Each juggler uses EXACTLY one object. No object used more than twice.

STEP 2: FORMAL RULES

The first rule is easy: Sam juggles either first or second.

$$1) \ S = 1 \text{ or } 2$$

The second rule says that, "Legolas juggles Mithril unless Gandalf juggles rings." Do you happen to recall what that means? To put it another way, what does the word, "unless," mean? It means "IF NOT." If you did not remember that, GET WITH THE PROGRAM! Make a flash card, write it down on the back of your hand... learn it. It translates to, "If not Gandalf juggles rings, then Legolas juggles Mithril." We *know* that this is an affirmative duty rule. So we put it into symbols and we contra-pose it.

$$2) \ -GR \supset LM$$
$$-LM \supset GR$$

The third rule says that Frodo juggles either Mithril or broadswords before Pippin and Gandalf juggle. Oooo! That is sneaky-dirty! It is two rules in one! Frodo has to juggle either Mithril or broadswords is the first part. We can denote this with F(M/B), remembering that the "/" means "one or the other." Since we know (from the hidden rules) that Frodo cannot do both, it is like an exclusive "or". The second part of the rule says that Frodo juggles before both Pippin and Gandalf, so that establishes a squishy order. We are going to re-write the rule thus:

3)

What kind of rule is the fourth rule? WHAT IS THE NAME WE HAVE FOR IT? It is called a bi-conditional. It says that Sam juggles broadswords if and only if Gandalf juggles rings. Recall that this means that SB is both an antecedent to GR and a consequent of GR. That is because the first "if" means antecedent and the "only if," means "then" which means consequent. It is two rules in one. It means "If GR then SB" and it means "If SB then GR." (If this is not ringing a bell, GO BACK TO THE SECTION ON LOGIC AND GET IT DOWN TIGHT!)

$$4) \; GR \supset SB$$
$$-SB \supset -GR$$
$$SB \supset GR$$
$$-GR \supset -SB$$

The fifth rule says that only the 4th juggler juggles Orc heads. In plain, everyday speak, we know what this means: O must go 4th and nowhere else. That is because, from our Jedi logic chapter, we learned that "only" means "then", and that means consequent. We could write, "If O then 4th" and contra-pose to, "if not 4th then not O." But seriously...what would we gain from that? Nada. It is an absolute. Let us write it as such:

$$5) \; ONLY \; 4 = O.$$

STEP THREE: DRAW
As always, our first objective in figuring out how to make a drawing is to identify the most definite or absolute element of the game. Any time there is an ordering element involved, that is the obvious choice. Here in particular, where all six jugglers must perform once, one at a time, we have a firm order to form the basis of our game. This is how we will always try to draw a double-order combo game:

	1	2	3	4	5	6
AFGLPS						
BMQRO						

Not to insult your intelligence, but the firm order runs across the top from left to right (before on left, after on right...remember that?). Below that are the two rows for the things we are ordering: jugglers in the top row and the objects in the second.

MEMORIZE THAT! People first, stuff second. That is a convention that we want to stick with always. Even when we re-write the rules, the person comes before the object (GO stands for Gandalf - Orc heads).

Knowing in advance how to create the drawing gives us another SUPER advantage. For example, rule 2 says if -GR, then LM. The way that we rewrote it above will suffice, but many people (yours truly included) "see" the meaning better by writing it this way:

$$2) \ \ \text{-G} \supset \text{L}$$
$$\ \ \ \ \ \text{R} \ \ \ \ \text{M}$$

People on top, objects below. This way is more visually consistent with the type of game we are dealing with, and that is one of the rules for rewriting the formal rules.

Here is why it may matter to you.
Let us suppose that we are given a rule that looks like this:

> 99) The person who juggles Mithril must juggle immediately before Gandalf and immediately after Aragon.

We can write that rule in at least two ways:

1) A_ _M G_
(A with an object, a person with Mithril, Gandalf with an object)

Or

2)

Which version of that rule makes more intuitive sense and seems more useful to you? Some people see A as adequate whereas others (like US) prefer the B version because it is more *visually consistent with the nature of the game*. You cannot do the B version if you are not clear as to the nature of the game and how it is going to lay out as a drawing. This is another reason why Step One is so bloody important.

As we said, so long as you stick to the conventions and you do not confuse yourself, you can write it either way, all other things being equal. IF YOU FIND, however, that you are consistently making mistakes because you did not realize that the rules mean something more or different than your rewriting of them indicated to you, try changing the way that you rewrite.

LASTLY, it is okay to use both methods at the same time. Our rule #2 does not really need to be drawn like pretend rule 99. YOU have the ability to select the tool that best fits the job at hand. Please do so, and practice that mightily.

STEP 4: INFERENCES
Here are all of our rules again. YOU MUST NOT FORGET TO INCLUDE THE HIDDEN RULES IN YOUR INFERENCES!

* All jugglers play EXACTLY once, one at a time.
* Each juggler uses EXACTLY one object.
* No object more than 2X

    1) S = 1 or 2

    2) $-GR \supset LM$

        $-LM \supset GR$

    3)

$$F(M/B) \cdots \overset{\cdot\cdot\cdot\; P}{\underset{\cdot\cdot\cdot\; G}{}}$$

    4) $GR \supset SB$

       $-SB \supset -GR$

       $SB \supset GR$

       $-GR \supset -SB$

    5) ONLY 4 = O

Absolutes? Rule 1 is NOT an absolute as far as S having to juggle first or second. It does tell us that S cannot go in spaces 3 through 6. We do NOT want to get sucked into thinking that two drawings are needed. If we redrew our original picture and put S in space 1 in one version and S in space two in the other, would that tell us anything additional and highly useful? It does not appear to at this point. Instead, let us just put an "S/" in 1 and 2 for the time being and check off rule #1:

	1	2	3	4	5	6
AFGLPS	S/	S/				
BMQRO						

Rule three says that F has to come before both P and G. That means that F cannot go in spaces 5 or 6 because there need to be at least two spaces after F for P and G to go into. It ALSO means that neither P nor G can go into slot 1, because F has to come before both of them. We must add these notes to our drawing, but we cannot check off rule three because it is not ***completely*** in our drawing.

	1	2	3	4	5	6
AFGLPS	S/ -P-G	S/			-F	-F
BMQRO						

Rule five is most definitely an absolute. Plug it into the drawing, making sure to cross "O" off of the list of players (because there can only be one), and check off the rule:

	1	2	3	4	5	6
AFGLPS	S/ -P-G	S/			-F	-F
BMQRØ	-O	-O	-O	(O)	-O	-O

We marked all of the other object spaces as "-O" to be 1000% certain that we don't make the mistake of overlooking the fact that O has to be in 4 and only in 4. Call us crazy, but it is better to be thorough than to screw up.

There are no more absolutes.

Bundles? YES! F is bundled with either B or M. Can we use that to our advantage? YES! If F can only be with B or M, then F cannot juggle fourth because that person has to use O. We can add another –F to position 4:

	1	2	3	4	5	6
AFGLPS	S/ -P-G	S/		-F	-F	-F
BMQRØ	-O	-O	-O	(O)	-O	-O

Any other Bundles? THERE ARE NONE! Do not get sucked into the trap of thinking that rules 2 or 4 create any Bundles. They do NOT. A bundle is a group of players that always have to be together. Rules 2 and 4 are *conditional statements*. Rule 4 says that IF G juggles R then we know L juggles M. That tells us *nothing* about any other G combination. If G juggles O then S can juggle anything other than B, AND according to rule 2, L will have to juggle M.

What all of this should *should* be telling you is that Calculators and Double-ups are going to be pay dirt for us.

Do we have any Calculators? Heck ya! We have six jugglers and five objects to juggle. Of those five, "O" can only go one time, and it is pinned down in the fourth position.

That means that there are four objects for five spaces. Our hidden rules tell us that no object can play more than twice. So what is the *least* number of objects that can play? Here is an easy way to calculate this: O has to play once exactly. We can have another object twice (hypothetically, X, X) and that, added to "O" makes three of the six. We can make another go twice (Y, Y) and that is five of six (i.e. O, X, X, Y, Y). So we need another object (Z) to fill all six spots. That means the fewest objects we can have is four: O, X, Y and Z, and in that case, two of the three X, Y, Z must go twice. THAT ALSO MEANS that the greatest number of objects that cannot be used is exactly ONE. That is good to know.

The trickier Calculator comes on the maximum side. In other words, can we get all five of the objects into the game? O has to go in exactly once. There are four other objects for the five spaces, so *something must always play twice.* If two objects go twice then only four can play (just like in the "minimum" calculation we did a second ago). So it looks as though we *ought to be able* to get them all in. The one thing that should make us slightly apprehensive is that there are six conditional rules. They might force us into always using two pairs. SNOZBERRIES!

Not really. Again, the Test Mentors Method saves the day. Remember how, every time we solve a problem, we **gain knowledge**? Some answer along the way may show us that five objects are allowed. WE DO NOT WANT TO SPEND BUCKETS OF TIME trying to hash out all of the conditionals when Double-ups are right around the corner. We know that four is the minimum that must play. Let us see if we can figure out more, and in an expedient manner.

Double-ups? Oodles. Rules 2, 3 and 4 all have common players in them. We must be careful. Let's first draw inferences from 2 and 4.

$$2) -GR \supset LM \cdot -SB$$
$$-LM \supset GR \cdot SB$$
$$4) GR \supset SB$$
$$-SB \supset -GR \cdot LM$$
$$SB \supset GR$$
$$-GR \supset -SB \cdot LM$$

We can see here that which would have been very easy to miss if we did not have a hard and fast methodology that includes looking for double-ups. Rule 3 says that F must be with M or B (F(M/B)). Rules 2 and 4 say that if GR then SB, and if −GR then LM. G can only do two possible things relative to R: G can be *with* R, and G can *not be with* R. Those are the only two ways G and R can possibly relate. In *either* event, LM will result or SB will result...ONE of those things *will* happen. Because of the F(M/B) rule, we should be able to sniff out an easy trap: using up two M or two B and then tricking you into thinking F can use that object as well. No object can go more than twice. If GR then SB. In that situation, if F juggles B, then nobody else can have B, but if someone else does use B, F must use M. Same thing goes for the scenario where

–GR happens. Then LM will happen, and if FM happens then nobody else can juggle M. If someone else does, then FB. So we are going to anticipate questions with SB and GR as well as questions involving -GR or -SB.

Using the Double-up step to smell the issues, questions, traps and correct answers before we even get to the questions is what makes for great law students and dangerously good lawyers.

Extras? Again, yes. Work your way down the list, in order.

Are there any bi-conditionals? Definitely. Rule 4. We no longer use the Right-Side Rule™ and that is sad.

Forced dichotomies? Yes, there are three, and they vary in subtlety.
Not-so-subtle: From the first rule, we know the Sam must play and that he has to be in first or second position. So if anyone else juggles first, Sam is second. If anyone else is in second, Sam is first. Now you may be asking yourself, "Big deal...why do I care?" CLUE: Rule #1.

Let's pretend that Gandalf is in position 2. Who is in position 2? SAM. Can Frodo go before Gandalf as required by rule one? HELLS NO! So the forced S = 1 or 2 dichotomy helps us to see that neither G nor P can go into second position either...ever. Sweet. Add it to the drawing[5].

	1	2	3	4	5	6
AFGLPS	S/ -P -G	S/ -P -G		-F	-F	-F
BMQRØ	-O	-O	-O	Ⓞ	-O	-O

Kind of subtle: F *must* play (forced) and he must juggle either B or M (dichotomy). How does that help us? Well, if two other people have M, then F can not, forcing F to juggle B. If two other people have B then F cannot have B, forcing F to juggle M. This seems trivial and perhaps even pedantic, but these are the kinds of things that "average" scorers overlook, fail to account for and fail to anticipate. Guess what? *THEY ARE GOING TO PAY FOR YOUR LAW DEGREE!*

Really subtle: The GR / -GR and SB / -SB thang. We saw this before, and it is a muy forced dichotomy. Now to be honest, the same thing could generally be said about any person in the game: they either juggle Mithril or they do not, they juggle rings or they do not, yadda yadda yadda. But G and B are special because we have specific rules about them in both instances, and the consequences of those are potentially tricky and clearly defined: if we know that if Aragon juggles Mithril, Sam cannot

---

[5] You may have already picked this one up way back at Absolutes or, more likely, Double-ups. That is the beauty of the Test Mentors Method: there are many roads to Rome, and they are all winners.

because that would be –SB which would mean –GR and LM, so if Sam *was* SM, we would have AM, SM and LM, a violation of the hidden rules! If this confused you, "SKETCH IT UP… LEONARDO Da VINCI!"

Right-side rule? Killed by the bi-conditional.

Affirmative duties? YES! WE HAVE THREE! Recall that an Affirmative Duty exists when there is a negative antecedent and an affirmative (positive) consequent. Rule 2 and its contra-positive are affirmative duties *by design* (the LSAC fed it to you up front). The contra-positive of the first part of rule 4 is also an affirmative duty, one that we only are aware of because of the inference we drew back in Double-ups. WAIT AND SEE HOW MANY QUESTIONS REVOLVE AROUND THIS RULE!

Contradictions? – There are none…but you should see for yourself.

Lone Conditionals? No. There are technically three, because rule 4 is a bi-conditional (two at once) and then there is rule 2.

Free-Rangers? There are no rules at all about which jugglers and objects? Aragon is a free ranger (how appropriate) and the quarterstaff has no rules associated with it. Another reminder: just because you are a free ranger, that does not mean that the logic cannot force you into or out of some box. For example, If F is in 1, Free-Ranger A cannot go into 2. The drawing explains why: S has to be in 1 or 2. F1 means S2.

STEP FIVE: DESTROY THE QUESTIONS
Take all that you have learned from steps one through four and use them to their maximum advantage. Remember that you always want to GO WITH WHAT YOU KNOW first, and then make notes and drawings only if necessary. If you need to review the process for destroying the questions, we posit that *now* would be the ideal time.

PROB. SET 17 (Answers in Appendix "B")

Six jugglers, Aragon, Frodo, Gandalf, Legolas, Pippin, and Sam are each going to juggle exactly once, one at a time. They will each be juggling exactly one of the following types of items, none of which may be used more than twice: Broadswords, Mithril, Quarterstaffs, Rings and Orc heads. The order in which they juggle and the item each juggles is determined by the following constraints:

Sam juggles either first or second.

Legolas juggles Mithril unless Gandalf juggles rings.

Frodo juggles either Mithril or broadswords before Pippin and Gandalf juggle.

Sam juggles broadswords if and only if Gandalf juggles rings.

Only the fourth juggler juggles Orc heads.

1) Which one of the following could be a complete and accurate ordering of the jugglers and the items that they juggle?
 a) Aragon, broadswords; Frodo, quarterstaffs; Sam, rings; Pippin, Mithril; Gandalf, Orc heads; Legolas, Mithril
 b) Sam, Orc heads; Frodo, broadswords; Pippin, quarterstaffs; Legolas, Orc heads; Gandalf, rings; Aragon, Mithril
 c) Sam, broadswords; Frodo, broadswords; Gandalf, rings; Aragon, Orc heads; Legolas, Mithril; Pippin, quarterstaffs
 d) Gandalf, Mithril; Sam, broadswords; Frodo, Mithril; Aragon, Orc heads; Pippin, quarterstaff; Legolas, rings
 e) Gandalf, broadswords; Sam, broadswords; Frodo, Mithril; Pippin, Orc heads; Aragon, rings; Sam, quarterstaffs.

2) If Sam juggles Mithril second, which of the following could be true?
 a) Frodo juggles Orc heads third
 b) Frodo juggles Mithril third
 c) Gandalf juggles rings first
 d) Pippin juggles rings first
 e) Sam juggles quarterstaffs fourth

3) If Frodo juggles Mithril third, which of the following is a complete and accurate list of all of the jugglers who could juggle first?
 a) Sam
 b) Sam, Legolas
 c) Sam, Legolas, Pippin
 d) Aragon, Legolas, Sam
 e) Aragon, Gandalf, Legolas, Sam

4) If Gandalf and Pippin juggle fifth and sixth respectively, and they juggle Mithril and rings respectively, then which of the following must be false?
 a) Frodo juggles before Sam
 b) Sam juggles before Frodo
 c) Aragon juggles before Frodo
 d) Frodo juggles before Aragon
 e) Sam juggles before Aragon

5) If Legolas juggles broadswords first, the for how many other people can their position in the order and the objects they juggle be determined?
 a) zero
 b) one
 c) two
 d) three
 e) four

6) Which of the following could be true?
 a) Both Aragon and Legolas juggle broadswords, and both Pippin and Sam juggle rings.
 b) Both Aragon and Sam juggle broadswords and both Pippin and Legolas juggle rings
 c) Both Gandalf and Aragon juggle rings, and both Sam and Frodo juggle broadswords
 d) Both Legolas and Aragon juggle quarterstaffs and both Gandalf and Sam juggle rings
 e) Both Gandalf and Aragon juggle rings, and both Sam and Frodo juggle Mithril

7) Which of the following is an item that both Gandalf and Sam can both juggle?
 a) Broadswords
 b) Mithril
 c) Orc heads
 d) Rings
 e) Quarterstaffs

8) If Sam and Frodo juggle broadswords second and third respectively, then which of the following could be true?
 a) Legolas juggles Mithril fourth
 b) Legolas juggles Mithril fifth
 c) Pippin juggles Orc heads first
 d) Pippin juggles broadswords fifth
 e) Aragon juggles broadswords fourth

PROB. SET 18 – YOU DO THE FACT PATTERN! Read the explanation to check your work AFTER you have finished. Then, re-do all five steps and do all seven questions on the full game that follows this fact pattern practice.

Exactly four different math classes are being taught, one during each quarter of the school year, at a community college: Algebra, Bayesian Statistics, Calculus, and Discrete Mathematics. At least one and at most two teachers are assigned to each course, and each teacher will be assigned at least one course. Algebra may be taught only by Flanders, Marge, Smithers or Willie. Bayesian Statistics may be taught only by Marge or Smithers. Calculus may be taught only by Homer, Marge or Willie. Discrete Mathematics may be taught only by Flanders, Homer or Smithers. The order in which the classes are taught and the assignment of teacher to them must comply with the following constraints:

　　No teacher may teach during more than two
　　　quarters, and they may not be consecutive.
　　Discrete Mathematics must be taught before
　　　Calculus and after Algebra.
　　None of Marge's classes may be taught later in the
　　　year than any of Smithers'.

STEP ONE: Nature of the Game = COMBO (Firm Order/ Buckets). Players: Quarters 1, 2, 3, 4. CLASSES = A, B, C, D. Teachers = F, H, M, S, W. Hidden Rules: ** All classes play (The setup says that exactly four different classes are taught, and there are exactly four classes listed and there are only four quarters). **1/2 Teachers per Class. **All Teachers Play.

"And now for something completely different.."[1]
Notice how the setup went to great lengths to confuse us with the players. THAT is where Marcus Aurelius saves the day. We must come back and organize the non-obvious after we do the Formal Rules and draw the Picture. There is a good reason for this madness, and you will be oh so pleased when you see what it is. They tell us which courses each teacher is qualified to instruct. If we write all of that out now, we are wasting time. You will see the truth of which we write in just a moment.

STEP TWO – Formal Rules (REMEMBER TO NUMBER THEM AND TO REWRITE THEM WITH THE NUMBERS TO MAKE SURE THAT YOU DO NOT SKIP A RULE.

Rule 1 is a compound rule: it gives two directives simultaneously. SEPARATE THEM OUT. Reason: half of the compound may Double-up with other rules and that is easy to miss if you have one big jumble rule.

1) Teach = 2X max
　　No teach consec. quarters

---

[1] Columbia Pictures et seq. 1971. "... Spam, Spam, eggs and Spam..."

Rule number 2 gives us a partial order for the teaching of the classes; three out of four to be precise. When you are getting used to doing these rules, SLOW DOWN and DO IT IN PARTS. D must come before C: D...C and D must come after A: A....D....C

2) A....D....C

Rule three tells us that M can never come after S. Many people mistakenly interpret this rule to mean M....S. Another classic blunder! Did you notice what this rule is NOT saying? It is not saying that M cannot teach in the *same quarter* as S. We need to rewrite the rule so that it is visually consistent with what we are going to draw later AND we need to make certain that we capture the entire meaning of the rule:

3) M....S or
      SM together

That is it for the formal rules. All tolled, our rules look like this:

> ** All classes play.
> **1/2 Teachers per Class.
> **All Teachers Play.
> **MARCUS!
> 1) Teach = 2X max
>   No teach consec. quarters
> 2) A....D....C
> 3) M....S or
>   SM together

STEP THREE: Draw

This game draws out just like the last one. REMEMBER that the picture is drawn around the most absolute thing we have to work with. In this case, that would be the four consecutive quarters, 1-4. Remember that PEOPLE COME FIRST!

	1	2	3	4
F, H, M, S, W				
A, B, C, D				

So there we have our game drawing... and now we have to follow up on Marcus Aurelius. Back in the setup, we were told which classes each person was allowed to teach. The formal rules told us that (rule 2) the class order must be A....D....C, with B going anywhere it wants to, or so it seems. If we organize our teachers in a manner that is consistent with rule 2, we can see something very powerful.

```
   A │  D  │  C
   F │  F  │  H
   M │  H  │  M
   S │  S  │  W
   W │     │
     ┼──┬──┼
        B
        M
        S
```

Notice that we put the teachers underneath the set order, and then we put class B and the possible teachers underneath. That allows us to visualize "sliding" it to the left of A, between A and D, between D and C or to the right of C.

TIME OUT!
Recall how we keep telling you that the rules are there to dictate *ISSUES*. In the present game, we can see what the issues are clearly: the A….D….C order, the "no teacher twice in a row," rule, and the "No M *after* S rule.

NOW look at the arrangement of the teachers. Look at F for a moment. We can see that the two classes that F is allowed to teach are A and D, which happen to be consecutive in the A…D…C order required by rule 2. Ha ha ha! We can just *smell* the stink of the question coming: "If Flanders teaches exactly two classes, what must be true?" We KNOW that it is coming because the ISSUE is right there in front of us! F cannot go twice in a row, so if F teaches twice, the B class has to be taught between A and D. That means that M or S or both would teach second… WE OWN THIS BAD BOY!

Had we done the INCORRECT thing and drawn out all of the classes and players in the order presented to us in the setup back in step 1, we would have missed this, because the two classes that F can teach are presented first (Algebra) and fourth (Discrete Mathematics) with Bayesian Statistics and Calculus in between. LOOK AT IT THE WAY THAT PEOPLE WHO ARE GOING TO PAY FOR YOUR SCHOLARSHIP DO IT:

```
  A │ B │ C │ D
  F │ M │ H │ F
  M │ S │ M │ H
  S │   │ W │ S
  W │   │   │
```

> **WARNING!**
> **THIS DRAWING**
> **IS VERY**
> **DANGEROUS!**

Notice how Marge runs in three consecutive classes in this bad drawing. Disorganized people think that they are looking at an "inference" that if M teaches twice, she cannot teach B, just A and C, which is completely incorrect.

You cannot spot the major issues of the game if you are not organized, disciplined and above all, ***MARRIED TO THE TEST MENTORS METHOD!***

STEP FOUR : Inferences

Now we can move on to the Inference step in total control of the highly organized information.

Absolutes – Are there any? A cannot be taught in the third or fourth quarters. C cannot be taught during the first or second quarters. B cannot be taught… It can be taught during any quarter! It is the people who are teaching the classes that may limit where B can go. As a general proposition however, B can be taught in any quarter. D cannot be taught in the first or fourth quarters. We can mark all of that into our drawing like so:

	1	2	3	4
F, H, M, S, W				
A, B, C, D	-C -D	-C	-A	-A -D

But now we must ask the question, "Is that really necessary?" If we look at the player charts that we made,

A	D	C
F	F	H
M	H	M
S	S	W
W		

B
M
S

is it not very obvious that A can be taught during the first (A1, B2 or D2) or second (B1, A2) quarters, but not during the third or fourth quarters? The same follows for all of the other Absolutes. We pwn this game![2]

Bundles? Not a one.

Calculators? Actually, yes, there is a calculator. We can see from the drawing that the four classes have to be taught in exactly one of four possible orders:

B,A,D,C
A,B,D,C
A,D,B,C
A,D,C,B

---

[2] To the uninitiated, "pwn" and its various forms appear to be a typographical error. It is not. "Pwn" (pronounced PŌN) means to own, and oddly enough, is originally the product of a typographical error (some World of Warcraft player, probably jacked up on Red Bull or Rock Star, fat-fingered the "p" rather than the "o" next door with his Cheeto-stained chubby-digits) but has become part of the modern lexicon. When you crush a logic game, you say, "I pwned that pig!"

Again, do we *need* to write that down? Is it not obvious from the listing of the players? HECK YA!

Double-ups? YA, and this is a big time tricky one. It has to do with the hidden rule that says that every teacher must play, and the fact that all of Marge's classes have to precede Smithers', although we can have S&M together.[3] Essentially, once Smithers teaches a class, Marge is out of the game. So if B is during the first quarter, S cannot teach it alone because M would have to teach a class in a later quarter but would not be able to. So the only way B can be taught in the first quarter by a single teacher is if M is that teacher. Otherwise, there must be both S and M teaching it, and in that case, M is done for the year.

By the same token, if B is taught in the 4th quarter, either S teaches it alone or S&M are together, because M comes before or with S. **Make a not of both!**

$$** B1 = M \text{ or } SM$$
$$** B4 = S \text{ or } SM$$

Extras? Let's run down the list. Are there any bi-conditionals? No. Are there any forced dichotomies? Sort of, but they are not really useful. Look at Flanders. He has to teach once or he can teach twice. He is forced to play, and there are two places he can play (A or D) however he can play in A or D or both (so long as the order is A, B, D, C to keep F from going twice in a row). So really there are no forced dichotomies, and we do not want to imagine them where they do not exist. Does the Right-Side Rule apply? There is no conditional logic in use, so no. Affirmative duties? All of the players have a duty to participate, right? That is not much help. Contradictions? None. Free rangers? None.

STEP FIVE – Destroy the Questions! Remember that when you are Destroying the Questions, you first Go With What You Know. We have provided you with a super-chunky problem set to help flesh out all of the processes and to demonstrate the power of the Test Mentors Methods.

---

[3] Letter combinations on the LSAT are often distracting. We surmise that they must be deliberately so. There are too many examples in the historical record of the LSAT having S&M, FO, MF and the like for it to merely be coincidental.

REMEMBER THE MARCUS AURELIUS QUOTE FROM THE BEGINNING OF THE SECTION!

PROB. SET 18 (Answers in Appendix "B")
Exactly four different math classes are being taught, one during each quarter of the school year, at a community college: Algebra, Bayesian Statistics, Calculus, and Discrete Mathematics. At least one and at most two teachers are assigned to each course, and each teacher will be assigned at least one course. Algebra may be taught only by Flanders, Marge, Smithers or Willie. Bayesian Statistics may be taught only by Marge or Smithers. Calculus may be taught only by Homer, Marge or Willie. Discrete Mathematics may be taught only by Flanders, Homer or Smithers. The order in which the classes are taught and the assignment of teacher to them must comply with the following constraints:

No teacher may teach during more than two quarters, and they may not be consecutive.

Discrete Mathematics must be taught before Calculus and after Algebra.

None of Marge's classes may be taught later in the year than any of Smithers'.

1) Which of the following could be a complete and accurate list of the classes taught, in order, and the teachers assigned to them?
 (a) Algebra: Marge, Flanders
   Bayesian Statistics: Marge, Smithers
   Calculus: Homer, Willie
   Discrete Mathematics: Homer
 (b) Algebra: Flanders, Willie
   Bayesian Statistics: Marge
   Discrete Mathematics: Homer, Flanders
   Calculus: Marge, Willie
 (c) Algebra: Flanders, Willie
   Bayesian Statistics: Smithers
   Discrete Mathematics: Homer, Flanders
   Calculus: Willie, Marge
 (d) Bayesian Statistics: Homer, Smithers
   Algebra: Flanders, Willie
   Discrete Mathematics: Homer, Smithers
   Calculus: Willie, Flanders
 (e) Algebra: Flanders, Willie
   Discrete Mathematics: Homer
   Calculus: Willie
   Bayesian Statistics: Marge, Smithers

2) If Flanders teaches in two different quarters, which of the following must be true?
 (a) Calculus is taught in the third quarter
 (b) Algebra is taught in the third quarter
 (c) Algebra is taught in the first quarter
 (d) Bayesian Statistics is taught in the first quarter
 (e) Bayesian Statistics is taught in the fourth quarter.

3) Which of the following, if known, would allow the order of the four courses to be completely determined?
 (a) Calculus is taught in the third quarter.
 (b) Algebra is taught in the first quarter.
 (c) Discrete Mathematics is taught in the second quarter.
 (d) Discrete Mathematics is taught by Homer and Flanders.
 (e) Bayesian Statistics is taught by Smithers only.

4) If Algebra is taught only by Flanders, and only Smithers teaches Bayesian Statistics, which of the following must be false?
 (a) Willie teaches Calculus with Marge.
 (b) Marge teaches Calculus with Homer.
 (c) Homer teaches Discrete Mathematics.
 (d) Bayesian Statistics is taught in the fourth quarter.
 (e) Smithers does not teach Discrete Mathematics.

5) Which of the following must be false?
 (a) Willie teaches during the first quarter.
 (b) Willie teaches during the second quarter.
 (c) Homer teaches during the first quarter.
 (d) Homer teaches during the second quarter.
 (e) Homer teaches during the third quarter.

6) Which of the following must be true?
 (a) Algebra is not taught in the second quarter.
 (b) Algebra is not taught in the first quarter.
 (c) Bayesian Statistics is not taught in the second quarter.
 (d) Calculus is not taught in the second quarter.
 (e) Discrete Mathematics is taught in the third quarter.

7) If Bayesian Statistics are taught by one teacher in the first quarter, which of the following could be true?
(a) Marge teaches calculus.
(b) Flanders teaches both Algebra and Discrete Mathematics.
(c) Smithers teaches both Algebra and Discrete Mathematics.
(d) Algebra is taught by Flanders and Willie, and Discrete Mathematics is taught only by Homer.
(e) Homer and Willie teach Calculus.

8) What is the greatest number of classes that can be taught by a single instructor during the four quarters?
(a) zero
(b) one
(c) two
(d) three
(e) four

9) Suppose that the condition which says that no teacher is allowed to teach more than twice is suspended. If all other rules remain in effect, then what would be the maximum number of teachers who could teach twice?
(a) One
(b) Two
(c) Three
(d) Four
(e) Five

10) If Homer teaches two classes by himself, Which of the following could be true?
(a) Smithers and Willie teach Algebra During the first quarter.
(b) Flanders and Willie teach Algebra during the first quarter.
(c) Smithers teaches two classes.
(d) Marge and Smithers each teach two classes.
(e) Flanders teaches one class and Smithers teaches two classes.

11) Which of the following is an acceptable ordering of the teachers of the classes, by quarter taught?
(a) First: Smithers, Willie
   Second: Homer, Flanders
   Third: Homer, Willie
   Fourth: Smithers, Marge
(b) First: Marge
   Second: Homer, Flanders
   Third: Smithers
   Fourth: Homer, Willie
(c) First: Homer, Willie
   Second: Marge, Smithers
   Third: Flanders
   Fourth: Homer, Smithers
(d) First: Marge, Smithers
   Second: Flanders, Homer
   Third: Willie
   Fourth: Homer, Marge
(e) First: Smithers
   Second: Flanders, Willie
   Third: Homer, Smithers
   Fourth: Willie

12) If Marge teaches during both the first quarter and the last quarter, which of the following must be false?
a) Marge teaches Algebra
b) Marge teaches Bayesian statistics
c) Marge teaches Calculus
d) Smithers teaches Calculus
e) Smithers teaches Discrete Mathematics

223

The Shape of Your Subdivision

Sometimes a logic game will do something like this:

A group of nine divers, B, C, D, E, F, G, H, J and K, is being broken up into three teams, X, Y and Z of at least two divers per team. Four of the divers, B, C, E and G, are master divers. Two of the divers, D and F, are intermediate divers. The remaining divers are novices. The teams must conform to the following conditions:

There must be at least one master diver on each team.
No team can have all of the novice divers.
K cannot be on the same team as B nor G.
D cannot be on the same team as C nor E.
H and K must be on either team X or Y.

We have nine divers, and those divers are sub-divided into three sub-groups: master, intermediate and novice. Here is the way to handle them: group them and apply *shapes* to them in Step One of the Test Mentors Method.

You can see that we have used a square, a triangle and a double-bar (above and below) to demark the three sub-divisions. We DO NOT use circles, because circles indicate that something is *absolute*. **The numerically smallest group, the intermediate, gets the triangle**. This is because the triangle, though easy to draw, is a bit annoying to draw around a letter. We recommend drawing the triangle first and putting the letter into the shape after. Squares and double-bars can be done in any order, though we recommend using the square for the largest sub-group. In Steps Two and Three we are going to use these shapes to clarify the logic and make inferences easier later.

1) @ least 1 ☐ per team

2) No team has 3 =

3) K̲ NEVER with B nor G

4) △ NEVER with C nor E

5) H̲ K̲ MUST be on X or Y

The shapes allow is to clearly, visually and easily see connections between rules (which are really just premises in an argument that we are supposed to draw inferences from). We will go through this entire game in one of the problem sets *infra.* For now, the thing that you must know is that :

WHENEVER A CATEGORY OF PLAYERS IS SUBDIVIDED, USE SHAPES. ***MEMORIZE THAT!***

This applies to things that are distinguished by gender, species, profession... whatever. It does not apply when the gender, experience level, etc. is itself the player, i.e. "A shaman, a monk, a priest, a deacon and a rabbi are walking into a bar..." That is not sub-dividing. Contrast that with: "Six religious officials, two priests, two rabbis and two monks are playing golf..." That is a group of six that is subdivided into subgroups.

Take a good look at the page number. In less than 230 pages you have learned *everything* you need to know to destroy the LSAT logic games section. You know every step, every rule, all of the logic, all of the processes and check-lists... *everything.* The logic will make you a great student. Being a great student will make you an excellent lawyer.

Knowing the Test Mentors Method is not enough: you must now **master** it. The way that you master it is by ***doing it.*** Hence, we have provided you with a plethora of additional games along with step-by-step analyses as to the proper application of the Test Mentors Method.

The following games are designed to challenge you to apply the methods as perfectly as you can. Going through the detailed explanations of each and every problem set is IMPERATIVE. We teach you more about the process, more about the subtleties of the Test Mentors Method and more about issue spotting in every explanation. In doing these problems, have two objectives in mind:

   a) Mastering the Test Mentors Method
   b) Learning something new from every set of problems.

We doubt that we can emphasize the following enough, but we are going to try:

1) Your entire future is dependent upon your knowledge of the methods taught in this book.
Doing problems and looking up the answers is pointless if you are not using the methods completely and properly.

2) The *issues* identified by the process are the _exact same kind_ that you will encounter in law school and in the practice of law: knowing the Test Mentors Method™ inside and out will make you a killer at games as well as in law school, the office and the courtroom.

3) DO NOT, UNDER ANY CIRCUMSTANCE, DELUDE YOURSELF INTO BELIEVING THAT THERE IS ANY SUBSTITUTE FOR COMPETENCE. WHEN IT COMES TO THE LSAT, THERE ARE NO SHORTCUTS, THERE ARE NO TRICKS. THERE IS ONLY COMPETENCE.

"DO OR DO NOT; THERE IS NO 'TRY.' "[1]

---

[1] Yoda, the greatest puppet-philosopher in the history of the universe. Star Wars, *The Empire Strikes Back*, 1980. He also makes a mean rootleaf stew (same movie) and is a killer banjo player (tragically left on the cutting room floor).

Problem Set 19

(Answers in Appendix "B")

Eight political candidates, Arthur, Ford, Grunthos, Hotblack, Marvin, Prostetnic, Trillian and Zaphod, are each to give a speech to a community organization. The speeches will be presented one at a time and must comply with the following conditions:

Ford speaks before Arthur but after Trillian.
Both Prostetnic and Zaphod speak after Grunthos.
Either Hotblack speaks before both Marvin and Zaphod, or else he speaks after both Marvin and Zaphod.
Marvin speaks before Ford.

1) Which one of the following could be the order in which the candidates speak?
A) Marvin, Trillian, Ford, Arthur, Hotblack, Grunthos, Zaphod, Prostetnic.
B) Trillian, Marvin Ford, Arthur, Grunthos, Zaphod, Prostetnic, Hotblack.
C) Hotblack, Marvin, Zaphod, Grunthos, Prostetnic, Trillian, Ford, Arthur.
D) Grunthos, Zaphod, Hotblack, Prostetnic, Marvin, Trillian, Ford, Arthur.
E) Hotblack, Grunthos, Marvin, Zaphod, Prostetnic, Trillian, Arthur, Ford.

2) How many candidates can speak either first or eighth?
A) Zero
B) One
C) Two
D) Three
E) Four

3) If Zaphod speaks after both Grunthos and Hotblack, which of the following must be false?
A) Hotblack speaks first
B) Hotblack speaks second
C) Hotblack speaks third
D) Hotblack speaks fourth
E) Hotblack speaks fifth

4) If Marvin is the sixth speaker, which of the following must be true?
A) Arthur speaks eighth
B) Hotblack speaks eighth
C) Trillian speaks fifth
D) Zaphod speaks fifth
E) Grunthos speaks fifth

5) If the first three speakers are Trillian, Marvin and Grunthos, respectively, then the sixth, seventh and eighth speakers, respectively, could be:
A) Hotblack, Arthur, Ford
B) Zaphod, Ford, Arthur
C) Prostetnic, Ford, Hotblack
D) Ford, Arthur, Hotblack
E) Ford, Hotblack, Zaphod

6) The earliest position that Arthur can speak in is:
A) Second
B) Third
C) Fourth
D) Fifth
E) Sixth

7) If Ford is the third speaker, which of the following could be the order of the fourth, fifth and sixth speakers respectively?
A) Arthur, Hotblack, Prostetnic
B) Hotblack, Grunthos, Zaphod
C) Grunthos, Prostetnic, Hotblack
D) Arthur, Grunthos, Prostetnic
E) Zaphod, Hotblack, Prostetnic

8) If Arthur speaks sixth and Prostetnic speaks seventh, which of the following must be true?
A) Either Hotblack or Grunthos speaks first
B) Either Hotblack or Zaphod speaks first
C) Either Hotblack or Zaphod speaks last
D) Either Trillian or Marvin speaks first
E) Either Trillian or Marvin speaks last

Problem Set 20 (Answers in Appendix "B")

A sixty story hotel has nine guests- A, B, C, D, F, G, H, J, K- that will only take rooms on one of the top three floors. Floor sixty has two rooms available, floor fifty-nine has one room available, and floor fifty-eight has two rooms available. Each room can fit a maximum of two guests. All guests must have a room and rooms must be assigned according to the following rules:

> D shares a room with another guest.
> If A does not share a room with C then B shares a room with F
> If H is on floor sixty, she has no roommate
> G and J share a room but not on floor 58.
> K is on floor 60 and does not share a room.
> A and B cannot be on the same floor.

1. Which one of the following could be a complete and accurate list of the guests staying on floor fifty-eight?
   A) B, C, A
   B) A, D, C, F
   C) G, J, B, C
   D) A, F, B, C
   E) A, C, D, J

2. Each of the following guests could be placed in a room on any floor EXCEPT:
   A) C
   B) F
   C) G
   D) H
   E) K

3. If A and C are on floor 60 which one of the following must be true?
   A) B and F share a room on floor fifty-eight
   B) C and H share a room on floor fifty-nine
   C) B and H are on the same floor
   D) F and H are on floor fifty-nine together
   E) H and F share a room on floor fifty-eight.

4. If D is on the same floor as K, which of the following must be true?
   A) Either G or J or both are on the sixtieth floor
   B) Either F or B or both are on the fifty-ninth floor
   C) Either C or F share a room with D
   D) Either C or F share a room with H
   E) Either A or D shares a room with F

5. Which one of the following is a complete and accurate list of guests who can share rooms together?
   A) B with F; A with C; G with J; D with H
   B) A with F; B with C; G with J; C with H
   C) A with C; B with J; G with H; D with F
   D) C with F; A with D; B with F; G with J
   E) A with B; C with D; F with H; G with J

6. Suppose floor fifty-nine now has two rooms available. If all of the other conditions remain in effect, which of the following must be false?
   A) H and F share a room on floor fifty-nine and A and C share a room on floor fifty-nine
   B) A and D share a room on floor sixty and K is on floor sixty
   C) G, J and K are all on floor sixty and there are no empty rooms in the hotel
   D) G, J and K are all on floor sixty and there is one empty room in the hotel
   E) G, J and K are all on floor sixty and there are two empty rooms in the hotel.

7) Which one of the following, if substituted for the rule requiring H, if on floor sixty, to have a room by herself, would have the same effect as that rule?
   A) H must be on floor fifty-eight
   B) H must be on floor fifty-nine.
   C) H is on either floor fifty-eight or floor fifty-nine.
   D) B and C cannot be on the same floor.
   E) D shares a room with H.

PROBLEM SET 21 (Answers in Appendix "B")

There are seven toppings available for an ice cream sundae- almonds, bananas, cherries, fudge, Heath bar©, peanuts, and sprinkles. Selection of the toppings must comply with the following constraints:

If almonds are selected peanuts are not.
If cherries or almonds are selected then bananas are as well.
If fudge is not selected then peanuts and sprinkles must be.
If sprinkles are selected then so are almonds and Heath bar.
If Heath bar is selected then cherries are also selected.

1. Which one of the following CANNOT be a complete and accurate list of the toppings selected?
   A) Almonds, Bananas, Fudge
   B) Peanuts, Fudge, Heath bar
   C) Fudge, Bananas, Cherries
   D) Heath bar, Fudge, Cherries, Bananas
   E) Heath bar, Fudge, Almonds, Bananas, Cherries, Sprinkles.

2. If sprinkles are selected which one of the following must be false?
   A) Heath bar is included
   B) Fudge is included
   C) Cherries are not included
   D) Peanuts are included
   E) Bananas are included

3. Which one of the following could be the only topping selected?
   A) Fudge
   B) Sprinkles
   C) Peanuts
   D) Heath bar
   E) Cherries

4. If exactly three toppings are selected, which one of the following CANNOT be one of the three?
   A) Bananas
   B) Fudge
   C) Almonds
   D) Cherries
   E) Heath Bar

5. If bananas are not selected which one of the following must be true?
   A) Peanuts are selected
   B) Heath bar is not selected
   C) Almonds are selected
   D) Fudge is not selected
   E) Peanuts are not selected

6. If peanuts are selected which of the following CANNOT be selected?
   A) Fudge
   B) Bananas
   C) Sprinkles
   D) Cherries
   E) Heath bar

7. Which one of the following toppings must be selected?
   A) Almonds
   B) Bananas
   C) Cherries
   D) Fudge
   E) Heath bar

8. Which one of the following could be a complete and accurate list of the toppings selected?
   A) Bananas, Fudge, Heath bar, Peanuts
   B) Bananas, Cherries, Heath bar
   C) Almonds, Cherries, Fudge, Peanuts, Sprinkles
   D) Cherries, Fudge, Heath bar, Sprinkles
   E) Almonds, Bananas, Cherries, Fudge

9. Which of the following is the minimum and maximum number of toppings that may be selected for the sundae?
   A) 0, 7
   B) 1, 7
   C) 1, 6
   D) 1, 5
   E) 2, 6

10. If bananas are not selected, which of the following must be true?
   A) At most, two toppings are selected
   B) At most, three toppings are selected
   C) At most, four toppings are selected
   D) At least two toppings are selected
   E) At least three toppings are selected

229

Problem set 22 (answers in Appendix "B")

Six campers, Brian, Joe, Lois, Peter, Quagmire and Stewie, are being assigned to beds in three bunks at camp Giggity, one person per bed. The bunks are numbered one, two and three. Each bunk has a top and a bottom bed. The assignment of campers to beds conforms to the following conditions:
  Brian and Joe share a bunk but are in different beds.
  Quagmire and Stewie are in different bunks.
  If Peter is in bunk two, then Lois is not in bunk three.

1) Which of the following could be a complete and accurate listing of the assignments to bunks and beds?
  A) Bunk 1: Brian top, Joe bottom
    Bunk 2: Peter top, Lois bottom
    Bunk 3: Quagmire top, Stewie bottom
  B) Bunk 1: Joe top, Brian bottom
    Bunk 2: Stewie top, Peter bottom
    Bunk 3: Quagmire top, Lois bottom
  C) Bunk 1: Peter top, Quagmire bottom
    Bunk 2: Lois top, Brian bottom
    Bunk 3: Joe top, Stewie bottom
  D) Bunk 1: Peter top, Quagmire bottom
    Bunk 2: Stewie top, Lois bottom
    Bunk 3: Joe top, Brian bottom
  E) Bunk 1: Joe top, Brian bottom
    Bunk 2: Lois top, Peter bottom
    Bunk 3: Stewie top, Quagmire bottom

2) Which one of the following must be false?
  A) Peter shares a bunk with Lois
  B) Peter shares a bunk with Quagmire
  C) Quagmire shares a bunk with Lois
  D) Stewie shares a bunk with Lois
  E) Stewie shares a bunk with Peter

3) If Joe is in the top of bunk 1, which of the following must be true?
  A) Peter is in bunk 2
  B) Quagmire is in bunk 3
  C) Lois is in bunk 2
  D) Lois is in bunk 3
  E) Stewie is in bunk 2

4) If Peter is in the bottom of bunk 3, then for how many other campers can their bunk and bed be determined?
  A) zero
  B) one
  C) two
  D) three
  E) four

5) If Lois is in bunk 1, which of the following must be false?
  A) Quagmire is in bunk 1
  B) Quagmire is in bunk 3
  B) Stewie is in bunk 1
  C) Stewie is in bunk 3
  E) Peter is in bunk 1

6) If Peter is in the bottom of bunk 2, which of the following is a complete and accurate list of all of the campers who could be in the top of bunk 3?
  A) Stewie
  B) Lois
  C) Lois, Stewie
  D) Lois, Quagmire
  E) Brian, Joe

7) Which of the following rules, if substituted for the rule which says that if Peter is in bunk 2, Lois cannot be in bunk 3, would have the same effect?
  A) If Lois is not in bunk 3, Peter must be in bunk 3.
  B) If Joe is in bunk 3, Lois is in bunk 1.
  C) If Quagmire is in bunk 1, Stewie is in bunk 2.
  D) If Peter is not in bunk 2, Joe is in bunk 2.
  E) If Quagmire is not in bunk 3, he is in bunk 1.

Problem set 23 (Answers in Appendix "B")

Seven astronauts, Allen, Cooper, Deke, Gus, John, Scott, and Wally, are to be assigned to zero-G training during a single week, Monday through Sunday, one astronaut per day. The astronauts trained on Monday and Tuesday will be assigned to the Mars mission. Those trained on Wednesday, Thursday and Friday will be assigned to the moon mission. Those trained on Saturday and Sunday will be assigned to the asteroid intercept mission (AIM). Training must conform to the following:

Wally is assigned to the Mars mission.

Deke and Scott train earlier in the week than Allen.

If John trains on Tuesday, either Deke or Scott trains on Saturday.

Gus cannot be assigned to the Mars mission.

1) Which of the following could be the astronaut training schedule, Monday through Sunday, respectively?
   A) Allen, Cooper, Deke, Scott, John, Gus, Wally.
   B) Wally, John, Gus, Deke, Scott, Cooper, Allen.
   C) Wally, Deke, Scott, Allen, Gus, John, Cooper.
   D) Gus, Wally, Cooper, Deke, John, Allen, Scott.
   E) Wally, Gus, John, Scott, Cooper, Deke, Allen.

2) If Deke is assigned to AIM, which of the following must be false?
   A) Allen trains on Sunday.
   B) John trains before Wally.
   C) Cooper trains on Wednesday.
   D) Wally trains on an earlier day than Gus.
   E) Gus trains earlier than Wally.

3) Which of the following is a complete and accurate list of the astronauts none of whom can be assigned to the Mars mission?
   A) Gus
   B) Allen, Deke
   C) Allen, Gus
   D) Allen, Gus, Deke
   E) Allen, John, Scott

4) If the moon mission consists of Allen, Deke and Scott, which of the following must be false?
   A) John trains before Wally.
   B) John trains after Wally.
   C) John Trains on Monday.
   D) John trains on Tuesday.
   E) John trains on Sunday.

5) Which of the following is the earliest day of the week on which Allen can train?
   A) Wednesday
   B) Thursday
   C) Friday
   D) Saturday
   E) Sunday

6) Which of the following can never be true?
   A) Gus trains on Saturday
   B) Wally trains on Monday
   C) Allen trains on Friday
   D) Scott trains on Sunday
   E) Allen trains on Thursday

7) If the training schedule for Tuesday, Wednesday and Thursday is John, Gus, Cooper respectively, how many possible different arrangements of the training schedule are possible?
   A) Two
   B) Three
   C) Four
   D) Five
   E) Six

Problem set 24 (Answers in Appendix "B")

Each of nine divers, B, C, D, E, F, G, H, J and K, will be assigned to one of three teams, X, Y and Z of at least two divers per team. Four of the divers, B, C, E and G, are master divers. Two of the divers, D and F, are intermediate divers. The remaining divers are novices. The teams must conform to the following conditions:

There must be at least one master diver on each team.

No team can have all of the novice divers.

K cannot be on the same team as B nor G.

D cannot be on the same team as C nor E.

H must be on either team X or Y as must K.

B is never on the same team as G.

1) Which one of the following is an accurate assignment of divers to teams?

A) X: B, D, G, H
   Y: C, E, K
   Z: F, J

B) X: C, F, J
   Y: B, D, E
   Z: G, H, K

C) X: D, H, J
   Y: B, C, F
   Z: E, G, K

D) X: D, G, H
   Y: C, E, K
   Z: B, F, J

E) X: D, E, H, K
   Y: B, C
   Z: G, F, J

2) If D is on team X, which one of the following must be false?

A) B is on team X
B) B is on team Z
C) H is on team X
D) K is on team X
E) K is on team Y

3) Which one of the following must be true?

A) If B is on team Y, G is on team Z
B) If C is on team X, E is on team Z
C) If K is on team Y, C is on team Y
D) If D is on team Y, H is on team Y
E) If F is on team X, G is on team Z

4) If C, E, F and J are on team Y, which one of the following could be true?

A) H is on team Z
B) H is on team Y
C) D is on team Z
D) Both H and D are on team X
E) Both H and D are on team Z

5) Which one of the following must be false?

A) K is on team Z
B) D is on team X
C) F is on team X
D) E is on team Y
E) B is on team Z

6) If D is assigned to team X, then which one of the following divers must be assigned to the same team as K?

A) B or G or both
B) F or H or both
C) J or G or both
D) J or H or both
E) C or E or both

7) If B and C are the master divers on team X, and if every team has one novice diver assigned to it, then it must be true that:

A) Team X has four or five divers.
B) Team Y has four or five divers.
C) Team Z has four or five divers.
D) Team X has at least as many members as team Z.
E) Team X has at least as many members as team Y.

8) Which of the following is a complete and accurate list of all of the divers who could be on team Z?

A) B, D
B) B, D, G
C) B, C, E, D, G
D) B, D, F, G, J
E) B, D, F, G, J, K

Problem set 25 (Answers in Appendix "B")

A display of six pumpkins sit next to each other as shown below:

1   4

2   5

3   6

Each pumpkin is white or else orange.
Pumpkin 1 is orange.
Each pumpkin has either a bat or else a face carved on it, but not both
Each bat must be directly above, directly beside, or directly below another bat.
Each face must be directly above, or directly below another face.
Pumpkin 5 has a bat.
Pumpkin 2 has a face.

1. If all pumpkins with bats are orange which one of the following must be true?
   A) Pumpkin 4 is orange.
   B) Pumpkin 1 is a bat.
   C) There is at least one orange pumpkin.
   D) There are at least two orange pumpkins
   E) There are at least three orange pumpkins.

2. If exactly three pumpkins are orange, and no white pumpkin is next to, above or below another white pumpkin, which one of the following cannot be true?
   A) There is an orange Bat.
   B) Pumpkins 3 is white.
   C) Pumpkins 1, 4, and 6 are orange.
   D) Pumpkin 2 and 6 are white.
   E) Pumpkin 1 has a bat

3. If there are only two pumpkins with bats, and every bat is white, which one of the following must be true?
   A) Pumpkin 4 is orange.
   B) Pumpkin 6 has a face.
   C) Pumpkin 4 is white or else pumpkin 2 is white.
   D) Pumpkin 6 is white or else pumpkin 3 is white.
   E) Pumpkin 4 is orange and pumpkin 2 is orange.

4. If pumpkin 3 has a face, which one of the following cannot have a face?
   A) Pumpkin 1
   B) Pumpkin 2
   C) Pumpkin 4
   D) Pumpkin 5
   E) Pumpkin 6

5. If pumpkins 1 and 6 are carved with bats and are white, which one of the following could be true?
   A) Pumpkin 4 is a white bat.
   B) Pumpkin 5 has a face.
   C) Pumpkin 3 is a white bat.
   D) Pumpkin 3 has an orange face.
   E) Pumpkin 4 is an orange bat.

6. If a rule is added that requires every orange pumpkin to be above, below or beside an orange pumpkin and each white pumpkin to be above, below or beside a white one, which one of the following CANNOT be true?
   A) Pumpkin 1 has a bat.
   B) Pumpkins 4 and 6 are white
   C) Pumpkins 2 and 4 are orange.
   D) Pumpkins 5 and 6 are orange.
   E) Pumpkins 2 and 3 are white.

233

Problem set 26 (Answers in Appendix "B")

Five dogs- R, S, T, V, and W- will each compete in a different dog sport- Agility, Conformation, Disk, Hare Coursing, and Obedience. Each dog is also assigned a level in the following order lowest to highest- Junior, Intermediate, or Expert, with at least one dog at each level. The following conditions apply:

The dog that competes in agility is intermediate level.

V is a lower level than the dogs that compete in Disk and Obedience.

R competes in agility if and only if W competes in conformation.

S and W are the only dogs at the expert level.

1. Which one of the following is a possible assignment of sports to dogs?
   A) R: Agility, S: Conformation, T: Hare coursing , V: Disk, W: Obedience
   B) R: Conformation, S: Disk, T: Hare coursing, V: Agility, W: Obedience
   C) R: Disk, S: Hare coursing, T: Agility, V: Obedience, W: Conformation
   D) R: Agility, S: Disk, T: Conformation, V: Hare coursing, W: Obedience
   E) R: Obedience, S: Agility, T: , V: Hare coursing, W: Conformation

2. If T is assigned to the intermediate level which one of the following must be false?
   A) S competes in agility
   B) V competes in agility
   C) R is assigned to the intermediate level
   D) W competes in disk
   E) S competes in conformation

3. Which one of the following CANNOT be a complete and accurate list of the dogs at the junior level?
   A) V
   B) T
   C) T, R
   D) V, R
   E) V, T

4. If V is assigned to the junior level which one of the following could be true?
   A) R competes in coursing.
   B) V competes in agility.
   C) V competes in disk.
   D) V competes in obedience.
   E) W competes in agility.

5. What is the greatest number of dogs that could be assigned to the junior level?
   A) 1
   B) 2
   C) 3
   D) 4
   E) 5

6. If T competes in agility which one of the following is a complete and accurate list of the sports W could compete in?
   A) Hare coursing
   B) Disk, Hare coursing,
   C) Disk, Hare coursing, Obedience
   D) Conformation, Disk, Hare coursing, Obedience
   E) Conformation, Obedience, Hare coursing

7) What is the maximum number of ways that the dogs can be arranged in different levels?
   A) 3
   B) 4
   C) 5
   D) 6
   E) 7

Jack Black is selecting new members for his garage band. He can choose from three guitar players- H, J, and K- three bass players- L, M, and N- and four drummers- O, P, Q, and R. The following conditions apply:

Exactly one bass player and one drummer must be selected.

Two guitar players maximum can be selected.

If M is not selected then P is selected.

J is selected.

If H is selected then Q and R are not.

1. Which of the following CANNOT be a complete and accurate list of the members selected?
   A) Guitar: J, K Bass: L Drums: Q
   B) Guitar: H Bass: L Drums: R
   C) Guitar: J, H Bass: M Drums: P
   D) Guitar: J, K Bass: L Drums: R
   E) Guitar: J Bass: N Drums: O

2. If there is only one guitar player selected, which of the following must be false?
   A) M and P are selected
   B) L and P are selected
   C) L and R are selected
   D) M and R are selected
   E) H and M are selected

3. Which of the following must be true?
   A) K is selected
   B) M and J are selected
   C) If M is selected O is selected
   D) If H is selected P is selected
   E) If N is selected P is selected

4. If R is selected then which of the following could be true?
   A) H is selected
   B) K is selected
   C) L is selected
   D) Q is selected
   E) N is selected

5. Which of the following could be a complete and accurate list of possible members that are NOT selected?
   A) M, O, Q, R, K
   B) N, L, P, Q, O, K
   C) J, O, P, Q
   D) M, N, O, P, Q, R, K
   E) O, P, Q, L, M

6. If the condition is added that two guitar players are selected N is also selected, which of the following must be false?
   A) N and H are selected
   B) N and K are selected
   C) N and P are selected
   D) N and O are selected
   E) H and P are selected

Problem set 28 (Answers in Appendix "B")

Five girls- A, B, C, D, and E- and six boys- F, G, H, J, K, and L- will each be placed on one of two soccer teams- Team 1 and Team 2. Each team can have seven players maximum including one team captain in accordance with the following constraints:

> If the captain of Team 1 is a girl then the other captain must be a boy.
>
> J is the captain of his team.
>
> If A is on Team 1 then C and H are on Team 2.
>
> If H is on Team 2 then J and L are also.
>
> If F is on Team 1 then B and D cannot be captains.
>
> E is one of two girls on her team and is not a team captain.

1. Which one of the following could be a complete and accurate list of the members for each team?

   A) Team 1: A, G, B, K, C
       Team 2: H, J, L, E, D, F
   B) Team1: H, L, F, B, E
       Team 2: C, A, J, G, K
   C) Team 1: J, C, E, G, K
       Team 2: B, D, H, A, F, L
   D) Team 1: L, E, C, F
       Team 2: J, H, A, B, D, K, G
   E) Team 1: H, E, A
       Team 2: F, G, J, K, L, B, C, D

2. If B is the captain of Team 1, which of the following could be true?

   A) E and D are on Team 2
   B) E and A are on Team 1
   C) C and A are on Team 1
   D) J is on Team 1
   E) C and E are on Team 2

3. If A and E are on Team 1 which of the following must be false?

   A) 5 boys are on Team 2
   B) 2 girls are on Team 1
   C) 4 boys are on Team 2
   D) 3 boys are on Team 1
   E) 3 girls are on Team 2

4. Which one of the following CANNOT be true?

   A) H is the captain of Team 2
   B) A is the captain of Team 1
   C) K is the captain of Team 1
   D) F is the captain of Team 1
   E) C is a captain

5. Which one of the following is a complete and accurate list of players that cannot be captains of team 2?

   A) A, E, H
   B) H
   C) J, A, C, D, B, F
   D) H, E
   E) J, H

6. If the condition that J is a captain is suspended which of the following could be the captains of Team 1 and Team 2 consecutively?

   A) F, D
   B) E, H
   C) B, C
   D) G, K
   E) F, E

236

APPENDIX "A" - THINGS TO MEMORIZE

1) The most important of all of the laws of life as a lawyer: FIGURE IT OUT FOR YOURSELF!

2) Always go with what you already know.

3) The "**fact pattern**" is the little paragraph at the very start of a game. It is separate and distinct from the "**formal rules**" of the game, which are listed right after the fact pattern.

4) *"There are only SIX kinds of logic games. They are all simple. Every problem can be reduced to an exact outcome when I follow the rules precisely. I will defeat them all. What one fool can do, so can another."*

5) Kinds of games
   1) ORDERING – firm or squishy
   2) BUCKETS – definite numbers and types
   3) WINNERS & LOSERS – What is in and what is out
   4) PROCEDURE - following a set of procedural steps
   5) DRAWING – repeating a process through cycles
   6) COMBO – two or more of the above, combined.

6) The more information we have and the more rules and requirements that there are, the fewer possible outcomes there can be.

7) The single most important key to LSAT success is to know the answers to the questions before you look at the answer choices.

STEPS FOR SOLVING ANY GAME
8) STEP ONE: Get a Grip
   1) What kind of game is it?
   2) Who are the players?
   3) What are the hidden rules?

9) HURRYING IS A SIN. Never rush. Ever.

10) STEP TWO: Re-write the rules.

11) The slash "/" means, "either - or".

12) STEP THREE: Drawing.
   The four kinds of basic drawings:

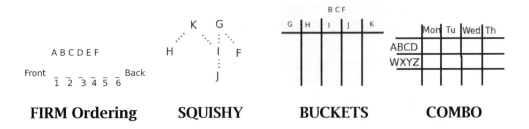

| FIRM Ordering | SQUISHY | BUCKETS | COMBO |

13) Numbering Things in Ordering Games
   A) Unless otherwise instructed, the first position is on the left, last is on the right.
   B) Top position is always at the top, bottom position is always at the bottom.
   C) "Higher" is always drawn above lower.
   D) Sometimes the bottom position is number one, sometimes it is number last. A hotel is a good example: bottom floor equals #1, top floor equals the highest number.

14) **Find, Bubble, Move** - For EVERY question on the LSAT there is _exactly one correct answer_. If you find an answer in any logic game that both fits your picture and complies will the rules that are not in the picture, it MUST be the correct answer, and all of the other choices **_must be incorrect!_** Ergo, if you deem "C" to be the correct answer, NEVER, EVER, EVER read "D" or "E", as they cannot be correct.

15) STEP FOUR: INFERENCES = **ABCDEF**
   1) Absolutes
   2) Bundles
   3) Calculators
   4) Double-ups
   5) Extras
   6) Free-rangers

16) In order to be correct, an answer has to comply with both the picture(s) and the rules not incorporated into the picture(s) EVERY TIME!

17) There can only be one correct answer, so FIND, BUBBLE, MOVE! (Pg.26).

18) STEP FIVE: Destroy the questions.
   a) Read and interpret the _call of the question completely_.
   b) Go with what you know already. If you do not have the answer, based upon all of the work you have done,
   c) Apply the _Pencil Protocols_
        i) Re-picture whatever it is that you are using for a picture. In the case

of winner/loser games, there is no picture, there are just players. So you write them all out.

   ii) Apply the "if" that the call of the question provides ***to your re-picture***.

      Remember to NEVER touch an original picture with all of the work that you did to it.

   iii) Go to the rules and see what the rules indicate must happen.

      A) If the rules tell you that something else must occur, apply that change to your re-picture and repeat step iii.

      B) If the rules do not indicate that anything else is to occur (i.e. no further changes need to happen to your re-picture) then you have the answer.

Don't get cocky, and don't walk away from all of the hard work you did in steps one through four.

19) In squishy ordering games, **THE DOTTED LINES DEFINE EVERYTHING.**

20) ALWAYS re-draw your pictures to plug in hypothetical information (from "if" questions) and NEVER TOUCH YOUR ORIGINAL PICTURES! RE-PICTURE THEM!

21) **The Multiple-Picture Rules**
   a) Draw two pictures when there are ONLY two ways for the game to be played AND the two drawings provide valuable additional information.
   b) You had better have a damn good reason for making three pictures.
     NEVER make more than three pictures: you are wasting precious time.

22) Unless otherwise indicated, "or" is used *inclusively* (steak, chicken or both steak and chicken) on the LSAT. If "or" is intended to be used *exclusively* on the LSAT, the statement will clearly indicate, "steak or chicken, but not both."

23) **SYMBOLS**

"X ⊃ Y" means "if X then Y"
"X · Y" means "X and Y" (the " · " is the "***conjunction***" symbol)
"X v Y" means "X or Y" (the "v" is the "***disjunction***" symbol)
"- X" means "not X" (the "-" is the "***negation***" symbol)

The terms on the left side of a conditional are called the ***antecedents*** and the terms on the right side are called the ***consequents***.

24) The LEFT side tells us SOMETHING absolute. The RIGHT side tells us NOTHING absolute. If you have a conditional statement, and then you are told that the thing(s) on the right side did in-fact happen, that does not mean that the thing(s) on the left happened.

25) You cannot say that if the *antecedent* (thing on the left) fails to occur that the consequent (thing on the right) did not happen.

26) If an "if" does not fulfill the antecedent condition then *the rule does not apply.*

27) EVERY CONDITIONAL STATEMENT should be put into symbols and immediately contra-posed. If there are no bi-conditionals, we circle the consequents of each rule-contra pair to remind ourselves of the right-side possibilities. This keeps us from affirming the consequents and denying the antecedents.

28) Contra-posing involves a three-step process:
   a) Flip everything
   b) Negate everything
   c) Swap all " · " and "v" symbols

29) **RIGHT SIDE RULE:** Everything on the right side is *possible.* Nothing on the right side tells us anything for absolutely certain.

30) "Only" = "then", and words that come after "then" go on the right hand side.

31) "Unless" = "if not".

32) **Bi-CONDITIONALS** - The phrase, "if, and only if," turns both of the categories of things in the rule into both a sufficient and necessary condition of each other.

33) When we have an "if and only if," rule, we circle the whole thing to avoid screwing up and thinking that the right side is possible, and to remind us that all four of these bad boys play as a schizophrenic team: IT IS THE EXCEPTION TO THE RIGHT-SIDE RULE.

34) "If and only if," is NOT an all or nothing situation in all cases.

35) Whenever there is a negative antecedent with an affirmative consequent, you have an *affirmative duty to do something:* something must be done, and "nothing" is not an option.

36) We must check every rule and its contra-positive for merger possibilities with all other rules.

37) EXTRAS form the inference step: When doing the A, B, C, D, E, F of the *Inferences* step, EXTRAS must be looked for in the following order:
   a) Bi-conditionals – if there are any, then the right-side rule is going to be ignored.
   b) Forced dichotomies – if there are only two choices, and if everyone must play, then the logic becomes binary. For instance, if everyone in the game has to eat either steak or chicken, -S means CHICKEN, and –C

means STEAK.

c) Right Side Rule – If there are no bi-conditionals, the Right Side Rule applies (see 27 above).

d) Affirmative duty rules – Find and note them. They are rules with negative antecedents and affirmative consequents.

e) Contradictions – Creating a situation where something must be true and false at the same time. The antecedent that brings about the consequent cannot happen.

f) Lone conditionals – When there is a single conditional rule, we may want to do a re-picture just for that rule.

38) When doing the Inference step in Winner/Loser games, do the double-up step first.

39) ALWAYS follow the pencil protocols whenever you are using your pencil to solve logic games problems!

40) When rewriting rules, the convention is, PEOPLE FIRST, STUFF SECOND.

41) "The secret of all victory lies in the organization of the non-obvious."

42) When categories of players are sub-divided, USE SHAPES!

APPENDIX "B" - ANSWERS TO PROBLEM SETS

Problem Set #1

Answers and explanations provided in the problem set.

PROBLEM SET #2 – SQUISHY ORDERING

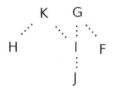

1) Which one of the following is an accurate possible ordering of the detergents, from highest to lowest?

 A) Fresh, Good Smellin', Ivy Soft, Juniper, Koala Dew, Happy Clothes
 B) Koala Dew, Good Smellin', Juniper, Ivy Soft, Fresh, Happy Clothes
 C) Good Smellin', Ivy Soft, Juniper, Koala Dew, Happy Clothes, Fresh
 D) Good Smellin', Koala Dew, Fresh, Ivy Soft, Juniper, Happy Clothes
 E) Koala Dew, Ivy Soft, Juniper, Good Smellin', Fresh, Happy Clothes

A) Can F ever go first? Nope.

B) K can be first and G can be second. Can J be third? NOPE. I has to be higher than J.

C) G can be first. Can I be second? What has to be ranked higher than I? Both G and K. Co this one is a loser.

D) G and K 1-2? It works. F third? It has to come after G, which it does. Can I go next? Is it coming after K and G? Yes! J has to come after I, which it does here, and H is allowed to be last. Hence, this is the answer we are looking for. Circle it and move on.

E) K can go first, but I cannot be ranked higher than G. Wrongo-bongo, but to be honest, you should have quit this problem once you found that "D" works. Naughty.

2) If Koala Dew is the second-highest ranked detergent, which of the following must be true?

 A) Happy Clothes is ranked third
 B) Ivy Soft is ranked third.
 C) Fresh is ranked third.
 D) Good Smellin' is ranked first.
 E) Juniper is ranked sixth.

What do we know already? We determined at the very outset of this game that only K and G can be ranked number one. If K is ranked number two, then we know for certain that G must be ranked first! A quick scan of the answers shows us that D) says precisely that! Circle it and move on.

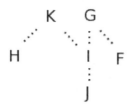

3) Which of the following is a complete and accurate list of all of the detergents which cannot be ranked second?

    A) Juniper
    B) Ivy Soft
    C) Ivy Soft, Juniper
    D) Ivy Soft, Juniper, Good Smellin'
    E) Juniper, Ivy Soft, Good Smellin', Koala Dew

What doe we know already? THE DOTTED LINES DEFINE the relationships. Any player that has more than one set of dotted lines coming out of the top of it has to have more than one player before it. J, for example, has three sets of dotted lines running out of the top of it: one directly from J to I, then two from I to K and G. If three players have to come before it, then it cannot be second. We can also see that I, having the two lines coming out of it has to have K and G before it, so the soonest it could come is third, meaning that it can never be second. We also know that either K or G could be first, which also means that they could go 1-2 in either order. This means that any answer with J and I can be the correct answer, any answer without both them has to be incorrect, and that answers with K and/or G have to be incorrect. Feel free to cross them all off. Our remaining is... THE answers: "C" must be correct.

4) If Fresh is ranked second, what cannot be true?

    A) Koala Dew is ranked third.
    B) Juniper is ranked fifth.
    C) Happy Clothes is ranked last.
    D) Koala Dew is ranked fourth.
    E) Ivy Soft is ranked fifth.

What do we already know? If F is second, which detergent has to be first? "G". So G is first and F is second. Quickly scan the answers for anything involving F or G. Poop! There are none. This only means that it is a good time to re-picture, using our *PENCIL PROTOCOLS* as we do so. G is above I, and the rules say what? "I" still has to come after G, but F is second, so "I" has to be after the G=1, F=2 line-up.

G
.
.
.
F
.
.
.
I

We changed the picture, so we look back at the rules and they tell us that "I" still has to go after K, and J has to go after I. Also, H still has to go after K.

Now that we have a visual representation of the new condition, we can answer the question easily.

    A) Can K be third? Certainly. In fact, it has to be, because K still has to come before I!

    B) Can J be 5th? J or H could be 6th, so either could be fifth as well. G,F,K,I,J,H would work.

    C) H last? Duh! We just saw that in "B".

    D) Can K be 4th? Uh....NO! At lowest, it can be third! This is our answer!

    E) Of course I can be 5th. G,F,K,H,I,J.

5) Which of the following is a complete and accurate list of all of the detergents which cannot be ranked third?

    A) Juniper

    B) Ivy Soft

    C) Juniper, Ivy Soft

    D) Juniper, Ivy Soft, Good Smellin'

    E) Juniper, Ivy Soft, Good Smellin', Happy Clothes

What do we already know? DO YOU REMEMBER DOING PROBLEM #3 a few minutes ago? IT'S THE SAME BLEEDIN' DEAL! Count the lines coming out of the top! We know that J has four, so it cannot ever be third. We can cross off (b) because it has no J in it.

Here is where we might screw things up if we rush. Every other detergent can be third. We can have G and F as 1-2 and make K 3rd. We can have K and H as 1-2, with G 3rd. F can be third if K and G go 1-2 in no particular order. Than means that H can also. "I" *LOOKS* problematic, unless you just count the lines. K and G come before it, and it could be third. Here, the truth is absolute. J is the only one that cannot be third.

We want to point out another little trick the test employs in order to see whether or not you have you wits about you. This question comes on the heels of question #4. If we re-pictured #4 and then mistakenly relied upon that drawing, we would end up with an incorrect answer to a very simple problem. There is a great reason for this: people who screw up simple problems are a malpractice nightmare down the road. They don't belong in a law school classroom, well enough a courtroom.

PROBLEM SET #3: PUTTING THINGS INTO BUCKETS

Answers and explanations provided in the problem set.

PROBLEM SET #4: BUCKETS, PART 2

B C F

G	H	I	J	K

1) I = C
2) G more than H
3) K&G 2 exact comm.
4) 1 ingred. min/ baker

2/3   1/2   3/2   G&K NEVER BOTH 3!

If H=2
G=3

1 MIN/BAKER

Recall that our primary inference was the Calculators issue:

G	H	K
2	1	2
2	1	3
3	1	2
3	2	2

G can never have just one ingredient, H can never have three and K can never have just one ingredient, and can only have three if G has two.

6) Which one of the following is a possible assignment of ingredients to bakers?
A) Gina: butter, cocoa, flour
   Henry: butter, cocoa
   Ida: butter, cocoa, flour
   Jason: flour
   Kelly: butter, cocoa, flour
B) Gina: butter, cocoa, flour
   Henry: butter, cocoa, flour
   Ida: butter, cocoa, flour
   Jason: flour
   Kelly: butter, cocoa
C) Gina: butter, cocoa
   Henry: butter, cocoa
   Ida: butter, cocoa, flour
   Jason: flour
   Kelly: butter, cocoa, flour
D) Gina: butter, cocoa
   Henry: butter
   Ida: butter, cocoa, flour
   Jason: flour
   Kelly: butter, cocoa, flour
E) Gina: flour
   Henry: butter, flour
   Ida: butter, cocoa, flour
   Jason: flour
   Kelly: butter, cocoa, flour

In (a) Gina has three and Kelly has three, so it is incorrect.

In (b) Gina has three, and Kelly has two, so rule #3 is complied with. G and H have the same number of ingredients, violating rule #2.

(c) has the same problem as "B" only here they both have two. Naughty.

In (d) G has more than H, K and G have exactly two in common, I has cocoa and two other ingredients (allowed!) and everyone has at least one. "D" is correct! CIRCLE IT AND GET OUT!

(e) is incorrect because H has more than G, but we just wasted critical time evaluating

7) If Jason has more ingredients than Gina, which of the following must be false?
A) Kelly has three ingredients
B) Kelly has two ingredients
C) Henry has one ingredient
D) Henry has two ingredients
E) Jason has three ingredients

How can J have more than G? Simple, because WE ALREADY KNOW IT! It works provided G has more than H. That means J has three, G has two and H has one. If G has two, K can have two (exactly what G has) or K can have all three. So what must be false? "A" and "B" could both be true, so kill them off. H must have one, so kill "C". "D" has Henry with two. False. Duh.

8) Which of the following, if known, would allow us to completely determine how many ingredients each baker has?
A) Kelly has three ingredients
B) Kelly has two ingredients and Henry has one
C) Jason has two ingredients and Ida has only cocoa
D) Jason has only flour, Ida has cocoa and butter only and Kelly has cocoa, butter and flour
E) Jason has only butter, Ida has only cocoa and Henry has cocoa only.

PAY PARTICULAR ATTENTION TO THIS PROBLEM! The LSAT has been using this kind of question in recent years to effectively stymie all but the best test takers, i.e. YOU. Remember, luck favors the prepared, and prepared we are! The question wants us to pin down the number of ingredients, not the kinds. So despite the wording of the answers, this is all just a calculator problem.

We know that J is a free-ranger, so he needs to be pinned down otherwise it is just free-ranging around and screwing everything up. We also need to pin down the exact number I has, and the G, H and K relationship.

"A", "B" and "C" fail to address all three issues and must be incorrect, so it is down to "D" and "E". Test one. If it works, circle it. If not, circle the other.

"D" gives J flour only and it pins down Ida's two. It then says K has all three. If K has three, G must have two and H must have one. "D" is correct.

BCF

	G	H	I	J	K

1) I = C
2) G more than H
3) K&G 2 exact comm.
4) 1 ingred. min/ baker

2/3   1/2   3/2 G&K NEVER BOTH 3!

If H=2
G=3

1 MIN/BAKER

"E" pins down J and I. If H has one ingredient, does that determine how many G and K must have? Not hardly. G could have two or three, and so could K. It is incorrect.

9) Which of the following must be true?
A) If Henry has butter, Jason must have flour
B) If Ida has cocoa and butter, Henry must have butter
C) If Gina has cocoa and flour, Kelly must have butter
D) If Henry has cocoa, Gina must have butter and flour
E) If Henry has cocoa and flour, Gina must have butter

A NAKED QUESTION! It does not give us any additional information to form a hypothetical; it simply asks what must be true based only upon the information in the original problem. This means that if we did the inferences correctly, we know the answer. The original problem told us that it is all about the Calculator, and that the actual ingredients are irrelevant.

"A" – If H has one, J is irrelevant.
"B" - If I has two, J is still irrelevant.
"C" – If G has two, K can have two or three.
"D" – If H has one, G can have two or three.
"E" – Must be correct. CIRCLE IT WITHOUT READING IT. PROOF: If H has two, G must have all three, i.e. G must have butter (and flour and cocoa). Notice that "E" does not say that G must have ONLY butter. Those test makers are a devious lot!

10) If the condition is added that nobody may have more ingredients than Jason, which of the following must be false?
A) Jason has Flour and cocoa only while Henry has flour
B) Jason has Flour and cocoa only while Kelly has flour and cocoa
C) Jason has Flour and cocoa only while Gina has flour and cocoa
D) Jason has Flour and cocoa only while Ida has flour only and Henry has butter and cocoa
E) Jason has Flour and cocoa only while Ida has flour and cocoa and Henry has butter

Here is a problem which is so typical of the last question in a game, the rule change or rule addition. Here is what you need to know about these questions: they are merely an attempt to mess with your head! They want you to believe that you have to start all over again and figure the whole thing out from scratch... but that is not in-fact the case almost all of the time. Why? Because, to quote the question, "If the

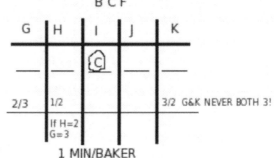

1) I = C
2) G more than H
3) K&G 2 exact comm.
4) 1 ingred. min/ baker

condition is added..." It is *added*. That means that all of the other conditions are still in effect. Given all that we already know, what does this extra condition mean? It means that we have a *further* restriction on possible outcomes! When this happens in the context of a game with two pictures, the "new rule" usually eliminates one of the two pictures and provides enough information to fill in the remaining picture.

Can J have one ingredient? NO! If J has one, G and K will have more, because G and K have to have two or three. If J has two, then H has to have one so that G and K have two and nobody has more than J. If J has three, then H can have one or two, and G or K can have three.

Which scenario sounds like one which will yield a "must be false" answer? Anything giving J just one, or anything giving J and H the same number (because G has to have more than H, so if H and J have the same number, G will have more than H and J, violating the new rule).

"A" gives J two and H one. No big deal. G and K can have two.
"B" gives J two and tells us that K has two. Again, no biggie.
"C" gives J two and G two. That is allowed so long as H has one and K has two.
"D" gives J two, I one and H two. J and H the same number? NEVER, because if H has two, G has to have three, which is more than J's two.
"E" has J with two, I with one and H with one. Completely acceptable.

248

PROBLEM SET #5

1) Everybody at the park has on red pants.

Categorical? Yes: there are two categories of things here, people in the park and red-pants wearers.
Universal? Yes: It says that everybody at the park has on red pants, ergo any person we find in the park will have on red trousers.
CONDITIONAL STATEMENTS: "If a person is in the park, then that person has red pants on." Also, "If a person is not wearing red pants, then they are not in the park."

2) There are not any people in my class with halitosis.

Categorical? Yes: It tells us about the people in my class and it tells us about people with halitosis.
Universal? Yes: It is telling us that *nobody* in my class has halitosis.
CONDITIONAL STATEMENTS: "If a person is in my class, then that person does not have halitosis." Also, "If a person has halitosis, then that person is not in my class."

3) The only things Hyundai makes are high quality cars.

Categorical? Yes: It tells us about things Hyundai makes and it tells us about high quality cars.
Universal? Yes: It is telling us that Hyundai makes but one thing: high quality cars.
CONDITIONAL STATEMENTS: "If it is made by Hyundai, then it is a high quality car." Also, "If it is not a high quality car, then it is not something made by Hyundai."

4) Many fast foods give one gout.

Categorical? Yes: It tells us about fast foods and about things that cause gout.
Universal? NO! "Many" is not "all". Also, we do not know about all things that cause gout, just one, "many" fast foods.

5) None of the people in the top ten-percent of the class are non-speed readers.

Categorical? Yes: It says that nobody (universal) in the top ten percent are people who are non-speed readers.
Universal? Yes: We know about every member of the top-ten percent.
CONDITIONAL STATEMENTS: "If a person is in the top-ten percent of the class, then they are not a non-speed-readers." You might be asking yourself, "Don't the two negatives cancel each other out?" Duh. Of course they do. It might be the LSAT, but the usual rules of reality apply. "Not non-speed-reader" is "speed reader." So it means, "If a person is top 10%, they are a speed reader." Also, "If a person is a non-speed reader, then they are not in the top-ten percent of the class," or "No non-speed-readers are in the top 10%."

6) Each child is special.

Categorical? Yes: It tells us about children and about special things.
Universal? Yes: It tells us about every child.
CONDITIONAL STATEMENTS: "If it is a child, then it is special." Also, "If it is not special, then it is not a child."

7) Catastrophes never strike Delaware.

Categorical? Yes: It tells us about disastrous things and about things that do not strike Delaware.
Universal? Yes: "Never" tells us that it is absolute.
CONDITIONAL STATEMENTS: "If it is something that strikes Delaware, then it is not a disaster." Also, "If it is a disaster, then it will never be a thing that strikes Delaware."

8) Leprechauns are mostly benign.

Categorical? Yes: It tells us about Leprechauns and about things that are mostly benign.
Universal? Yes: It is telling us about all Leprechauns.
CONDITIONAL STATEMENTS: "If it is a Leprechaun, then it is mostly benign." Also, "If it is not mostly benign, then it is not a Leprechaun."

9) Chickens make lousy house pets.

Categorical? Yes: It tells us about chickens and about things that make lousy house pets.
Universal? Yes: It is telling us about all chickens.
CONDITIONAL STATEMENTS: "If it is a chicken, then it is a lousy house pet." Also, "If it is not a lousy house pet, then it is not a chicken."

10) There are no Vogons who are unencumbered by administrative inertia.

Categorical? Yes: It tells us about Vogons and about things unencumbered by administrative inertia.
Universal? Yes: The "no" tells us that there are none of a certain thing anywhere in the universe, and that makes it universal (because we know about every one of them).
CONDITIONAL STATEMENTS: "If it is a Vogon, then it is not unencumbered by administrative inertia." (And once again, "not unencumbered" means that they are encumbered). Also, "If it is unencumbered by administrative inertia, then it is not a Vogon."

PROBLEM SET #6

1) If Jerry wears pants, Delores wears a hat.

$$JP \supset DH$$
$$-DH \supset -JP$$

So if Dolores has NO hat, Jerry is NOT wearing pants, and if Jerry is wearing pants, Dolores must wear a hat. Dolores can wear a hat while Jerry wears no pants (Right Side Rule).

2) If Bill does not have roast beef, Nancy has pie or ice cream.

$$-BR \supset (NP \vee NI)$$
$$-NP \cdot -NI \supset BR$$

So if Nancy does not have pie and she does not have ice cream, Bill DOES eat roast beef, because if Bill had roast beef, Nancy would have had pie or ice cream. Nancy CAN have pie or ice cream while Bill has the roast beef (Right Side Rule).

3) Janet skydives and swims if Raoul knits.

$$RK \supset (JSKY \cdot JSW)$$
$$-JSW \vee -JSKY \supset -RK$$

Tricky, huh? The "if" came in the middle. That is why you have to stop and think about what the rule means. The test makers are brutal about trying to trick you, so SLOW DOWN and figure it out first! If Janet does not swim or she does not skydive, we know that Raoul does not knit, because if he had, Janet would have done one or the other (or both!).

4) Estevan will not play guitar if Celine is hit by a meteor.

$$CM \supset -EG$$
$$EG \supset -CM$$

If Estevan does play guitar, Celine was not hit by a meteor, because if Celine had been hit, Estevan would not play. Estevan can not play guitar even though Celine is not hit (Right Side Rule).

5) If Sigfried buys steak sauce, Roy has meat but not potatoes.

$$SS \supset (RM \cdot -RP)$$
$$RP \vee -RM \supset -SS$$

If Roy has potatoes or he does not eat meat, then Sigfried did not buy steak sauce, because if he had, Roy would eat meat and not eat potatoes. Roy can eat meat and not eat potatoes while Sigfried does not buy steak sauce (Right Side Rule).

6) Ronnie eats jelly beans whenever Nancy skinny dips.

$$NSD \supset RJB$$
$$-RJB \supset -NSD$$

"Whenever" just means that "any time that Nancy...." Ergo, *if* Nancy skinny dips, Ronnie will eat jelly beans. So if Ronnie is not eating the jelly beans, we know that Nancy is not skinny dipping. This also means, by the Right Side Rule, that Ronnie *can* eat jelly beans even when Nancy is out of the water.

7) Alan Scott will have a ring and a lantern if Bill drinks whiskey or Martin does not.

$$BW \lor -MW \supset AR \cdot AL$$
$$-AR \lor -AL \supset -BW \cdot MW$$

So if Bill has whiskey OR Martin does not drink whiskey, then Alan will have a ring AND Alan will have a lantern. So if Alan has no ring or if Alan has no lantern we know that Bill had no whiskey and that Martin did. The Right Side Rule reminds us that Alan can have the ring and the lantern even if Bill does not have whiskey and Martin does.

8) Rain will cause the ball game to be cancelled.

$$R \supset -B$$
$$B \supset -R$$

The Right Side Rule tells us that the ball game can be cancelled even if it does not rain. That makes sense, because we do not want to have a ball game in the middle of the zombie apocalypse or a simple hail storm.

9) Licensed dogs are required to have vaccinations.

$$LD \supset V$$
$$-V \supset -LD$$

If the dog is licensed, then it has a vaccination. The word "required" means that the vaccinations are a required "ingredient" of being a licensed dog. Ingredients are consequents, so they go on the right side. If the dog has no vaccination then it cannot be licensed. The Right Side Rule tells us that a dog can have its vaccinations and still not have a license at the same time... perhaps its owner got it a shot and then went to a bar and got drunk.

10) Non-citizens and convicted felons are not allowed to vote.

$$-C \lor F \supset -V$$
$$V \supset C \cdot -F$$

Notice how we used the "-C" for "non-citizen"? Cute, huh? But non-citizen is the complement to citizen, and that is a true dichotomy. The contra-positive tells us that a person can be a citizen and a non-convicted-felon and still not vote... in our universe it usually it involves them being a non-sober, non-felon citizen.

PROBLEM SET #7 : Splitting "or" Conditionals

1)   If Veronica lays carpet, Robert installs drywall or does framing.

$$VL \supset RD \lor RF$$
$$-RD \cdot -RF \supset -VL$$

There are no "or" antecedents (conditions on the left side), so there is no splitting to do. If you tried to split it, REMEMBER: we cannot split an "and" antecedent because both conditions must occur in order for it to be sufficient to prove the right side, so – RD alone proves jack squat, as does –RF.

2) If Jill wins the high jump or the pole vault, Xavier runs the triple jump and the long jump.

$$JWH \lor JWP \supset XRT \cdot XRL$$
$$-XRT \lor -XRL \supset -JWH \cdot -JWP$$

Both the original rule and the contra-positive have disjunctive "or" antecedents, so they can both be split up. They look like this:

$$JWH \lor JWP \supset XRT \cdot XRL$$
$$JWH \supset XRT \cdot XRL$$
$$JWP \supset XRT \cdot XRL$$

And

$$-XT \lor -XL \supset -JH \cdot -JP$$

$$-XT \supset -JH \cdot -JP$$
$$-XL \supset -JH \cdot -JP$$

Our original rule is split and contra-posed into six rules! We could further split up the conjunctive consequents... but as was stated in the call-out box on this subject, that is very counter-productive (trust us, you will thank us later for dissuading you from doing it).

3) If Steven waits tables and busses them, Anthony vacuums or polishes silverware.

$$SW \cdot SB \supset AV \, v \, AP \cdot -(AV \cdot AP)$$
$$-AV \cdot -AP \, v \, (AV \cdot AP) \supset -SW \, v \, -SB$$

Again, we have no "or" antecedents, so we cannot split it apart.

4) If Donovan is assigned to Tuesdays or Thursdays, Miles is not assigned to Wednesday.

$$DT \, v \, DH \supset -MW$$
$$MW \supset -DT \cdot -DH$$

The original rule has an "or" in the conditional, and so we can elect to split it apart. If we contra-pose the parts, we end up with the equivalent of the contra-positive, just in less confusing form.

$$DT \supset -MW$$
$$MW \supset -DT$$
$$DH \supset -MW$$
$$MW \supset -DH$$

That is a lot tastier to most folks' intellectual palates, though we do hope that you will eventually make yourself more comfortable with the original, compound rule.

5) If Fred fails to pay child support or does not show up for visitation, Gail gets custody of the children.

$$-FP \, v \, -FV \supset GC$$
$$-GC \supset FP \cdot FV$$

Again we have a rule that can be split apart in the original form. Yea.

$$-FP \supset GC$$
$$-GC \supset FP$$
$$-FV \supset GC$$
$$-GC \supset FV$$

Splitting the disjunctive antecedent rule up and contra-posing the parts gives us four absolute and crystal clear rules. If Fred does not pay support, Fred loses junior to Gail. If Gail does not have custody of the kid, Fred paid support. If Fred does not show up for his visitation, he loses custody of the kid to Gail. If Gail does not have custody, then Fred showed up for visitation.

PROBLEM SET #8

1)   Quincy gets the twelve-gauge if and only if Janet has a forty-four caliber.

$$Q12 \supset J44$$
$$-J44 \supset -Q12$$
$$J44 \supset Q12$$
$$-Q12 \supset -J44$$

We now have four different antecedents. Notice that all of the signs in each individual rule are identical on both sides, so this compound rule means, "all or nothing." We must have Q12 and J44 together or we cannot have either.

2)   Peter runs the marathon if and only if Tanya swims or bikes.

$$PM \supset TS \text{ v } TB$$
$$-TS \cdot -TB \supset -PM$$
$$TS \text{ v } TB \supset PM$$
$$-PM \supset -TS \cdot -TB$$

We could break the second part of the rule apart and contra-pose the results into

$$TS \supset PM$$
$$-PM \supset -TS$$
$$TB \supset PM$$
$$-PM \supset -TB$$

Even though each individual rule has the same signs on both sides of the argument, we can see that this is *not* an, "all or nothing," situation, because having –TS by itself has no consequence, and the same applies to –TB. It is only when they *both occur* that –PM results. Remember, "All or Nothing" only applies when we have a simple premise with one term on each side.

3) Uma stocks shelves and dusts if and only if Yvette is the manager.

$$US \cdot UD \supset YM$$
$$-YM \supset -US \lor -UD$$
$$YM \supset US \cdot UD$$
$$-US \lor -UD \supset -YM$$

We can break the rule with the "or" antecedent apart:

$$- US \supset -YM$$
$$- UD \supset -YM$$

Is it, "all or nothing?" NO! We can have US only, or we can have UD alone and suffer no consequence.

4) Eve buys a Ferrari if but only if Kim does not buy a Porsche.

$$EF \supset -KP$$
$$KP \supset -EF$$
$$-KP \supset EF$$
$$-EF \supset KP$$

Is this an, "all or nothing?" No! So what *is* it? It's an "Exactly One"!

Problem Set #9

Write out the following rules in symbols, contra-pose them and then circle the right side to note what you are allowed to have at the same time.

1) If there are no bananas there must be cherries.

$$-B \supset C$$
$$-C \supset B$$

We have to have bananas or we have to have cherries because if both are missing, we are violating the rules. We are not prohibited from having cherries and bananas at the same time (Right Side Rule).

2) If she selects disco and she does not select funk, she must also select classical.

$$D \cdot -F \supset C$$
$$-C \supset -D \lor F$$

CURVE BALL! The original rule has the conjunctive antecedent (if both D and –F) as sufficient to force C. The contra-positive says that –C is sufficient to prove *either* –D or F, but we do not know which, and it could be *both*, because *or* is *inclusive* on the

LSAT. We are not prohibited from having C, -D and F all at the same time because if we have F, the antecedent side tells us that the rules do not apply. If we have –D, the left side says that the rules do not apply. If we have C, the antecedent side says that the rules do not apply. Thus they are allowed simultaneously.

3) If she buys nothing from Blerg, she buys chairs from Ikea.

$$-B \supset I$$
$$-I \supset B$$

She has to buy something from B or I or both, because if she does not buy anything, she is in violation of the rule.

4) Tom inherits no decorative plates unless Becky inherits the silver service.

$$-BS \supset -TP$$
$$TP \supset BS$$

Say it: that was *sooooo* evil! *Unless* means, "if not." So if not Becky inherits silver, Tom does not inherit decorative plates. If Tom gets the plates, Becky has to have received the silver because Tom could not have gotten them unless Becky did. The right-side rule still applies, and this is *not* an affirmative duty rule.

1) Unless Gaius is a republican, Cicero is.

$$-GR \supset CR$$
$$-CR \supset GR$$

One or the other or both must be Republican, because there is an affirmative duty, because *unless* means *if not*.

PROBLEM SET #10 – Merging Conditional Logic
A) Sponge Bob and Patrick are going to the movies.

> If Sponge Bob sees *Jaws*, Patrick sees *Free Willy*.
> If Patrick Does not see *Free Willy*, he sees *The Abyss*.
> If Sponge Bob sees *The Little Mermaid* he also sees *Jaws*.

The rules in symbols, contra-posed, right-side rule applied and merged:

$$SJ \supset PF$$
$$-PF \supset -SJ \cdot PA \cdot -SL$$
$$-PF \supset PA$$
$$-PA \supset PF$$
$$SL \supset SJ \cdot PF$$
$$-SJ \supset -SL$$

i) Patrick wants to see both *Free Willy* and *The Abyss*. Is he allowed to? ANSWER: **YES**.

These questions are typical of the type of analyses you are asked to perform on the LSAT logic games. Most people screw this up by thinking that somewhere within the second, third and fourth rules on our list there is the requirement that Patrick goes to one movie or the other but not both. There are two ways to look at the situation.

First, pretend Patrick did go to *Free Willy*, or PF. What do the rules say happens if PF? JACK SQUAT! There are no rules where PF serves as an antecedent. The same goes for the situation where Patrick sees *The Abyss* or PA. If no rules prevent it, then it is allowed.

The other way of looking at the problem is better because it is more efficient and equally as accurate. The Right Side Rule has PA and PF circled. Both are allowed. This works because there are no bi-conditionals that would limit our ability to use the right-side rule. REMEMBER, my darlings, that if there is a bi-conditional, either overt or latent, we do not use the Right Side Rule.

ii) What do we know FOR ABSOLUTE CERTAIN if Sponge Bob does *not* see *The Little Mermaid*?

What do our rules tell us about Sponge Bob not seeing *The Little Mermaid* (-SL)? NADA! ZILCH! ZIP! If Sponge Bob does not see *The Little Mermaid*, the **ONLY** thing we know for sure is that he did not see *The Little Mermaid*. Perhaps he did not see *The Little Mermaid* because he did not see *Jaws*. Perhaps he did not see *The Little Mermaid* because Patrick did not see *Free Willie*. MAYBE he did not see *The Little Mermaid* because he was DRUNK and could not find the theater. –SL is a consequent, but the right side only tells us that MAYBE the antecedent brought about that consequent. If we do not know the antecedent, we cannot say that the consequent proves the antecedent. Remember our basic example:

If I shoot you, you will die.

If you are dead, that does not prove that I shot you. Maybe I did, because if I had, you would be dead according to the rule. But maybe you just expired because all of this logic stuff made your brain melt.

iii) If Patrick does not see *Free Willy*, what must be true?
The second rule on our list says it all:

$$-PF \supset -SJ \cdot PA \cdot -SL$$

Sponge Bob cannot see *Jaws*, Patrick must see *The Abyss*, and Sponge Bob cannot see *The Little Mermaid*.

iv) BONUS QUESTION! – If Sponge Bob gets sick from having eaten too many Crabby Patties and decides to go home, can Sponge Bob and Patrick leave having not seen any movies?

The answer is clear if you use what you already know (we had to write those words in order to stop people from "inadvertently" looking down and seeing the answer in one or two words). What you are really being asked is, "Do either of these aquatic twits have an *affirmative duty* to see a movie?" In other words, are there any negative antecedents with affirmative consequents? The answer to that question is... affirmative. Patrick has to see *The Abyss* or *Free Willie* or both (rules 2, 3 and 4). Sponge Bob has no affirmative duties, so he can go home and wretch (which is what Patrick will do after watching *Free Willie*).

B) Tony, Christopher and Paulie are, "doin' family business."

> If Christopher hijacks a truckload of Blu-Ray players, Tony gets paid.
> If Paulie robs a bank, Christopher does not hijack a truckload of Blu-Ray players.
> If Paulie does not rob a bank, Tony fixes a fight.
> If Tony does not fix a fight, Tony does not get paid.

Our rules in symbols, contra-posed, right-side rule applied and merged:

$$CH \supset TP \cdot -PR \cdot TF$$
$$-TP \supset -CH$$
$$PR \supset -CH$$
$$CH \supset -PR \cdot TP \cdot TF$$
$$-PR \supset TF$$
$$-TF \supset PR \cdot -TP \cdot -CH$$
$$-TF \supset -TP \cdot PR \cdot -CH$$
$$TP \supset TF$$

i) What must be true if Tony does not fix the fight? SIMPLE! The rule that says what happens if we know for sure that Tony does not fix the fight (-TF) tells us that Paulie is going to rob the bank, Tony is not going to get paid and Christopher is not going to hijack the truckload of Blu-Ray players. Sweeeeet!

ii) If Tony does get paid, what must be true? The TP rule tells us that Tony also fixes the fight.

iii) Can it be true that Paulie did not rob the bank and that Christopher did not hijack the Blu-Ray player truck? This is asking us whether or not two things can happen at the same time. SIMPLE! Can we have –PR and –CH at the same time? If we know –PR, the rules tell us only that Tony will fix the fight: It tells us nothing about Christopher. If we also know –CH, the rules tell us…. JACK SQUAT! That means that it is possible for both to happen, because they are both allowed, and neither one of the things we know makes the other "illegal."

iv) Is it possible for Tony to *not* fix the fight and for Christopher to hijack a load of Blu-Ray players? Our rules tell us that if Tony does not fix the fight (-TF) we know for sure that one of the consequents is that Christopher *cannot* hijack the Blu-Ray truck (-CH). Thus, the answer is a definitive, "No!" We can also see that if Christopher *does* hijack the truck, Tony *must* fix the fight. EACH THING THAT WE KNOW DISPROVES THE HYPOTHETICAL –TF and CH.

Problem Set 15 – Procedure Games

The software company Macrotrugid, in an effort to keep people from pirating its grossly inefficient programs, is creating a security code algorithm. Each "code" consists of four "clusters" arranged A through D, from left to right. Each "cluster" consists of four non-negative numerical digits. Each code must satisfy the following conditions:

  No more than two of the clusters can have the same first digit.
  No more than two of the clusters can have the same last digit.
  Each code is created by having an initial cluster A, and each
     succeeding cluster is the result of one of three operations
     performed on the cluster immediately preceding it: replace a
     single digit with a different one, swapping the first digit and the
     last digit of the preceding cluster, reversing the order of the
     digits in the cluster before it.
All three operations must be used in creating a code.

STEP ONE: GET A GRIP

What is the nature of the game? It looks like an ordering game when we read over the fact pattern, but it is not. We know this because of rule 3. VALUABLE LESSON: sometimes we have to read the formal rules in order to determine the nature of the game. Occasionally the test problems are designed so that the fact pattern looks like the game is one type and then the rules change all of that. This is a trap for the undisciplined speed-freaks out there. They see the, "...arranged A through D, left to right...," language and ASSUME[1] that it has to be an ordering game. THIS IS A VERY BAD AND DANGEROUS HABIT TO BE IN! Many games (Combo games, most notably) combine ordering with some other kind of game. DO NOT BE A FOOL. BE THOROUGH.

This is not a trivial point because in Step Two, we re-write the rules in a manner visually consistent with the nature of the game. If we have already screwed up the nature of the game and write out our rules incorrectly, we freak out when we realize our error.

Who are the players? Four clusters, A, B, C and D. There will be four non-negative numbers in each cluster (0-9).

Hidden rules? A – D clusters go left to right. If you called this or the four-digit numbers "hidden rules," that is okay. The point is that you saw them and you noted them as being important (which they are).

STEP TWO: FORMAL RULES

1) 2 clusters MAX w/same first digit
2) 2 clusters MAX w/same last digit
3) Each cluster except A is result of operating on prior cluster:

---

[1] Every time you *assume*, you make a Wal-Mart greeter out of a lawyer.

3 operations- REPLACE a digit w/different, SWAP first / last digit, FLIP
entire cluster.

4) All operations play.

STEP THREE: DRAW

$$\overline{} \quad \overline{} \quad \overline{} \quad \overline{}$$

A   B   C   D

4 Digit/cluster

STEP FOUR: INFERENCES

RECALL that the rules are not just there to mess with your head. They DEFINE THE
ISSUES! Here, the rules define the issues to be the two ends of the clusters and the
three operations. Do the middle two digits matter at all? Not really. In fact, the
middle two digits are irrelevant. If cluster A=1234 and we do an inversion operation
making B=4321, then we change one of the middle digits so that C=4351, then we
swap the ends to make D=1354, we have not violated the only really limiting rule,
the one that says that we cannot have three or four identical first or last digits. THE
ISSUE IN THIS GAME IS ABOUT WHAT HAPPENS TO THE ENDS!

Absolutes – Is there anything that definitely has to go in a particular place, or which
absolutely cannot go into a particular place? If there are, we do not see them.

Bundles – Each cluster is a bundle, but that is no help.

Calculators – Remember that Calculators are where we check for numerical
combinations, permutations etc. There is a great deal of potential for Calculators
here. There are three operations, all of which must be used, and there are only four
clusters to apply them to. They are going to have to give us at least one cluster to
work with (or part of a cluster) in able for us to do anything. That means that we are
just going to have to apply the three operations to the three remaining slots to figure
out what must/could be in them, or we are gong to have to deduce the operation(s)
used for cluster values. Fortunately the rules look like they will make this simple, if
we use our brainpower to its fullest.

We know that every cluster will have four digits, that only two clusters can have the
same first digit, and that only two can have the same last digit. It does not matter if
they are the same two; i.e. if A = 2372 and B= 2732 those would be the only two that
can begin with two. They would also be the only two that can end with two.

We have three operations: End Swap, Invert and Digit Change. The first thing we
need to note is that Digit Change is the only way to make the two middle digits
different. Invert will switch the *order* of the middle two, but they will be the *same*

digits. So any time a middle digit is different, it has to be that a Digit Change happened. That means that (a) only one of the middle digits can be different between any of the four clusters, and (b) that those middle digits have to be the same in three of the four clusters (because there is only one Change Digit allowed), and (c) the middle digits have to change positions exactly one time. The other two operations have to effect the first and fourth digits only.

We should think about this. If the ENDS of cluster "A" are the same, let us say A=7127, what happens to the cluster as we do all three operations? If we change one of the digits in the middle to make cluster B, let us say to 7X27 (using X to show any number), then A and B have the two ends pinned down and no other cluster can have a 7 at either end. But we would only have two operations left for C and D: End Swap (giving us 7X27 again, with 7 on both ends for a third time, which is illegal), or Invert B to make C, which would give us 72X7, the identical violation.

But what if, rather than change a middle digit (which we suspect are meaningless in this little charade) we changed one of the ends? A=7127 could become B=0127. But then the Invert and End Swap to get C and D would get C=7210 and D=0217...three 7's in the fourth digit. SNOZBERRIES[2]!

We can see two things from this. The first is that B CAN NEVER HAVE the same digit on both ends! Even if A had started out with different ends, such as 1112, if the A to B operation changes the leading 1 to a 2 to make 2112, then we have to invert and swap ends for C and D, giving us 2 on both ends in B, C and D. We can add this to our picture.

B ends NEVER SAME

$$\overline{} \quad \overline{} \quad \overline{} \quad \overline{}$$

A   B   C   D

4 Digit/cluster

This also might indicate something else to you, which it should: A cannot have the same number on both ends either. If it did, two operations (invert or switch ends) would put identical ends in B, which we just figured out cannot happen. If we use the third operation to change one of the ends, we would have a problem too. Let us pretend A=1991. We change the last 1 to a 2: 1992. Our two remaining operations will just flip the ends around two times, regardless of the order we do them in. If we invert then swap ends we get A=1991, B=1992, C=2991, D=1992. Three clusters begin with 1. Hopefully you can see that the same result occurs if we use end swap and invert for C and D. If we had changed the first digit from 1991 to 2991, we

---

[2] See *Charlie and the Chocolate Factory*, Chapter 22, and *My Uncle Oswald*, Chapter 23, both by Roald Dahl. Be prepared to have your mind blown... or something... In fact, if you are a fan of the movie *Charlie and the Chocolate Factory* starring Gene Wilder and Jack Albertson and you remember the lines from said flick about Snozberries with a fond smile, you do **_NOT_** want to check these references.

would have ended up with three clusters with the same fourth digit: A=1991, B=2991, C=1992, D=2991. SHAZAM!

A&B ends NEVER SAME

—— —— —— ——
A   B   C   D

4 Digit/cluster

You also may have noticed something else from that last two little walk-throughs. No matter what digits A starts out with, if we use the Digit Change operation to get B, we end up with the same bloody problem. For example, if A=1234 and we change the last digit to 5, B=1235, then the last two operations flip the ends twice, which gets us C=5321, D=1325 (invert, end swap, where A, B and D all have 1 as the first digit) or C=5231, D=1325 (end swap, invert, where A, B, and D all have 1 as the first digit). *So the A to B operation can never be the Digit Change!* It has to be the Invert or the End-Swap!

A&B ends NEVER SAME

—— —— —— ——
A   B   C   D
Inv/End Swap
4 Digit/cluster

If we Invert or End Swap from A to B, then we only have two operations left for C: the other of End Swap or Invert that we did not use going from A to B, and the Digit Change. If we flip it again going from B to C, then we have a problem. If we started A=1234, B=4321 then we Swapped Ends, C=1324, BOTH ends of A and C are the same, and in going from C to D we can only change one digit, meaning that there will either be three first digits the same or three last digits the same. Any way you slice it, you are *ewedscray*. That means that the B to C operation MUST be the Change Digit. And if that is the case, then the C to D has to be whichever of the End Swap or Inverse we did not do in going from A to B. We should note this in our drawing. The "delta" under C is the symbol for "Change".

A&B ends NEVER SAME

—— —— —— ——
A   B   C   D
Inv/End Swap   Δ   Inv/end Swap
4 Digit/cluster

We own this bad boy now!

DOUBLE-UPS – None of the rules really double-up. Remember that on this step we are looking for two or more rules that talk about the same player(s). None of the rules do that, so we are good.

EXTRAS – Bi-conditionals? None. Forced dichotomies? None. Right Side Rule? Nada. Affirmative duty rules? None. Contradictions? Zippo. Lone conditional? ZILCH!

FREE RANGER(s) – There are none. A, B, C and D are all constrained. The 4 digits are too, especially in A and B. We are soooo going to crush this game!

STEP FIVE: DESTROY THE QUESTIONS!

A&B ends NEVER SAME

____   ____   ____   ____

A   B   C   D
Inv/End Swap   Δ   Inv/end Swap
4 Digit/cluster

1) Which of the following could be a complete and accurate code?
       a) A: 2437 B: 2737 C: 2612 D: 2962
       b) A: 3325 B: 3327 C: 7327 D: 7237
       c) A: 2112 B: 2119 C: 9112 D: 9212
       d) A: 9775 B: 5779 C: 5799 D: 9975
       e) A: 6427 B: 7426 C: 8426 D: 9426

A) INCORRECT! The A to B move is a digit change.
B) INCORRECT! The A to B move is a digit change.
C) INCORRECT! The A to B move is a digit change.
D) A to B is an Inverse or an End Swap... we can call it either because the center two digits are the same! The B to C move is a Digit Change. C to D Inverses. Do we have more than two clusters with the same first number or last number? NO! D wins. BUBBLE IT AND MOVE ON!

E) A to B End Swaps. B to C Digit Changes, but so does C to D. Naughty.

2) If cluster B is 2643 and cluster D is 3467, then cluster C must be:
       a) 2647
       b) 3647
       c) 3764
       d) 7643
       e) 7463

Again, our hard-won knowledge saves the day. We know that the B to C has to be a digit change. How can we determine which digit was changed? THEY TELL US! D has one different digit, 7. That has to be it because there can only be one digit change. C to D has to be End Swap or Invert, both of which change the end values. So if, as we were told, D has the 7 on the right end, 7 had to be on the left end in C, followed by all of the rest of B, i.e. 7643. That is (d). Gone Daddy Gone.

3) If cluster A is 7832 then cluster B can be which one of the following?
        a) 2387
        b) 9832
        c) 7839
        d) 8832
        e) 9832

Ha ha ha! The A to B has to change 7832 into what two possible numbers? Invert = 2387 or End Swap = 2837. If you need us to tell you which answer choice is the correct one, perhaps law is not for you.

4) Each of the following could be cluster A except:
        a) 2000
        b) 2771
        c) 2772
        d) 2773
        e) 2774

What do we already know? A can never have identical ends. (c) is the answer. Move along.

5) If cluster A is 8609 and cluster C is 9678, which of the following must be true?
        a) B is an inversion of A.
        b) C is an inversion of B.
        c) C is a swap of the first and last digits of B.
        d) D is a swap of the first and last digits of C.
        e) D is an inversion of C.

What do we already know? A to B was an Invert or End Swap, and B to C has to be Digit Change. An Invert will change the order of the middle two digits the one and only time they can change places. The call of the question says that 6 is in the same place in A and C, meaning the A to B move was End Swap, making B 9608. B to C was Digit Change 0 to 7. That which remains, Invert, had to be used to obtain D.

6) Which of the following must be false?
        a) B is an inversion of A.
        b) B is a swap of the first and last digits of A.
        c) C is an inversion of A.
        d) C is a change of one digit form B.
        e) D is a swap of the first and last digits of C.

_____   _____   _____   _____

A   B   C   D
Inv/End Swap   Δ   Inv/end Swap
    4 Digit/cluster

After all we have learned about this game, they are going to slow pitch us?!? YES! (a) and (b) can both be true or false. (c) can never be true. (c) could be an inversion AND a Digit Change of A, but not just an inversion. (d) MUST be true. (e) may or may not be true.

Problem Set 16 – Practicing Steps 1-4 of the Method

(A) LSAC RELEASED LSAT #7, SECTION 2

> Seven types of pies will be served, one at a time. The pies are Apple, Blueberry, Cherry, Dewberry, Elderberry, Fig and Gooseberry. A complete pie is served before the next pie is served. The order of the serving of pies is subject to the following limitations:
> Cherry pie is served immediately before Dewberry.
> The Gooseberry pie must be served before the Cherry pie.
> Exactly two pies are served between the serving of the Elderberry pie and the Apple pie.

STEP 1: GET A GRIP

The nature of the game- Ordering for sure, but is it Firm or Squishy? The rules seem to indicate that it is a little bit of both: Firm because of rule 3 and squishy because of the "relative positioning" rules. Hence, as you may recall from wayyy back, this is a "Squirm" game, or squishy-firm. The players are A, B, C, D, E, F and G. Hidden rule(s): Pies served one at a time, whole pie before next served, ALL PLAY. You may be asking yourself, "How do we know that all of the pies will play?" The fact pattern says, "Seven types of pies *will be served*..."

STEP 2: FORMAL RULES

Rule 1 says C is *immediately* before D. Put them together:

  1) CD

Rule 2 says that G is before (not immediately before, which means that it can be immediately before or way before) C.

  2) G...C

Rule 3 says that there are two pies between E and A. It does NOT tell us that E is before A or vice-versa. So we have to account for either:

  3) E/A _ _ A/E

STEP 3: DRAW

Recall that in Squishy games we turn the rules into our drawing, and that in firm games we draw out a visual representation of the ordering. In *Squirm* games we have to make a judgment call: if drawing some of the rules into a squishy order looks *efficient and useful* then we should do it. Here, our two squishy rules don't really give us much if we put them together. We can just draw the seven-space firm order and keep the three rules in place until we get to the inferences and save time. REMEMBER that we are trying to be *efficient*, not fast. Fast and unhelpful is inefficient, as is wasting time on unnecessary (i.e. redundant) work.

```
__  __  __  __  __  __  __
1   2   3   4   5   6   7
```

STEP 4: INFERENCES

Absolutes? Heck ya! Nothing has to go anywhere, but there are things that cannot go places. Rule 1, CD, means that C cannot be last and that D cannot be first. Also, rule 2, G ... C, means that G cannot be last and C cannot be first.

```
__  __  __  __  __  __  __
1   2   3   4   5   6   7
-C                      -G
-D                      -C
```

Bundles? Rule 3, E/A _ _ A/E is a bundle of four. We can see that the bundle is going to have a limited number of places that it can go, which we will ferret out in in Calculators. CD is also a Bundle. This is a pair that can go in between the E/A _ _ A/E, before it (if space allows) or after it (also if space allows).

Some of you savvy test takers have already spotted that G...CD is going to end up being our "Double-up". This is very true and it is not a bad thing that you spotted it. WHAT YOU MUST REMEMBER is that great LSAT performance requires discipline. So if you are thinking of those three letters as a G...CD Bundle, make VERY CERTAIN that when you get to the Double-up step that you do not skip it, thinking that you have hit upon every Double-up because you got the easy one already. In this case it will not kill you to make that mistake. In real sets of games things are much more challenging. So be disciplined.

Calculators? Yes sirree! We have that E/A _ _ A/E bundle that eats up four spaces. There are only four places we can put it in. It has to go into 1 and 4, 2 and 5, 3 and 6 or 4 and 7. That is not the important feature of this game though, is it? This game is checking to see whether or not we understand how the G...CD and the E/A _ _ A/E bundles work around (or between) each other. Guess what that is going to turn upon? Almost certainly the placement of the Free Rangers or the position of a bundle. Let us just THINK for a second (and not draw).

- If the E/A _ _ A/E is in 1 and 4 then the G...CD can go G in 2/3 and the CD in two of 5, 6 or 7 (i.e. C in 5 or 6 with D in 6 or 7).
- As the E/A _ _ A/E moves to the right into 2 and 5, the G can slip into 1 with the CD in 3 and 4 or 6 and 7. Also, the G could go into 3 or 4 and CD would have to go into 6

269

and 7. BUT IF EITHER E or A IS IN 2, the other of the pair has to be in 5, and if either is in 5, the opposite has to be in 2.

- With E/A _ _ A/E in 3 and 6 G can go 1 or 2, but CD MUST go 4 and 5 (because there is only one space, 7, to the right of 6). So if EITHER E or A is in 3, its partner has to go into 6 (because there have to be three spaces, two empty and then the other letter, and going left there are only 2 and 1) and if either is in 6 its partner has to go to 2.

With E/A _ _ A/E in 4 and 7, it's a free for all unless a Free Ranger clogs up things and forces the CD pair to go somewhere.

So we make a quick note about the four possible arrangements of E/A _ _ A/E:

```
___  ___  ___ ___
 1    2  3   4  5  6   7
-C                     -G
-D                     -C

1,4 or 4,7 ⎤
2,5        ⎬  E/A _ _ A/E
3,6        ⎦
```

Double-ups? Any more of you bad boys out there? Nope. But remember to ALWAYS check bot the formal rules and the hidden rules for Double-ups. There have been many occasions where the big ugly score killer came in the form of a hidden rule. Extras? No Bi-conditionals. No Forced dichotomies. No Right-side rules. No Affirmative Duties. Contradictions? None. No Lone Conditionals either. Tally ho!

Free Rangers? YES! B and F. They will be the ones that are used to wreak havoc on us. For example: *"If A is in 4 and B is in 7, which one of the following could be true?"* A4 and B7 means our E/A _ _ A/E MUST GO E1, A4. That would FORCE the CD pair into 5 and 6 (because if we put them in 2 and 3 the G could not go before them as required. G would have to go into 2 or 3 along with F in 2 or 3.

(B)

> Exactly four people must attend Johnny Sack's funeral. The four are selected from the group of: Artie, Carmela, Furio, Paulie, Silvio, Tony and Vito. Who attends depends upon the following limitations:
> Artie attends the funeral if and only if Carmela does not.
> Silvio will not attend the funeral unless Furio goes.
> Vito does not attend the funeral unless Carmela does.
> Either Tony or Silvio, but not both, must go to the funeral.

STEP ONE: GET A GRIP

Nature of the game – WINNER/LOSER. Players – A, C, F, P, S, T, V. Hidden rules – EXACTLY 4 are selected out of 7 (we would write 4 Win / 3 Lose).

STEP TWO: FORMAL RULES

1) THIS IS A BI-CONDITIONAL! Recall that "if and only if" means "If and Then." So If Carmela does not go, then Artie does, and if Artie does, Carmela does not. BOTH MUST BE WRITTEN AND CONTRA-POSED.

$$(1) \ -C \supset A$$
$$-A \supset C$$
$$A \supset -C$$
$$C \supset -A$$

2) AN "UNLESS" RULE! Unless = "if not" so "If not Furio, then Silvio will not go."

$$(2) \ -F \supset -S$$
$$S \supset F$$

3) Same as (2), it is an "unless":

$$(3) \ -C \supset -V$$
$$V \supset C$$

4) Tony or Silvio MUST go. We know that "or" is inclusive, unless they specifically say otherwise (which they DID) by saying that one must, but both cannot. Again we have a bi-conditional. If you did not catch that this is a bi-conditional, WORK ON IT. You cannot miss these.

It is easy to spot that if Tony goes, Silvio cannot, and vice-versa:

$$(4) \ T \supset -S$$
$$S \supset -T$$

But the right-side (consequent side) of this says that –S and –T are allowed at the same time, which is a direct violation of the rule. That is why it is bi-conditional. If Silvio does NOT go, Tony must, and contra:

$$(4) \ T \supset -S$$
$$S \supset -T$$
$$-S \supset T$$
$$-T \supset S$$

Together they form a bi-conditional. Our list of rules is thus:

$$(1) \ -C \supset A$$
$$-A \supset C$$
$$A \supset -C$$
$$C \supset -A$$
$$(2) \ -F \supset -S$$
$$S \supset F$$

$$\text{(3) } -C \supset -V$$
$$V \supset C$$
$$\text{(4) } T \supset -S$$
$$S \supset -T$$
$$-S \supset T$$
$$-T \supset S$$

STEP THREE: DRAW

Recall that in Winner/Loser games we do not always make a drawing. When they just tell us that we are going to have to figure out who wins and who loses, we just draw out a list of all of the players and identify who wins and who loses according to the call of the question and the rules.

Here, however, we are NOT being asked just to identify winners and losers. We are given a hidden rule that says that exactly four winners go and three losers do not. To many of you this smells like it is going to turn into inference GOLD when we get to the calculator step (and you are soooo correct). We can represent the 4:3 relationship in a picture like so:

We know that there are four winners and three losers and it is perfectly clear where everybody has to be.

STEP FOUR: INFERENCES

Absolutes? Well actually, YES! Rule 1 tells us that one of the "Winner" positions has to be filled by either A or C and that the other of that pair has to be a loser. So the first position on both sides of the line will have one of them. We can plug that into our picture and we can cross A and C off of the list:

Rule 4 does the same bloody thing with Tony and Silvio! We can plug them into the picture and whack them as well:

WIN   LOSE

A/C   T/S ___ ___ | C/A   S/T ___

Now notice that we have but three players left to place. SWEET!

Bundles: Are there things that always have to be together? No. Rule 2 looks like it might be a bundle of Silvio and Furio, but the consequent side tells us that we can have –S and F at the same time, so they are NOT a bundle. We have none.

Calculators? Look at our picture now. There are two spots for winners and there is one spot for a loser. There are three players to fill the two winner spots (i.e. 2/3). ANY time we know that F or P or V is a LOSER, then the other two MUST be going to the funeral! Any time we know that two of F, P or V is a winner, the third is a loser. This is HUGE because that is the issue we are being tested upon according to the rules. We are going to see situations where one of those three are forced to not go, thus forcing the other two to go (i.e. win). THESE ARE THE THINGS WE ARE GOING TO BE LOOKING FOR WHEN WE ARE DEALING WITH THE CONDITIONAL LOGIC!

Double-ups? JEEZ! We have them all over the place. The biggest problem most people have with games like this is that they are UNDISCIPLINED and they stampede to the double-ups, missing all of the juice in the calculators. We cannot allow ourselves to do that. The double-ups here in the rules go like so:

$$(1) -C \supset A \cdot -V$$
$$-A \supset C$$
$$A \supset -C \cdot -V$$
$$C \supset -A$$
$$(2) -F \supset -S \cdot T$$
$$S \supset F \cdot -T$$
$$(3) -C \supset -V \cdot A$$
$$V \supset C \cdot -A$$
$$(4) \ \ T \supset -S$$
$$S \supset -T \cdot F$$
$$-S \supset T$$
$$-T \supset S \cdot F$$

RIGHTEOUS! Rule 1 says that if C is a loser, then A is a winner AND V is a loser. According to our picture, if V fills the third loser spot then F and P have to win. THOSE MUST BE ADDED TO RULE #1!

Any time that V, F or P are losers, then the others are winners and that has to be added to the rules. The same thing applies when two of them win: we have to throw

273

the other one out. Each one of those additional consequents can also drag in other things, so we have to check them to see whether or not they are also antecedents and add on any additional consequents. So here is what the rules finally look like:

$$(1) \; \text{-C} \supset \text{A} \cdot \text{-V} \cdot \text{F} \cdot \text{P}$$
$$\text{-A} \supset \text{C}$$
$$\text{A} \supset \text{-C} \cdot \text{-V} \cdot \text{F} \cdot \text{P}$$
$$\text{C} \supset \text{-A}$$
$$(2) \; \text{-F} \supset \text{-S} \cdot \text{T} \cdot \text{P} \cdot \text{V} \cdot \text{C} \cdot \text{-A}$$
$$\text{S} \supset \text{F} \cdot \text{-T}$$
$$(3) \; \text{-C} \supset \text{-V} \cdot \text{A} \cdot \text{F} \cdot \text{P}$$
$$\text{V} \supset \text{C} \cdot \text{-A}$$
$$(4) \; \text{T} \supset \text{-S}$$
$$\text{S} \supset \text{-T} \cdot \text{F}$$
$$\text{-S} \supset \text{T}$$
$$\text{-T} \supset \text{S} \cdot \text{F}$$

NOW we know that any time that F is a loser, S and A are also losers and everyone else has to go to the funeral.

EXTRAS? Boy howdy! We have bi-conditionals up the kazoo, so the Right Side Rule does not apply. We are going to carefully check every rule any time it is necessary. To be honest, it is no big deal because we got soooo much out A, B, C and D that the E's can take the day off. There are no forced dichotomies. There are affirmative duties galore (if you do not remember what an affirmative duty is, GO FIGURE IT OUT RIGHT NOW!), but they are a product of the bi-conditionals. We need not be intimidated by these because the "affirmative duty" here is to get four bodies to the funeral to pay respect. And just to be complete, there is not a lone conditional. Duh. Are there any contradictions? No there are not. Lone conditionals? Ha ha ha!

FREE RANGERS? None! Everyone is constrained by the CALCULATOR. P lose, F, V win. F lose, P, V win...etc.

C) A funky-fresh Hip-Hop artist is creating three new experimental music tracks. He has four kinds of instruments to work with, and he wants each track to have three kinds of instruments on it. His available instruments are: Cow Bells, Marimbas, Piccolos and Xylophones. Each track must be made in accordance with the following limitations:

Track 3 cannot have any Marimba.
Track 1 uses exactly two types of instruments.
All four types of instruments must be used
  amongst the three tracks at least once.
Cow Bell must appear at least on Track 3.
Piccolo must be on Track 2.
For every Marimba that is used among the
  three Tracks, there must be at least twice as
  many Piccolos, whether or not they are on the
  same Track as the Marimba.

STEP ONE: GET A GRIP
Nature of the game: BUCKETS. Players: Trax 1, 2, 3 and Instruments C, M, P, X.
Hidden Rules: 3 instrument / Trax.

STEP TWO: RULES
  (1) NO M on Trax 3.
  (2) Trax 1 = TWO kinds
  (3) ALL PLAY
  (4) C = TRAX 3 MIN.
  (5) P = TRAX 2 MIN.
  (6) @ least twice as many P as M

NOTES ON THE RULES: Notice how we put "Trax" before references to Tracks? That is because numbers come up both as ordinals and cardinals in the rules and we want to minimize confusion. Look at rule 4. If we put "C = 3 min" that might confuse us into thinking, when we are doing inferences, that there have to be at least three cow bells. But the rule is that at least track 3 has a cow bell. This has to be something that the test makers are doing on purpose. Having Trax 1, 2, 3 and then telling us numbers of instruments. It is to see whether we make careless mistakes by confusing our data. NOT US! Also from the "NOT US," department, rule 6. We used "twice as many," rather than 2X because THERE IS A PLAYER CALLED X! ***They are just double-dog-daring you to fall for that idiotic error. Do not.***

STEP THREE: DRAW

```
        C M P X
     1  |  2  |  3
     ___|_____|___
     ___|_____|___
     ___|_____|___
```

We have our three "Buckets," which are the tracks we are supposed to record. In each bucket there are exactly three lines for each of the requires instruments. Above the buckets are the four instruments we have to choose from. Notice how this particular variety of Bucket game is the variation mentioned back in the Bucket Games section, where there do not seem to be any limits upon how many of each instrument there are. We know that there has to be at least one of each, but not much else.

STEP FOUR: INFERENCES

Absolutes? OODLES! Rule 1 says there are no marimbas on track 3. Rule two says that Trax 1 has two kinds of instruments. Rule 4 says that cow bell has to be on Trax 3. Rule 5 says that there must be a piccolo on Trax 2. Get them all into your picture!

Bundles? Nope. There are not any players that always have to be with other players.

Calculators? Heavens YES! WARNING! HERE IS A GREAT EXAMPLE OF A TRAP THAT THE LSAT HAS SET FOR YOU. The LSAC is **_NOT_** being evil by doing this. On the contrary, they are seeing whether or not you are sharp enough to avoid a pretty blatant error. We will walk you through how people fall into it.

Where do we see the greatest potential for the Calculator? We are hoping that you are at least *thinking* rule 6. That is not the trap. There have to be at least twice as many piccolos as there are marimbas. Marimbas cannot go into Trax 3, so they are limited to Trax 1 and 2. There are only seven empty spaces left, and all four instruments have to play.

THE ERROR
If there is one marimba, there have to be two or more piccolos. That will fill up a minimum of three of our seven remaining spaces. We can put in a ton of piccolos (between two and five), which are limited only in that they have to leave at least one space for the xylophone to get in there somewhere. If there are two marimbas, there

have to be at least four piccolos. That would jam up six of our seven spaces, and that would mean that the last spot would have to be reserved for the xylophone.[3]

The "classic blunder," committed in that last paragraph was that *we already have a piccolo in the drawing.* Forgetting that one of the required P's is already there can screw up your inferences. Sometimes the consequences are mostly harmless, sometimes they are tragic.

THE REAL CALCULATORS

We can never have three marimbas, because that would require at least five more piccolos and that is eight additional instruments for seven spaces in our buckets. If we have one marimba, we need a minimum of two, which means we need at least ONE more. If we have two marimbas, we need at least three more piccolos for four total **and** that will leave us two spaces, at least one of which must be reserved for xylophones. We need to make a note of this!

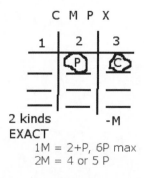

We have another Calculator as well. Trax 1 must have two types of instruments exactly. When we look at that in conjunction with what we just deduced from the marimba- piccolo Calculator, we anticipate that the test makers could try to set up a scenario that forces three different instruments into Trax 1 or (and more likely) a scenario where Trax 1 can only have one type of instrument. For example, "Which one of the following must be false?" An answer choice that said something such as, "Track 2 has two marimbas and track 3 has two xylophones," would force our three required additional piccolos into track 1, giving it one kind of instrument only.

We can smell the pain ahead. When there is one marimba, all is open and flexible. When there are two marimbas, things get tight and we only have one or two extra spaces. ANTICIPATE THIS ISSUE BEING KEY!

Double-ups?

---

[3] Once again, this must be said in the voice of Wallace Shawn, portraying Vizzini in *The Princess Bride,* Act III Communications, Buttercup Films Ltd., et. seq. 1987: *"You fell victim to one of the classic blunders - The most famous of which is "never get involved in a land war in Asia" - but only slightly less well-known is this: "Never go against a Sicilian when death is on the line!"*

Rules 1 and 4 talk about Trax 3. 5 and 6 mention P. There do not appear to be any meaningful deductions associated with them, so let's move to Extras.

Extras? No bi-conditionals. No forced dichotomies. No right-side rule. No affirmative duties. No contradictions. No lone conditionals.

Free Rangers? Xylophones.

D)
Seven proctors, Mary, Nancy, Peter, Quintin, Robert, Larry and Tanya, are each being assigned to supervise exactly one of three exams: the ACT, the GRE or the SAT. The assignment is consistent with the following conditions:

   The SAT may not be proctored by Quintin.
   If Nancy proctors the ACT then Quintin and
      Tanya proctor the GRE.
   Peter proctors the ACT.
   Robert may not be assigned to proctor any
      test Quintin proctors.
   Quintin may not be assigned to proctor any
      test that Tanya proctors.
   The SAT may not be proctored by Robert.
   Each test must have at least two proctors.

STEP ONE: GET A GRIP
Nature of the game: Buckets. Players? Proctors = M, N, P, Q, R, L, T; Tests = A, G, S. Hidden rules? All play EXACTLY once.

STEP TWO: FORMAL RULES
   1) Q= A or G
   2) NA ⊃ QG · TG
         -TG v –QG ⊃ -NA
   3) P=A
   4) R ⊃ -Q
         Q ⊃ -R
   5) Q ⊃ -T
         T ⊃ -Q
   6) R = A or G
   7) 2 proctors min/ test

STEP THREE: DRAW
Here is the part that throws people for a loop. We have two sets of players: tests and people. Which ones are the buckets, and which ones are the things that get thrown into the buckets? It is harder in this game to decide when contrasted against the last one. In the last one, the instruments could vary in number wildly, so it made sense to make them the thing that gets thrown into the buckets. But here, the game itself tells us to assign proctors to tests. IF THERE IS ANY DOUBT, just chillax and take a

second to think it through: three tests with two proctors under each covers 6 of the 7 proctors, with a "rover" that can be a third in any test. If you draw the seven people, and then you put the tests underneath them, you have to keep track of the A's, G's and S's. BOOOO! BOOOOO!

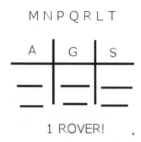

STEP FOUR: INFERENCES

Absolutes? Rule 1 says that Q has to be A or G (i.e. it cannot be SAT). Rule 3 says that P does the A test. Rule 6 says that R does A or G (i.e. not SAT). Put all of that into the picture, making sure that when you put the P into test A that you circle it to show that it cannot move:

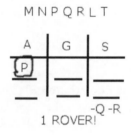

Rules 2, 4 and 5 are the only ones left to deal with!

Bundles? None.

Calculators? We sussed out the fact that there is a "rover" based upon the seven proctors, two per test, three tests total. We can also see that any time any person other than P, Q or R are assigned to the ACT, they have to be the third person doing the ACT, i.e. no more "rover."

Double-ups? Oh ya! Here is where the money is! We already have our drawing showing that neither Q nor R can do the SAT. They both have to do either A or G, and rule 4 says they cannot be together! So one of them must be A and the other must be G.

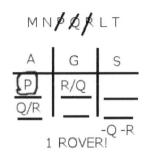

What we are beginning to see is that whichever test gets the "roving" third proctor (and whoever the rover is) is going to play a heap big role in the outcome.

If we Double-up the conditionals we get:

> NA ⊃ QG · TG · RA · MS · LS
> -TG v –QG ⊃ -NA
> R ⊃ -Q
> Q ⊃ -R · -T
> Q ⊃ -T · -R
> T ⊃ -Q

Look at the first rule. It says that if N does ACT, Q and T both do GRE. We know (from the picture we drew) that (1) if N does the ACT, that has to be the third ACT along with P and Q or R, (2) if Q does the GRE, then R has to do the ACT (making the ACT = P, R, N). Q and T have to be doing the GRE, which just leaves L and M to do the SAT! THAT is how Double-ups work. We use the rules, the hidden rules and all of the inferences we drew before we got to the Double-ups to spank this bad boy.

Extras?
Bi-conditionals? None. Forced dichotomies? Just Q and R, which we have handled. Right Side Rule? YES, and in three rules, 2, 4 and 5. But Q and R are part of a forced dichotomy, so any rule(s) involving them are right-side problems. For example, the right side of rule 5 and it's contra-positive say that we can have a test that has neither Q nor R. Well that would be the SAT. But because neither of them can do the SAT, they have to split between the ACT and the GRE. The both cannot be absent from the ACT and GRE because of the forced dichotomy. How about affirmative duties? None. Contradictions? Zero. Lone conditionals are out as well.

Free Rangers?
L and M are foot loose and fancy free-ranging...ish. The cannot both do the ACT, because there is only one possible space there. But we noted that with our "1 ROVER" note.

E) Five candidates for the legislature, Beretta, Colt, Glock, Kimber and Remington, are campaigning in Bakwatir County, which is divided into exactly five overlapping cities: Alcas, Freemont,

Leatherman, Mantis and Ontario. The five cities comprise the entirety of Bakwatir County, which can be drawn as follows: Leatherman and Mantis are square cities of equal size and share one border completely. Ontario is a square the same size as Leatherman and Mantis, half of which is inside both Leatherman and mantis in equal parts and half of which is outside of Leatherman and Mantis. Alcas is circular. No part of it is outside of Leatherman, and part of it is also inside of Ontario. No part of Alcas touches any part of Mantis. Freemont is a circular city which partially lies in Mantis and no other city. The five candidates campaign in a manner consistent with the following::

  All candidates are within the County.
  Colt is in Alcas but not Ontario.
  Glock and Remington are never in the same city.
  Kimber and Beretta are never in the same city.
  Kimber is always in exactly two cities.

STEP ONE: GET A GRIP

Nature of the Game – Drawing. Players – CITIES = L, M, F, A, O CANDIDATES = B, C, G, K, R. Hidden Rules – Uh... WOW! The entire drawing is one fat hidden rule. We have to CAREFULLY draw the picture the way they described it, making sure that it complies with every rule and that no hidden rules are missed. Essentially we are doing step THREE before we do step TWO.

First they tell us that Leatherman and Mantis are square cities of equal size and share one border completely.

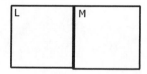

Next we are told that . Ontario is a square the same size as Leatherman and Mantis, half of which is inside both Leatherman and mantis in equal parts and half of which is outside of Leatherman and Mantis.

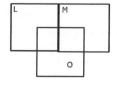

Then we are told that Alcas is circular. No part of it is outside of Leatherman, and part of it is also inside of Ontario. No part of Alcas touches any part of Mantis.

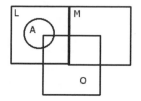

281

And finally we are told that Freemont is a circular city which partially lies in Mantis and no other city.

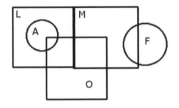

Seriously: how difficult was that?

STEP TWO: FORMAL RULES
1) ALL PLAY
2) C = A but not O
3) G & R NEVER IN SAME CITY
4) K & B NEVER IN SAME CITY
5) K = EXACTLY 2 CITIES.

STEP THREE: DRAW
Er....uh.....

STEP FOUR: INFERENCES
Absolutes? Rule 1, C=A but not O. Stuff that bad boy in there:

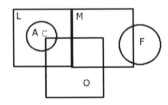

There are also a four places that, according to rule 5, K cannot go:

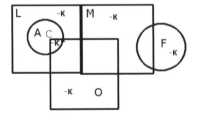

Bundles? None

Calculators? We can see that there are single, double and triple zones. SINGLES = L, M, F, O. DOUBLES = LA, FM, LO and MO. TRIPLE = LAO.

Double-ups? Rules 4 and 5 both talk about K. Wherever K is located, B cannot be in ANY of them. So if B is in the triple zone (LAO) then K has to be in FM because that is the only two city zone left.

Extras? No bi-conditionals. No forced dichotomies. No Right Side Rules. No affirmative duties. Contradictions? None. No lone conditionals either.

Free Rangers? NONE!

F) The magazine, *Reports on Things People Consume* is releasing its most recent rankings of eight bagged snack chips sold in U.S. markets. The chips, Angioplasties, Bypassers, Chlorester-alls, Diabitees, Elegies, Fatboys, G'outaheres and Heart Attackers, will be ranked from most favorable (first) to least favorable (eighth). The ratings are consistent with the following conditions:
Angioplasties are either lower ranked than
  both Heart Attackers and Bipassers or they
  are higher ranked than both.
G'outaheres are higher ranked than both
  Elegies and Angioplasties. rated than Diabitees.
Fatboys and Elegies are both higher ranked
  than Heart Attackers.
Diabitees are lower ranked than
  Bipassers.

STEP ONE: GET A GRIP
Nature of Game? Squishy Ordering. Players? A, B, C, E, F, G, H. Hidden Riles? Rank 1 – 8, hi – low. All play.

STEP TWO: FORMAL RULES

1)

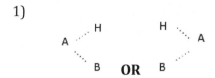

2)

3)

4)   B ..... D

STEP THREE: DRAW

Remember how we build up a Squishy game. We are essentially doing our Double-up Inference step and our picture at the same time. Notice how the way that WE drew the rules handed us the two-option scenario. Rule 1 tells us that the A – H – B relationship can only work in two ways. Those are the only two ways that the game can be played, so we Double-up the other rules onto them and *voila!* We get the big prize. So we can put the first part of rule 1 together with rule 3:

Then we can tack on rule 2:

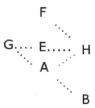

Then tack on rule 4:

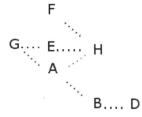

And there you have it, one of the two ways to play the game. We repeat the process for the other "or" in rule 1 by combining it with rule 4:

Then we tack on rule 3:

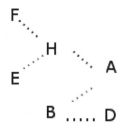

And then we tack on rule ... 2... which makes us a little bit crazy. Rule 2 says that G comes before both E and A. Visually, a lot of people freak out. This is, once again, a great time to KEEP YOUR COOL! We can already see that in this picture, E comes before H and H comes before A. If G has to come before E and A, that is, logically, the same as saying that G has to come before E. If G comes before E, and E comes before A, then G comes before E and A. THINK BEFORE YOU TOUCH PENCIL TO PAPER!

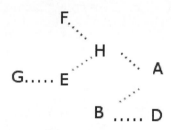

Now we have two pictures that show us the ONLY two ways this game can play out:

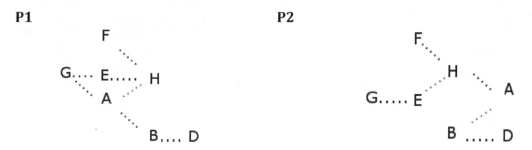

STEP FOUR: INFERENCES

Do not give in to the temptation to skip this step! Yes, we have made some really sweet inferences thus far with the pictures we drew. Victory depends upon regimented, disciplined attack because we know that the rules dictate the issues of the game, and the Inference step points out most if not all of them.

Absolutes? Remember that in a Squishy game, one of the key issues we have to grasp is the "endpoints." Who can be first and who can be last? In P1 only F and G can be first. In P2 B, F and G can be first. This is a big deal. The average schmo taking the LSAT does not grasp that B can be first, and that if B is first (P2) A or D MUST be last (and H cannot be last, as it can in P1). So we make a note:

$$1 = B, F, G$$

Then we pin down #8:

$$8 = A, D, H$$

As always in Squishy games, the money is in the middle. We are not going to waste our time trying to figure out who can be second, seventh etc.

Bundles? None.

Calculators? They are almost all in the pictures, as plain as the nose on your face. There are a LOT of ways this could play out, so we will rely upon the pictures when we get to the questions.

Double-ups? DONE.

Extras? No bi-conditionals. FORCED DICHOTOMY! We spotted it before in rule 1. H and B are either both before or both after A. And that, ladies and germs, is the big victory point of this lesson: SQUISHY ORDERING GAMES ARE ALWAYS FORCED DICHOTOMIES! A only has two positions it can take relative to H: before and after. They don't give us rules that say things like, "X is either before or after Y," in Squishy games because... DUH, that is the only it can work. If ties are allowed, then it is no longer a dichotomy. The good news is that any time that there has EVER been a Squishy Ordering game on the LSAT, ties were not allowed. There have been Bundles (X and Y always go the bathroom together) but that makes them ONE PLAYER in the Squisht-branchy-bush.
Right Side Rule? Nada. Affirmative duties? None. Contradictions? None. Lone conditionals? Zip.

Free rangers? C! C is a bloody Free Ranger. It can be First or last or second or... "I'm bad. I can do what I want." Had we skipped the Inference step and gone right to the question, we would possibly have missed this. Imagine totally dorking up a question like, "Which of the following could be a complete and accurate list of the chips ranked X?" First, last… it does not matter. If Chlorester-alls are not in the answer choice, then the answer choice is INCORRECT! If you were relying upon the incomplete inference from the Absolutes step, you could have pulled a serious boner. So amend your notes:

$$1 = B, F, G, C$$
$$8 = A, D, H, C$$

NOW we are ready to DESTROY THE QUESTIONS!

PROB. SET 17

Six jugglers, Aragon, Frodo, Gandalf, Legolas, Pippin, and Sam are each going to juggle exactly once, one at a time. They will each be juggling exactly one of the following types of items, none of which may be used more than twice: Broadswords, Mithril, Quarterstaffs, Rings and Orc heads. The order in which they juggle and the item each juggles is determined by the following constraints:

Sam juggles either first or second.
Legolas juggles Mithril unless Gandalf Juggles rings.
Frodo juggles either Mithril or broadswords before Pippin and Gandalf juggle.
Sam juggles broadswords if and only if Gandalf juggles rings.
Only the fourth juggler juggles Orc heads.

	1	2	3	4	5	6
AFGLPS	S/ ⁻P⁻G	S/ ⁻P⁻G		-F	-F	-F
BMQRØ	-o	-o	-o	⊙	-o	-o

** ALL PEEPS PLAY **NO OBJ. More than 2X!

1) S = 1/2
2) −GR ⊃ LM · −SB
 −LM ⊃ GR · SB
3)

F(M/B) ⸴⸴ P
 ⸴⸴ G

4) GR ⊃ SB
 −SB ⊃ −GR · LM
 SB ⊃ GR
 −GR ⊃ −SB · LM
5) 4="O" = ONLY "O"

1) Which one of the following could be a complete and accurate ordering of the jugglers and the items that they juggle?

a) Aragon, broadswords; Frodo, quarterstaffs; Sam, rings; Pippin, Mithril; Gandalf, Orc heads; Legolas, Mithril

b) Sam, Orc heads; Frodo, broadswords; Pippin, quarterstaffs; Legolas, Orc heads; Gandalf, rings; Aragon, Mithril

c) Sam, broadswords; Frodo, broadswords; Gandalf, rings; Aragon, Orc heads; Legolas, Mithril; Pippin, quarterstaffs

d) Gandalf, Mithril; Sam, broadswords; Frodo, Mithril; Aragon, Orc heads; Pippin, quarterstaff; Legolas, rings

e) Gandalf, broadswords; Sam, broadswords; Frodo, Mithril; Pippin, Orc heads; Aragon, rings; Sam, quarterstaffs.

REMEMBER THAT HE FIRST PROBLEM IN THE SET IS TO BE DONE TOP-TO-BOTTOM! Begin with (a) and work your way down the list so you *learn more about the game.* So we read the call of the question and we GO WITH WHAT WE KNOW before we start using our pencils.

(a) cannot be correct. It fails to put S in the first or second position.

(b) Looks more promising. It has S in 1... but is has S juggling O, but our drawing and rule 5 says that "O" can only go in fourth position.

(c) SB is first. FB is Second, putting F before P and G. GR is third and rule 4 requires GR. AO is fourth, so the O in fourth place is fulfilled. LM is okay because we do not have any other people juggling M. PQ in sixth works because P is after F. This is not in violation of any rule, ergo it must be correct. Circle it and go to the next question, because (d) and (e) must be incorrect.

For those of you who need proof: (d) is incorrect because G is before F, and (e) is incorrect because G is before F.

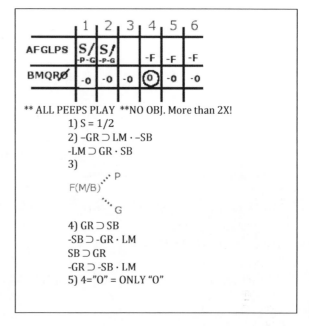

** ALL PEEPS PLAY **NO OBJ. More than 2X!

1) S = 1/2
2) –GR ⊃ LM · –SB
-LM ⊃ GR · SB
3)

F(M/B) ⸽ P
⸽ G

4) GR ⊃ SB
-SB ⊃ -GR · LM
SB ⊃ GR
-GR ⊃ -SB · LM
5) 4="O" = ONLY "O"

2) If Sam juggles Mithril second, which of the following could be true?
 a) Frodo juggles Orc heads third
 b) Frodo juggles Mithril third
 c) Gandalf juggles rings first
 d) Pippin juggles rings first
 e) Sam juggles quarterstaffs fourth

What do we already know? If Sam is juggling Mithril, then Gandalf cannot juggle rings and Legolas has to juggle Mithril (rule 4). Also, Frodo has to juggle Mithril or broadswords first or third. We know quite a bit...in fact we know so much that:
(a) must be false (No FO allowed).
(b) could be true. Circle it and be done with it.
(c) Cannot happen.
(d) Pippin can never go first.
(e) The fourth juggler has to juggle Orc heads, not quarterstaffs.

3) If Frodo juggles Mithril third, which of the following is a complete and accurate list of all of the jugglers who could juggle first?
 a) Sam
 b) Sam, Legolas
 c) Sam, Legolas, Pippin
 d) Aragon, Legolas, Sam
 e) Aragon, Gandalf, Legolas, Sam

We already know that P and G cannot go first. (c) and (e) are incorrect. Sam is in all answers, so we can ignore him (besides, we already know that he can always go first). The three remaining answers (a) Sam, (b) Sam, Legolas and (d) Aragon, Legolas, Sam points us to an easy solution. Sam is a winner. Aragon is a free ranger who could only be squeezed out of position 1 if someone else was in position 2, thus requiring Sam to be in 1. Since that is not the case, Aragon can go into 1. Legolas is in both (b) and (d). Thus (d) must be correct. We do not need to check Legolas at all, because Aragon can go, and (d) is the only answer with Aragon.

4) If Gandalf and Pippin juggle fifth and sixth respectively, and they juggle Mithril and rings respectively, then which of the following must be false?

289

a) Frodo juggles before Sam
b) Sam juggles before Frodo
c) Aragon juggles before Frodo
d) Frodo juggles before Aragon
e) Sam juggles before Aragon

REMEMBER what our process is! First, we go with what we know. If we do not have the answer already (or if keeping everything straight in our head is too difficult) we

re-draw our picture. We have to apply the rules to the information that the problem gives us, and then, if the rules make us change the re-pictured scenario, we add the change(s) and check the answers.

Here is where we start to really see the benefit of having taken the time to draw the inferences in Step Four of the Test Mentors Method.
We can see that GM is 5 and PR is 6.
O is still in 4.
Rule two says that because G is not juggling R, L must be juggling M.
F still has to be 1, 2 or 3, but F can no longer juggle M because two Ms are in play. F must be with B.
S still has to be 1 or 2.
This MIGHT be just a bit overwhelming for you. If it is, do this:

$$
\begin{array}{cccccc}
L & F & & & & \\
M & B & & & & \\
\underline{S/} & \underline{S/} & \underline{} & \underline{} & \underline{G} & \underline{P} \\
 & & & O & M & R \\
\end{array}
$$

This quick, truncated re-picture helps us to see an obvious truth: S, F and L all must go in the first three positions, so Aragon, the free ranger, is no longer so free: he must go with O in 4. The answer should be obvious.
(a) F can go 1, 2 or 3. INCORRECT
(b) If F can go 1, 2 or 3, then S can go 1 or 2. INCORRECT
(c) Aragon must be in position 4 juggling Orc heads. CORRECT
(d) Must be true
(e) Must be true.

5) If Legolas juggles broadswords first, the for how many other people can their position in the order and the objects they juggle be determined?
  a) zero
  b) one
  c) two
  d) three
  e) four

Here is another question that should be a snap for us as long as we are careful and we do not fall into the big trap set for us.

If LB is in 1, we already know that GR and SB are a must (contra-positive of rule 2). We also know that SB has to go into 2. That means that F has to go with M in 3 because both of the B's are used up, and F has to be in 1, 2 or 3, but 1 and 2 are full. Again, you can take notes as you go:

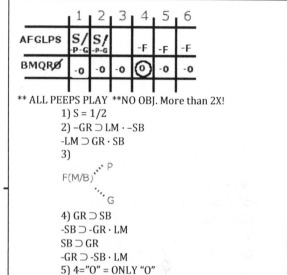

** ALL PEEPS PLAY **NO OBJ. More than 2X!
1) S = 1/2
2) –GR ⊃ LM · –SB
   -LM ⊃ GR · SB
3)
F(M/B) ⋯ P
        ⋰ G
4) GR ⊃ SB
   -SB ⊃ -GR · LM
   SB ⊃ GR
   -GR ⊃ -SB · LM
5) 4="O" = ONLY "O"

$$\frac{L \quad S \quad F}{B \quad B \quad M \quad O} \;-$$

The rules tell us nothing else for sure other than that Gandalf cannot go into 4. We do not know, however, whether he goes into 5 or 6. The same can be said of A and P. So we can see that LB = 1, SB = 2, and FM = 3. So the answer is... (c)! Did you fall into the trap? Many people incorrectly say that the answer is (d), which is not correct. The call of the question asked us, "...how many *other* people..." as in, other than L. If you fell into the trap, do not let it happen again. If you did, pour yourself a nice, tall, cool and refreshing Fresca.

SIDE NOTE: Many of you might be thinking that L cannot juggle M. He can. –LM forces GR. GR does not force –LM. GR only forces SB. That error is called *affirming the consequent*, and that is a logic error... a HUGE logic error, and one of the main ones they are testing...which you would **_know_** if you had paid attention back In the logic section. So if you missed that, REVIEW!

6) Which of the following could be true?
 a) Both Aragon and Legolas juggle broadswords, and both Pippin and Sam juggle rings.
 b) Both Aragon and Sam juggle broadswords and both Pippin and Legolas juggle rings
 c) Both Gandalf and Aragon juggle rings, and both Sam and Frodo juggle broadswords
 d) Both Legolas and Aragon juggle quarterstaffs and both Gandalf and Sam juggle rings
 e) Both Gandalf and Aragon juggle rings, and both Sam and Frodo juggle Mithril

A NAKED QUESTION! No "if," no information, just a straight-up test of competence. We be competent. This should be easy.

(a) Can we have AB and LB? No. Why? Rule 2. If –LM then GR and SB (the SB is what we care about here). So LB gets SB, and AB would be three B's. Ooops.
(b) Notice how, once we spot the issue in (a), the same issue is manifested in (b), just in a slightly different way. L is put in the back half of the problem with R, which

is just another flavor of –LM. So AB and SB up front works (not too many B's) but –LM forces GR again, and GR, PR and LR makes 3 R's.

(c) GR, AR, SB, FB. Hmmmmm. GR forces SB. Sweetness. AR is good because that makes two R's only. FB is consistent with the rules. NOW JUST ONE LAST THING before we cavalierly circle (c): who does that leave to squeeze in, and can it be done without breaking any rules? L and P still need to play, and one of them has to play with O in slot 4. That is no big deal. This is our answer!

(d) is an easy kill. LQ is –LM, and that again forces GR and SB. But this answer has SR. KILL IT (and a kitten while you are at it, because we already found the correct answer, and every time you keep reading answers after you have found the correct one, you are killing a kitten… and KILLING YOUR SCORE BY WASTING TIME).

(e) GR means SB. This has SM, which Hobbits are not into.

We have one final note about this question. Many people head into this problem set with the faulty assumption that one, *and only one* object may play more than once. That is an error on their part. Here we see how the LSAC, whether deliberately (probably) or otherwise (not) uses such common errors to test something more subtle about applicants. If you made this mistake, the problem set does not point out the error until you get to the sixth question. Imagine for a moment that you are some mouth-breathing, slack-jawed troglodyte. You assume that, because O goes one time, and all of the people have to play, that all of the objects must be used, so one of them will go twice and all of the objects will be used. You get through the first five questions and you are feeling pretty good about life, and then question six comes along. ALL of the answer choices say that two of the objects can go twice. You become panicked. You freak out. You lose your composure. You cannot concentrate. That sick feeling hangs with you for the rest of the exam, killing your score, your chances of getting a scholarship, getting into law school, impressing your dates…. You should not be a lawyer if this happens to you. Here is why.

That two objects can go twice did not in any way impact any of the other answers. If you are going to freak out and lose your cool during one of the most important events in your life and allow that lack of composure to tank your future, should you really be responsible for the lives, futures and fortunes of other people?

THIS IS A BIG DEAL because the LSAC puts this very sort of thing on every LSAT. Your first line of defense is to NOT LET IT BE AN ISSUE. You do that by learning how to do things properly, systematically, intelligently and maturely. In other words, you learn to do it our way.

7) Which of the following is an item that both Gandalf and Sam can both juggle?
a) Broadswords
b) Mithril
c) Orc heads
d) Rings
e) Quarterstaffs

We know that we have the bi-conditional rule four: GR proves SB, and SB proves GR. This kills (a) and (d) right out of the gates.

Think for a second. WHAT ELSE DO WE ALREADY KNOW? There can only be one O. KILL (c).

So it comes down to Mithril vs. Quarter... Quarterstaffs? They have been awfully quiet throughout this entire affair, wouldn't you say? What do we know about them? FREE RANGER! If we go GQ and SQ, the only thing we are forced to do is... have LM. That leaves another M for F, or two B's for F. Q HAS TO BE THE ANSWER!

For the sake of argument (but not the kittens) Mithril is a dog. If we have GM and SM we learned long ago that GM is –GR, and that means we have to have LM, and that makes three M's, GM, SM and LM. Poor dead kitty.

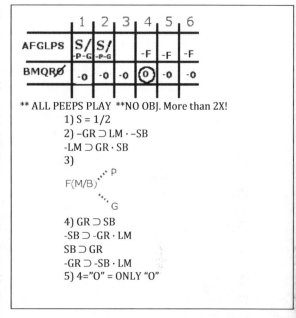

	1	2	3	4	5	6
AFGLPS	S/ -P-G	S/ -P-G		-F	-F	-F
BMQRØ	-O	-O	-O	Ⓞ	-O	-O

** ALL PEEPS PLAY **NO OBJ. More than 2X!

1) S = 1/2

2) –GR ⊃ LM · –SB
   -LM ⊃ GR · SB

3)
$$F(M/B) \begin{array}{l} \cdots P \\ \cdots G \end{array}$$

4) GR ⊃ SB
   -SB ⊃ -GR · LM
   SB ⊃ GR
   -GR ⊃ -SB · LM

5) 4="O" = ONLY "O"

293

PROBLEM SET 18

Exactly four different math classes are being taught, one during each quarter of the school year, at a community college: Algebra, Bayesian Statistics, Calculus, and Discrete Mathematics. At least one and at most two teachers are assigned to each course, and each teacher will be assigned at least one course. Algebra may be taught only by Flanders, Marge, Smithers or Willie. Bayesian Statistics may be taught only by Marge or Smithers. Calculus may be taught only by Homer, Marge or Willie. Discrete Mathematics may be taught only by Flanders, Homer or Smithers. The order in which the classes are taught and the assignment of teacher to them must comply with the following constraints:

No teacher may teach during more than two
   quarters, and they may not be consecutive.

Discrete Mathematics must be taught before
   Calculus and after Algebra.

None of Marge's classes may be taught later in the
   year than any of Smithers'.

** All classes play.
**1/2 Teachers per Class.
**All Teachers Play.
** B1 = M or SM
** B4 = S or SM
1) Teach = 2X max
   No teach consec. quarters
2) A....D....C
3) M....S or
   SM together

A	D	C
F	F	H
M	H	M
S	S	W
W		

B
M
S

	1	2	3	4
F, H, M, S, W				
A, B, C, D				

1) Which of the following could be a complete and accurate list of the classes taught, in order, and the teachers assigned to them?

(a) Algebra: Marge, Flanders
   Bayesian Statistics: Marge, Smithers
   Calculus: Homer, Willie
   Discrete Mathematics: Homer

(b) Algebra: Flanders, Willie
   Bayesian Statistics: Marge
   Discrete Mathematics: Homer, Flanders
   Calculus: Marge, Willie

(c) Algebra: Flanders, Willie
   Bayesian Statistics: Smithers
   Discrete Mathematics: Homer, Flanders
   Calculus: Willie, Marge

(d) Bayesian Statistics: Homer, Smithers
   Algebra: Flanders, Willie
   Discrete Mathematics: Homer, Smithers
   Calculus: Willie, Flanders

(e) Algebra: Flanders, Willie
   Discrete Mathematics: Homer
   Calculus: Willie
   Bayesian Statistics: Marge, Smithers

** All classes play.
**1/2 Teachers per Class.
**All Teachers Play.
** B1 = M or SM
** B4 = S or SM
1) Teach = 2X max
   No teach consec. quarters
2) A....D....C
3) M....S or
   SM together

```
  A   D   C
  F   F   H
  M   H   M
  S   S   W
  W
   B
   M
   S
```

```
              1   2   3   4
F, H, M, S, W
A, B, C, D
```

REMEMBER that the first question in the set is addressed by working it from (a) to (e). WE DO NOT jump around. Rather, we learn about the game.

(a) says: Algebra: Marge, Flanders; Bayesian Statistics: Marge, Smithers; Calculus: Homer, Willie; Discrete Mathematics: Homer.

All we need to do is reference our drawing to see that A = M, F is allowed.

```
  A   D   C
  F   F   H
  M   H   M
  S   S   W
  W
   B
   M
   S
```

WE MUST ALSO CHECK the rules to make sure that there is no violation of any rule that did not make its way into the drawing. AGAIN, we must emphasize the *importance of good habits.*[4] In this particular case, it would not necessarily kill you to not check the rules (as none of them apply). It is the habit of doing every step, every time that is important. If you skip any part of the method when it *does* count and *can* hurt you, you lose points...usually EASY points. Do not slip into bad habits. Practice the good ones always.

B = M, S is allowed by the drawing. Check the rules. VIOLATION of rule #1: Marge is in consecutive quarters. KILL IT!

(b) Algebra: Flanders, Willie; Bayesian Statistics: Marge; Discrete Mathematics: Homer, Flanders; Calculus: Marge, Willie. We know that A can go first, and F, W works. All rules are followed. B second is allowed by the drawing, and Marge is good to go. No rule violations. D can go third (it has to if A and B are 1 – 2) and H & F are

---

[4] One of the most horrific videos you will ever see is of a cameraman who skydives with a helmet-cam to document the first parachute jumps of others. The cameraman, cutting corners and NOT doing every step, every time, jumped from 10,000 feet without a parachute. BAD HABITS KILL. Always use good habits.

okay. Fourth has to be C, which it is, and Marge and Willie can teach it...but, "Houston, we have a problem here."[5] ONE OF OUR INFERENCES tells us that M cannot go in the fourth quarter unless she is teaching B (because she would be coming after S, which is a violation of rule 3). ALSO, S is nowhere in the answer choice, which is a violation of hidden rules. KILL IT!

(c) Algebra: Flanders, Willie; Bayesian Statistics: Smithers; Discrete Mathematics: Homer, Flanders; Calculus: Willie, Marge. We know from (b) that A = F, W works. B= S fits the picture and the rules... BUT WE KNOW THAT (c) MUST BE INCORRECT! M has not taught yet, so she will have to come after S, and that is a rule violation! KILL IT!

(d) Bayesian Statistics: Homer, Smithers; Algebra: Flanders, Willie; Discrete Mathematics: Homer, Smithers; Calculus: Willie, Flanders

WRONG! B can go first, but Homer cannot teach it. DOH!

At this point, you MUST circle E and move on to the next question. If a, b, c and d are incorrect....
Do not waste time checking an answer that MUST be the correct answer.
PROOF:
(e) Algebra: Flanders, Willie; Discrete Mathematics: Homer; Calculus: Willie; Bayesian Statistics: Marge, Smithers

A = F, W. Good. D second is allowed, and H can teach it. C third is cool, and W is okay to teach it. That means that C ahs to be fourth with M and S, which it is.

NOTICE SOMETHING: Some people begin with answer choice (e) and work up the list. Those who misinterpret rule 3 to mean that M must come before S blow this problem. We work top to bottom. If WE screwed up rule 3, we would have eliminated (a) through (d) and then, because (e) must be the answer, we would learn about our mistake quickly and efficiently. Answer choices, especially with the first problem, work that way.

---

[5] This quote is NOT from astronauts Jack Swigert, Jim Lovell or Fred Haise on their Apollo 13 flight. It was stated as such in the recreation of that flight in the movie *Apollo 13*, Universal Pictures, 1995, and was stated in the movie by Tom "F-bomb" Hanks (and almost certainly was constantly uttered in some variation by singer Bobby Brown). Most importantly, Swigert (played by Kevin Bacon) said, "Okay, Houston ..." followed by Lovell, "I believe we've had a problem here." Thus bringing this book well within six degrees of Kevin Bacon.

** All classes play.
**1/2 Teachers per Class.
**All Teachers Play.
** B1 = M or SM
** B4 = S or SM
1) Teach = 2X max
No teach consec. quarters
2) A....D....C
3) M....S or
SM together

			1	2	3	4
F, H, M, S, W						
A, B, C, D						

2) If Flanders teaches in two different quarters, which of the following must be true?
(a) Calculus is taught in the third quarter
(b) Algebra is taught in the third quarter
(c) Algebra is taught in the first quarter
(d) Bayesian Statistics is taught in the first quarter
(e) Bayesian Statistics is taught in the fourth quarter.

WHAT do we already know? Look at the drawings. F can teach A and D, which are together. *"We gotta keep 'em separated!"*[6] So the order of the classes has to be A, B, D, C, with F teaching A and D. Hence, (a) is incorrect. KILL IT! (b) is incorrect. KILL IT! (c) is correct. Done. Next problem.

3) Which of the following, if known, would allow the order of the four courses to be completely determined?
(a) Calculus is taught in the third quarter.
(b) Algebra is taught in the first quarter.
(c) Discrete Mathematics is taught in the second quarter.
(d) Discrete Mathematics is taught by Homer and Flanders.
(e) Bayesian Statistics is taught by Smithers only.

What do we already know? The order really turns on "B" and where it goes. So B can lock it down, but two other things can lock B down: if C is third, B has to be fourth, and if A is second, B has to be first. This is one of those things that we *could* have taken a bunch of time to calculate out back at the *Calculators* step, but it was not necessary. Now that the need arises, we can do it. Had the need not arisen, we would have been wasting tons of time.

Again, our method saves the day. Our drawings allow us to visually "slide" B around and see that if A is first, B can go anywhere else but if A is second, there is nothing left to figure because there is only one way for A to go second. That is precisely the same thinking that applies to C being third; there is only one way for that to happen,

---

[6] The Offspring, *Smash,* Epitaph / Ada Records, 1994.

but there are several ways for C to go 4th. This also allows us to see that D is worthless, because it cannot go first or fourth, but there are several ways for it to go second or third.

(a) says C is third. That means B is 4th, making A first and D second. Circle it, bubble it, move to the next problem.

4) If Algebra is taught only by Flanders, and only Smithers teaches Bayesian Statistics, which of the following must be false?
  (a) Willie teaches Calculus with Marge.
  (b) Marge teaches Calculus with Homer.
  (c) Homer teaches Discrete Mathematics.
  (d) Bayesian Statistics is taught in the fourth
        quarter.
  (e) Smithers does not teach Discrete Mathematics.

NOTICE how the call of the question is 1000% consistent with what we have been screaming at you: the rules define the issues that will be queried. The inferences we draw point them out ahead of time. Here, we already know a ton and we must use it.

Look at the drawing. If A is only taught by F, then M, S, and W do not teach their one minimum… yet. If B is taught only by Smithers, we know that B cannot go in the first quarter (M needs to teach before or with S per rule 3). And there is the answer. A has to go in first quarter. B has to go somewhere that allows M to teach before S. The only option is to put B in the 4th quarter so M can do C third (because M cannot teach A, according to the call of the question, and M cannot teach D according to the rules). BUT NOTICE SOMETHING ELSE! A = F alone in the 1st quarter means that Willie *must* teach C with M 3rd. It is the only other class Willie can teach! THAT means that Homer *must* teach D, because he just got pushed out of C!

If this is a bit confusing, fear not. Let's use our pencil to re-picture things. Here is what the call of the question told us to be true:

WHENEVER we re-picture things, we have to check the new drawing against the rules. The rules say that all teachers must play, and that M teaches before or with S. Can M teach with S now? Nope. She must, ergo, teach before S. The only class she can teach before S is… C. So for C to come before B, B must be last and M must teach C.

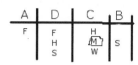

The rules still say that everyone must teach a class. W can only teach C, and the rules say that two people maximum can teach a class, so W does C with M.

** All classes play.
**1/2 Teachers per Class.
**All Teachers Play.
** B1 = M or SM
** B4 = S or SM
1) Teach = 2X max
   No teach consec. quarters
2) A....D....C
3) M....S or
   SM together

			1	2	3	4
F, H, M, S, W						
A, B, C, D						

The rules *still* require everyone to teach a class. Who has not gone? H. What can he teach? Only D.

We made a change to the drawing, so we check the rules. No teacher can go twice in a row, so F cannot do D, and S cannot do D because M must do C before S teaches.

Ta-da! There is nothing left for the rules to tell us.

(a) Willie teaches Calculus with Marge.
HA HA HA HA HA! This is the sucker-trap! This is the answer to a, "...what must be true?" Question. That is *precisely* what you have to expect when there is a complex

question like this. They want to know whether you can both handle the multiple levels of analysis *and* avoid careless errors. The call of the question asked for what must be *false.*

(b) Marge teaches Calculus with Homer. Done. Circle it. Next question that needs destroying, please.

META-NOTE:
And this, ladies and germs, is a perfect example of how the LSAC makes a question "harder": they make several issues operative at the same time and they give you a question call to shoot yourself with. This is precisely like how, on the SAT math section, a problem is "easy" if it wants you to do one thing only (for example, solve for X) and "difficult" if it calls on you to do two or three things (like solve for X, then insert that value into another equation, solve it, then factor the answer).

WE ARE ABLE TO DO EVERYTHING THAT THE TEST MAKERS CAN AND WILL ASK OF US. So long as we stick to the Test Mentors Methods, use our heads, do not rush, and do not spaz out, we will always *DESTROY THE QUESTIONS.*

5) Which of the following must be false?
  (a) Willie teaches during the first quarter.
  (b) Willie teaches during the second quarter.
  (c) Homer teaches during the first quarter.
  (d) Homer teaches during the second quarter.
  (e) Homer teaches during the third quarter.

Again we see a naked question: no additional information is provided. So unless the answer choices are squirrely, we already have the answer in front of us in our drawing, rules and inferences.
(a) says that Willie teaches during the first quarter. Must that be false? NO! Willie can do Algebra. KILL IT!
(b) Willie teaches during the second quarter. If W can do the 1st, he can do the 2nd. KILL IT!
(c) Homer teaches during the first quarter. He can only teach D and C, neither of which can go first. Done. Next question.

6) Which of the following must be true?
  (a) Algebra is not taught in the second quarter.
  (b) Algebra is not taught in the first quarter.
  (c) Bayesian Statistics is not taught in the second quarter.
  (d) Calculus is not taught in the second quarter.
  (e) Discrete Mathematics is taught in the third quarter.

You have got to *love* these naked questions by now!
(a) Algebra is not taught in the second quarter. Can A go first? Duh. KILL IT!
(b) Algebra is not taught in the first quarter. KILL IT!

** All classes play.
**1/2 Teachers per Class.
**All Teachers Play.
** B1 = M or SM
** B4 = S or SM
1) Teach = 2X max
   No teach consec. quarters
2) A....D....C
3) M....S or
   SM together

(c) Bayesian Statistics is not taught in the second quarter. KILL IT!
(d) Calculus is not taught in the second quarter. DONE! C must be taught in the third quarter or the fourth quarter.

7) If Bayesian Statistics are taught by one teacher in the first quarter, which of the following could be true?
   (a) Marge teaches calculus.
   (b) Flanders teaches both Algebra and Discrete Mathematics.
   (c) Smithers teaches both Algebra and Discrete Mathematics.
   (d) Algebra is taught by Flanders and Willie, and Discrete Mathematics is taught alone by Homer.
   (e) Homer and Willie teach Calculus.

What to we already know? If B is taught by one person (an issue we spotted earlier) it *must* be taught by M. Do you remember why? Because if S teaches it, M cannot teach in an earlier quarter. So if B is taught by M first quarter, the class order is B, A, D, C. This means that M cannot teach Algebra because she would be teaching two consecutive semesters.

Take a good look at the drawing and rules and see if you catch anything else:

** All classes play.
**1/2 Teachers per Class.
**All Teachers Play.
** B1 = M or SM
** B4 = S or SM
1) Teach = 2X max
   No teach consec. quarters
2) A....D....C
3) M....S or
   SM together

B, A, D, C with M teaching B means no M teaching A. But it also means M cannot teach C because then she would be teaching after S. Perhaps some of you saw that way back when we were doing the Inference step. We did, but we left it out on purpose to demonstrate a **_HUGE_** point: even if you do not hit *every single inference within a given step*, you are still safe so long as you keep using all of the other steps, every single time. They form a safety net, with lots of built-in redundant back-stops.

So, (a) Marge teaches calculus is incorrect. KILL IT!

(b) Flanders teaches both Algebra and Discrete Mathematics. A and D are consecutive in the B, A, D, C line up. KILL IT!

(c) Smithers teaches both Algebra and Discrete Mathematics. Same problem as (b). KILL IT!

(d) Algebra is taught by Flanders and Willie, and Discrete Mathematics is taught only by Homer. Look at your pictures carefully. B is taught by M first quarter. If A is taught by F and W, and D is taught by H alone, what does that mean? S cannot teach any classes! KILL IT! Circle (e), bubble it on the answer form and run off to the next question.

(e) Homer and Willie teach Calculus. Could be true, because F and S can teach A or D. We just killed a kitten.

8) What is the maximum number of teacher assignments that can be made during the four quarters?

(a) four
(b) five
(c) six
(d) seven
(e) eight

A	D	C
F	F	H
M	H	M
S	S	W
W		

B
M
S

No freaking out! What do we already know? This is the perfect place to ... look back at the other correct answers we have obtained! Question #1 has six teaching assignments in it. That means that (a) and (b) are incorrect answers. SHAZAM! KILL THEM! Now we have to figure out whether 7 or 8 will work.

WORK FROM HIGH TO LOW

Let's see if we can get eight. If not, that should at least help us to see whether or not there are any intricacies to the rules that allow us to determine whether or not seven will work.

As has been the case throughout, we already know that the M...S or MS (rule 3) problem is the key. In order to get eight assignments, how many of the five people have to be assigned to two classes? THREE! Generically speaking, we need VV, WW, XX, YZ to get five letters to fill eight spaces. So three of our teachers have to go twice, and they all have to avoid going consecutively.

The drawing reveals out true issue: Bayesian Statistics only has two possible teachers. To get eight assignments, that MS (our problem children) have to appear together. We now need to do something... atypical. THINK in reverse order. We need to push B toward the 4th quarter, it appears, in order to get eight. We saw back in question 4 how this kind-of worked, with B in the 4th quarter, only there it could only be taught by S

** All classes play.
**1/2 Teachers per Class.
**All Teachers Play.
** B1 = M or SM
** B4 = S or SM
1) Teach = 2X max
   No teach consec. quarters
2) A....D....C
3) M....S or
   SM together

A	D	C
F	F	H
M	H	M
S	S	W
W		

		1	2	3	4
F, H, M, S, W					
A, B, C, D					

B
M
S

We can do a quick re-picture with B 4th and M, S teaching it.

A	D	C	B
F	F	H	M
M	H	M	S
S	S	W	
W			

If this were the scenario, working backwards to the third quarter, we would have to have C = H, W in order to avoid the "two M in a row" problem. But that would create a problem. If C=H, W, then D = F, S to avoid two consecutive H's in C and D. But if D = F, S, the B = M, S violates rule 3 because M teaches B way after S teaches D. So B = M, S will not get us 8 in the 4th quarter, but it could get us seven assignments if D = F only, and A=M, W. So we know (c) is incorrect. KILL IT!

If we put the B between D and C that changes things slightly.

A	D	B	C
F	F	M	H
M	H	S	M
S	S		W
W			

We MUST have B = M, S to get eight. If that is so, we can have C= H, W in the 4th quarter and D = F, H in the 3rd. Algebra in the 1st has four candidates to choose from, but F is out and so is S (because M is later in the year). So A = M, W is our only hope. Does it violate any of the rules? NO! M, W and H all go twice, F and S go once. Circle (e), bubble it on the answer form and move on.

NOTE: We promised you that there would be problems like this, problems that rest upon inferences that are too time-consuming to do in the actual Inference step of the Test Mentors Method. We *could* take the time in the Inference step to figure out every possible combination possible, but that would be a complete waste of time. Why? We are only going to be asked about one or two of them. We are better off waiting for these "tough" questions and spending 90 seconds pounding them out than wasting four minutes creating a list of things, ninety percent of which are not getting us any closer to our goal.

YOU MUST REMEMBER THIS! There are always a few questions that you just have to roll your sleeves up and get dirty with. If you did all of the other steps in the process well, these questions are much easier than if you are doing them from next-to-scratch (which is what almost everyone else is doing). The test makers put these questions in on purpose for the best test takers to distinguish themselves. DO IT! Don't panic about the time. Don't "go rogue" and start making stuff up *ad hoc*. Stay cools, work them out, and know that you are better than everyone else.

AGAIN, this is why it is critical to do **_everything_** perfectly, by the Test Mentors Method. That is how you get the other questions quickly and have the time to do the hardest of the hard. As we just saw, they are not impossibly difficult. They are just challenging.

9) Suppose that the condition which says that no teacher is allowed to teach more than twice is suspended. If all other rules remain in effect, then what would be the maximum number of teachers who could teach twice?
  (a) One
  (b) Two
  (c) Three
  (d) Four
  (e) Five

Ordinarily a "rule change" or a "new rule" question is the last question in the problem set. Here, because we gave you twelve questions as opposed to the usual six or seven, this one appears as number nine. Just remember that when you come across these questions, you need to remember that they usually change very little about the game, and that they are mostly psychological warfare by the test makers. They want you to think that you have to start over from scratch and re-figure everything. Suckers leap right to that conclusion. We will DESTROY THE QUESTION systematically.

Take a look at what we already know. There are four quarters and there are two teachers per quarter maximum. That is eight teachers. If four teachers could go twice, that would be eight teachers. HOWEVER, the "all play" rule is still in effect also. Oops. KILL (d) and (e). The last problem, question 8, showed us that three can go twice even under the *old* rule. Three must be the answer. Circle it, bubble it in and go to the next question.

10) If Homer teaches two classes by himself, which of the following could be true?
  (a) Smithers and Willie teach Algebra During the first quarter.
  (b) Flanders and Willie teach Algebra during the first quarter.
  (c) Smithers teaches two classes.
  (d) Marge and Smithers each teach two classes.
  (e) Flanders teaches one class and Smithers teaches two classes.

** All classes play.
**1/2 Teachers per Class.
**All Teachers Play.
** B1 = M or SM
** B4 = S or SM
1) Teach = 2X max
   No teach consec. quarters
2) A....D....C
3) M....S or
   SM together

```
A | D | C
F   F   H
M   H   M
S   S   W
W

    B
    M
    S
```

	1	2	3	4
F, H, M, S, W				
A, B, C, D				

Again, this is a piece of cake for us. We already can see from our original drawing that if H teaches two classes *by himself,* those classes must be D and C. They have to be separated by B, our "consecutive player breaker-upper." Once we realize that H is alone teaching both D and C, we know that F, S, M and W have not taught any classes. If this is getting to be a bit much for you to follow, make a quick re-picture. BUT WE ARE WARNING YOU that this takes time, and you want to try, as best as you can, to try to do this without becoming overly dependent upon your pencil. A still has all four of F, M, S and W. However, it can only have two of them. That means that B has to have the other two, and that means that B = M, S because those are the only two B can have. Thus we must have A = F, W in order to get all five teachers a gig for the year. So it turns out that everything is completely resolved, and there are not any "could be true" things, just "must be true" and "must be false" things. We win again.

(a) is grossly incorrect, as A is taught 1st quarter by F and W.
(b) is correct. Circle it, bubble it on the answer form and move on to the next question.

For those of you who might need a visual, we give you this:

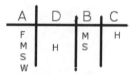

Now that you can see D and C with H only, we have four teachers left to place and only two classes with a two-teacher maximum to put them in. So the M, S pair *must* go with B. That leaves F and W to go with A.

11) Which of the following is an acceptable ordering of the teachers of the classes, by quarter taught?
  (a) First: Smithers, Willie; Second: Homer, Flanders; Third: Homer, Willie; Fourth: Smithers, Marge
  (b) First: Marge; Second: Homer, Flanders; Third: Smithers; Fourth: Homer, Willie
  (c) First: Homer, Willie; Second: Marge, Smithers; Third: Flanders; Fourth: Homer, Smithers
  (d) First: Marge, Smithers; Second: Flanders, Homer; Third: Willie; Fourth: Homer, Marge
  (e) First: Smithers; Second: Flanders, Willie; Third: Homer, Smithers; Fourth: Willie

Here again, they are checking your ability to orient yourself to the call of the question and to remain cool. They give us the teachers *without* the class order. So we have to figure that out. *CHILD'S PLAY!* What do we already know? For beginners, THIS:

We also know that this question is simply a matter of determining which quarter B is taught in and making certain that the rules are complied with. Pretty awesome, huh?

(a) First: Smithers, Willie; Second: Homer, Flanders; Third: Homer, Willie; Fourth: Smithers, Marge
This must be incorrect because we already know that S cannot go before M.

(b) First: Marge; Second: Homer, Flanders; Third: Smithers; Fourth: Homer, Willie
There is no S before M issue here. If M is in the 1st quarter, we have to figure out whether or not she is teaching A or B (the two classes M can teach first). We cannot tell this without making reference to the 2nd quarter, H, F. The only way H and F can teach together in the 2nd quarter is how? *If they are teaching D!* So A is 1st and D is 2nd. Is B 3rd or 4th? It would have to be 3rd. That is because the 4th class in this answer choice has H and W, and the only way that can happen is if B is 3rd and C is 4th. IT WORKS! Circle it, bubble it in on the form and move to the next question.
(c) is incorrect because H and W can never teach together in the 1st quarter. You just killed a kitten.
(d) is incorrect because there is an S before an M. Another dead kitten.
(e) is incorrect because S can never teach the 1st quarter alone, as M would never be able to teach. That is an entire litter. Nice job.

CONTINUED ON NEXT PAGE

12) If Marge teaches during both the first quarter and the last quarter, which of the following must be false?
a) Marge teaches Algebra
b) Marge teaches Bayesian statistics
c) Marge teaches Calculus
d) Smithers teaches Calculus
e) Smithers teaches Discrete Mathematics

What do we know already? If we look at the line-up of our players, we notice the big issue that these weasels are playing at: There are *four* ways that M can teach both first and fourth quarters:

B, A, D, C
A, B, D, C
A, D, B, C
A, D, C, B

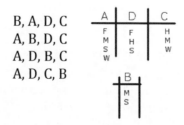

Those are the only four ways this game can be played anyway! In other words, there is nothing here that we do not already have figured out. This should be a piece of pie![1] We are being asked about what cannot ever possibly be true and we have that down cold.

a) Marge teaches Algebra. Could be true. KILL IT!
b) Marge teaches Bayesian statistics. Could be true. KILL IT!
c) Marge teaches Calculus. Could be true. KILL IT!
d) Smithers teaches Calculus. Seriously? That's it? Yep. Sometimes it is just that easy. Circle it, bubble it in on the answer form and move on to the next question.

---

[1] Ya, we know that the "traditional" idiom is about cake. But seriously, pie is sometimes just... better. Sure, there is no frosting, but pie has fruit like apples and cherries. Do not even bother with the, "Oh, you can put fruit into a cake..." argument because that is just wrong. Putting fruit into a cake just turns it into a fruitcake, and you are what you eat, and ... sorry. We digress...

Problem Set 19

Eight political candidates, Arthur, Ford, Grunthos, Hotblack, Marvin, Prostetnic, Trillian and Zaphod, are each to give a speech to a community organization. The speeches will be presented one at a time and must comply with the following conditions:
  Ford speaks before Arthur but after Trillian.
  Both Prostetnic and Zaphod speak after
    Grunthos.
  Either Hotblack speaks before both Marvin
    and Zaphod, or else he speaks after both
    Marvin and Zaphod.
  Marvin speaks before Ford.

STEP ONE: GET A GRIP

The nature of the game is ordering, and from a glance at the formal rules we can tell that it is pure Squishy. Remember that a "Squirm" game has a mixture of Squishy and Firm rules (both formal and hidden). Here, the only thing we have that resembles a "firm" rule is that they speak one at a time and in order, which is useless in and of itself. *The Players* are A, F, G, H, M, P, T and Z as our candidates, and positions one through eight. The *Hidden Rules* are that ALL PLAY ("... are each to give a speech..."), and that they speak one at a time (so all eight positions get filled).

DO NOT be fooled into thinking that because there *might* be a definite order that this is a Firm Ordering game. The formal rules all betray the truth of the treachery afoot here.

STEP TWO: FORMAL RULES

Because they are all squishy, we will just draw them out, like so:

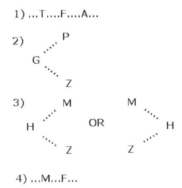

Let us make certain that our brains are firmly wrapped around these rules. Rule 1 says that F is before A and after T. There are leading and trailing dots. We can use those to remind us that T need not be first, nor does A need to be eighth. Rule 2 shows G coming before both P and Z. Notice how we did not use the leading and trailing dots. That was on purpose, just to show you that they are optional.

ALERT 1! ALERT 1! ALERT 1!

Rule 3 is an *awesome* rule, the type that you ought to always be on the lookout for. It says that H is either before both M and Z, or it is after both M and Z. What does that mean to your *test taking* brain? Allow us to give you a hint: think about the *Extras* from Step Four.

Rule 3 is a *forced dichotomy*! Under normal circumstances, H could come *between* M and Z. Now it is only allowed to come *before or after both.* This is a gift from the test gods! They have just told us that there are exactly two ways to play this game. So when we get to Step Three, we are going to make TWO drawings, one with H before M and Z, the other with H after M and Z

ALERT 2! ALERT 2! ALERT 2!

This rule could just have as easily (actually, more easily) been written, "H cannot come between M and Z." Because they all have to play and there can be no ties, the effect would have been the same. A huge pile of people would not have seen the dichotomy though. Essentially, this shows that the people who make this test are actually somewhat kind. **The bigger point is this: when a rule says that X cannot come between Y and Z, and when everyone has to play, and when there can be no ties (i.e. one at a time), it means that there is a FORCED DICHOTOMY, which means two pictures only, which means you are going to DESTROY the questions.**

Rule 4 just says that M is before F. How mundane.

STEP THREE: DRAW

Recall that in a Squishy Ordering game, we combine all of the rules into a drawing by finding common players within the various rules to connect together.

We are going to have two drawings, P1 and P2. P1 will be based around H being before M and Z. P2 will be based around H being after M and Z.

Rule 4 says that M comes before F, so we can add that right away to both:

Rule 1 stay that T comes before F and that F comes before A, Add it to the F in the picture:

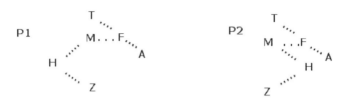

Finally, rule 2 says that G is before P and Z:

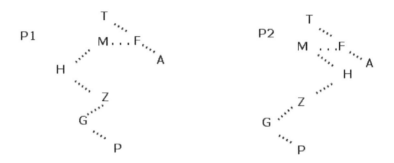

Voila! Two pictures, and the only two ways that the game can be played.

STEP FOUR: INFERENCES
Remember to do **EVERY** part of **EVERY** step **EVERY** time. There is a real temptation to skip the inferences once the two wicked-bad-awesome pictures are drawn. *"CLASSIC BLUNDER!"*

ABSOLUTES: Recall that we are looking for players that must go in a specific place or who can never go in a specific place. In the Squishy game, NEVER FIRST and NEVER LAST are easy pin-downs. We can easily determine who is eligible to be first and last, thus telling us who cannot. Recall that anyone without a dotted line coming out to the left can be first and that anyone without a line coming out to the right can be last.

We just have to check both P1 and P2 to make sure that we do not miss some key difference or similarity. P1 allows T, H and G to be first. P2 allows for T, M and G to be first. How about that! Nobody else can be first. Equally as important is the fact that the distinction between P1 and P2 is H vs. M in first position. If H is first, we are in P1. If M is first, we have to be in P2.

For the eighth position, P1 allows A, Z or P. P2 allows for A, H or P. Again we have a subtle difference that tells us a TON of juicy information. If Z is last, we are in P1. If H is last, we are in P2. Something else is very noteworthy: H can be first and H can be last. There has *got* to be a question based on that! Write all of that down!

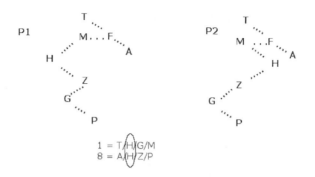

Bundles? None

Calculators? We done did them earlier when we did absolutes.

Double-up? We did them when we built the pictures in Step Three.

Extras? Bi-conditionals? Not really. Forced Dichotomies? YES! That is precisely how we ended up with two pictures. Otherwise this bad boy looks like a free-for-all. Right Side Rule? None. Affirmative duties? Everyone plays... big deal. Contradictions? Zip. Lone Conditionals? None.

Free Rangers? Not a one of them.

STEP FIVE: DESTROY THE QUESTIONS! Remember to *ALWAYS GO WITH WHAT YOU ALREADY KNOW FIRST!*

1) Which one of the following could be the order in which the candidates speak?
 A) Marvin, Trillian, Ford, Arthur, Hotblack,
        Grunthos, Zaphod, Prostetnic.
 B) Trillian, Marvin Ford, Arthur, Grunthos,
        Zaphod, Prostetnic, Hotblack.
 C) Hotblack, Marvin, Zaphod, Grunthos,
        Prostetnic, Trillian, Ford, Arthur.
 D) Grunthos, Zaphod, Hotblack, Prostetnic,
        Marvin, Trillian, Ford, Arthur.
 E) Hotblack, Grunthos, Marvin, Zaphod,
        Prostetnic, Trillian, Arthur, Ford.

The first problem in the set should be attacked from (A) through (E) so we can learn more about what is going on. (A) has M, T, F, A, H, G, Z, P. P1 won't work, but P2 allows for the M, T, F, A, just not the H, G, Z, P. Both G and Z need to come before the H in P2. But we did learn something interesting: M, T, F, A works.

(B) T, M, F, A, G, Z, P, H – Again we are in P2 with T, M, F, A still working for us (just swapping the T and M). (B) also resolves the G and Z before H problem. This is our winner!

(C) is incorrect because it has Z before G.

(D) is incorrect because it has G, Z as 1-2, which means we have to be in P2 (in P1, H must come before Z), and that means that H has to come after M.

(E) is incorrect because it has A before F... too bad, because otherwise it was a good answer.

THIS ANSWER (E) is a "speed trap". People will see that the first five or six work properly and they circle it in a rush to get to the next question. They fail to see A is before F and they miss an easy point. This is a great trap for the people who work backwards, E to A.

2) How many candidates can speak either first or eighth?
 A) Zero
 B) One
 C) Two
 D) Three
 E) Four

What do we already know? H is the only one. Circle (B) and move on.

3) If Zaphod speaks after both Grunthos and Hotblack, which of the following must be false?
 A) Hotblack speaks first
 B) Hotblack speaks second
 C) Hotblack speaks third
 D) Hotblack speaks fourth
 E) Hotblack speaks fifth

What do we know already? If Z is after both G and H, we must be looking at P1. We also know that T, H or G could go first. That is important because it also means that any one of them could also go second or third. Think about it: T, H, G or T, G, H or H, T, G or ... We hope you see that point. That makes our problem much easier, because (A), (B) and (C) all must be incorrect. So we are down to (D) and (E). The real question is, can we get H into the 4th spot? And the answer is affirmative. P can go after G but before H. So they could speak in the order G, P, T, H. Eliminate (D), circle (E), bubble it and move on.

4) If Marvin is the sixth speaker, which of the following must be true?
 A) Arthur speaks eighth
 B) Hotblack speaks eighth
 C) Trillian speaks fifth
 D) Zaphod speaks fifth
 E) Grunthos speaks fifth

What do we know already? If M=6, we have to be in P1. How do we know that? SAY IT OUT LOUD AND MAKE SURE YOU UNDERSTAND IT!

In P2, F, H and A al have to come after M. Thus M cannot be 6th in P2. In P1, if M is 6th to speak, then F must be 7th and A must be 8th. Does that answer our problem? Yes it does. (A) is correct. Bubble it in and move on. We know that all of the other answers

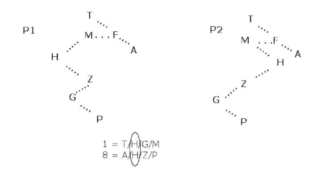

have to be incorrect. We can see why if we just look back to question 3 above. T, H, G, Z and P have buckets of freedom. They are a tiny bit constrained (Z can be third, fourth or fifth, etc.) , but none of them is pinned down to a "must be true" by the mere fact that M is 6th.

5) If the first three speakers are Trillian, Marvin and Grunthos, respectively, then the sixth, seventh and eighth speakers, respectively, could be:

A) Hotblack, Arthur, Ford
B) Zaphod, Ford, Arthur
C) Prostetnic, Ford, Hotblack
D) Ford, Arthur, Hotblack
E) Ford, Hotblack, Zaphod

ALERT! THE "KUSO" MOMENT[73]

Before we dive into the actual explanation of this problem, we would like to look at a pattern that you will want to familiarize yourself with. No, what we meant to say is, ***you need to recognize this pattern on site***. This is what we call a "Kuso!" moment for many a test taker. Imagine that you are a person who did not write out the two different pictures, P1 and P2. Rather, you missed the big inference altogether, or you drew one picture and decided to try to keep track of the other rule 3 possibility on the fly (as insanely stupid as that sounds). Question five alerts you to the fact that T, M and G can go 1, 2, 3 respectively, a fact that you were probably oblivious to. This comes as quite a shock to your brain. You flip out, wonder how many of the prior questions you screwed up, begin to panic, feel your entire future sliding from the court rooms of New York to the break rooms of Wal-Mart... in other words, things turn to *kuso* in a big hurry for these poor saps.

The test makers could have made this the first question in the problem set, thus humanely pointing out the error of the test taker's ways at the start. However we surmise that this is not the point of the exercise. Rather, we think that they are trying to do something rather interesting. They are seeing whether or not the mediocre test taker at least has the composure to keep their wits about them and

---

[73] Long story short: "Kuso" is the Japanese word for "crap." The author coined it as a term for playing chess: it is the moment in the game when you realize that, if your opponent is doing what they are doing on purpose and for the reason(s) you think that they are, you are absolutely, positively, inextricably, screwed. All one can do is say, "Kuso!" and resign.

not freak out. The average test taker gets the answer to question #1 by the ad-hoc checking of each rule against the answer choices (something we tell you to never do, and this is one of the reasons why). This "average" person gets the answer correct, but sets themselves up to get kicked in the crotch on question number five. Finding the correct answers to questions one through four did not depend on having the two drawings. If these test takers do not freak out, they can continue to function at maximal mediocrity. If it does freak them out, they sink lower and lower into the left half of the bell curve because they waste time re-figuring the first four questions, become psychologically rattled by the belief that they have screwed up the entire game, become panic stricken because of the time they are losing, or some combination of the three.

Three of the many things that great LSAT takers have in common are, (1) they follow every procedure for destroying the test on every problem, every time, (2) they never have the *kuso* moment and (3) someone else pays for their law degrees. Be a great test taker.

So now we have question 5 to deal with. We are in P2, and we already know that P, A or H has to be eighth. Eliminate (A) for having Ford eighth and (E) because it has Z eighth. Now we have to do a little work. A LITTLE.
(B) is incorrect because if Z is sixth, H has to come after it but does not in (B).
(C) is incorrect because if F is seventh, A must be after it.
(D) is the only one left, so we circle it and we move along.

6) The earliest position that Arthur can speak in is:
  A) Second
  B) Third
  C) Fourth
  D) Fifth
  E) Sixth

Smooth sailing. Now P2 is *required*. We can see that, in P2, F, T and M have to fo before A. That means A can go 4th. In P1, A can go 5th at the soonest. (C) wins.

7) If Ford is the third speaker, which of the following could be the order of the fourth, fifth and sixth speakers respectively?
  A) Arthur, Hotblack, Prostetnic
  B) Hotblack, Grunthos, Zaphod
  C) Grunthos, Prostetnic, Hotblack
  D) Arthur, Grunthos, Prostetnic
  E) Zaphod, Hotblack, Prostetnic

If question 6 was a *kuso* moment, seven prolongs the magic. Without P2, F being third makes no sense. We know already that if M is third, T and M have to be first and second, though not in that order. We can see from P2 that H has to come after G and G, making (A), (B) and (E) incorrect *ab initio*[74]. (C) has H in the correct place, but G and P are before it, not G and Z. (D) must be the correct answer.

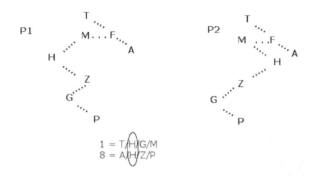

Notice how the correct answer had A as the 4th speaker, then G and P as 5ht and 6th? That is the kind of thing they do to see whether you know that *the dotted lines define the relationships*. A has relationships with M, T and F but none whatsoever with anyone else in P2. *Visually* it looks like it has to come after G and P, but that is an illusion. THAT is the bigger issue being tested here.

8) If Arthur speaks sixth and Prostetnic speaks seventh, which of the following must be true?
 A) Either Hotblack or Grunthos speaks first
 B) Either Hotblack or Zaphod speaks first
 C) Either Hotblack or Zaphod speaks last
 D) Either Trillian or Marvin speaks first
 E) Either Trillian or Marvin speaks last

What do we already know? P1 and P2 help us a little, if we want to do it by brute force. But we also know that A and P are on our "who can speak eighth" list. If they are not eighth, then H or Z must be. That is answer choice (C). Done.

---

[74] LOOK IT UP! It gets thrown around in law all of the time. That's just one more way you can make your life easier in law school: get a legal vocabulary so the words do not add to your workload.

Problem Set 20

A sixty story hotel has nine guests- A, B, C, D, F, G, H, J, K- that will only take rooms on one of the top three floors. Floor sixty has two rooms available, floor fifty-nine has one room available, and floor fifty-eight has two rooms available. Each room can fit a maximum of two guests. All guests must have a room and rooms must be assigned according to the following:

   D shares a room with another guest.
   If A does not share a room with C then B shares a room with F
   If H is on floor sixty, she has no roommate
   G and J share a room but not on floor 58.
   K is on floor 60 and does not share a room.
   A and B cannot be on the same floor.

STEP ONE: GET A GRIP – Nature of the game? They are asking us to take people and to put them into rooms... just like putting "stuff" into "buckets." This is a bucket game, albeit a bit unusual. Players? People = A, B, C, D, F, G H, J and K. Floors/rooms = 58 (2 rooms), 59 (one room) and 60 (two rooms). We *should*, at this very moment be *anticipating* that this is going to be an issue that the test makers mess with us with. There are five rooms and nine people. Already we are seeing the *Numbers* inference looming on the horizon. Hidden rules? All of the people have to play. Maximum of two people per room. (NOTICE WHAT THE HIDDEN RULES DO *NOT* SAY! Not every room is required to have a person in it).

STEP TWO: FORMAL RULES –

* All Play
* MAX 2 peep/room

1) $\boxed{D \_}$

2) $-AC \supset BF$
   $-BF \supset AC$

3) H 60 $\supset$ H alone
   $\cdot - $ H alone $\supset$ - H 60

4) $\boxed{GJ}$ 59/60

5) K = 60 = ALONE

6) $\dfrac{A}{B} \Big/ \dfrac{B}{A}$

Let us take a few moments to look at what we did and *why.*

First, we put our Formal Rules directly under our Hidden Rules. We want everything lined up when we get to step four, the Inferences. Not including the Hidden rules in that process is a recipe for a career as a non-lawyer.

Second, we circled the first and fourth rules to highlight that D and his pal will occupy one entire room and that G and J are always and forever roommates (unless there is a question breaking them apart).

Third, rule number six is drawn to visually represent A and B being on different floors. If you wrote something like, "A & B Different Floors," go punish yourself appropriately. We are going to have a three-floor picture of a hotel and we want our representation of the rules to reflect that.

Fourth, rule four was written to show us where the GJ bundle *MUST* go. That is far more useful to us than "GJ Not on 58," especially come inference time.

STEP THREE: DRAWING

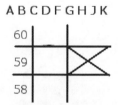

How is that for simple? That is precisely what a hotel with floors looks like, no? So that is how we draw it. Note that we had to block off one of the rooms on the 59th floor. So now we have our two on 60, two on 58 and one on 59.

IF YOU DID NOT LIST OUT ALL OF THE PEOPLE, GIVE YOURSELF A SPANKING.

STEP FOUR: INFERENCES
Absolutes? – YES. Rule #5 tells us that K must be solo on 60.

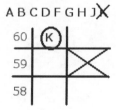

So now K is placed and we have crossed it off of the list of available players. Do we have any other Absolutes? NO! Don't get ahead of yourself and start doing Double-ups or Calculators ahead of schedule. It may be tempting to jump on the obvious things that will come later, but that is indicative of a lack of discipline. Discipline is what is required to hit the 85%+ mark. So pretty please with sugar on top, stick to the game plan.

Bundles? – YES! GJ is a bundle. RECALL how we are to use Bundles: they have to work around the Absolutes. GJ has the additional property of being limited to floors 59 and 60. Do we want to draw two different pictures, one with GJ on 60 and one with it on 59? Look at the drawing and the rest of the rules and think about it: will it net us a bunch of additional information?

Actually, it will. If GJ is on 60, rule 3 is taken out of commission and rule 6 is easy to draw in. If GJ is on 59 then rule 6 is also easy to pencil in. First, let's put GJ in 60, then re-picture it with the GJ on 59, remembering to cross them off of the "player" list once they have their new, permanent home:

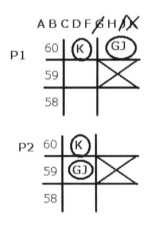

Now it should be easy to see that, in P1, either A or B has to go on 59 and its opposite number has to go on 58. In P2 one of them has to go onto 60 and the other has to go to 58. Let's put them in and cross them off:

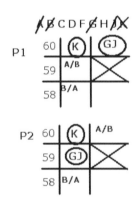

RIGHTEOUS! Are there any other Bundles? DO NOT FOOL YOURSELF INTO THINKING that rule 2 or rule three represents a bundle. They do not. They are **CONDITIONAL**. They create "bundles" only in the one, narrow circumstance defined by the *antecedent* (the left, "if" side).

Calculators? – HECK YA! Now is the time to really dig deep into our energy reserves and concentrate. Look at our P1 and P2. They include rules 4, 5 and 6 completely. We now have to see if rules 1 or 2 or 3 in any way create "combinations, permutations or numerical issues." Do they?

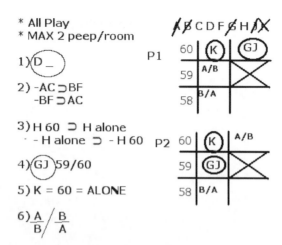

Look at rule 3. It says that **IF** H is on 60, H is alone. *Can H be on 60 in P1?* No way! H has to go to 58 or 59 in P1. *Can H be on 60 in P2?* Er, uh… NO! In P2, A or B has to be on 60, and that would not allow H to be *alone*. Daaaaannnnngggg, bayyyy-beeee! H cannot go to 59 in P2 either: "No room at the inn!" GJ have clogged up the works. So in P2, H **must** be on 58!

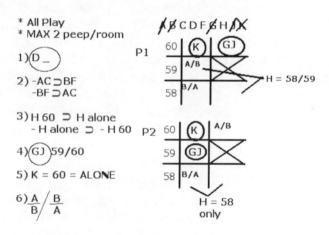

We don't have H pinned down quite enough to cross H off, but we are getting closer by the minute, and for all intents and purposes, rule 3 is dead.

How many players are left to place? FOUR: C, D, F and H. How many spaces are left in out hotel? P1 has one space on 59 and three on 58… for a total of *four!* P2 has one space on the 60th floor and three on the 58th. Again, *four spaces for four people!* There can be no other single rooms. MAKE A NOTE OF THAT!

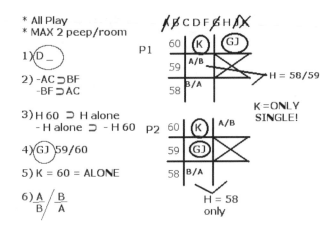

This is HUGE! We know that we have rule 2 just waiting to be the pain in our backsides! Someone must go with A and with B! That will always trigger rule 2.

Seeing as how we are still on the Calculator step, let's think for a second. A and B can only go with C, D, F or H. If A rooms with C, or if B rooms with F then Rule 2 is irrelevant: it only comes into play when A is not with C, or B is not with F. *BUT* what if A and F room together? Rule 2 says that if A is not with C then B must be with F... but if A is with F, how can B room with F? DUH! B cannot. Ergo, A can never go with F. Are you seeing it? AF is the "-AC" antecedent that has a BF consequent. In other words, AF proves BF, but there is only one F. So A and F cannot room together.

The same thinking should apply to B and C. The contra-posed rule 2 says that if –BF then AC. If B rooms with C, that is "-BF". How can we have BC and AC at the same time? WE CANNOT! Thus B can never be with C.

If you ate your Shredded Wheat this morning you might have picked up on one more idea that flows from this Calculator: F and C cannot room together either. If they did, we would have –AC and –BF (because F and C would be tied up together, as it were). The –AC would force the BF, but F would be with C. The –BF would force the AC, but again, C and F would be together. IN OTHER WORDS, F and C can never room together.

If most of that did not come to you when you did the game on your own, try not to let it get you down. This stuff takes time. IT ALSO TAKES EFFORT. DO NOT DELUDE YOURSELF INTO THINKING THAT, BECAUSE YOU CAN FOLLOW OUR EXPLANATION THAT YOU UNDERSTAND HOW TO DO IT ON YOUR OWN. You will know that you can do it on your own just as soon as you do it on your own, and not a moment sooner.

So here is where we are at with the addition of our Calculators:

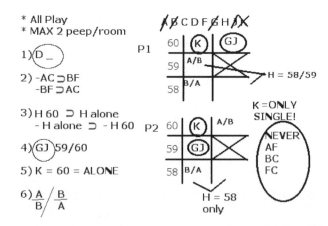

Double-ups? – We are looking for two or more rules that reference the same player(s). Rules 2 and 6... but we beat them to death a while ago. Rules 4 and 5 talk about the 60th floor... but we have that covered as well.

Extras? – ALWAYS! Is there a bi-conditional? No.

Are there any forced dichotomies? SCADS of them! A or B can go on any of the floors, but one of them always has to be on 58. So A or B are on 58-59 or 58-60. That smells like a "must be true" question in the making, no? GJ is another: 59/60. H is 58/59.

Right Side Rules? YES! Rule 2 allows AC and BF. Be looking for that question to pop up as well...or more likely, be looking for a *correct* answer choice that includes both AC and BF to trip up the mouth breathers. CIRCLE THAT BAD BOY, but do not waste your time with the right side on rule 3 because we already know the H cannot be on 60 and H cannot possibly be alone (due to the hidden rules).

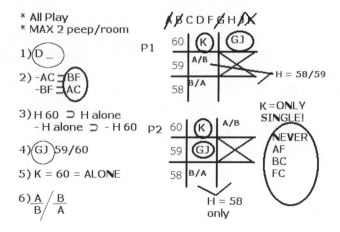

Affirmative Duties? YES! Rule 2 is an affirmative duty. We have to have either BF or AC or both. Have we beat that horse to death yet? It is also Right-Side Rule! Contradictions? None.

Lone Conditionals? Nope. We have two conditional rules, and it is going to be very easy to deal with rule 2.

Free Ranger(s)? – C, D, F and H are the four that we have not placed, but they are all so heavily constrained that to call them "free" would be a bit... disingenuous.

STEP FIVE: DESTROY THE QUESTIONS!

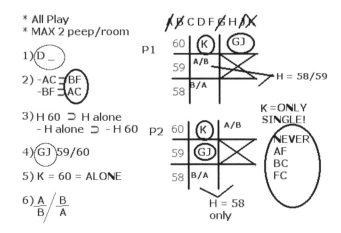

1. Which one of the following could be a complete and accurate list of the guests staying on floor fifty-eight?
   A) A, B, C
   B) A, C, D, F
   C) G, J, B, C
   D) A, F, B, C
   E) A, C, D, J

What do we already know? Well we know that each room has to have two people in it (except for K on 60). So (A) is incorrect. Answer choice (B) has A, C, D and F. If they were on 58, then A would have to go with C or D because AF is, as we already know, illegal. But AC is allowed. AC in a room, DF in the other. That would put us in P1. BH would be on 59 and in full compliance with rule 2. GJ and K on 60 and we are done. Circle that bad mamma jamma and go on to the next question!

(C) is incorrect because G and J are restricted to 59 and 60. IF YOU PICKED THIS ANSWER, that means that you are not paying attention to what you already know, i.e. a flippin' formal rule. Even if you missed all of the Inferences, rule 4 is pretty plain on its face.
(D) is incorrect because A and B cannot be on the same floor. IF YOU PICKED THIS ANSWER, that means that you are not paying attention to what you already know, i.e. a flippin' formal rule. Even if you missed all of the Inferences, rule 6 is pretty plain on its face.
(E) is incorrect. (C) above should explain why.

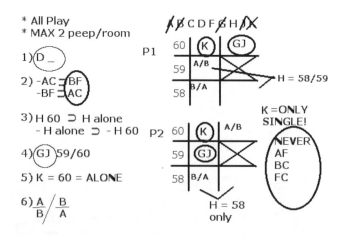

2. Each of the following guests could be placed in a room on any floor EXCEPT:
   A) A
   B) B
   C) C
   D) F
   E) H

Pay dirt! We know this one already. A, B, C and F have that weird relationship going on that allows them (or forces them) to interchangeably flip places in P1 and P2. Knowing that the right side rule allows them to both happen at the same time (AC and BF) makes this very easy. H on the other hand, cannot go on the 60th floor... ever. (E) wins.

3. If A and C are on floor 60 which one of the following must be true?
   A) B and F share a room on floor fifty-eight
   B) C and H share a room on floor fifty-nine
   C) B and H are on the same floor
   D) F and H are on floor fifty-nine together
   E) H and F share a room on floor fifty-eight.

What do we know already? AC = 60 means that we are in P2. B is on 58 and so is H. Guess what? That is answer choice (C).

(A) is incorrect. B and F could share a room on the 58th, but they do not *have to*. That is why you go with what you know first, so you do not get sucked into bad answers like (A).
(B) is incorrect because the 59th floor has to be GJ.
(D) is incorrect because ... read (B).
(E) is incorrect because H and F *could* share a room, but they do not have to. That is why you go with what you know first, so you do not get sucked into bad answers like (E).

4. If D is on the same floor as K, which of the following must be true?
   A) Either G or J or both are on the sixtieth floor
   B) Either F or B or both are on the fifty-ninth floor
   C) Either C or F share a room with D
   D) Either C or F share a room with H
   E) Either A or D shares a room with F

Really? REALLY!?!?! If D is on the same floor as K, what do we already know? They are on the 60th floor and that means that we are looking at P2. That means that G and J are occupying the 59th floor. What else do we already know? D has to be with A or B on 60. Either way we are having to deal with rule 2. If it is AD=60, then it is BF=58. If it is BD=60, then it is AC=58. In either event, H has to be on 58 in the room that A or B is not in. USE THAT to see if you can see where the answer most likely lies. We are thinking that (D) is probably money, because it has H in it, and coming up with H was a long way down our chain of reasoning. (D) says that C or F has to be

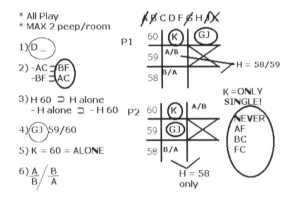

with H, which is precisely true. AD or BD on 60 means BF or AC respectively on 58. If it is BF on 58, then the C goes with H. If it is AC on 58, then the F that would have gone with B now goes with H. (D) is our spot-on-perfect answer. We killed it.

If that answer is hard for you to get your head around, we understand. This question is what we call a BoB (Baddest of the Bad). What makes a question a BoB? We are glad that you made inquiry. **BoBs are problems that have multiple solutions but some common element between the various solutions.** Here, the A/B flip potential between 60 and 58 gave us huge BoB issues: C or F was going to have to be in the same room with A or B respectively on 58 (again, because A or B was going to have to be with D on 60, thus triggering rule 2. So C or F was going to be on 58 with A or B and the one of them that was not with A or B would have to take the only room left, and that is with H on 58 as well. BoB.

DO NOT FRET, however! There was a less efficient though equally deadly method (SBD: Slower But Deadly). We already know that (A) has to be incorrect, because G and J are on 59 in P2. (B) must be incorrect because nobody can be on 59 other than G and J. (C) must be incorrect because P2 show us that A or B shares a room with D on 60, not C or F. (E) is incorrect, but it is the "challenge" answer for people taking

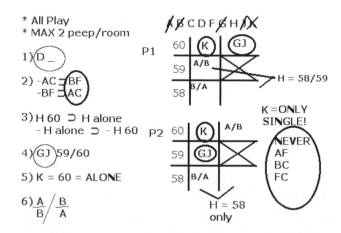

this ad hoc approach... and it is only a *challenge* if, in the process of thinking about (E), you get sloppy. P2 tells us that A or B is with D, so D cannot share a room with F. Some disoriented student might think, "Well, if B and D are together on 60, that might force A to go with F." If you are sitting next to that person, please slap him or her right now, just on principle. BD is, per rule 2, -BF and that means AC and that in turn means that (E) is muy-mucho-incorrecto.

5. Which one of the following is a complete and accurate list of guests who can share rooms together?
   A) B with F; A with C; G with J; D with H
   B) A with F; B with C; G with J; C with H
   C) A with C; B with J; G with H; D with F
   D) C with F; A with D; B with F; G with J
   E) A with B; C with D; F with H; G with J

This looks like a toughie. What do we already know? Well, we know that AF, BC and FC are impermissible roomies, that GJ is a bundle, that AC and BF can happen at the same time, and that K is always alone. We win. (A) is the perfect answer. Mark it and move before you get sucked into a bad answer. Speaking of which:
(B) is incorrect because... wow... where to begin with this pantload. Let's just kill it at AF.
(C) is incorrect because of the BJ
(D) is incorrect because of the FC
(E) is incorrect because of the AB: they cannot even be on the same floor as each other, well enough alone share a room. Sounds like an H.R. issue, to be sure.

6. Suppose floor fifty-nine now has two rooms available. If all of the other conditions remain in effect, which of the following must be false?
   A) H and F share a room on floor fifty-nine and A and C share a room on floor fifty-nine
   B) A and D share a room on floor sixty and K is on floor sixty
   C) G, J and K are all on floor sixty and there are no empty rooms in the hotel
   D) G, J and K are all on floor sixty and there is one empty room in the hotel
   E) G, J and K are all on floor sixty and there are two empty rooms in the hotel.

You had to have seen something like this coming. *Everything* in this game was completely hashed out in advance. Changing the rule(s) is the only way that they can "up the ante," so to speak.

Rule changes are introduced to *mess with your head and your inferences.*[75] In other words, there were key inferences that we made in Step Four of the Test Mentors Method that were the result of there only being one room on 59. That is the heart of what we have to look at.

DON'T PANIC! When there is a change like this, we have to remain calm, keep our wits about us and above all else, **THINK**. The situation has changed and now there is a second room on the 59th floor. *How does that change things, if at all?* Sometimes there is no practical effect whatsoever. Let's look at P1 for starters.

We saw in the Inferences step that, in P1, the only reason GJ has to go to 60 is because A and B have to be on different floors. In P1, with one of A or B on 59, GJ has to go to 60 only because there was no other room on 59. Now GJ can go to 59 or 60 because there are two rooms. In P2 we had the reverse situation, where GJ was on 59, thus forcing A or B to 60. Now GJ and A or B can be in separate rooms on 59. We could re-picture the entire scenario, but that would not be a very efficient use of our time...yet.

We ended up with a P1 and a P2 because of that missing room on 59: we could not get a third picture with A or B on 60 and B or A on 59 because One of them on 60 meant GJ filled the only room on 59. Now we can have A on 60 and B on 59, or vice-versa.

Also, we determined that everyone but K had to be doubled-up into a room because there were eight spaces for eight people after K was cemented onto the 60th floor. Now we have 10 spaces for eight people, so two people could go solo now. But that also means that everyone can still share rooms and there can be one empty room.

REMEMBER that all of the other rules have to be complied with as well. Sometimes the game that is afoot is that the test distracts you into overlooking a rule that did not change (i.e. D still cannot have a single room).

Do these insights actually answer the question?

Yes! (E) says that there could be two empty rooms, but we know that is not possible because the most people we can pack into a room is still two. If there are five empty rooms, and all eight of our people are doubling up, they need four of the five rooms. (E) cannot be true.

---

[75] People who do not make inferences, only partially draw them or who do them poorly are suddenly struck with fear.

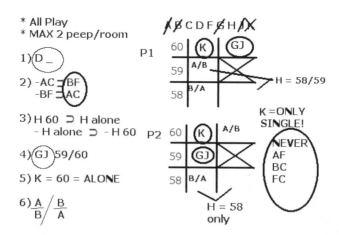

7) Which one of the following, if substituted for the rule requiring H, if on floor sixty, to have a room by herself, would have the same effect as that rule?

A) H must be on floor fifty-eight

B) H must be on floor fifty-nine

C) H is on either floor fifty-eight or floor fifty-nine.

D) B and C cannot be on the same floor.

E) D shares a room with H.

Here is another question call that really throws people for a loop. They are asking us for another rule that would *have the exact same effect* as an existing rule, in this case, rule 3.

DON'T PANIC! **THINK!** What *is the complete effect* of rule #3? It is that H cannot be on the 60th floor, but can be on either 58 or 59. That is all there is to it. So find an answer choice that *means* the same thing (i.e. "H must be on 58 or 59," etc.). If there are different or additional consequences to the answer choice then it must be incorrect because we are looking for the *exact* same effect.

(A) is a trap because the effect is *different*. Locking H onto 58 takes away P1's ability for H to go on 59.

(B) is incorrect because... well, you ought to be able to see that based on the wrongness of (A).

(C) is ... very correct. It kicks H off of 60 and it allows all of the other rules to function exactly as they did before. Circle it, bubble it on your form and MOVE!

(D) Would this little gem force H off of 60? No! It would change things substantially because it would allow H to be on 60, and would allow H to be there with a roommate. Incorrect! Besides, what does separating B and C have to do with anything? Nothing, actually. It is tied to rule 2, but (D) would change the application of the H rule substantially.

(E) This could be a tricky one, and one that we should not even be looking at (because (C) was the correct answer and we should have moved on by now). D sharing a room with H would force H off of 60 because, as we can see in our two pictures, either GJ has to fill the other room on 60, or one of A or B must. It would also, however, have a whole bunch of additional collateral changes. D is allowed to pair up with several other players as the rules stand originally. If we force D and H into a bundle, that changes a whole bunch of the dynamics of the game (A and B can no longer room with D). Incorrect.

PROBLEM SET 21

There are seven toppings available for an ice cream sundae- almonds, bananas, cherries, fudge, Heath bar©, peanuts, and sprinkles. Selection of the toppings must comply with the following constraints:

> If almonds are selected peanuts are not.
> If cherries or almonds are selected then bananas are as well.
> If fudge is not selected then peanuts and sprinkles must be.
> If sprinkles are selected then so are almonds and Heath bar.
> If Heath bar is selected then cherries are also selected.

STEP ONE: GET A GRIP - Nature of the game: Winner/Loser. Players: A, B, C, F, H, P, S. Hidden rules: *none!*

STEP TWO: FORMAL RULES – Oooo! Looky what we have here!

> 1) $A \supset -P$
> $P \supset -A$
> 2) $C \lor A \supset B$
> $-B \supset -C \cdot -A$
> 3) $-F \supset P \cdot S$
> $-S \lor -P \supset F$
> 4) $S \supset A \cdot H$
> $-H \lor -A \supset -S$
> 5) $H \supset C$
> $-C \supset -H$

Rule 2 has a disjunctive antecedent AND the "A" will Double-up with rule 1. That means we should separate out the antecedents.

> 1) $A \supset -P$
> $P \supset -A$
> 2) $C \supset B$
> $A \supset B$
> $-B \supset -C \cdot -A$
> 3) $-F \supset P \cdot S$
> $-S \lor -P \supset F$
> 4) $S \supset A \cdot H$
> $-H \lor -A \supset -S$
> 5) $H \supset C$
> $-C \supset -H$

STEP THREE: DRAW –

Since this is a winner/loser game, and we do not have any numbers prescribed, there is nothing to draw! All we can do is list out all of the players and then circle them when they have to play, or cross them off when they cannot. Hence, we have no drawing per se.

STEP FOUR: INFERENCES –

Absolutes? Nothing is obvious.

Bundles? Nothing that is not conditional. In other words, some people might look at rule three and think that there is a bundle. There is not. It only is known to be true when we know that fudge is not selected. Otherwise there is not necessarily a bundle.

Calculators? We cannot really calculate anything until *after* we have done the double-ups.

Double-ups? Only about a jillion.

1) $A \supset -P \cdot B \cdot F$
   $P \supset -A \cdot -S \cdot F$
2) $C \supset B$
   $A \supset B \cdot -P \cdot F$
   $-B \supset -C \cdot -A \cdot -H \cdot -S \cdot F$
3) $-F \supset P \cdot S \cdot -A \cdot -S \cdot F \cdot A \cdot H \cdot C \cdot B \cdot -P \cdot B$
   $-S \vee -P \supset F$
4) $S \supset A \cdot H \cdot -P \cdot B \cdot F \cdot C$
   $-H \vee -A \supset -S \cdot F$
5) $H \supset C \cdot B$
   $-C \supset -H \cdot -S \cdot F$

Now is that not delicious? Let us look over what we have just done. The first, most glaring thing we should notice is that rule 3 is a *contradiction*. It says that if we know that we do not have Fudge, then we know that we do have F. Oops. That means that we cannot have a situation in which we do not have Fudge! Fudge must always be selected (and we can be absolutely certain that there will be a question about it). So now we can go down our list of rules and tack on an " $\cdot F$ " to every one of them (most have it already), because fudge is always on the sundae!

1) $A \supset -P \cdot B \cdot F$
   $P \supset -A \cdot -S \cdot F$
2) $C \supset B \cdot F$
   $A \supset B \cdot -P \cdot F$
   $-B \supset -C \cdot -A \cdot -H \cdot -S \cdot F$
3) $-F \supset P \cdot S \cdot -A \cdot -S \cdot F \cdot A \cdot H \cdot C \cdot B \cdot -P \cdot B$
   $-S \vee -P \supset F$
4) $S \supset A \cdot H \cdot -P \cdot B \cdot F \cdot C$
   $-H \vee -A \supset -S \cdot F$
5) $H \supset C \cdot B \cdot F$
   $-C \supset -H \cdot -S \cdot F$

Of course this also means that rule 3 and its contra positive are worthless: the no-fudge scenario can never happen. Fudge must always be on the sundae, hence the contra-positive giving us a specific situation in which fudge must appear is somewhat misleading. We should cross them both off, just to make sure we do not make the mistake of referencing them later).

1) $A \supset -P \cdot B \cdot F$
    $P \supset -A \cdot -S \cdot F$
2) $C \supset B \cdot F$
    $A \supset B \cdot -P \cdot F$
    $-B \supset -C \cdot -A \cdot -H \cdot -S \cdot F$
3) ~~$F \supset P \cdot S \cdot -A \cdot -S \cdot F \cdot A \cdot H \cdot C \cdot B \cdot -P \cdot B$~~
    $-S \vee -P \supset F$
4) $S \supset A \cdot H \cdot -P \cdot B \cdot F \cdot C$
    $-H \vee -A \supset -S \cdot F$
5) $H \supset C \cdot B \cdot F$
    $-C \supset -H \cdot -S \cdot F$

We can also see that rule 1 is a, "mutual exclusion" rule. Recall that this is a rule that says that, at most, Almonds and Peanuts count as one topping for counting purposes. So we really don't have seven toppings, we have six to choose from, because we cannot have both A and P (but the right-side rule tells us that we could have neither!).

Now we can re-visit the Absolutes, Bundles and Calculators. Fudge is an *Absolute*. We still have no real bundles, but there is a calculator issue: one is the minimum number we can have (FUDGE!) and the maximum number appears to be... RULE 4! Six is the maximum!

We can also see that rule 4 is a complete answer: S banishes P and then everything else must be on the sundae. So sprinkles is a key player.

EXTRAS? Bi-conditionals? None.

Forced dichotomies? None.

Right side rule? TONS OF 'EM (well, three). Our big right side rule insight is that B and F can be together with or without A or C. The BF combo is one to keep an eye on.

Affirmative Duty rules? Just that F always has to play.

Contradictions? GREAT SCOTT! We were undisciplined! We caught it already though, and for that we are to be given kudos. We will find, over time, that as we get better at using the Test Mentors Methods, we will spot things almost instantly. Doing them out of order is actually not fatal. What is potentially dangerous however is ***failure to do all of the steps.*** In this case, we found the contradiction a while ago, did our work on it and then hit the Contradiction extra when its turn came up later anyway, just to be thorough. That is what the best test takers do.

Lone conditional? Nope. Four of them.

FREE RANGER(s)? There are none. Every player appears in at least two or three rules.

STEP FIVE: DESTROY THE QUESTIONS!

1. Which one of the following CANNOT be a complete and accurate list of the toppings selected?
   A) Almonds, Bananas, Fudge
   B) Peanuts, Fudge, Heath bar
   C) Fudge, Bananas, Cherries
   D) Heath bar, Fudge, Cherries, Bananas
   E) Heath bar, Fudge, Almonds, Bananas, Cherries, Sprinkles.

REMEMBER! First question, work top to bottom!

A) A, B, F – Rule 1 says yes.
B) P, F, H – Rule 5 says that H has to have C and B with it. There's your winner right there!

DON'T READ THE REST OF THE ANSWERS! GET THE HELL AWAY FROM THE PROBLEM!

For those of you who are too thick-skulled to listen to expert advice:
   C) F, B, C – Rule 2 says yes.
   D) F, H, B, C – Rule 5 still says yes.
   E) H, F, A, B, C, S – Rule 4.

2. If sprinkles are selected which one of the following must be false?
   A) Heath bar is included
   B) Fudge is included
   C) Cherries are not included
   D) Peanuts are included
   E) Bananas are included

Oh my! Oh my! Oh my! Are you not oh so glad that you did all of your inferences? Peanuts cannot play and everything else must. That makes "D" an easy kill.

3. Which one of the following could be the only topping selected?
    A) Fudge
    B) Sprinkles
    C) Peanuts
    D) Heath bar
    E) Cherries

Ha ha ha! It has to be fudge, because everything else has to bring fudge along with them, meaning that nothing else can be the "only" topping.

4. If exactly three toppings are selected, which one of the following CANNOT be one of the three?
    A) Bananas
    B) Fudge
    C) Almonds
    D) Cherries
    E) Heath Bar

This is easier than it looks if we remember to think about what we already know. Fudge has to be on the list, so kill "B". Rule one says that almonds bring bananas and fudge, and that makes three, so "A" and "C" are out. We only need to check Cherries. Rule two says that cherries bring bananas and fudge as well, so "E" must be the answer. If you are still not capable of stopping yourself from checking Heath Bar, spank yourself. It has to be the answer, as the other four are incorrect. Rule 5 proves it, just in case you do know.

5. If bananas are not selected which one of the following must be true?
    A) Peanuts are selected
    B) Heath bar is not selected
    C) Almonds are selected
    D) Fudge is not selected
    E) Peanuts are not selected

What do we already know? The contra-positive of rule two, for starters. Here again the problem is messing with your head, sy-ko-lahj-ik-lee. It is trying to make you think that you overlooked something having to do with peanuts, the only ingredient not rolled up in this rule. Well you did not overlook jack squat. Peanuts are irrelevant, and the rule tells us everything else we need to know. "A" is out (if you are so ADD that you forgot what we said one sentence ago, seek help). "B" is confirmed by the rule. Circle it and get out of here. "C" is incorrect based upon the rule. "D" is for the people who did not Sherlock out the fact that fudge is always on the sundae. "E" is out (if you are so ADD that you forgot what we said five sentence ago and then called out four sentences ago, seek help).

6. If peanuts are selected which of the following CANNOT be selected?
   A) Fudge
   B) Bananas
   C) Sprinkles
   D) Cherries
   E) Heath bar

Really? REALLY?!? Try to remember that there have to be some easy ones in the mix. Rule one tells us the answer, which has to be either almonds or sprinkles, with almonds being the no-braineriest of the two. The answer is "C". Move along.

7. Which one of the following toppings must be selected?
   A) Almonds
   B) Bananas
   C) Cherries
   D) Fudge
   E) Heath bar

That was one of our big inferences. Most people will be *dying* right now. We know that it is fudge. Circle "D" and move.

8. Which one of the following could be a complete and accurate list of the toppings selected?
   A) Bananas, Fudge, Heath bar, Peanuts
   B) Bananas, Cherries, Heath bar
   C) Almonds, Cherries, Fudge, Peanuts, Sprinkles
   D) Cherries, Fudge, Heath bar, Sprinkles
   E) Almonds, Bananas, Cherries, Fudge

YES! A totally legit question with two tricky issues posed, ones that we can easily navigate. Which of the two we are forced to deal with depends upon the order in which we test ingredients. But we have gotten ahead of ourselves.

What do we already know? Fudge must be on any sundae, and any sundae with sprinkles is a complete Sunday with six toppings minus peanuts. "B" has no fudge, so kill it, please. Both "C" and "D" have sprinkles, but not the requisite six total. Take them out, while you are crossing things off. Now we can just check "A" and if it works, we are done; else-wise, "E" must be correct. You could check "E" and if it is incorrect circle "A". It is up to you. Here is where the issues come into play. If we check "E" we have a different issue than if we check "A". We will do them both, just to show you what we are prattling on about.

"A" has bananas, fudge, Heath Bar and peanuts. We know that we can ignore fudge: it does nothing other than, like a lame brother in law, show up all of the time. The bananas have no rule. We may recall that peanuts require us to get rid of almonds and sprinkles and to have fudge, all in the contra-positive of rule one. The rule says nothing about Heath Bars or bananas. Because it says nothing, that means that they are allowed, correct? Yes! So does that mean that "A" is the correct answer? NO! It means that one or the other is allowed and that *possibly* both are allowed. But you would have to bring the consequents of them along. The consequent of having the

Heath Bar might force us to not have bananas. It might also force us to have other ingredients that would make "A" incomplete. In this case, because we just said that bananas being on the sundae is not covered by a rule, we have only to check the Heath Bar. It requires cherries, which are not in "A". Ergo, "E" must be correct.

Had we elected to check "E" first, the issue presented has to do with the inclusive "or" in rule two. Cherries or almonds proves bananas and fudge. Some people might fell a bit trepidatious or (inclusive) paranoid about relying upon rule two. THAT OUGHT NOT BE YOU! Rule two says cherries or almonds or both are sufficient to prove bananas and fudge. Done. End of story.

9. Which of the following is the minimum and maximum number of toppings that may be selected for the sundae?

    A) 0, 7
    B) 1, 7
    C) 1, 6
    D) 1, 5
    E) 2, 6

What do we already know? THE FLIPPIN' ANSWER! Fudge is the only required ingredient sprinkles forces six total (and we can never have seven because of rule one). Mark it "C" Smokey!

10. If bananas are not selected, which of the following must be true?

    A) At most, two toppings are selected
    B) At most, three toppings are selected
    C) At most, four toppings are selected
    D) At least two toppings are selected
    E) At least three toppings are selected

What do we know? The contra-positive of rule two tells us about everything except peanuts. Fudge has to be on the sundae, peanuts can come and go as they please. You should be able to smell this one for what it is: an attempt to see whether or not you will get flustered about denying antecedents. Not having bananas means that, amongst other things, we cannot have almonds. Some people might be tempted to say (by denying the antecedent of rule one) that peanuts have to be on the sundae and select "D". That would be incorrect. Peanuts can come or go as they please. That makes "A" correct.

PROBLEM SET 22

Six campers, Brian, Joe, Lois, Peter, Quagmire and Stewie, are being assigned to beds in three bunks at camp Giggity, one person per bed. The bunks are numbered one, two and three. Each bunk has a top and a bottom bed. The assignment of campers to beds conforms to the following conditions:

Brian and Joe share a bunk but are in different beds.
Quagmire and Stewie are in different bunks.
If Peter is in bunk two, then Lois is not in bunk three.

STEP ONE: GET A GRIP – Nature of the game: . Players: B, J, L, P, Q, S. Three Bunks, 1, 2, 3. Beds per bunk, Top, Bottom. Hidden Rules: One person per bed.

STEP TWO: FORMAL RULES –
    1) B, J same bunk
    2) Q different bunk S
    3) P2 ⊃ -L3
       L3 ⊃ -P2

STEP THREE: DRAW – We need top and bottom beds on each of three bunks:

B, J, L, P, Q, S

STEP FOUR: INFERENCES –

Absolutes? – None. Remember that an *absolute* is some player that must always be in some place or be doing some thing. B and J sharing a bunk gives us exact-ish information, but it does not tell us something absolute, as they could be in any of the three bunks.

Bundles? – B and J is a bundle however. We can segregate them off to the side and cross them off of the player list to make a really clear picture of what is going on:

B, J, L, P, Q, S

Calculators? - HERE is how we want you to be thinking about this game now that you are a little more experienced with the Test Mentors Methods.

We know that we have six people for six beds, so we realize that there are no *numerical* issues: everybody will end up in a bed and every bed will end up with a body. However we can also see that, because of our bundle of BJ, we will really have four people filling four beds and a BJ clogging up one entire bunk. The rules do not mention, in any way, that the "topness" or "bottomness" of a bed actually matters. They do not. So the real *issues* being tested here are the rule two separation of Q and S and the lone conditional in rule three, which we are going to kill when we get to the Extras. Rather than look at this as a nasty, challenging problem that has to be dealt with while the heat is rising, we need to look at it like a simple problem with very few possible outcomes. Even though we might not be able to actually calculate out the exact number, we can sense that it is going to be small: four people in four beds does not seem that imposing. Here is how to get an intuitive sense of the simplicity of it.

Because of the BJ bundle, we know that there could, under ordinary circumstances, be exactly six ways to "pair off" the remaining players: LP, LQ, LS, PQ, PS and QS. Any time that we know one of the combinations, we know the other: if L and Q share a bunk, then P and S have to share another and the BJ bundle will be in the third, etc.

Rule two tells us that there are less than six possible pairings because Q and S have to be in different bunks. But if Q and S have to be apart, that means that L and P have to be separated as well, for if they were together that would force Q and S into the same bunk. Q has to go with L or P and S has to go with L or P. Hence there are only four possible pairings (QL, QP, SL, and SP) AND in actuality, there are only TWO that we need to be concerned with. This is because if Q is with L, S must be with P and if Q is with P then S has to be with L. We need to add a note to rule two in order to make sure that we do not lose this very important insight.

1) B, J same bunk
2) Q different bunk S - P different bunk L (QL PS BJ / QP LS BJ)
3) P2 ⊃ -L3
   L3 ⊃ -P2

Any given set of the three pairings can be put into bunks in six different ways. Two pairings times six arrangements equals twelve possible combinations... and even that is not so because of rule three.

THE POINT here is not that you need to know all of this (though to be honest, it would be sweet if you would take the time to think it through, practice it and get to the point where you can see such things very clearly, very quickly). The point *is* that this is a very manageable game and that there are only two possible ways to put Q, L, P and S together: QL, PS, BJ and QP, LS and BJ.

Double-ups? - Nada. All six people are mentioned and so are bunks 2 and 3, but none more than once.

Extras?

Bi-conditionals – none.

Forced dichotomies – none.

Right-side rules? There is one. We can have –L3 and –P2 at the same time... which is not very helpful.

Affirmative duties? There are no negative antecedents with affirmative consequents. Contradictions? NADA.

Lone conditionals? YES! Would it get us much in the way of useful information if we were to draw out the lone conditional? THINK about it for a second. If P2, then –L3. How would that look? This should draw our attention to something important that ties to what we learned back in the "calculators" section: P and L have to be separated. Many people who are only nominally learned in the art of logic will look at rule three and think that if P2, then –L3, which means L2 or L1. But if P is in 2 and L cannot be in 3 and L cannot be with P, then L has to go to 1. If P2 and L1, then the BJ pair has to go to 3. We just have to divide up the QS between bunks one and two.

So now the sixty-four thousand dollar question becomes this: do we want to draw out our lone conditional or do we want to rely upon the fact that we know that when P is in bunk two, then rule three applies, putting L in bunk one and BJ into three?

The *best* answer (i.e. most efficient use of our time and the most solid fundamental habit) is to *not* draw it out. We know that if P is in bunks one or three, then the BJ fills a different bunk, the L fills half of the remaining bunk and the Q and S get divvyed up between the P and L.

What we can do to make matters a bit more certain is to tack an additional notation onto the end of the original rule 3 so that it is more complete and serves the function of ensuring that we do not drop the ball:

1) B, J same bunk
2) Q different bunk S - P different bunk L (QL PS BJ / QP LS BJ)
3) P2 ⊃ -L3 · L1 and BJ3
   L3 ⊃ -P2

Once we have done that, we can see that the right-side reminds us that BJ can be in bunk three even though P is not in bunk two (i.e. P and L can flip-flop between one and two).

FREE RANGERS? – Boy howdy, there are no players with "free rangerness," even the bunks. If BJ is in bunk one, P has to be in three and L has to be in two. If BJ is in two, then the P and L split bunks one and three. Q and S are constrained to be separated but distributed to P and L, and vice-versa. But now WE OWN THIS BAD BOY!

STEP FIVE – DESTROY THE QUESTIONS!

1) B, J same bunk
2) Q different bunk S - P different bunk L (QL PS BJ / QP LS BJ)
3) P2 ⊃ -L3 · L1 and BJ3

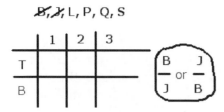

~~B, J,~~ L, P, Q, S

1) Which of the following could be a complete and accurate listing of the assignments to bunks and beds?
 A) Bunk 1: Brian top, Joe bottom
    Bunk 2: Peter top, Lois bottom
    Bunk 3: Quagmire top, Stewie bottom
 B) Bunk 1: Joe top, Brian bottom
    Bunk 2: Stewie top, Peter bottom
    Bunk 3: Quagmire top, Lois bottom
 C) Bunk 1: Peter top, Quagmire bottom
    Bunk 2: Lois top, Brian bottom
    Bunk 3: Joe top, Stewie bottom
 D) Bunk 1: Peter top, Quagmire bottom
    Bunk 2: Stewie top, Lois bottom
    Bunk 3: Joe top, Brian bottom
 E) Bunk 1: Joe top, Brian bottom
    Bunk 2: Lois top, Peter bottom
    Bunk 3: Stewie top, Quagmire bottom

First question, complete and accurate list, top to bottom.
   A) BJ in one, PL in two – INCORRECT! P and L have to be separated.
   B) JB in one, PS in two (RULE THREE ALERT!) INCORRECT! PS in two means BJ in three.
   C) PQ in one, LB in two… INCORRECT! B is with J always.
   D) PQ in one, LS in two, JB in three. Works perfectly. Correct.
   E) WHY ARE YOU READING "E"?!? MOVE ALONG!

2) Which one of the following must be false?
 A) Peter shares a bunk with Lois
 B) Peter shares a bunk with Quagmire
 C) Quagmire shares a bunk with Lois
 D) Stewie shares a bunk with Lois
 E) Stewie shares a bunk with Peter

What do we know already? QS separated, PL separated, BJ together. Answer (A) must be false. Move along.

3) If Joe is in the top of bunk 1, which of the following must be true?
 A) Peter is in bunk 2
 B) Quagmire is in bunk 3
 C) Lois is in bunk 2
 D) Lois is in bunk 3
 E) Stewie is in bunk 2

Notice how they are messing with the non-hackers here? If Joe is in the top of bunk one, then B and J are in 1, and we do NOT care about top or bottom... but there will be people out there who are intimidated or confused by the call of the question. That is why it is so bloody imperative for us to be on top of the *issues* the problems present to us.

What do we know already? BJ in one, L in two, P in 3, Q and S split between two and three. Money.
A) Incorrect.
B) Incorrect
C) Yee-haw! Next question.

4) If Peter is in the bottom of bunk 3, then for how many other campers can their bunk and bed be determined?
 A) zero
 B) one
 C) two
 D) three
 E) four

The ultimate mind game! Again, top and bottom do not matter. If a person still thinks that they do, they are ood-scrayed! For us this is a freebie. We know that no other person can be pinned down to a bed because Q or S has to be with P, on top, in three... we just do not know which one it is. As far as everyone else is concerned, top or bottom is optional. (A) has to be the answer.

5) If Lois is in bunk 1, which of the following must be false?
 A) Quagmire is in bunk 1
 B) Quagmire is in bunk 3
 C) Stewie is in bunk 1
 D) Stewie is in bunk 3
 E) Peter is in bunk 1

Notice how this is now a more complex issue. If L is in 1, we could have the P two, BJ three, or we could have BJ in two and P in three. But that is all stuff that we already know!
 A) Q in one works (Q or S with L is acceptable).
 B) Wherever P can go, so can Q or S. Could be true.
 C) Same as (A)
 D) Same as (B)
 E) MUST BE THE ANSWER!

1) B, J same bunk
2) Q different bunk S - P different bunk L (QL PS BJ / QP LS BJ)
3) P2 ⊃ -L3 · L1 and BJ3

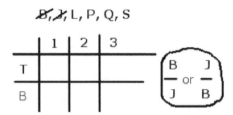

B̶,̶ J̶, L, P, Q, S

REMEMBER that when you have eliminated four answer choices, you must circle the remaining one, bubble it in on your answer form and GET MOVING TO THE NEXT QUESTION! There is no excuse for wasting time. Here, it would be a TOTAL waste of time because (E) just restates that which we already know: P and L can *never* go together.

6) If Peter is in the bottom of bunk 2, which of the following is a complete and accurate list of all of the campers who could be in the top of bunk 3?
  A) Stewie
  B) Lois
  C) Lois, Stewie
  D) Lois, Quagmire
  E) Brian, Joe

Another rule 3 problem. B or J has to be in the bed. Mark (E) and move!

7) Which of the following rules, if substituted for the rule which says that if Peter is in bunk 2, Lois cannot be in bunk 3, would have the same effect?
  A) If Lois is not in bunk 3, Peter must be in bunk 3.
  B) If Joe is in bunk 3, Lois is in bunk 1.
  C) If Quagmire is in bunk 1, Stewie is in bunk 2.
  D) If Peter is not in bunk 2, Joe is in bunk 2.
  E) If Quagmire is not in bunk 3, he is in bunk 1.

Remember that with these types of questions, the *issue* being probed is one of *equivalent effect.* You are looking for a new rule which will have the same effect as the original. We already know what the effect of the original rule was: P2 meant L1 and BJ3, with S and Q split between P and L in no preferred manner.

  (A) is an easy kill. It puts L in 3.
  (B) puts J (and thus B) in 3, and L in 1. L and P have to be separated and 3 is full, so P is in 2. That just means sharing S and Q between 1 and 2... EXACTLY THE SAME EFFECT! Circle it, mark it on your answer form and MOVE!
  (C) WHY are you reading (C) ? It is incorrect because it has *sort-of* the same effect, but not exactly. The original rule allows either S or Q to go with either

P or L. Choice (C) forces Q into 1 and S into 2, which does force B and J to 3, but P and L can go in 1 or 2: P is not forced into 2 etc.

(D) Peter being in 1 or 3 has NOTHING to do with what we are talking about.

(E) This is just (C) all over again because it locks down Q in 1. Q has to be able to go to 1 or 2 in order for the new rule to function in the same way.

Problem set 23

Seven astronauts, Allen, Cooper, Deke, Gus, John, Scott, and Wally, are to be assigned to zero-G training during a single week, Monday through Sunday, one astronaut per day. The astronauts trained on Monday and Tuesday will be assigned to the Mars mission. Those trained on Wednesday, Thursday and Friday will be assigned to the moon mission. Those trained on Saturday and Sunday will be assigned to the asteroid intercept mission (AIM). Training must conform to the following:
  Wally is assigned to the Mars mission.
  Deke and Scott train earlier in the week than
    Allen.
  If John trains on Tuesday, either Deke or Scott
    trains on Saturday.
  Gus cannot be assigned to the Mars mission.

STEP ONE: GET A GRIP - Nature of the game: We are being asked to assign astronauts to days of the week, and that sounds like firm ordering (but remember, the firm/squishy/squirm distinction comes from the formal rules). We are also told that certain days of the week have certain other aspects associated with them: certain missions are assigned to certain days.

What is helpful is that the days that the missions are assigned are set in stone: Mars is Monday and Tuesday, Moon is Wednesday, Thursday and Friday, and AIM is Saturday and Sunday. This is very helpful because the mission order is firm and we do not have to mess with it. This allows us to see what the big ISSUE of this game is: figuring out each of the astronauts' mission assignments given the days of the week. This should be as easy as eating pie.

PLAYERS are the days, the missions and the astronauts, A, C, D, G, J, S, W.

The HIDDEN RULES are that: ALL astronauts play (it said that "Seven astronauts *are assigned...*"). There is exactly one week, Monday through Sunday. One astronaut is assigned per day. Monday and Tuesday are the Mars mission. Wednesday, Thursday and Friday are the Moon mission. Saturday and Sunday are the AIM. Recall that whenever we are given complex information, we are being challenged: do we have the maturity and steel to organize the information in a calm, cool manner? We do and we will.

A, C, D, G, J, S, W = Astro
Mon thru Sun = days
*1 Astro/ day
*All play
* M/Tu = Mars
*Wed - Fri - Moon
Sat/Sun = AIM

STEP TWO: FORMAL RULES – DO NOT FORGET TO NUMBER THEM!
The first rule says that Wally goes to Mars. Easy enough.
The second rule says that both Deke and Scott go early on the schedule than Allen. That is a squishy rule. Because we know that it is firm ordering with at least one

squishy rule, it is officially a "squirm". Remember that you should have drawn this rule out with the dots defining the relationships, earlier on the left, later on the right. Rule three says that IF John trains on Tuesday, THEN Deke or Scott train on Saturday. Ordinarily, "or" is inclusive (D or S or BOTH on Saturday). But here, because every astronaut has their own day, it is an "exclusive or," meaning exactly one of them goes, not both.

Rule four has Gus on AIM or Moon and never on Mars.

> 1) W = Mars (Mon/Tu)
> 2) D
>   A
>   S
> 3) J Tu ⊃ D Sat v S Sat
>   -D Sat · -S Sat ⊃ -J Tu
> 4) G = AIM/Moon (Wed - Sun)

STEP THREE: DRAWING

First, we know what the most definite element of the game is, and that is what we want to base our drawing upon: Monday through Sunday.

A, C, D, G, J, S, W

Mon	Tu	We	Th	F	Sa	Su

We also can add in the information about the different missions and the days that they fall upon. Some of you out there in student land might be saying, "Isn't that an "absolute" from step four: inferences?" In fact, yes it is. The key thing to remember is that we have all of the steps in the order that we have them in order to avoid *missing* any critical issues. If we do one of the steps early, it is, technically speaking, a break in discipline. However the critical thing that we must remember is that it is only a ***failure of discipline*** if we then skip the *absolutes* in step four because we assume that because we got one, we got them all. So the key is this:

HIT EVERY STEP, EVERY TIME. ***Memorize that!***

A, C, D, G, J, S, W

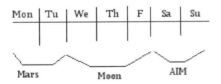

STEP FOUR: INFERENCES – Absolutes? Yes! Rule 1 says that Wally goes to Mars. Rule two has Deke and Scott before Allen, which means that Allen cannot go on Monday or Tuesday, and that neither Deke nor Scott can go on Sunday. Also, rule

four says that Gus cannot go on Monday or Tuesday as they are the Mars mission days.

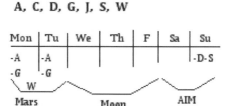

Bundles? Sort of, but we hit them (and if we did not, we would hit them right now). Mars is "bundled" with Monday and Tuesday, the Moon is bundled Wednesday through Friday, and AIM is the weekend bundle. Also, Wally is "bundled" with Monday or Tuesday. Yay. As we said just moments ago, so long as we maintain the discipline of hitting every step every time, we will never miss any essential issue in any game.

Calculators? Remember that when we get to calculators and there are squishy elements, we want to look at the *ends* of things, i.e. first and last. To be sure there does not appear to be much here, mostly because we only have one squishy rule. Deke or Scott could go first, Allen could go last... big whoop. However, we see that Allen cannot go on Monday or Tuesday because two others, Deke and Scott must go before Allen. But Wally *must* go on Monday or Tuesday. So if Wally is Monday, then Deke or Scott could go on Tuesday (and vice-versa) and the other of Deke-Scott could go on Wednesday, but Allen can never go on Wednesday. Essentially Wally, Deke and Scott all must come before Allen because we cannot get both Deke and Scott before Wally.

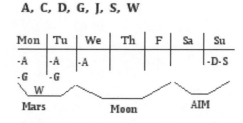

Double-ups? The obvious double-up is the connection between rule two and rule three because they *both* reference Deke and Scott. On top of that, if we are really on top of our game, we realize that we will have a lone conditional on the "extras" step, and that could work to our advantage.

If John is on Tuesday, Deke or Scott has to go on Saturday. Rule two says that Allen has to be scheduled after both Deke and Scott, so whichever one is on Saturday, Allen has to be on Sunday. We already determined earlier that, because Wally has to be scheduled for Monday or Tuesday (Mars), John on Tuesday means Wally on Monday. So our lone conditional that doubles-up gives us this:

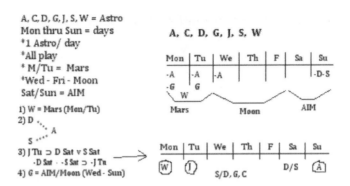

EXTRAS? Do it by the numbers.

Bi-conditionals? None.

Forced dichotomy? YES! Wally *must* be scheduled for Monday or Tuesday. But either way, we do not gain much in the way of useful information. Right side rule? Yes, and you can bet there will be ample opportunity for them to trick mouth-breathers into affirming consequents and denying antecedents. **_NOT US!_** We can see that Deke or Scott on Saturday can occur without John on Tuesday.

Affirmative Duties? None. Lone conditional? Beaten like an egg at a meringue party. Contradictions? None. Lone conditionals?

FREE RANGERS? We have one: Cooper.

STEP FIVE: Destroy the questions, remembering to GO WITH WHAT YOU KNOW!

1) Which of the following could be the astronaut training schedule, Monday through Sunday, respectively?

- A) Allen, Cooper, Deke, Scott, John, Gus, Wally.
- B) Wally, John, Gus, Deke, Scott, Cooper, Allen.
- C) Wally, Deke, Scott, Allen, Gus, John, Cooper.
- D) Gus, Wally, Cooper, Deke, John, Allen, Scott.
- E) Wally, Gus, John, Scott, Cooper, Deke, Allen.

The first question in the problem set means what, boys and girls? We begin with "A" and we work our way down the list, in order, making sure that we avail ourselves of all of the gifts the LSAC hath provided.

A) has A and C as the Monday-Tuesday combo. We know that W has to be in there, so we can kill it.

B) has W on Monday (a Mars day as required) which checks out. It also has J on Tuesday, which we ALREADY KNOW (because we worked out the lone conditional) that either D or S has to be on Saturday and A has to be last. "B" has Cooper on Saturday. Kill it.

C) has W Monday, D Tuesday, S Wednesday (so D and S are before A), A on Thursday, G on Friday (which is a Moon day and in compliance with the rules), J on

Saturday and C on Sunday. This works. Circle it, bubble it in on the answer form and move on.

2) If Deke is assigned to AIM, which of the following must be false?
- A) Allen trains on Sunday.
- B) John trains before Wally.
- C) Cooper trains on Wednesday.
- D) Wally trains on an earlier day than Gus.
- E) Gus trains earlier than Wally.

DO NOT BE QUICK ON THE DRAW WITH YOUR PENCIL! We have worked this one out already! We figured it out when we did the lone conditional and the right-side rule. If D or S is on the AIM, it has to be a Saturday so that A can go on Sunday (rule 2). The **trap** set here is that they are going to try to get you to affirm the consequent (i.e. D can be on Saturday without J being on Tuesday). W still has to be Monday or Tuesday, but for the most part, it is a wide opened set of possibilities that just forces us to look for a rule violation.

Do not lose sight of the call of the question. They want to know what cannot ever possibly happen. So if we *can* make the answer choice work it is incorrect.

A) Must be true. Kill it.
B) Here is the trap! J can go on Monday or Tuesday with impunity, and Monday is before Wally. Kill it.
C) Cooper is the free ranger. Even if J was on Tuesday (the lone conditional drawing) C can be on Wednesday, Thursday or Friday. Kill it.
D) We know, once again based on the lone conditional, that this can be true. Kill it, circle "E" and move along.
Just for clarity sake, "E" has to be false because Gus before Wally puts Gus on the Mars mission, which rule four prohibits.

3) Which of the following is a complete and accurate list of the astronauts none of whom can be assigned to the Mars mission?
- A) Gus
- B) Allen, Deke
- C) Allen, Gus
- D) Allen, Gus, Deke
- E) Allen, John, Scott

What do we already know? Gus and Allen cannot go to Mars. That is "C". Circle it and move.

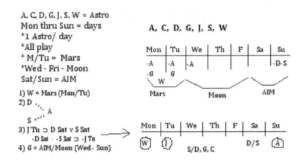

4) If the moon mission consists of Allen, Deke and Scott, which of the following must be false?
- A) John trains before Wally.
- B) John trains after Wally.
- C) John Trains on Monday.
- D) John trains on Tuesday.
- E) John trains on Sunday.

What do we know? The Moon mission is Wednesday, Thursday and Friday. D and S have to come before A, so A must be the Friday astronaut. This will also force Gus into the AIM (Saturday/Sunday). Cooper, John and Wally are the remaining astronauts, and Wally is trapped on Monday or Tuesday. Cooper and John have a bit of latitude, except that if J is scheduled for Tuesday, neither D nor S can go on Saturday as they are pinned down on Wednesday and Thursday.

That tells us that "D" has to be the correct answer.

Notice the "B" is a really nasty trap answer. J can train after W... on the weekend. If we *assume* that "B" means "Tuesday," we screw up badly. "A" and "C" are the same answer, and because there cannot be two correct answers, they must be incorrect.

5) Which of the following is the earliest day of the week on which Allen can train?
- A) Wednesday
- B) Thursday
- C) Friday
- D) Saturday
- E) Sunday

YES! We know the answer to this already. It is Thursday. People who cut corners on the inferences think that it is Wednesday. It sucks being them.

6) Which of the following can never be true?
- A) Gus trains on Saturday
- B) Wally trains on Monday
- C) Allen trains on Friday
- D) Scott trains on Sunday
- E) Allen trains on Thursday

Here is a grand example of how our previous work on the earlier problems would save the day had we missed an inference. Any way you slice it, this problem is a lay-down. We know from question four that Gus can go on Saturday or Sunday, so "A" is incorrect. Wally can go on Monday, as our lone conditional proves, so "B" is wrong. Question four also had Allen on Friday, so "C" is incorrect. Scott has to come before Allen, so "D" has to be correct: Scott can never go last. Circle it and move. To be complete, we know that Thursday is the earliest day that Allen can go, so "E" is incorrect.

7) If the training schedule for Tuesday, Wednesday and Thursday is John, Gus, Cooper respectively, how many possible different arrangements of the training schedule are possible?
  A) Two
  B) Three
  C) Four
  D) Five
  E) Six

Could it get any nicer than this? J on Tuesday is our lone conditional drawing. S and D have to go on Friday and Saturday, but in either order. W, J and A are all pinned down as well. So there are only two possible orders: W, J, G, C, S, D, A or W, J, G, C, D, S, A.
That is answer choice "A". Circle it, bubble it and move on.

Problem set 24
Each of nine divers, B, C, D, E, F, G, H, J and K, will be assigned to one of three teams, X, Y and Z of at least two divers per team. Four of the divers, B, C, E and G, are master divers. Two of the divers, D and F, are intermediate divers. The remaining divers are novices. The teams must conform to the following conditions:
  There must be at least one master diver on
    each team.
  No team can have all of the novice
    divers.
  K cannot be on the same team as B nor G.
  D cannot be on the same team as C nor E.
  H must be on either team X or Y as must K.
  B is never on the same team as G.

STEP ONE: Get a grip – NATURE = Buckets. PLAYERS = (1) divers B, C, D, E, F, G, H J and K, (2) dive teams X, Y and Z, (3) sub-division "master divers" B, C, E and G (squared), (4) sub-division "intermediate divers" D and F (triangles because they are the smallest sub-division), (5) sub-division "novices" H, J and K (double-bar). REMEMBER to think about sub-divisions just like they are their own category of player because the LSAT will test your ability to do logic based both upon the people and each person's characteristic. HIDDEN RULES = All play ("Each...will be assigned..."). Also, there must be at least 2 divers minimum per team. Here is what it should look like so far:

* All play
* MIN 2/ team

B, C, G, E = master = ☐

D, F = Intermed = △

H, J, K = novice = ▤

TEAMS = X, Y, Z

STEP 2: FORMAL RULES – Do **_NOT_** skip the part where you number the rules and then re-write the rules with a corresponding number.

1) @least 1☐ per team

2) NO team 3 ▤

3) Never $\overline{K}$ with B
    Never $\overline{K}$ with G

4) Never △ with C or E

5) Both $\overline{H}$ and $\overline{K}$ are on X v Y

6) Never B with G

Take a quick glance at rules three and four. They are the same type of rules (negative bundles) yet they are written in two different ways. *You can write them either way!* Remember what we are always trying to do: **_re-write the rules in a manner that is visually consistent with the nature of the game_** and to do so in a manner that does not confuse ourselves. For some people the approach of rule three is clearer, for others rule four is. Yet for others it does not matter. The point is that *WHEN YOU REWRITE RULES, DO SO IN THE MANNER THAT WORKS THE BEST FOR YOU.* Stick to the principles outlined in this book, but remember that ultimately, **you have to understand information in the best way possible for YOU**.

STEP 3: DRAW – We know that the "nature" of our game is buckets. We always build our bucket drawing around the most absolute element of our game. This means that the class of players that "moves around" the least is our "bucket" category. The three dive teams, X, Y and Z are the non-movers and shakers in this game, so they will be our buckets and we will move divers into them.

We need to be careful and THINK about what we are doing here. We are going to be putting shapes with letters into the drawing as we go. This means that we need to make sure that we leave ourselves enough room (especially in the middle buckets) to draw everything that we need to include without making a bloody mess out of it.

STEP 4: INFERENCES –

A) ABSOLUTES – Are there any players that *must* be in a particular place or *must not* be? Let us take a quick jaunt through the rules (formal and hidden!) to figure this out. Our hidden rules tell us that there must be at least two people on each team. We have to add that to the drawing:

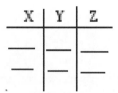

Formal rule 1 tells us that there has to be at least one master diver on each team, so we know that three of the four master-squares occupy one slot on each team:

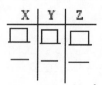

Make sure to put a check mark next to rule #1 to indicate that it has been incorporated into the drawing.

Rule 5 tells us that both H and K are on either teams X or Y. NOTE what the rule *does not say:* it does not say that they cannot both be on the same team. They could both be on X. They could both be on Y. They could be divided up between the two teams. What we know for **certain** is that neither one of them can be on team Z.

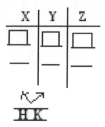

NOTE what *blunder* you are invited to commit here! H and K are two of our three novices. The rule was worded in such a way that one might interpret it to mean that they have to be separated and distributed amongst X and Y. That might lead one to make two drawings: one with H in X and K in Y, the other with K in X and H in Y. That would be a HUGE mistake, because they could both be together in either X or Y as well. Additionally, there are always some folks out there who incorrectly infer that J, our remaining novice, has to be placed on team Z. BLUNDER! There is no rule requiring that every team have a novice. Be careful, s'il vous plait.

Make sure to put a check mark next to rule #5 to indicate that it has been incorporated into the drawing.

B) BUNDLES – Do we have players that always have to be together in a group (positive bundles) or that can never be together (negative bundles)? Yes, there are scads of them.

Rule #3 says that K cannot be on the same team as B or G. B and G are both master divers, and every team has to have a master diver, so K has to be on a team with a master diver that is *not* B or G. As a practical matter that means that K must be on a team with C or E (the other masters) or both. We are going to use the "v" disjunction symbol to indicate B or G or both, because *"or" is always inclusive unless specifically made exclusive*. Rule #4 says that D has to be with dive masters B or G. Lastly, rule 6 says that B and G have to be separated onto different teams. We will do them all in similar fashion:

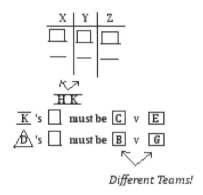

Different Teams!

HERE IS WHERE ***DISCIPLINE*** COMES INTO PLAY! Remember that while *learning* the Test Mentors Method©, we want to do every step in order. We do not want to skip around pell-mell[76]. We mention this because there is a real urge to skip to another step here and jump on something that might leap out at you as obvious. DO NOT DO IT! **Stick to the Method**. You will not forget the important thing(s) you see because

---

[76] Seriously, where did the phrase "pell mell" come from? Shakespeare used it in *Richard III*, and old French has "*pesle mesle,*" which is not defined anywhere we have been able to locate (and we spent way too much time investigating it, including a delightful conversation with an old Frenchman). It means, "...disorganized, confused, disoriented and haphazard," just in case you care. We just cannot tell you why it means that, or from whence it derives...it is what it is.

they will be extracted in later steps (often with greater benefit), provided you do them all thoroughly and in order.

Make sure to put a check marks next to rules #3, 4 and 6 to indicate that they have been incorporated into the drawing.

NOTICE that the only rule that is not checked off is rule number two: we cannot have all three novices on one team. SWEETNESS!

C) CALCULATORS – We have nine divers and they all have to play, so we will have nine total spaces for them on the teams. Does this mean that there are no calculation issues? NO! Think about why that is.

We do not necessarily have to have the same number of divers on each team: there is no rule stating that. Perhaps the logic will require it, but that is what calculators are all about. Our job at this point is to figure out whether or not there are numerical combinations that are required or are forbidden.

Each team has to have at least one master diver and at least one other person. Hmmm. There are four masters and three teams, ergo…. One of the three teams MUST have two master divers on it, and the other two must have one. We do not know which team will have the two masters, but we can make note that there has to be exactly on double-master team.

There are three teams total with two divers minimum per, so that means that six of our nine divers have to be assigned equally (2:2:2) amongst the three teams. That also means that there are three "left overs" to be distributed according to the logical limitations of the game.

THINK MINIMUMS AND MAXIMUMS – We know the minimum per team is two. Can we put five divers on one team (i.e. the two minimum plus all three left overs)? Look carefully at the drawing and at the remaining rule #2. Can we do it? It looks very possible if we have not misinterpreted our rules. K has to go with C or E, but C and E can be on the same team (the double-master team) and bring K along for the ride. As we saw earlier, H and K *can* go on the same team, so we could throw on H. **DANGER!** Remember that H and K are two of the three novices, so the third, J, cannot go on our super team. The other two masters, G and B, will anchor the other two teams, and so long as our C, E, H, K quartet is on team X or Y (H and K must be on X or Y per rule 5), the other teams are irrelevant (at least as far as calculations are concerned). D cannot join the quartet as it has to go with B or G on the mini-teams. That just leaves F to join the C, E, H, K party. Does it work? YES! So we can have a five diver team, C, E, F, H, K. Are there more? It sort of seems like it, but truth be told, ___WE DO NOT CARE!___ All we are trying to do is *calculate* the numerical possibilities. Five is the maximum and two is the minimum. Make a note and move on.

D) DOUBLE-UPS – Do we have two or more rules that talk about the same players? YES! And we can see by looking at the rules that we have several double-ups going on:

1) @least 1 ☐ per team

2) NO team 3 ⹀

3) Never $\overline{K}$ with $\boxed{B}$
   Never $\overline{K}$ with $\boxed{G}$

4) Never △ with $\boxed{C}$ or $\boxed{E}$

5) Both $\overline{H}$ and $\overline{K}$ are on X v Y

6) Never $\boxed{B}$ with $\boxed{G}$

I)   Rule 1 talks about master divers, as do rules 3, 4 and 6.
II)   Rule 2 talks about novices, as do rules 3 and 5.
III) Diver K is in both rules 3 and 5.
IV)   Divers B and G are in both rules 3 and 5.

This all has GOT to mean something important. Any time we are given so many rules that have logical connections, we should be very hesitant to walk away without thorough consideration. It would be easy to be glib or lazy or intimidated (remember, "or" is inclusive) but we cannot be any of those things because WE ARE BETTER THAN 90% OF ALL LSAT TAKERS!

Rule (1) says that we have to share the master-love, which we already have in our drawing. But (3) attaches actual expert players B and G and associates them, negatively, with K, a novice. K has to go *somewhere* (because they all have to play), so *wherever K is, B and G are not.* (5) tells us that K can only go onto Team X or Team Y (but not both, because everyone is on one team only). Add to the mix (6) which says that B and G have to be separated as well and we can smell that something ***BIG*** is brewing.

If we put K on team X, then B and/or G has to go on Y or Z. If we put K on team Y then B and/or G must go to teams X or Z. K cannot go to Z. That means that there are ONLY TWO WAYS THAT THIS GAME CAN BE PLAYED!

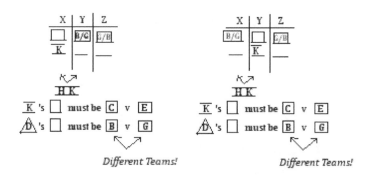

Now that we have that sorted out and crystal clear, we also have to add the fact that C or E have to be with K.

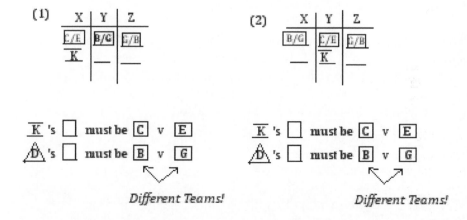

NOTICE that the first drawing has "B/G" and "G/B" in Y and Z. Switching them around indicates that they can swap, but that one goes in Y and the other goes in Z. The "C/E" appears one time (attached to K) and is the same in both the left and right drawing. That is because C or E or both can be in X or Y respectively.

The difference is HUGE! If we know that B or G is on team X, we KNOW that we are in the right drawing (we will call the left on #1 and the right one #2) and that the other of the B/G pair is on team Z, with K on team Y along with C or E or both. If we know that B or G is on team Y, we know that we are in drawing #1 and that the opposite of the B/G pair is on team Z, with K on team X with C or E or both. THIS points out the big issue that they can use to trick or trap us! G or B is ALWAYS on team Z, and knowing that one of them is on Z tells us JACK SQUAT! The same goes for C or E: if we only know where one of them is, we do NOT know where K is, nor do we know which drawing we are in. C could be on team X with K and E on team Y. Get it? K dictates where C or E or both go, but C and E do not dictate anything by themselves. If E is on team Z, we only know that C has to be on X or Y... very unhelpful.

We also have the other half of rule 5 (H still has to be in X or Y) and rule 4 (D has to go where C and E are not. Rule 4 is there right below the drawings, and we can change the rule 5 to look like this:

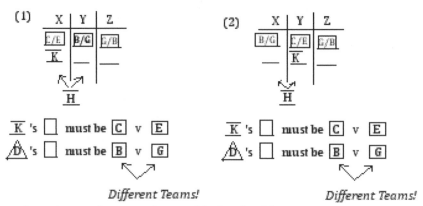

Different Teams!   *Different Teams!*

There we have it... and we are done with the double-ups.

E) EXTRAS – Any bi-conditionals? None. Forced dichotomies? None. Can we use the right side rule? Rules 3, 4 and 5 all have consequent sides and we can look at them to make doubly-sure we do not affirm consequents or deny antecedents. Are there affirmative duties? No. Are there contradictions? No. Is there a lone conditional? No. 3 is in the drawing and 4 is included below the drawing.

F) Free Rangers – YES! F has no rules associated with it, and neither does J.

STEP 5: DESTROY THE QUESTIONS! ***REMEMBER*** that we always *GO WITH WHAT YOU ALREADY KNOW!*

1) Which one of the following is an accurate assignment of divers to teams?
    A) X: B, D, G, H
       Y: C, E, K
       Z: F, J
    B) X: C, F, J
       Y: B, D, E
       Z: G, H, K
    C) X: D, H, J
       Y: B, C, F
       Z: E, G, K
    D) X: D, G, H
       Y: C, E, K
       Z: B, F, J
    E) X: D, E, H, K
       Y: B, C
       Z: G, F, J

REMEMBER that on the first question, we ALWAYS work our way from A through E.
A) Can team X have both B and G? Nope. Kill it.
B) Team X has C, F and J. We KNOW that if that is so, that K has to be on team Y. Oops. Kill it.
C) Same problem as B. Kill it.

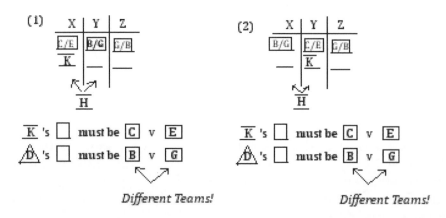

D) Team X has D, G and H. That puts us in drawing #2 AND it means that K has to be on team Y, which it is. NOTICE the little nasty trick? They put both C and E on Y for people who think (for whatever reason) that C and E cannot be together. Team Z has B, F and J. This all works perfectly with our #2 drawing. Circle it. Bubble it in. Move on.

For the sake of completeness, (E) is incorrect because it has D with E in violation of rule 4.

2) If D is on team X, which one of the following must be false?
   A) B is on team X
   B) B is on team Z
   C) H is on team X
   D) K is on team X
   E) K is on team Y

They want you to jump to the pencil and waste time re-drawing the whole damned mess. **BE DISCIPLINED!** WHAT DO WE ALREADY KNOW?

If D is on X, we have to be in drawing #2. The ONLY thing that is "iron-clad MUST be true" in that drawing is that K has to be on team Y. We can also see that G or B must be on team X, and that B or G must be on team Z etc. But look at the answer choices. They are declarative and definite and not "alternative" (i.e. "Either B or G...."). Because K on team Y is the only definite "must be true," we are looking for "K is on team X" or "K is on Z as our "must be false". That is answer choice D. Circle it. Bubble it. Move on.

3) Which one of the following must be true?
    A) If B is on team Y, G is on team Z
    B) If C is on team X, E is on team Z
    C) If K is on team Y, C is on team Y
    D) If D is on team Y, H is on team Y
    E) If F is on team X, G is on team Z

Yay, we think. A good old-fashioned naked, must be true question...NOT! The call of the question looks like a a simple must be true, but the answer choices are all conditional. Flippin' poo! If you scan them over, they give us five different "if" scenario. That stinks...if you did not do the first four steps properly. We did. Recall that we always want to go with what we know.

Answer choice (A) says that if B is on team Y, G is on team Z. Look at the two pictures. B can be on team Y in P1 only, and in that picture, G has to be on team Z. Done.

4) If C, E, F and J are on team Y, which one of the following could be true?
    A) H is on team Z
    B) H is on team Y
    C) D is on team Z
    D) Both H and D are on team X
    E) Both H and D are on team Z

What do we already know? If C and E are on team Y, we are in picture number two. So in actuality, C, E, F, J and K are on team Y. That is five divers, and that forces what two other things to be perfectly absolute? H has to go to team X and D has to go to team Z. How freakin' easy is that! (C) has to be the correct answer.

5) Which one of the following must be false?
    A) K is on team Z
    B) D is on team X
    C) F is on team X
    D) E is on team Y
    E) B is on team Z

Alas, an easy one. We already know the must-be-trues and the must-be-false answers. Answer choice A says that K is on team Z. We know that cannot be true, so we are done. Mark it and move on. If we look at our two pictures we can see that answers B through E are all possible. The only choice that might make us second guess ourselves is C, and that is because F is a free ranger and, possibly, by putting F on team X we might create a logically impossible scenario elsewhere. If this answer choice did make you think twice, LEARN YOUR LESSON HERE AND NOW! Answer choice A CANNOT be true, so it must be the answer and you should not be wasting valuable time looking at any other choices.

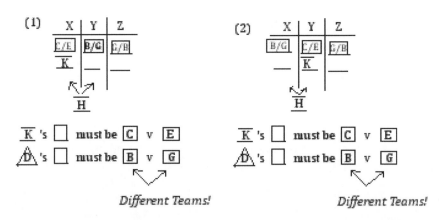

6) If D is assigned to team X, then which one of the following divers must be assigned to the same team as K?

    A) B or G or both

    B) F or H or both

    C) J or G or both

    D) J or H or both

    E) C or E or both

Another slam-dunk for us! Just look at the pictures and the rules then GO WITH WHAT YOU KNOW! D has to be on a team with B or G. So if D is on team X, we are definitely in the second picture because in P1 neither B nor G is on team X. And who has to be in bed with K in P2? C or E or both. That happens to be answer choice E. Mark it and go.

7) If B and C are the master divers on team X, and if every team has one novice diver assigned to it, then it must be true that:

    A) Team X has four or five divers.

    B) Team Y has four or five divers.

    C) Team Z has four or five divers.

    D) Team X has at least as many members as
        team Z.

    E) Team X has at least as many members as
        team Y.

Now we have a real problem to solve! We know everything that must be true and must be false based upon the raw logic, but they have added extra conditions, and so we cannot possibly know the answer without a little extra thinking. The real question is, can we do it without using our pencil, or is it required?

First, we have to figure out whether we are in one picture or both. If B and C are the masters on X, what does that indicate? We must be in P2 again, because that is the only one in which B can be on team X. From that drawing we can see two other things clearly. If B and C are on team X, then E and K are on team Y. However, we have also been asked to put a novice on each team, and there are only three of them, H, J and K. K is pinned down to team Y, and in P2 we know that H has to be on X or

Y. Because K is the novice on Y, H has to be the novice on X and J has to be the novice on Z.

Now perhaps you are thinking to yourself, "Your awesomeness," because that is how you ought to refer to yourself, "how in the name of the Face of Boe am I supposed to keep track of all of this...I mean, awesome though I am...."

Fear not! If you need it, NOW would be a great time to go to your pencil! Make a quick, tidy, small re-picture of P2 and put in the essentials:

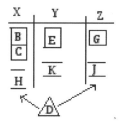

D has to go with B or G. That means that D is on team X or Z. F can go anywhere.

That is all there is to know, so let's destroy the answers. (A) is incorrect because team X may have three only. (B) is incorrect because team Y can have three maximum. (C) is incorrect because team Z can have two, three or four. (D) is incorrect because if Z has four, X has three. CIRCLE (E) AND MOVE! This is the correct answer because the most team Y can have is three and the fewest team X can have is three.

8) Which of the following is a complete and accurate list of all of the divers who could be on team Z?
   A) B, D
   B) B, D, G
   C) B, C, E, D, G
   D) B, D, F, G, J
   E) B, D, F, G, J, K

Here we are facing off against the question type that gave birth to the command, "Go with what you know." From our pictures, we know that C, E, H and K can never be on team Z. That eliminates answer choices C and E. Question 7 (which we penciled out!) shows us that J can go on team Z, so the correct answer has to contain J, and that is answer choice (D), as in "done."

360

Problem set 25

A display of six pumpkins sit next to each other as shown below:

1	2
3	4
5	6

Each pumpkin is white or else orange.
Pumpkin 1 is orange.
Each pumpkin has either a bat or else a face carved on it, but not both
Each bat must be directly above, directly beside, or directly below another bat.
Each face must be directly above, or directly below another face.
Pumpkin 5 has a bat.
Pumpkin 2 has a face.

STEP ONE: Get a Grip – This is completely new and different and challenging-ish. The set-up for this game does not tell us all of the information we have come to expect from a game. NERDS! We have to read the Formal Rules to determine who all of the players actually are. So we do what we must.

The nature of the game is COMBO! Buckets are provided by the drawing, and there is a definite (though atypical) Ordering going on. They provided us with a drawing, so we should use it. The players are the six pumpkins 1 – 6 and the colors (W, O) and the carvings (B, F). There are no hidden rules.

STEP TWO: Formal Rules- There is a HUGE new issue for us to wrap our brains around here. Rules 1 and 3 are opposite-sign bi-conditionals. Condition 1 says that if a pumpkin is white, it is not orange AND that if it is orange then it is not white AND if it is not white then it is orange AND that if it is not orange then it is white. Rule three does the same with Bat and Face carvings. The question we have is this: is there any point, given the context of everything we are seeing, in writing out the bi-conditionals? What do these two rules actually *do?*

The bi-conditionals just create a forced dichotomy. If you did not get that from the lengthy description of rule 1, you need to sharpen up or review. There is an "exclusive 'or' " employed. We can take advantage of the logical simplicity of the forced dichotomy without writing out the bi-conditionals in full because there are no other logical statements to connect them to AND they do not connect to each other.

Also, recall that we re-write all of the formal rules so that they reflect the meanings of the rules within the context of the game. We want them to be *visually consistent with the nature of the game.*

1) All pump. = W $\oplus$ O

2) $1 = 0$
3) All pump. $= B \oplus F$
4) All B must be B B / B
                           B
5) All F must be FF / F
                       F
6) $5 = B$
7) $2 = F$

STEP THREE: Draw a Picture – They have already done it for us. Angels. We always want to use the drawing that they provide for us. We do this because (1) it is free stuff and (2) they had a reason for giving it, and we ought not question their reasoning. We can however modify it a tad, just to make the "bucketness" stand out:

1	2
3	4
5	6

At least now we can see distinct buckets.

STEP FOUR: Inferences – Absolutes: Plenty. Rules 2, 6 and 7 can all be plugged right into the drawing.

1 ^{O}	2 ^{F}
3	4
5 ^{B}	6

Bundles – None.
Calculators – Interesting proposition. Faces must be next to Faces, Bats next to Bats. There is one Face and one Bat in the picture, so there will have to be a second of each at a minimum. So we could have 2, 3 or 4 of either.
Double-ups: Rules 3, 4 and 5 have players in common. What they are saying does not really connect together in any way other than to make a compound rule: each pumpkin is a face or bat, not both, and faces must be next to faces and bats must be next to bats. That does tell us something though, which we saw in the calculators. 1 or 4 or both have to be faces, 3 or 6 or both have to be Bats.

THE BIGGEST THING about the double-ups to note is the white / orange distinction does NOT double-up at all. It is the big beastie in this game, we can surmise.

Extras – There are no bi-conditionals. Forced dichotomies abound! Every pumpkin has to be one or the other of two different properties. There are no Right-Side rules. There **are** affirmative duties (because forcing players into action always creates an affirmative duty). There are no contradictions. There is no lone conditional.

Free Rangers - pumpkins 1, 3, 4 and 6. On top of that, the colors of the pumpkins is pretty wide opened.

STEP FIVE: Destroy the Questions – Remember to go with what you already know, and **_DO NOT_** get sucked into using your pencil unnecessarily. Remember how to use your fingers on the drawing rather than re-picturing things or drawing on your original.

1. If all pumpkins with bats are orange which one of the following must be true?
   F) Pumpkin 4 is orange.
   G) Pumpkin 1 is a bat.
   H) There is at least one orange pumpkin.
   I) There are at least two orange pumpkins
   J) There are at least three orange pumpkins.

What a grand opportunity to screw up! They have given us a hypothetical conditional:

$$B \supset O$$
$$-O \supset -B$$

Because we are dealing with dichotomies, "-O" really means "W" and "-B" really means "F":

$$B \supset O$$
$$W \supset F$$

Do you see where the "trap" is? It is in the Right-Side rule and the fact that pumpkin 1 is orange. Answer choice "B" is just screaming for you to pick it. That is evil! The condition says nothing about whether an orange pumpkin has to be a bat, and the consequent side says that a face can be orange. Cheeky!

If we look at the picture we made and the inferences we drew, we know that 5 is already a Bat, thus orange. At least one of pumpkins 3 or 6 (but not necessarily both) have to be Bats, thus orange. Pumpkin 1 is orange. That means that there have to be at least three orange pumpkins. Guess what? There is a choice that looks suspiciously like that.[77]

---

[77] For those of you who do not get it, "E" is the correct answer. Pumpkins 1 and 5 have to be orange. Either 3 or 6 must be a Bat, thus orange. Three minimum.

2. If exactly three pumpkins are orange, and no white pumpkin is next to, above or below another white pumpkin, which one of the following cannot be true?
   F) There is an orange Bat.
   G) Pumpkins 3 is white.
   H) Pumpkins 1, 4, and 6 are orange.
   I) Pumpkin 2 and 6 are white.
   J) Pumpkin 1 has a bat

Righteous! A real mystery! Except not. Three oranges mean three whites. Three whites that cannot touch other whites. The whites must be pumpkins 2, 3 and 6. So 1, 4 and 5 must be orange. The only way we can screw this one up is if we forget that we are being asked to find the thing that CANNOT be true. Got it?

A) Must be true: 5 is a bat and has to be orange.
B) Must be true.
C) Cannot be true. Circle it, bubble it in, run like hell.

$$
\begin{array}{c|c}
1^{\ O} & 2^{\ F} \\
\hline
3 & 4 \\
\hline
5^{\ B} & 6 \\
\end{array}
$$

3. If there are only two pumpkins with bats, and every bat is white, which one of the following must be true?
   F) Pumpkin 4 is orange.
   G) Pumpkin 6 has a face.
   H) Pumpkin 4 is white or else pumpkin 2 is white.
   I) Pumpkin 6 is white or else pumpkin 3 is white.
   J) Pumpkin 4 is orange and pumpkin 2 is orange.

Another easy one. Pumpkin 5 is a bat, so the second bat has to be wither 3 or 6. That means 5 and either 3 or 6 but not both are white bats. Pumpkins 1, 2 and 4 have to be faces, and so does either 3 or 6 (whichever one is not a bat). Again, we are presented with the opportunity to commit a logic error: the face pumpkins can be white or orange at will as there are no conditions in the call or otherwise to the contrary.
A) INCORRECT
B) INCORRECT
C) INCORRECT
D) Duh. Correct. One of them has to be a white bat. Circle it, bubble it, run.

4. If pumpkin 3 has a face, which one of the following cannot have a face?
  F) Pumpkin 1
  G) Pumpkin 2
  H) Pumpkin 4
  I) Pumpkin 5
  J) Pumpkin 6

Seriously? W should be laughing! We drew the inference long ago that 3 or 6 had to be a bat. If 3 is a face then 6 has to be a bat. SLAM DUNK.

If that did not leap right out at you, try the following plan "B". Put an "F" finger on 3 (you know which finger) and spot the issue: the two "F"s need to be touching another F. We must stick an F in 1 because it is isolated: if we put a B there, it would not be able to touch another B. Put an F finger there too. At this point it ought to be obvious that in order to comply with rule 4, pumpkin 6 has to be a bat. Pumpkin 4 can go either way. Shazam.

5. If pumpkins 1 and 6 are carved with bats and are white, which one of the following could be true?
  F) Pumpkin 4 is a white bat.
  G) Pumpkin 5 has a face.
  H) Pumpkin 3 is a white bat.
  I) Pumpkin 3 has an orange face.
  J) Pumpkin 4 is an orange bat.

Once again ladies and gentlemen, the fingers. Put fingers on 1 and 6 to represent the white bats. What do we know already? Pumpkin 1 is a bat, so it needs to touch a bat in 3. Put a third bat finger there. 2 and 4 have to be faces. We have the answer.
A) is incorrect. It is a face.
B) is just dumb.
C) is the correct answer. Color does not matter. It is a bat.

6. If a rule is added that requires every orange pumpkin to be above, below or beside an orange pumpkin and each white pumpkin to be above, below or beside a white one, which one of the following CANNOT be true?
  F) Pumpkin 1 has a bat.
  G) Pumpkins 4 and 6 are white
  H) Pumpkins 2 and 4 are orange.
  I) Pumpkins 5 and 6 are orange.
  J) Pumpkins 2 and 3 are white.

What do we know already? Pumpkin 1 is the only one that has a color assigned. As far as we are concerned, there can be six orange pumpkins. We also know that pumpkins 2 and 3 cannot be white, because that would isolate the orange in 1. We also know that the new condition made no connection between color and carving, so the face / bat distinction is mostly irrelevant, save for the ordinary reasons we care about them.

A) INCORRECT. No reason that cannot be true.
B) INCORRECT. We do not care about them.
C) INCORRECT. Pumpkins 1, 2 and 4 can be orange at the same time.
D) INCORRECT. They can all be bloody orange.
CIRCLE then BUBBLE (E) AND RUN.

Problem set 26

Five dogs- R, S, T, V, and W- will each compete in a different dog sport- Agility, Conformation, Disk, Hare Coursing, and Obedience. Each dog is also assigned a level in the following order lowest to highest- Junior, Intermediate, or Expert, with at least one dog at each level. The following conditions apply:

> The dog that competes in agility is intermediate level.
> V is a lower level than the dogs that compete in Disk and Obedience.
> R competes in agility if and only if W competes in conformation.
> S and W are the only dogs at the expert level.

STEP ONE: Get a Grip – What in the heck is going on here? We have dogs, sports, levels and an order. This has got to be a Combo game. So NOW we need to try to wrap our pea-brains around just what in the heck they are asking us to do. Remember that we want a rough idea as to how this is going to sketch up later so we can re-write the formal rules appropriately.

There is going to be an Ordering component, Junior, Intermediate, Expert, low to high. There is a Buckets component in that we are putting things together, dogs and sports. So there will be five dog/sport pairings and they will be ordered lowest to highest. There is nothing indicating that within a given "level" they need be in any particular order.

Players: DOGS: R, S, T, V, W. SPORTS: A, C, D, H, O. LEVELS: J, I, E.

Hidden Rules: Each dog plays one unique sport. At least one dog in each level.

STEP TWO: Formal Rules – This time we have some pretty advanced, shady looking rules. We simply have to remember that each rule has a ***meaning*** and that we are in the business of extracting said meaning and re-writing that out.

> Dog= R S T V W
> Sport= A C H D O
> Lev = J I E, (Lo - hi)
> 1) A = Int.
>
> 2)
>   V ⋰⋅⋅ D
>   ⋱⋅⋅ O
>
> 3) RA ⊃ WC
>   -WC ⊃ -RA
>   WC ⊃ RA
>   -RA ⊃ -WC
> 4) 2 Exp. EXACT: S and W

Take a look at rule number two. It tells us that V is lower than D and O, but it does not indicate that the rule is that DOG V is in a lower LEVEL than the dogs in SPORTS

D and O. That is going to lead to a TON of confusion (and incorrectness) if we do not clean it up.

Dog= R S T V W
Sport= A C H D O
Lev = J I E, (Lo - hi)
1) A = Int.

2)

V ⋯ D
LEVEL
⋯ O

3) RA ⊃ WC
-WC ⊃ -RA
WC ⊃ RA
-RA ⊃ -WC

4) 2 Exp. EXACT: S and W

STEP THREE: Draw a Picture

As always, ***thinking*** pays mega-dividends. We know that we are going to put the dogs into an "order" from Junior to Expert. We also know that ORDERING will go across the top of our drawing. The other two sets of players (dogs and sports) will go along the side, like so:

	J	I	E
DOG - RSTVW			
Sport - ACDHO			

STEP FOUR: Inferences

Absolutes: Rules 1 and 4. Pop them into the drawing and then check off the rules.

	J	I	E
DOG - RS̶T̶V̶W̶			S W only
Sport - A̶CDHO		A	

Next, take note of rule 2. Any time there is an order established, we know that the item on the left side cannot go last (in this case, V cannot be an expert) and that the things on the right end cannot go first (D and O cannot be Juniors). Obviously V cannot be an expert as that bucket is full, per rule 4.

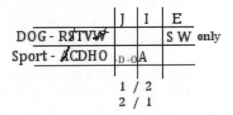

Bundles: Yes, but we captured the rule 4 bundle as an absolute.

Calculators: Oh BABY! This is going to be good. There are five dogs total. The "E" bucket must have exactly the two dogs S and W. The "J" and "I" buckets have to have at least one dog. That means that either "J" or "I" have two dogs and the other of them has one. Is it *really* worth the time and the effort to re-picture the entire game just to have that inference in front of us? The answer is NO! It would be very inefficient. We can simply make a note below the picture of the ratios thus:

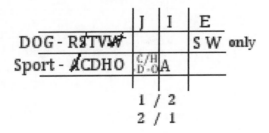

While we are, "all up in the math," let us look at the "J" column. D and O and A are out, so C and H are the only two candidates for the "J". Let us mark that in as well BECAUSE we can see another issue: IF there are two dogs in the "J" column, then they must be doing C and H, with A alone in the "I" column and D and O in the "E". We can expect that there will NOT be a ton of questions about "Two in Junior" because it is buttoned down like Malcom X's shirt[78].

	J	I	E
DOG - R~~S~~TV~~W~~			S W only
Sport - ~~A~~CDHO	C/H D-O	A	

1 / 2
2 / 1

What this means is that, as far as the dogs are concerned, we have ourselves a 2/3 scenario! R, T and V are the only remaining dogs. Two in J means one in I. Two in I

---

[78] First, Malcom *always* appeared in public looking fly, so this was a compliment. Second, if you felt some sort of twinge inside when you read that comment, as though you were about to get angry, bring it down a notch. Law school is going to be full of flesh flutes who want to turn your every comment into some sort of slight directed toward their oppressed-in-need-of-defense group of the day. Make a pledge to yourself right now: "When in law school, and for the rest of my life, I will always try to interpret the words of others in a light most favorable to them, and will not presuppose malice or ill will on their part, ever." That will help you to avoid falling into the trap.

means one in J. That has to be deliberate, and we probably ought to understand why. THINK for just a second. Is there anything *special* about any of those three dogs?

If we force two dogs into the J level, let us pretend that they are V and T, then the remaining dog, R, has to go to the I level and do activity A... RA. That triggers rule 3. But rule 3 cannot be complied with because if there are two dogs in level J, they have to be doing C and H: W cannot do C ! ERGO, IF there are two dogs at the junior level, one of them **must** be R. You can just smell the question looming like a bacon pancake.

Double Ups: Rules 1 and 3 talk about A. DO NOT BE A GIMP! Remember why we are doing what we do! We are here to try to spot the issues and anticipate the question traps that they are laying for us. Rule 3 says that RA is sufficient to establish WC. That also means that is sufficient to establish that R is in the I column. The "negative sign" component of the bi-conditional says that –RA is sufficient to establish –WC. We smell an issue here: R could still be in the I column, not doing A. It looks as though they may be baiting us into a possible bad inference where W is not doing C (so R cannot do A) and testing whether or not we believe that R must go into the J column. Those cheeky ... So we add on the columns to rule 3, and while we are at it, we can add on the "E" column for the W, because we are good test takers, and thorough:

Dog= R S T V W
Sport= A C H D O
Lev = J I E, (Lo - hi)
1) A = Int.

2)   ·D
       V⸱⸱⸱⸱⸱·   LEVEL
              · O

3) RA ⊃ WCE · RAI
   -WC ⊃ -RA
   WC ⊃ RAI · WCE
   -RA ⊃ -WC

4) 2 Exp. EXACT: S and W

Extras: Bi-conditional, check. It is a same-sign bi-conditional, so we know that we have both RA and WC or we have neither. Forced dichotomies? YES, we have them. Sports D and O must play and they cannot go into column J, so they are I or E. If one of them is in I with sport A, there will be two in column I, so the other must go to E. Affirmative duties? There are none in the sense that we do not have any conditional logic requiring things to occur. Everyone must play, however, so that is an affirmative duty. Right side rule: we are not using it. We are methodically working through each rule carefully to avoid the traps. Contradictions: Zero.

And then there is the Lone Conditional. Yes, we just have the bi-conditional. Is it worth drawing out a separate drawing that has RA and WC? What happens in that event, given all that we know? R is doing A, W is doing C. That means that H has to be in column J (because only C and H can possibly be there). On top of that, we have the D and O issue in hand: one is with A in column I, the other is in column E and linked to S.

This also tells us that Rule 2 is in the bag: if D and O are in the I and J columns, then V has to be alone in the J column doing H. That would leave dog T as the only possible dog to go with R.

SKETCH IT UP! Make sure that you indicate that this is not an "P2": it is NOT a general-purpose solution, but is specific to this one and only hypothetical condition.

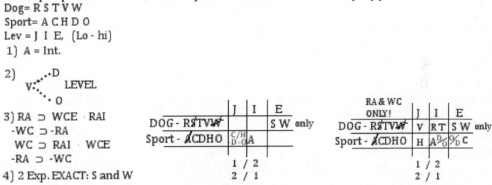

    Dog= R S T V W
    Sport= A C H D O
    Lev = J I E, (Lo - hi)
    1) A = Int.

    2)   ··D
         V:··   LEVEL
            ·· O

    3) RA ⊃ WCE · RAI
      -WC ⊃ -RA
      WC ⊃ RAI · WCE
      -RA ⊃ -WC
    4) 2 Exp. EXACT: S and W

Boom goes the dynamite.
Free Rangers? There are players without rules (sport H, dog T). As we have seen, the logic of the game really constrains their degrees of freedom. We posit that this game is in the bag.

STEP FIVE: Destroy the bloody Questions! Remember to Go With What You Already Know!

1. Which one of the following is a possible assignment of sports to dogs?
    A) R: Agility, S: Conformation, T: Hare coursing , V: Disk, W: Obedience
    B) R: Conformation, S: Disk, T: Hare coursing, V: Agility, W: Obedience
    C) R: Disk, S: Hare coursing, T: Agility, V: Obedience, W: Conformation
    D) R: Agility, S: Disk, T: Conformation, V: Hare coursing, W: Obedience
    E) R: Obedience, S: Agility, T: , V: Hare coursing, W: Conformation

Start from the top.
A) R is doing A, and that is our special drawing, and it is incorrect.
B) R is not doing A, nor is W doing C, so the special drawing is out and the general drawing is in play. This answer choice is a hum-dinger! We know that rule 3 is out of the mix, so we have to check it against the other rules. Rule 2 has V before D and O. Answer choice "B" has V doing A, which puts it in bucket I. That means D and O have

to be with S and W in bucket E. Are they? YES! Looking good, because H and T are free rangers here. CIRCLE IT, bubble it in, move along AND STOP LOOKING AT THE OTHER ANSWERS!

Just to help you see how you might have dorked things up:

C) has V doing activity O. That would put it in the same level as O, in breach of rule 2.

D) has R doing A but not W doing C, a violation of rule 3.

E) has W doing C without R doing A in contravention of rule 3.

2. If T is assigned to the intermediate level which one of the following must be false?
    A) S competes in agility
    B) V competes in agility
    C) R is assigned to the intermediate level
    D) W competes in disk
    E) S competes in conformation

Here is a lovely question! Can you see the big issue? T being intermediate works in out picture, but it also works in the special purpose Rule 3 picture as well! They are totally messing with us! Look at the drawings. If T is intermediate AND R is doing A, the Rule 3 drawing applies. If T is intermediate and R is NOT doing A AND W is not doing C, then we are in the original drawing. We are going to have to work carefully. NONE of that actually matters: we were asked what CANNOT be true. We can see, quite easily, all of the possibilities right before our eyes. Let us sally forth and NOT draw unnecessarily.

A) says that S competes in agility. Seriously? All hat and no cattle, as the saying goes. That is the answer. This was just a garden variety, rank amateur psych job. CIRCLE IT, bubble it in, MOVE!

3. Which one of the following CANNOT be a complete and accurate list of the dogs at the junior level?
    A) V
    B) T
    C) T, R
    D) V, R
    E) V, T

Now HERE is the money! We already know that the junior level has to have one or two puppies, and that there are only three available: R, T and V. We also know that the only sports available for them are C and H. We also know that IF we have C pinned down in the "J" level, then R cannot do A because that would force WC, which could not happen if C was back in the "J" level. We hashed all of this out a long time ago with the 2/3 Scenario discussion.

The choice that forces R to do A and that forces C to be in the J level (i.e. putting V and T in the J level) has to be correct. CIRCLE "E", bubble it in. NEXT!

Dog= R S T V W
Sport= A C H D O
Lev = J I E, (Lo - hi)

1) A = Int.

2)   ··D
      V:·   LEVEL
         ·· ·· O

3) RA ⊃ WCE · RAI
   -WC ⊃ -RA
   WC ⊃ RAI · WCE
   -RA ⊃ -WC

4) 2 Exp. EXACT: S and W

DOG - R S T V W	J	I	E
Sport - A C D H O	C/H D -O		S W only

| | 1 / 2 |
| | 2 / 1 |

RA & WC ONLY!	J	I	E
DOG - R S T V W	V	R T	S W only
Sport - A C D H O	H	A D-O C	

| | 1 / 2 |
| | 2 / 1 |

4. If V is assigned to the junior level which one of the following could be true?
   A) R competes in coursing.
   B) V competes in agility.
   C) V competes in disk.
   D) V competes in obedience.
   E) W competes in agility.

Here is one for the average test taker to prove their mediocrity. We already know that if V is assigned to the junior level, we could be in either the general picture or the RA/WC picture (and the average person does not). Advantage: us. V will do C or H.
A) Can R do coursing? Why the heck not?!? It would have to be in the I level, with some other doggie doing agility. Ain't no thang but a chicken wang!

5. What is the greatest number of dogs that could be assigned to the junior level?
   A) 1
   B) 2
   C) 3
   D) 4
   E) 5

They are kidding, right? (C) Three is the dumbass answer. (B) is correct.

6. If T competes in agility which one of the following is a complete and accurate list of the sports W could compete in?
   A) Hare coursing
   B) Disk, Hare coursing,
   C) Disk, Hare coursing, Obedience
   D) Conformation, Disk, Hare coursing, Obedience
   E) Conformation, Obedience, Hare coursing

GREAT SCOTT! Another easy one! Once agility is non-R, anything goes for W except... coursing! They are testing whether or not you understand bi-conditional, which you do because you paid attention. Thus D, H and O count and (C) must be the correct answer. CIRCLE IT, bubble it in, MOVE!

7) What is the maximum number of ways that the dogs can be arranged in different levels?
    A) 3
    B) 4
    C) 5
    D) 6
    E) 7

Here is a little Easter egg that we left for you. We *deliberately* did not figure this out back at the Calculators to prove a point. EVEN IF YOU MISS AN INFERENCE, there is no reason to EVER freak out and lose focus. It is a *balanced equation:* If the question was never asked, we would be no worse off. Because it was asked, we have to spend the time on it. However NOW we have more understanding of the problem, so it ought to be a breeze...or at least "breezier" than it was at square one.

What do we know already? We figured out that if there were TWO dogs in the junior class, they had to be VR or TR. Any of the R, T or V trio could be the lone junior, with the other two in the intermediate level. Remember that the issue is that if there are two in the junior level, that would pin down C in the juniors and that would not allow R to go intermediate because that would trigger the RA/WC rule 3. So two plus three equals five. That is (C). Circle it, bubble it, have yourself a double shot.

Problem set 27

Jack Black is selecting new members for his garage band. He can choose from three guitar players- H, J, and K- three bass players- L, M, and N- and four drummers- O, P, Q, and R. The following conditions apply:

    Exactly one bass player and one drummer must be selected.

    Two guitar players maximum can be selected.

    If M is not selected then P is selected.

    J is selected.

    If H is selected then Q and R are not.

STEP ONE: Get a Grip – What kind of a game is it? Winner/Loser WITH NUMBERS. Players are guitarists H, J and K, Bassists L, M and N and Drummers O, P, Q and R. Hidden rules are...non-existent. There are nine musicians and they are sub-divided into three sub-groups. We should use shapes when we get to the rules. Remember that the square is used for the most numerous category, which in this case is drummers. For the time being, we should list out the players like so:

$$\underline{\text{Guit} = \qquad \text{Bass} \triangle \quad \text{Drum} \square}$$
$$\text{H J K} \qquad \text{L M N} \qquad \text{O P Q R}$$

STEP TWO: Formal Rules –

1) Exact 1 $\triangle$
   Exact 1 $\square$

2) $2 = $ max

3) $-\underline{\underline{M}} \supset \boxed{P}$
   $-\boxed{P} \supset \underline{\underline{M}}$

4) $\underline{\underline{J}}$

5) $\overline{H} \supset -\boxed{Q} \cdot \cdot \overline{R}$
   $\boxed{R} \lor \boxed{Q} \supset -\overline{H}$

STEP THREE: Draw a Picture – It is Winner/Loser with numbers, so we know how to draw it. BUT HOLD THE PHONE! We don't know exactly how many winners and how many losers there are! It is not exactly clear (to some of us) what the numbers look like. We can save the Drawing step until *after* the inferences if we need to, and that raises a new, big-time issue: AGILITY.

Once we have learned each and every step of the Test Mentors Method® we need to be able to adapt it to any given scenario, as required, on the fly, calmly, coolly and with dispassionate purpose: every tool has multiple uses, and each tool may be better suited for a different chronological place. Recall how in a Winner/Loser game, we do the Double-up step first, then do the A, B, C, E, F? As it turns out, we may occasionally find ourselves in the position of having to adapt to a specific situation that is not precisely, "well behaved." Here we have a Winner/Loser with numbers, but we do not have an exact bead on the numbers yet. We would be better served to wait until after the Calculator inference in Step Four to try to draw a picture. Appendix "D" explains what this all is about. But if you are kind-of, sort-of getting our drift, you are in good shape.

STEP FOUR: Inferences – It is a Winner/Loser, so we will Double-Up first.
Recall that when we are using shapes, we have to look at the letters and the shapes to make logical connections. *After* we do that, we will make the drawing and then we may have *further inferences* based upon the calculators and the drawing. This is pretty big-time, hard-core.

Rules 1 and 2 do not seem to do much. They will be absolutes, and they may connect up with other rules.

Condition 3 says that if M loses, P wins. P is a square, and since rule 1 says that there can only be one square, the others must lose.

1) Exact 1 △
   Exact 1 □
2) 2‾ max
3) -M̶ ⊃ [P] • -[O] • -[Q] • -R̶
   -[P] ⊃ M̶
4) (J̶)
5) H̶ ⊃ -[Q] •• -[R]
   [R] v [Q] ⊃ -H̶

The contra of 3 says that if P loses, M wins. Again, rule 1 says that there can be but one triangle, so L and N lose.

1) Exact 1 △
   Exact 1 □
2) 2‾ max
3) -M̶ ⊃ [P] • -[O] • -[Q] • -R̶
   -[P] ⊃ M̶ • -△ • -N̶
4) (J̶)
5) H̶ ⊃ -[Q] •• -[R]
   [R] v [Q] ⊃ -H̶

The same shenanigan applies to the contra of rule 5, and this is where we probably ought to note that we might be well served to separate out the disjunctive antecedent. That is because if R wins, O, P and Q lose. If Q wins, then P, O and R lose. In other words, rule 1 turns the "or" in contra-5 into an *exclusive or.* We must address it, just to be safe.

1) Exact 1 △
 Exact 1 □
2) 2 ⁻ max
3) -△ ⊃ P • -O • -Q • -R
 -P ⊃ △ • -△ • -△

4) Ⓙ

5) H̄ ⊃ -Q • -R
 R ⊃ -H̄ • -O • -P • -Q
 Q ⊃ -H̄ • -O • -P • -R

NOTHING ELSE SEEMS TO DOUBLE-UP! Let us go back and blow away the rest of the inferences.

Absolutes: RULE 4! J always plays! It is a "constant, and we should ALWAYS tack it on to the end of *every rule* just to make sure we do not screw it up! The test makers are going to be looking to see whether or not we are careless and lose track of the simple stuff. That is a recipe for malpractice later, so they want to weed you out early if you are such a person.

1) Exact 1 △
 Exact 1 □
2) 2 ⁻ max
3) -△ ⊃ P • -O • -Q • -R • J̄
 -P ⊃ △ • -△ • -△ • J

4) Ⓙ

5) H̄ ⊃ -Q • -R • J̄
 R ⊃ -H̄ • -O • -P • -Q • J̄
 Q ⊃ -H̄ • -O • -P • -R • J̄

Bundles : None

Calculators: YES! There are ten possible musicians. There has to be exactly one drummer, one bassist and either one or two guitarists. That means there must be three or four winners and seven or six losers, respectively. We can sketch that up, and we can stuff in a ton of information based upon what we know.

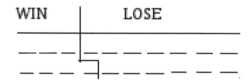

We know that J has to go into both of the drawings. We also know that in P1, there will be one of each sub-type (guitarist, drummer and bassist) on the winner side, whereas in P2 there will be two guitarists and one of each of the other.

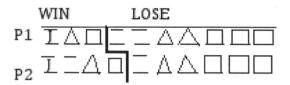

P2 is telling us something...about rule 5. H is sufficient to prove J, and that means that K is out!

1) Exact 1 △
   Exact 1 □
2) 2 ‾ max
3) -M̶ ⊃ P • -O̶ • -Q̶ • -R̶ • J̲
   -P ⊃ M̶ • -△ • -M̶ • J̲
4) (J̲)
5) H̄ ⊃ -Q • -R • J̲ • -K̄
   R ⊃ -H̄ • -O • -P̶ • -Q • J̲
   Q ⊃ -H̄ • -O • -P • -R • J̲

Extras: Bi-Conditionals: There are none.
Forced dichotomies? There do not appear to be any.
Affirmative duties? There are two. Rule 3 is a proper one, with a negative antecedent and an affirmative consequent. M or P or both must always be amongst the winners. Also, there has to be one J guitarist at all times.
Right side rule: P and M can be winners at the same time. J can win even thought H is not present. No big whoop. This looks like an easy game.
Contradictions? There are none.
Lone conditionals? Not at all.

Free Rangers: Whoa, Nelly! There are none! All ten of the players ended up in rules.

So what we can see is fairly simple and clear: rules 3 and 5 are all that there is to know. Keep track of the numbers and shapes in the drawing, and do NOT screw up on the rule. Should be a walk in the park.

STEP FIVE: Destroy the Questions. Remember to GO WITH WHAT YOU ALREADY KNOW.

1) Exact 1 △
   Exact 1 □
2) 2‾ max
3) -◭ ⊃ P • -0• -Q• -R • J
   -P ⊃ ◭ • -◭ • -◭ • J

4) J

5) H ⊃ -Q •- R • J • -K   Guit‾   Bass△ Drum□
   R ⊃ -H• -0• -P• -Q • J   H J K   L M N   O P Q R
   Q ⊃ -H• -0• -P• -R • J

	WIN						LOSE				
P1	I	△	□				△	△	□		□
P2	I		△	□			△	△	□		□

1. Which of the following CANNOT be a complete and accurate list of the members selected?
   A) Guitar: J, K Bass: L Drums: Q
   B) Guitar: H Bass: L Drums: R
   C) Guitar: J, H Bass: M Drums: P
   D) Guitar: J, K Bass: L Drums: R
   E) Guitar: J Bass: N Drums: O

Top-to-bottom:
A) INCORRECT. K is not a bass player.
B) INCORRECT. No J on guitar.
C) CORRECT. Simple test of the Right Side rule. M and P can bot win. J is present. CIRCLE IT. Bubble it. MOVE.

2. If there is only one guitar player selected, which of the following must be false?
   A) M and P are selected
   B) L and P are selected
   C) L and R are selected
   D) M and R are selected
   E) H and M are selected

What do we already know? If there is only one guitarist selected, then J is the winner, H and K are the losers.
E) has H winning. That must be false. Circle. Bubble. Move.

379

3. Which of the following must be true?
   A) K is selected
   B) M and J are selected
   C) If M is selected O is selected
   D) If H is selected P is selected
   E) If N is selected P is selected

This is sort of cute. A simple looking naked question can be a trap in disguise if you are not on top of your game.

A) Must " be selected? Hardly.

B) Must M and J be selected? No, unless P is not (contra 3).

C) Here is where the going gets interesting. If M is selected...there is no M antecedent. BUT, because the entire game is a forced dichotomy, and there can only be one drummer and one bass player, M winning means –L and –N. There are no antecedents for them either. INCORRECT.

D) Does H winning force P to win? Condition 5 says that H winning forces out drummers Q and R. O or P could be the winning drummer. INCORRECT.

E) CIRCLE IT! This must be correct. Bubble it on your answer form. Run. Why, you might be asking, is it correct? Because if N wins, M loses. Rule 3 says that if M loses, P wins. Congrats on wasting time.

4. If R is selected then which of the following could be true?
   A) H is selected
   B) K is selected
   C) L is selected
   D) Q is selected
   E) N is selected

FREEBIE (so long as we do not forget the call)! This is here to confuse the weakest of the weak. We know that if R wins, H, O, P and Q lose but J, as always, wins, and there could be a second guitar player.

A) INCORRECT.

B) K could be the second guitarist. CORRECT. Circle it, bubble it and run.

We realize that there may be some questions as to the other answers. We highly recommend that rather than being a lazy gimp, you figure out why C, D and E are incorrect on your own...THEY ARE.

C) is incorrect because L winning means M losing and that means R loses. The call of the question has R winning. Do the math.

D) has Q winning and that means R loses, just like (C).

E) is the same as (C) as well.

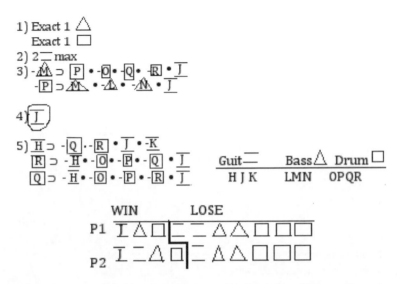

5. Which of the following could be a complete and accurate list of possible members that are NOT selected?

    A) M, O, Q, R, K
    B) N, L, P, Q, O, K
    C) J, O, P, Q
    D) K, M, N, O, Q, R
    E) Q, R, K, L, N, P

Ab Initio, which of these answers stink? A, C, and E. KILL THEM NOW! Why are they so malodorous? Because there must be six or seven losers at all times, so five, four and five losers respectively are INCORRECT. We only have to test (B). If it is correct, we are done. If it is incorrect, then (D) is correct.

(B) has N, L, P, Q, O and K losing. That means that M, R, H and J win. Are any of the winners antecedents? Oui. If H wins, Q and R lose. (B) is INCORRECT.

(D) must be correct. CIRCLE IT, BUBBLE IT, MOVE! To be thorough: K, M, N, O, Q, R losing means that H, J L and P win. Rule 3 says that M losing means P wins. Good. It also says that O, Q and R lose. Still good. It says that J wins. Gooder. Rule 5 says that H winning is sufficient to prove that K, Q and R lose and that J wins. Gooderer. Finally, there are one drummer, one bassist and two guitarists in the winner's circle. That was a lot harder than just eliminating (B).

6) If the condition is added that two guitar players are selected with N being one of the guitarists selected, which of the following must be false?

    A) N and H are selected
    B) N and K are selected
    C) N and P are selected
    D) N and O are selected
    E) H and P are selected

Does this or does this not smell like it might actually require us to get out our pencils? It seems as though there is too much going on to keep track of merely with our fingers. This is particularly true given that there will be four winners and six

losers, not to mention three sub-divisions of players to track. Suck it up, buttercup.
Do a quick re-picture of P2:

Jam in the N:

Now apply the rules. First off, M and L lose.

Do any other rules force changes to the picture? Yes! Rule 3. M losing is sufficient to
prove that P wins and that O, Q and R lose.

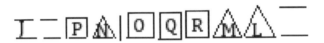

As for the other guitarist, it can be either H or K because H is sufficient to prove J
wins and K is a loser, and K is not an antecedent, nor is –H.

So then, what must be false?
A) N and H can both be winners. INCORRECT.
B) N and K can also. INCORRECT.
C) N and P must win. INCORRECT.
D) N and O cannot win because O loses. Correct. Circle it, bubble it, hit the showers.

Problem set 28

Five girls- A, B, C, D, and E- and four boys- F, G, H and J- will each be placed on one of three city league half-court basketball teams- Teams 1, 2 or 3. Each team will have three players one of which is the team captain. Assignment to teams is made in accordance with the following constraints:

If the captain of Team 1 is a girl then the captain of Team 3 must be a boy.

J is the captain of his team.

B and J are not on the same team.

D and B are not on the same team.

If H is on Team 2 then G and J are on team 3.

E is one of two girls on her team and is not a team captain.

STEP ONE: Get a Grip – What is the nature of the game? It is asking us to put people on teams, so that must be Buckets. The Players are girls A, B, C, D and E and boys F, G, H and J for a total of nine. Hidden Rules? ALL PLAY ("...will each be placed..."), three people per team, one captain per team.

$$\female\ A\ B\ C\ D\ E \qquad \male\ F\ G\ H\ J$$

Teams 1, 2, 3

* All play

*3 peeps/team

*1 capt/team $= \square$

Notice how we used the little universal symbols for female and male to designate the sub-divisions? We are guaranteed to have to deal with the issue of boy/girl combos. Also, we made the captains on each team a square to designate their specialness. After all, the hidden rule requires one per team, so we can anticipate, "...who could / must be the captain..." questions.

STEP TWO: Formal rules –

1) $\boxed{\ }1\female \supset \boxed{\ }3\male$
   $\boxed{\ }3\female \supset \boxed{\ }1\male$

2) $\boxed{J\male}$

3) $B\female\ /\ J\male$ diff. teams
4) $D\male\ /\ B\female$ diff. teams

5) $H\male 2 \supset G\male 3 \bullet J\male 3$
   $-G\male 3\ v\ -J\male 3 \supset -H\male\ 2$
6) $E\female$ on team w/ exact 1 other $\female$
   E is not $\square$

Let us take a few seconds to explain several things before moving on. Rule 1 says that a captain that is female on team 1 is sufficient to establish that a male is the captain of team 3. So far, it is pretty straight forward. Then something goofy looking happened when we contra-posed it. Strictly speaking the contra should say that if the captain of three is not a boy then the captain of 1 is not a female. But that is not what it says, and we are guessing that you can tell us why. Go ahead, say it out loud. Nobody is looking or listening. "Not girl" is the same as "boy," and "not boy" is the same as girl. So that is how the contra was written. The boy/girl distinction is a true dichotomy and we availed ourselves of its binary nature.

Rule 5 did NOT pull this little stunt because the rule is *different* from rule 1. Rule 5 talks about H♂2 etc. The rule turns upon their bucket number, not their gender. In other words, the letter in the bucket is the condition and gender is just there fo window dressing.

Also, notice how every player mentioned in every rule is also identified by gender. This is of great importance because questions will distinguish by letter or gender or bucket, inclusive.

STEP THREE: Draw a Picture –   This ought to be pretty easy. Three buckets, numbered 1, 2 and 3. Three slots in each. Ready, set ....

1	2	3
—	—	—
—	—	—
—	—	—

Simple as simple can be.

STEP FOUR: Inferences. Absolutes; do we have any? HECK YEAH! There has to be one captain on each team.

1	2	3
☐	☐	☐
—	—	—
—	—	—

Bundles – Are there any? Look carefully. Rule 6 says that there is a bundle of two women, E + 1 and that the third member of that team has to be male. It also says that E cannot be a captain. Let us put that below our drawing to make sure that we never miss it:

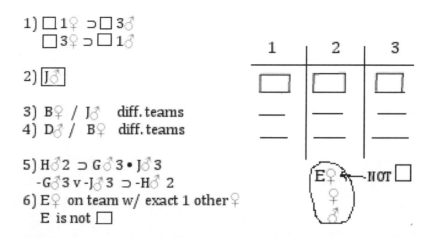

1) □ 1♀ ⊃ □ 3♂
   □ 3♀ ⊃ □ 1♂

2) [J♂]

3) B♀ / J♂ diff. teams
4) D♂ / B♀ diff. teams

5) H♂2 ⊃ G♂3 • J♂3
   -G♂3 v -J♂3 ⊃ -H♂2
6) E♀ on team w/ exact 1 other♀
   E is not □

There are a pair of *negative bundles* in rules 3 and 4 (things that can *never go together*) but those are just rules that we are going to need to watch out for, and re-writing them would be inefficient.

Calculators – You might be saying to yourself, "Three people per team, nine total, three teams. Done." But maybe we could turn up the gas under our brains just a smidgen more.

There are five girls. That means that there could theoretically be a team with three girls and two on another. There could also be three on one team with the remaining two split between the other two teams. There could be two girls on each of two teams and the last girl along with two boys on the third team. Let's write out those ratios quickly. Note that the order of the ratios (3:2:0 etc.) do not necessarily indicate that there have to be three girls on team #1, just that one team has three girls, another has two and the third has zero. We can then determine what the boy ratio would need to be to fill out the teams.

G	B
3:2:0	0:1:3
3:1:1	0:2:2
2:2:1	1:1:2

Double-ups: Rules 3 and 4 both talk about B♀. B♀ cannot be with J♂ nor D♀. HOWEVER J♂ and D♀ can be on the same team. Do not lose sight of that.

Extras – Are there any bi-conditionals? No. Are there any forced dichotomies? Only the boy / girl issue that we dispatched in rule 1. Are there any Right-side rule issues? Both rules 1 and 3 have them. We can have boys as the captains of teams one and three at the same time and G and J can be on team three even though H is *not* on team two. Are there any contradictions? No there are not. Is there a lone conditional? No.

Free Rangers – A♀, C♀, and F♂ are all rule-free. They can fill in any holes in any problem *so long as doing so does not force a rule violation.*

As we can see, there was not a lot to be learned from the inference step. Our picture is…rather Spartan (look it up). Al that means is that we are dealing with a **back-side game.** That is no big deal. It means that the time that we saved doing very little on the front side is going to be eaten up on the back side (i.e. doing the questions). There is always a balance.

STEP FIVE: Destroy the Questions – Remember to go with what you already know.

1. Which one of the following could be a complete and accurate list of the members for each team, with the captain listed first?
   A) Team 1: D, J, E
      Team 2: B, F, G
      Team 3: H, A, C
   B) Team 1: J, D, E
      Team 2: H, A, C
      Team 3: B, F, G
   C) Team 1: H, A, C
      Team 2: B, F, E
      Team 3: J, D, G
   D) Team 1: E, D, A
      Team 2: H, C, G
      Team 3: J, G, B
   E) Team 1: D, E, A
      Team 2: H, C, F
      Team 3: J, B, G

Welcome to the jungle. Notice anything completely *maddening* about the answer choices? You cannot tell the gender of the players by the way that they are listed. That is why we isolated them out at the beginning, so we could glance up at them to see whether or not the boy/girl components are complied with. Remember that because this is the first question in the set and it is a "complete answer" question, we want to work it top to bottom.

A) Can Team 1 have D, J and E with D as captain? Rule 2 says definitely not. J must always be the captain of any team he is on. INCORRECT.
B) Team 1: J, D, E – Now here is a juicy one. It fixes the issue from (A) and then throws a little taste of rule 6 in. E has to be with exactly one other girl and one boy. So far, so good. Because J is a boy, rule 1 is off of the table (it does not count because it tells us what to happen if there is a girl captain). Team 2: H, A, C – Both A and C are free-rangers, so we need not worry about them. It is the H in the captaincy that triggers rule 5: if H is on team 2 then J and G need to be on team 3. Are they? If you had to think about that, ***wake the hell up!*** We just talked about J being on team 1. INCORRECT!
(C) Team 1: H, A, C – H on 1 kills the problems from (B) and eliminates rule 5 from the menu. H is a boy, so rule 1 is out as well. Still worthless are A and C. Team 2: B, F, E – This seems to be poking at rules 3, 4 and 6. They are all complied with. Team 3: J, D, G – J is the captain… and here is where the average mouth-breather porks the pup on at least one of two accounts. They see J and G together on team 3 and think

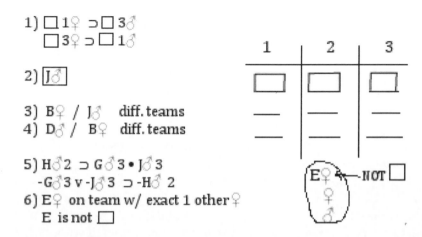

1) □ 1♀ ⊃ □ 3♂
   □ 3♀ ⊃ □ 1♂

2) |J♂|

3) B♀ / J♂   diff. teams
4) D♂ / B♀   diff. teams

5) H♂2 ⊃ G♂3 • J♂3
   -G♂3 v -J♂3 ⊃ -H♂ 2
6) E♀ on team w/ exact 1 other ♀
   E is not □

that H has to be on team 2. They also think that rules 3 and 4, taken together, mean that B, D and J must be on three separate teams. Admittedly, this would be a much less sophisticated game if this were true... but it is not. We saw that back in the inferences: D and J can be on the same team. Grin. Go ahead. Revel in the glory. They have to pay for your scholarship. CORRECT. Circle it, bubble it in on the answer sheet, then run like hell to the next question.

2. If B is the captain of Team 1, which of the following could be true?
   A) E and A are on Team 1
   B) D and A are on Team 1
   C) H and G are on Team 2
   D) J, E and G are on team 3
   E) J, E and C are on Team 2

HERE IS A TIME TRAP! They are *begging* you to waste time drawing a new picture, and they are testing whether or not you are going to be a spazztard and forget the basics. DO NOT PANIC, and do not be too hasty to go to the pencil. GO WITH WHAT YOU KNOW!

What is/are the possible issue(s) here (in other words, what do we already know)? B is a girl, and that triggers rule 1. There has to be a girl captain on team 3. Rules 3 and 4 tell us that D and J cannot be on the same team (team 1) as B. If E is on team 1, then she had better drag a dude with her.
A) Can E and A be on team 1 with B? No. Por why? They are all girls. That violates rule 6. INCORRECT.
B) D and A on team 1 with B. Do you see what they did? Tricking the people who just saw the rule six issue, dropped E out of it (to cure the rule 6 violation) and slam them. Now we have a rule 4 violation. INCORRECT.
C) H and G on team 2: can it be? No. Rule 5 violation. INCORRECT.
D) J, E and G on team 3? NO! Again there is a rule 6 violation. INCORRECT.
Circle E, bubble it in and MOVE!

3. If A, E and J are on Team 2, which of the following must be false?
A) C, F and H are on team 1.
B) B, C and H are on team 1.
B) B, C and H are on team 3.
C) C, F and D are on team 1.
D) C, F and D are on team 3

Again, they want you to waste time re-picturing every scenario. We just want to remind you, once again, not to panic. Look at the question call and the answer choices, then try to spot the issue(s) being raised by them. A, E and J on team 2 means that J is the captain (rule 2). Rule 3 is no longer applicable because J is on a team that B cannot be on. Rule 5 (if H2...) is off of the table because there is no room at the inn. Rule 6 is no longer a concern either as it is complied with.

So the issues have to do with rules 1 and 4. There are three girls and three boys left, so there is no way for three girls to fill up team 3 and have a girl be captain on team 1, triggering rule 1. Ergo, we are going to get a rule 4 violation somewhere, possibly one that puts three people on one team and forced B and D together on the remaing team.

A) C, F and H on team 1 forces B and D together on team 3. There it is folks. CORRECT. Circle it, bubble it in, run like hell.

This is a *prime* example of a tough question; it requires us to have a complete understanding of the game and the rules **and** it turns **not** on brute force, but upon an understanding of the issues raised as well as the fact that the answer comes from the *unstated information*. The call of the question and the answer choices give us six of the nine players. The correct answer turned upon the three that were never mentioned.

YOUR BRAIN IS YOUR GREATEST ASSET! Use it and abuse it at all times. Never turn away from your brain and toward your pencil unless absolutely necessary. Speaking of which...

4. Which one of the following could be true?
A) Team 3 is comprised of D, G and J.
B) Team 1 is comprised of A, C and E.
C) Team 2 is comprised of A, H and J.
D) Team 2 is comprised of A, H and G.
E) Team 3 is comprised of B, D and E.

Another BRUTAL looking problem! Our first rule of destroying the questions is what, again? "Go with what you already know!" Boy howdy, do we know a lot. In fact, by this point we know more than we did when we began question 1. We have a three questions that we have answered. Each of them taught us more, and each one of them gave us correct answers that we can rely upon as fact.

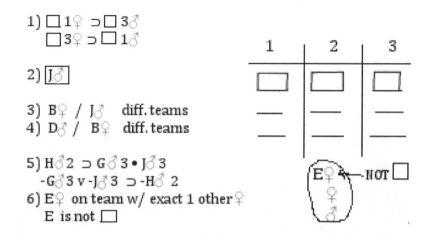

1) $\square$ 1♀ ⊃ $\square$ 3♂
   $\square$ 3♀ ⊃ $\square$ 1♂

2) $\boxed{J♂}$

3) B♀ / J♂   diff. teams
4) D♂ / B♀   diff. teams

5) H♂2 ⊃ G♂3 • J♂3
   -G♂3 v -J♂3 ⊃ -H♂ 2
6) E♀ on team w/ exact 1 other ♀
   E is not $\square$

A) asks us if team 3 can be made up of B, G and J. There are several different ways to skin this pig, the worst of which is to start drawing. THINK! D, G and J on 3 looks like **what issue** we have seen before? H on 2 from rule number 5. It forces J and G to 3, so things look promising. It also keeps J away from B.

Now, we could continue this little conversation...but we would be wasting our time. Why? Because the answer to question 1 had B, G and J on team three as the correct answer. **THAT,** boys and girls, is what we mean when we say that we have to go with what we know. We have to use **EVERYTHING** that we learn along the way to maximize our efficiency. Circle it, bubble it, go.

5. If the three team captains are G, H and J, and if E is on team 1, which of the following must be false?
   A) A is on team 1 and B is on team 2.
   B) A is on team 1 and B is on team 3.
   C) B is on team 1 and G is on team 3.
   D) G is on team 1 and H is on team 3.
   E) G is on team 1 and J is on team 3.

What do we already know? If G, H and J (all boys!) are the captains and we have no idea which teams they are on, that tells us that F is the only boy left to place. E is on team 1 with a boy, so team 1 has to have a girl in the third spot: F has to go to teams 2 or 3. Rule 1 is dead. **RULES 3 and 4 need to be watched.** We also know that if J and G have to be on different teams then **H cannot go onto team 2** because that would violate rule 5. Bag it.
A) A1 and B2 works. J can stay on 1, G2 and H3. Slap D3, sprinkle some free rangers... INCORRECT.
B) A1 and B3 works. We can stick H1, J2 and G3 with a D3 etc.
C) B1 and G3 works. J2 and H1 avoids rule 5 and pins B down comfortably. Throw D into 2 or 3... nobody cares about her.
D) G1 and H3 works. That means J2. Put B1 and D can go 2 or 3.

E) Circle it, bubble it, RUN to the final chapter of this nightmarish problem set. And just for kicks and grins, G1 and J3 means H2. Cheeky monkeys.

6. If J is on team 2 and A is the captain of team 3, which of the following could be true?
    A) B and E are on team 2.
    B) E and F are on team 2.
    C) B, C and D comprise team 1.
    D) B, C and E comprise team 1.
    E) B, C and F comprise team 1.

What do we know already? If J2 then J cannot be 3, so H2 is NOT HAPPENING. H must go to team 1 or 3. Sadly, none of the answer choices mention H. The captain of team 3 is A. Now we have an issue. A is a girl and the contra-positive of rule 1 says that if a girl is the captain of team 3, a boy must be the captain of team 1. We have three answer choices that talk about team 1. Start with them.
C) has B, C and D on team 1. That violates rule 4. INCORRECT.
D) has B, C and E on team 1. That is three girls on E's team. INCORRECT.
E) has B, C and F on team 1. B an J are separated as are B and D. So long as we can stick H on 3 and get E onto a team with a girl and a boy which we can (team 3) , we are good to go. CORRECT. Circle it, bubble it and break out a bottle of the good stuff.

APPENDIX "C": Bi-conditional Bonus

Wow! Check you out! You actually followed directions and came to the appendix to find out the answer! There is hope for you yet.

When a bi-conditional is a simple one (i.e. one category on either side of the if-then horseshoe) the rule is:

If the signs are the same $(X \supset Y \: / \: {-X} \supset {-Y})$ on both sides,
It is a "Both or neither rule."

If the signs are different $({-X} \supset Y$ or $X \supset {-Y})$ on either side,
It is an, "Exactly One of two rule."

Not to be pedantic, but let's do an example to make really good and sure that we are crystal clear.

Tyrion kills Joffrey when, and only when, Arya slaps Clegane.

In symbols, Tyrion killing Joffrey (TKJ) is both an antecedent and consequent of Arya slapping Clegane (ASC):

$$ASC \supset TKJ$$
$$-TKJ \supset -ASC$$
$$TKJ \supset ASC$$
$$-ASC \supset -TKJ$$

The signs are the same on both sides, so we have "Both or neither." There are no other possible outcomes: both will happen or neither will.

If we have:

Dumbledore does not kiss Grindelwald if and only if Ron kisses Hermione.

In symbols, Dumbledore not kissing Grindelwald (-DKG) is an antecedent and consequent of Ron kissing Hermione (RKH):

$$RKH \supset -DKG$$
$$DKG \supset -RKH$$
$$-DKG \supset RKH$$
$$-RKH \supset DKG$$

The first two tell me that if anyone does any kissing, it prevents the others from kissing. The second two says that if we know that any couple fails to kiss, then the other pair is forced to. In other words, EXACTLY one kiss is going to happen (and we all know how that turned out).

This raised a very important (and super relevant) point: WHEN THE LANGUAGE OF A RULE IN A LOGIC GAME *MEANS*, "One of X or Y must play, but not both." YOU KNOW THAT IT IS A BI-CONDITIONAL WITH DIFFERENT SIGNS ON EITHER SIDE OF THE HORSESHOE! WHEN THE LANGUAGE OF A RULE IN A LOGIC GAME *MEANS*, "EITHER BOTH X AND Y MUST PLAY OR NEITHER CAN." YOU KNOW THAT IT IS A BI-CONDITIONAL WITH THE SAME SIGNS ON EITHER SIDE OF THE HORSESHOE.

THE PARENTHETICAL DISJUNCTIVE CONSEQUENT THANG

So the real reason you popped by the hinterlands of this book is to resolve any lingering doubts about what conjunctions and disjunctions in a bi-conditional mean. The example we were looking at was:

$$
Bi \begin{cases} \text{1a) ST} \supset \text{BJ} \cdot \text{BU} \\ \quad \text{-BJ v -BU} \supset \text{-ST} \\ \text{1b) BJ} \cdot \text{BU} \supset \text{ST} \\ \quad \text{-ST} \supset \text{-BJ v -BU} \end{cases}
$$

1a) tells us that ST is sufficient to prove BJ and BU. So ST proves all three. The contra-positive says that if BJ is missing or if BU is missing or both are missing then we know –ST for certain. If we have –BJ and BU that is sufficient to establish –ST. The same goes for if we have –BU and BJ. So 1a says that we have ALL if ST is true, and the contra-positive says that we do NOT have to have nothing.

1b) says that if we do have both BJ and BU then we have ST: knowing that we have the two forces the third. If we only have BJ there is no consequence, and the same can be said of BU. The contra-positive of 1b says that if we have –ST then we have no BJ (-BJ) or we have no BU (-BU) or both. –ST could just have the consequent of –BU with BJ still happening. –ST could have the consequent of –BJ with BU still happening.

So this is tricky stuff. Throwing conjunctions and disjunctions into bi-conditionals is the stuff of hard-core law students. Here is the rule from before, just in case you have forgotten it:

When you have bi-conditionals, the right side rule does not apply to any rule in the game.

ALSO remember that this rule is only a rule for the LSAT, and that it is a safety precaution. In the real world, the right side rule still applies to all of the rules / laws that do not have any connection to the bi-conditionals. Rules that "touch" or connect to the bi-conditionals are "polluted" with the taint of the bi-conditional, and so we cannot use the right side rule with them. Under the combat stress of the LSAT, you do not have the time to go through and make sure that any particular rule is or is not connected to the bi-conditional, so we just adopt a prophylactic (look it up) rule against the use of the right side rule.

A Jedi You Are...almost.

Yoda: No more training do you require. Already know you, that which you need.
Luke: Then I am a Jedi.
Yoda: No. Not yet. One thing remains. Vader. You must confront Vader. Then, only then, a Jedi will you be. And confront him you will.

And this, ladies and gentlemen, is the moment at which you have arrived at the pinnacle of logic gamedom. You need to practice and practice and then practice some more. After you have obtained and done every single logic game that the LSAC has published AND figured out how to quickly and efficiently use the Test Mentors Method™ in every one of them, you will be ready to face Vader.

Practice allows you to see patterns. Practice allows you to learn how to adapt to subtleties. Practice allows you to see that there is nothing to fear but yourself, meaning that you are your own worst enemy. If YOU CONTROL YOU, there is nothing to fear. If you allow yourself to cheat, be lazy, cut corners or be undisciplined, then you have something to fear.

Then you will be ready to face Darth Vader, or more aptly, the LSAT itself. And when you do, you need to remember this one simple fact: **there is NOTHING different about the "actual" LSAT.** It is all LOGIC. It is all of the same issues. All of the same tools apply. It is like a doctor practicing on a bunch of people and then getting a "different" person: there is no reason to freak out. There may be tiny cosmetic differences, but under the hood, they are all the same.

STICK TO THE TEST MENTORS METHODS.
TRAIN HARD.
BE DISCIPLINED.
CRUSH THE LOGIC GAMES!